Wealth, Power and Inequality in World History

GLOBAL AND COMPARATIVE HISTORY

Wealth, Power and Inequality in World History

VOLUME 1

James R. Farr
Patrick J. Hearden

Purdue University

cognella
SAN DIEGO

Bassim Hamadeh, *CEO and Publisher*
David Miano, *Specialist Acquisitions Editor*
Michelle Piehl, *Senior Project Editor*
Rachel Kahn, *Production Editor*
Emely Villavicencio, *Senior Graphic Designer*
Trey Soto, *Licensing Specialist*
Natalie Piccotti, *Director of Marketing*
Kassie Graves, *Senior Vice President, Editorial*
Jamie Giganti, *Director of Academic Publishing*

Copyright © 2022 by Cognella, Inc. All rights reserved. No part of this publication may be reprinted, reproduced, transmitted, or utilized in any form or by any electronic, mechanical, or other means, now known or hereafter invented, including photocopying, microfilming, and recording, or in any information retrieval system without the written permission of Cognella, Inc. For inquiries regarding permissions, translations, foreign rights, audio rights, and any other forms of reproduction, please contact the Cognella Licensing Department at rights@cognella.com.

Trademark Notice: Product or corporate names may be trademarks or registered trademarks and are used only for identification and explanation without intent to infringe.

Cover image copyright © 2018 iStockphoto LP/hyejin kang.

Printed in the United States of America.

cognella® ACADEMIC PUBLISHING
3970 Sorrento Valley Blvd., Ste. 500, San Diego, CA 92121

BRIEF CONTENTS

Introduction xix

CHAPTER 1 THE BEGINNINGS OF SOCIAL INEQUALITY, 6,000,000 TO 4,000 YEARS AGO 1

CHAPTER 2 THE AGRICULTURAL REVOLUTION, 9000 BCE–1 BCE 20

CHAPTER 3 THE URBAN REVOLUTION AND STATE FORMATION, 4000 BCE–1000 BCE 40

CHAPTER 4 EARLY EMPIRES IN ASIA, AFRICA, AND MESOAMERICA, 1200 BCE–1 BCE 61

CHAPTER 5 THE MEDITERRANEAN WORLD, 2000 BCE–500 BCE 84

CHAPTER 6 THE CLASH OF EMPIRES IN THE ANCIENT WORLD, 550 BCE–1 BCE 108

CHAPTER 7 CONQUEST, CRISIS, AND RECOVERY: THE ROMAN WORLD, 27 BCE–400 CE 131

CHAPTER 8 THE UNIFICATION OF CHINA: THE QIN AND HAN DYNASTIES, 221 BCE–220 CE 155

CHAPTER 9 EMPIRES AND THE SILK ROAD IN ASIA, CA. 200 BCE–CA. 850 CE 173

CHAPTER 10 IMPERIAL CHINA UNDER THE TANG DYNASTY, 618–907 190

CHAPTER 11 THE FRAGMENTATION OF EUROPE, CA. 400–CA. 750 210

CHAPTER 12 CONVERSION, CONQUEST, AND COMMERCE IN THE ISLAMIC WORLD, 610–CA. 1000 231

CHAPTER 13	THE SONG DYNASTY AND CONQUERORS FROM THE NORTH: CHINA FROM 900–1300	253
CHAPTER 14	TERRITORIAL EXPANSION AND ECONOMIC GROWTH IN EUROPE, 750–1300	278
CHAPTER 15	TRADE AND STATES IN SUB-SAHARAN AFRICA, 8000 BCE–1500 CE	300
CHAPTER 16	FRAGMENTED STATES AND COMMERCE IN THE ISLAMIC WORLD, CA. 900–1500	324
CHAPTER 17	THE AMERICAS, CA. 1 CE–1533	343
	Glossary: Volume 1 (Chapters 1–17)	367
	Bibliography	379
	Index	381

DETAILED CONTENTS

	Introduction	xix
CHAPTER 1	THE BEGINNINGS OF SOCIAL INEQUALITY, 6,000,000 TO 4,000 YEARS AGO	1
	The Emergence of Humans in Africa	1
	Hominin Evolution	2
	The Emergence and Dispersal of New Hominin Species	3
	The Appearance of Modern Humans	4
	The Beginning of Modern Behavior	5
	Language and Social Evolution	5
	Homo sapiens Colonize the World	6
	The Great Human Diaspora	7
	Mammoth Hunters in Eastern Europe	8
	Modern Humans Replace the Neanderthals	9
	The Colonization of the Western Hemisphere	9
	Egalitarian Groups of Hunters and Gatherers	11
	The Sharing Ethic	11
	Technology and Trade	12
	Ice Age Warfare	13
	Affluent Ice Age Foragers	13
	The Emergence of Self-Interested Households	14
	A Remarkable Ice Age Burial	15
	The Spread of Social and Economic Inequality	16
	Social Stratification and Warfare Before Agriculture	17
	Affluent Foragers in Asia and Europe	17
	Stratification and Warfare in North America	18
	Review Questions	18

	Additional Readings	19
	Figure Credits	19
CHAPTER 2	**THE AGRICULTURAL REVOLUTION, 9000 BCE–1 BCE**	**20**
	The Origins and Spread of Agriculture	20
	The Domestication of Plants and Animals and the Production of Surplus Food	21
	The Spread of Farming Throughout the World	22
	The Invention of Irrigation	23
	Agriculture and Social Inequality	24
	Southwest Asia, Europe, and Central Asia	24
	One Starting Point: The Fertile Crescent	25
	The Farming Settlement of Catalhoyuk	26
	Expansion into Europe	27
	Expansion into Central Asia	29
	East Asia, Southeast Asia, and the Pacific	30
	Another Starting Point: East Asia	30
	Expansion into Southeast Asia	31
	Expansion into the Pacific Basin	32
	Africa, South Asia, and the Americas	34
	Africa: Farming and Pastoralism	34
	Farming in South Asia	36
	The Americas: Independent Centers of Food Production	37
	Review Questions	38
	Additional Readings	39
	Figure Credits	39
CHAPTER 3	**THE URBAN REVOLUTION AND STATE FORMATION, 4000 BCE–1000 BCE**	**40**
	Mesopotamia: City-States and Empires	40
	A Great Transformation: Urban Growth and Temple Development	40
	Intercity Warfare	42
	The Gap Between Rich and Poor	43

Regional Empires and Long-Distance Trade	44
Egypt: Unification and Disintegration	46
Gifts of the Nile: Plenty and Power	46
Egyptian Rulers: The Pharaohs	46
Cycles of Centralization and Fragmentation	49
A Prosperous and Patriarchal Society	50
The Urban Revolution in South Asia	50
Urban Growth in the Indus Valley	51
Agricultural Intensification and Craft Production	52
Urban Plans and Public Works	53
Political Organization and Urban Decline	54
Cities and States in East Asia	55
The First Chinese State	55
The Rise of the Shang Kingdom	56
A Strong and Stratified Kingdom	57
The Changjiang State	58
Review Questions	59
Additional Readings	59
Figure Credits	60

CHAPTER 4 EARLY EMPIRES IN ASIA, AFRICA, AND MESOAMERICA, 1200 BCE–1 BCE — 61

The Unification of China	61
The Zhou State and the Rise of Regional Warlords	61
The Warring States and the Northern Tribes	62
The Rise of the Qin Empire	64
The First Emperor of China	65
The Collapse of the Qin Empire	66
Empire Building in South Asia	66
Chiefs and Brahmans	67
The Second Urbanization	67
Chiefdoms and Kingdoms	68
The Rise of the Mauryan Empire	69
King Ashoka and His Quest for Social Harmony	71

Early Urbanization and States Formation in Tropical Africa ... 73
   The Rise of the Napatan Empire ... 73
   The Formation of the Meroitic State ... 75

Early Urbanization and State Formation in Mesoamerica ... 77
   Agricultural Villages and Long-Distance Exchange ... 77
   The Rise and Fall of Olmec Chiefdoms ... 78
   A Great Transformation in the Valley of Oaxaca ... 80
   State Formation in the Basin of Mexico ... 81

Review Questions ... 82

Additional Readings ... 82

Figure Credits ... 83

CHAPTER 5 — THE MEDITERRANEAN WORLD, 2000 BCE–500 BCE ... 84

The Eastern Mediterranean Exchange Network ... 84
   Minoans and Mycenaeans ... 84
   Trade and Diplomacy in the Eastern Mediterranean ... 86
   Social Stratification in the Eastern Mediterranean ... 88

The Phoenician Commercial Empire ... 89
   The Phoenicians and the Israelites ... 90
   Royal Authority and Merchant Oligarchy ... 91
   The Phoenician Commercial Empire ... 92
   The Colonization of the Western Mediterranean ... 94
   The Demise of the Israelites and the Phoenicians ... 95

The Greek Agrarian Governments ... 96
   Dark Age Chieftains ... 96
   The Polis ... 97
   The Hoplites and City-State Governance ... 98
   Solon and His Reforms in Athens ... 99
   A Stratified Society ... 100

The Greeks Overseas ... 101
   Greek Colonization ... 101
   Competition with the Etruscans ... 103
   Into the Black Sea ... 104

	Review Questions	106
	Additional Readings	106
	Figure Credits	107
CHAPTER 6	**THE CLASH OF EMPIRES IN THE ANCIENT WORLD, 550 BCE–1 BCE**	**108**
	The Persians and the Greeks	108
	The Achaemenids Forge a Vast Empire	108
	Ruling the Multiethnic Empire	110
	The Persian and Peloponnesian Wars	112
	The Recovery of Athens: A Stratified Society	114
	The Hellenistic World	115
	The Macedonians: Philip II and Alexander the Great	115
	Seleucus, Antigonus, and Ptolemy	116
	The Antigonid Kingdom	117
	The Seleucid Kingdom	117
	The Ptolemy Kingdom	118
	The Rise of Rome	118
	From Monarchy to Republic	119
	Early Roman Expansion	120
	New Period of Military Conquest	122
	The Imperial Republic	123
	Carthage and the Three Punic Wars	123
	The Polarization of Wealth and Social Unrest	125
	Civil Wars in Rome	126
	The End of the Roman Republic	128
	Review Questions	129
	Additional Readings	129
	Figure Credits	130
CHAPTER 7	**CONQUEST, CRISIS, AND RECOVERY: THE ROMAN WORLD, 27 BCE–400 CE**	**131**
	The Countryside and the City	131
	Landed Aristocrats	131

Peasants and Slaves	132
City Dwellers	133
The Power of the State	134
The Emperor and the Army	134
Taxes and Money	138
Infrastructure	139
Religion and the Power of the State	141
The Economy of the Roman Empire	142
Conditions of Economic Growth	143
Specialization, Export, and Investment	145
Markets and Profits	146
Long-Distance Trade with the East	148
To the East	148
India, the Indian Ocean, and the Red Sea	149
The Overland Trade to Arabia and Central Asia	151
Review Questions	153
Further Readings	153
Figure Credits	154

CHAPTER 8 THE UNIFICATION OF CHINA: THE QIN AND HAN DYNASTIES, 221 BCE–220 CE — 155

Imperial Unification in Classical China	155
From Qin to Han: Central Control and the Warlord	155
Ideology and Legitimacy: Heaven's Mandate, Law, and Confucianism	157
Taxes and Infrastructure	159
The State, the Peasant, and the Landlord	161
Land and Taxes	161
The Growth of Landed Estates	163
Peasant Unrest and the Fall of the Eastern Han Dynasty	164
The Economy of Classical China	165
Technology and Production	165

	The Importance of Cities	167
	Trade and Tribute	168
	The Role of Merchants	168
	The Xiongnu, Silk, and Horses	168
	The Silk Road	170
	Review Questions	171
	Further Readings	172
	Figure Credit	172
CHAPTER 9	EMPIRES AND THE SILK ROAD IN ASIA, CA. 200 BCE–CA. 850 CE	173
	The Ecosystem of Central Asia	173
	People of the Steppe	175
	Horse-Riding Nomads	175
	The Xiongnu Empire	176
	The Türkic and Uighur Empires	177
	Empires of Southwestern Asia	179
	The Kushan Empire (ca. 124 BCE–ca. 230 CE)	179
	The Parthian and Sassanian Empires (224–651 CE)	181
	Connections and Transfers Across Asia	184
	Trade in the Ancient World	184
	Nomads, Chinese, and Sogdians	185
	Kushans, Parthians, and Sassanians	186
	Review Questions	188
	Further Readings	189
	Figure Credits	189
CHAPTER 10	IMPERIAL CHINA UNDER THE TANG DYNASTY, 618–907	190
	Unification, Expansion, and Governance	190
	The Emergence and Consolidation of the Tang Dynasty	191
	Tang Governance	191
	Taxes	193

xiii

Militarism and Civilian Governance	194
Tang Armies	194
The An Lushan Rebellion	195
Imperial Weakness and Collapse	195
Producing Wealth: Agriculture and Manufacturing	197
The Conditions for Economic Growth	197
The Great Estates	198
Rice and Tea	199
Technology	200
Manufacturing	201
Moving Wealth: The State, Cities, and Commerce	202
State Regulation and Commercial Growth	202
Credit and Domestic Trade	205
Long-Distance Trade	206
Review Questions	208
Further Readings	208
Figure Credits	209
CHAPTER 11 THE FRAGMENTATION OF EUROPE, CA. 400–CA. 750	210
After the Roman Empire in the West	210
Barbarians and the Disappearance of the	
Imperial State in the West	210
Barbarian Kingdoms	212
Rich and Poor	215
The Roman Empire in the East	216
The Byzantine State	216
Social Stratification	219
The Economy in the West	220
Production: Plague, Population, and Technology	221
Trade in the West	222
The Economy in Byzantium	226
Production: Agriculture and Manufacturing	227
Trade in the East	228
Review Questions	229

Further Readings	230
Figure Credits	230

CHAPTER 12 CONVERSION, CONQUEST, AND COMMERCE IN THE ISLAMIC WORLD, 610–CA. 1000 — 231

The Prophet Muhammad and Early Islam	231
The Man and the Revelation	231
The Mission	232
The Quran and the State	233
Conquest and Expansion	234
Arab Armies and Non-Arab Lands	235
Political Decentralization and the Emergence of Inequality	236
The Caliphates: Governance and Legitimacy	237
The Rightly Guided Caliphs, 632–661	238
The Umayyad Caliphs, 661–750	240
The Abbasid Caliphs, 750–1258	242
The Fruits of Conquest: Cultural Unity, Agricultural Revolution, and the Emergence of a Commercial System	245
An Agricultural Revolution	246
Cultural Unity and Commercial Growth	247
Cities and Markets	248
Islamic Economic Principles	250
Review Questions	251
Further Readings	251
Figure Credits	252

CHAPTER 13 THE SONG DYNASTY AND CONQUERORS FROM THE NORTH: CHINA FROM 900–1300 — 253

The Northern Song Dynasty (960–1127): Warlords and Bureaucratic Governance	253
The Collapse of the Tang Dynasty	253
The First Song Emperor, Taizu	254
Civilian Governance of the Northern Song	255

Conquerors from the North and the Southern Song Dynasty 256
    The Khitan Liao Empire 257
    The Jurchen Jin Empire 258

The Song Economic Revolution: A Market Economy 260
    Agriculture and Urbanization 261
    Manufacturing 263
    A Commercial Revolution 265
    The Role of the State 267
    Foreign Trade 268

The Mongols 270
    Genghis Khan and Mongol Conquests 270
    Death, Succession, and the Four Khanates 271
    Kublai Khan and the Yuan Dynasty in China 272
    Commerce Under the Mongols 274

Review Questions 275

Further Reading 276

Figure Credits 277

CHAPTER 14 TERRITORIAL EXPANSION AND ECONOMIC GROWTH IN EUROPE, 750–1300 278

The Carolingians 278
    Wars of Conquest 278
    The Carolingian Economy 281

Raiders, Traders, and Settlers 284
    Raiders from the North 285
    From Raiders to Traders and Settlers 287

The Byzantines 287
    The Resurgent State 288
    The Aristocracy and the Peasantry 289

Political Recovery and Economic Growth 289
    New States in the West 290
    Population Growth and Migration in the West 293
    Quickening Economic Activity in the East 294
    Trade 295

Review Questions	298
Further Reading	298
Figure Credits	299

CHAPTER 15   TRADE AND STATES IN SUB-SAHARAN AFRICA, 8000 BCE–1500 CE — 300

Geography, Ecology, and Human Settlement	300
Pastoralism and Agriculture	300
Expansion of Bantu-Speaker Culture	302
The Nile Valley and the Ethiopian Highlands	303
The Kingdom of Kush	304
The Kingdom of Aksum	306
Nubia	308
West Africa	309
Trans-Saharan Trade	309
The Kingdom of Ancient Ghana	310
The Kingdom of Mali	313
East Africa	315
Coastal Port Cities and Indian Ocean Trade	315
The Mapungubwe Kingdom and Great Zimbabwe	317
Slavery in Africa Before 1500	319
Slavery, the Slave Trade, and Islam	319
The Status of Slaves	321
Review Questions	322
Further Reading	322
Figure Credits	323

CHAPTER 16   FRAGMENTED STATES AND COMMERCE IN THE ISLAMIC WORLD, CA. 900–1500 — 324

The Muslim Regimes in North Africa	324
The Fatimids	325
The Almoravids, Almohads, Ayyubids, and Mamluks	326

The Muslim Regimes in Southwest Asia		328
The Mongol Ilkhans and Tamerlane		328
The Ottomans		330
The Commercial Economy of the Islamic World		332
The Growth of Trade		333
Egypt and the Supremacy of the Red Sea Route		334
The Ottoman Economy		337
Al-Andalus		339
Review Questions		341
Further Reading		341
Figure Credits		342

CHAPTER 17   THE AMERICAS, CA. 1 CE–1533   343

The Indians of North America		343
The Woodland Hopewell		344
Mississippian Culture		345
The Indians of Southwest North America		347
The Indians of Mesoamerica		349
Teotihuacán		349
Maya		351
Toltecs		352
Aztecs		353
The Andean Indians of South America		356
The Nazca and Moche Cultures		357
The Tiwanaku Empire		360
The Wari Empire		360
The Inca Empire		361
Review Questions		364
Further Reading		364
Figure Credits		365
Glossary: Volume 1 (Chapters 1–17)		367
Bibliography		379
Index		381

INTRODUCTION

Wealth is power, and power is wealth.
—Philosopher Thomas Hobbes, 1651

While comprehensive in scope, this book maintains a sharp focus on political and economic affairs. Rather than treating each one as a separate topic, we will demonstrate the close interaction between these two subjects throughout the course of world history. Our text has a central theme: the ever-changing allocation of wealth and power both within individual societies and among different political entities, such as city-states, nations, and empires.

In this study, we discuss both wealth and power in relative terms. We say that A has power over B if A can get B to do something that B would not otherwise do. We likewise say that individuals or countries are wealthier than others if they have more material possessions, longer life spans, higher literacy rates, or other such blessings. When analyzing economic developments in recent centuries, we use estimates of per capita gross domestic product to indicate the relative wealth of different countries.

This account of the history of humans living around the world is comprehensive with respect to both time and space. It covers all chronological periods from the emergence of the human species in Africa to the present era of accelerated globalization. And it analyzes important economic, social, and political transformations in every geographical area that *Homo sapiens* eventually inhabited.

Anatomically modern humans, who could think and speak like people living today, began migrating out of Africa around 100,000 years ago. As successive groups settled in different parts of the world and adapted to diverse environments, they developed many distinct patterns of learned behavior. But while residing in different regions, these people also acted in similar ways because they possessed the same basic dispositions and abilities despite superficial variations in skin color caused by exposure to different climates.

The accumulation of surplus food had a critical impact on the course of world history. In most hunting and gathering societies, food remained scarce, and people had a strong incentive to share with other members of their group in order to reduce the risk of starvation. But in all societies, whether foraging or farming, that possessed an abundance of food, a few individuals found ways to acquire more than others. Such acquisitive behavior, which began in many places well before the invention of writing about 5,000 years ago, invariably led to an unequal distribution of wealth and power in surplus-producing societies on every continent.

While discussing the relationships among various groups living in hierarchical societies, we demonstrate that ruling elites have frequently used force or the threat of force to preserve or enhance their power and privileges. We also show that the extraction of surplus products from the lower classes to support the upper classes has sometimes provoked revolutionary upheavals.

During our analysis of the relationships among numerous political entities, we point out that wealth and power have been closely linked throughout the course of world history. Wealth has been used to establish strong armies and navies, while military power has been employed to gain access to valuable resources and lucrative markets. To achieve their economic objectives, societies have often engaged in military conquest as well as peaceful commerce. Thomas Hobbes, the astute English philosopher, observed long ago that wealth and power are inseparably joined together. Indeed, our study reveals a common pattern in which the rich use their wealth to get stronger, and the strong employ their power to get richer.

Though concentrating on political and economic issues, we discuss both religion and gender in terms of their impact on the accumulation of wealth and the exercise of power. Political leaders in many different times and places have used religion to provide an ideological justification deemed necessary for the preservation of the established social order. They have also made religious appeals to incite their followers to fight against foreigners for the protection of strategic and economic interests.

Although women have traditionally occupied subservient positions in hierarchical societies all over the world, some did enjoy political and social prominence. Countless others have made significant contributions to the global output of agricultural and industrial products.

By maintaining a global perspective, this book avoids the pitfalls of a Eurocentric bias. We reject the concept of a universal world history in which people everywhere pass through the same stages of sociocultural evolution. Rather than portraying Western countries as occupying the highest stage in a progressive march from savagery to civilization, we point out that societies have taken different pathways in their efforts to achieve similar political and economic aims. The histories of communities in different parts of the world, by revealing uniformities as well as diversities in behavior, undermine assertions of Western intellectual, cultural, or moral superiority.

While discarding notions of Western uniqueness or exceptionalism, we point out that the geographical center of wealth and power has shifted over time. China was once the richest and strongest country in the world, and the Indian Ocean was for many centuries the heart of a worldwide trading network. Eventually, the regional seat of wealth and power moved from Asia and the Middle East to western Europe and the United States. But the economic and political center of gravity may shift yet again if China, India, Japan, and other Asian nations continue their rapid industrial development.

While analyzing many important developments in different times and places, this text covers the major watersheds that have shaped the contours of world history. The transition from foraging to farming about 10,000 years ago and the subsequent spread of agriculture resulted in the production of enormous quantities of food. This Agricultural Revolution provided the economic foundation for urbanization, state formation, and a global population explosion. Around 2,000 years ago, the long-distance exchange of agricultural commodities and manufactured goods linked for the first time the eastern and western ends of the vast Eurasian landmass. These transitions led not only to accelerated economic growth but also to greater inequality both within individual societies and between different societies.

Modern humans, as this book will show, have been purposeful actors on the stage of world history. As agents of change since their emergence in Africa, they have interacted with a wide variety of environments around the globe. These ecological niches have presented communities with a range of constraints and opportunities. For example, the soil and climate in some areas served as obstacles to the development of intensive agriculture, while conditions in other locations enabled farmers to produce enough food to support large urban populations.

Ambitious individuals and aggressive nations, while operating in diverse ecosystems, have exhibited a deep-seated desire to become prosperous and powerful. Some have succeeded; others have failed. Their actions, moreover, have often had unintended consequences. On many occasions, for example, human efforts to manipulate the environment have produced not only short-term benefits but also long-term problems, such as soil erosion, water pollution, and increasing levels of carbon dioxide in the atmosphere. Furthermore, as this study will reveal, the pursuit of wealth and power has repeatedly led to economic, social, and political inequities in many different regions of the world.

CHAPTER 1

The Beginnings of Social Inequality, 6,000,000 to 4,000 Years Ago

The Emergence of Humans in Africa

Humans are members of the **primate** family, and chimpanzees are their closest relatives among the African apes. Molecular evidence suggests that humans and chimpanzees living today share a common ancestor that existed somewhere in Africa around six or seven million years ago. These apes spent much of their time living in trees. Their opposable thumbs and big toes helped them grasp branches with a firm grip, and their stereoscopic vision gave them excellent depth perception, allowing them to leap from one branch to another without falling.

As a long period of colder and drier climate led to shrinking forests in Africa, one ape **species** began spending more time on the ground and evolved into **bipedal** creatures that anthropologists call **hominins**. Early hominins, while walking upright on two feet, retained some of the anatomical features of tree dwellers, such

FIGURE 1.1 Hominin Footprints. This trail of hominin footprints was fossilized in volcanic ash in Tanzania about 3.6 million years ago.

as long fingers and toes along with short hind limbs. For the first several million years of their history, these bipedal apes did not develop brains that were larger than those possessed by chimpanzees.

Hominin Evolution

Anthropologists view hominin **evolution** not as a ladder ascending in a direct line from apes to humans but rather as a tree with many branches and one small human twig. In a series of **adaptive radiations**, hominins diverged to fill different environmental niches, resulting in the emergence of a variety of new bipedal species. **Fossil** discoveries indicate that at least six different hominin species existed in Africa between three and two million years ago. These hominin species all became extinct except for those that included the *Homo* lineage, whose members gradually evolved into modern humans. While possessing a mixture of anatomical features that allowed for both tree climbing and upright walking, the early *Homo* species had brains that ranged from 600 to 700 centimeters in size, or almost half as large as modern humans.

The first appearance of stone tools in the archaeological record approximately 2.5 million years ago coincides with the earliest fossil evidence for the emergence of the *Homo* lineage. These stone implements, originally discovered in Tanzania and known as Oldowan tools, consisted of small flakes made by banging one rock against another. Experiments with replicas of Oldowan tools reveal that short flakes with sharp edges can be used to slit the hide of large mammals like zebras or gazelles, to slice through tendons, and to strip flesh from bones. In addition, heavy cores can be employed to crack bones to gain access to fatty marrow and nutritious brains. The oldest stone tools that archaeologists have discovered so far were often found in close proximity to the bones of large animals, and cut marks left on the bones at these sites offer positive evidence that from the very outset manufactured flakes were used for butchering animals.

The intimate connection between tool production and meat consumption represents an economic revolution that many anthropologists believe had a profound impact on human evolution. Although early hominins and apes had brains that were similar in size, modern humans have brains that are about three times larger than would be expected for apes of the same weight. What made it possible for the brains of the members of the genus *Homo* to grow larger over time? Many anthropologists think that the answer lies in an increase in the amount of meat in their diet. Apes and early hominins ate small quantities of meat and large amounts of less nutritious plant food. But the use of stone tools enabled members of the *Homo* line to butcher large animals, to eat more meat, and to ingest greater amounts of protein.

The Emergence and Dispersal of New Hominin Species

A new species in the human lineage made a dramatic appearance about two million years ago in tropical areas of eastern Africa. Known as *Homo ergaster*, the new species was more like modern humans than all previous hominins with respect to limb proportion and brain dimension. Their short arms and long legs suggest a final abandonment of any ape-like dependence on trees for food or refuge and a nearly exclusive commitment to bipedal walking and terrestrial living. The microwear pattern on the surface of teeth shows that *H. ergaster* ate much more meat than any of its ancestors. And fossilized skulls reveal that compared to earlier hominins *H. ergaster* had larger brains that ranged in size from about 850 to a little more than 1,000 cubic centimeters.

An important technological advance occurred around 1.5 million years ago when *H. ergaster* began manufacturing more sophisticated stone tools that required greater manual dexterity and intellectual ability. First discovered in Ethiopia and later named Acheulean tools, most were large tear-shaped hand axes used to perform a variety of tasks, including heavy-duty butchering. Unlike the simple Oldowan flakes without any consistent shape, Acheulean hand axes were more symmetrical in form and had a bigger cutting edge. The degree of standardization of these two-sided implements indicates that the tool manufacturers had a well-defined image of the final product in mind before they started to transform the stone into the desired shape.

Shortly after emerging in the grasslands and relatively open woodlands of eastern Africa, *Homo ergaster* began expanding its range not only by migrating into other parts of the continent but also by embarking on a remarkable exodus out of Africa. Small bands radiated from their tropical homeland to nearby areas in Africa with ample flora and fauna but with somewhat greater seasonal differences in climate. After establishing settlements in north Africa during periods when rainfall was sufficient for sparse populations to survive, *H. ergaster* groups traveled along a land route through the Sinai Peninsula and moved at different times between 1.7 and 1.3 million years ago into different regions of Eurasia. These pioneers evolved into *Homo erectus*, a new hominin species that survived in East Asia for about a million years.

Between 800,000 and 600,000 years ago, *Homo ergaster* gave rise in Africa to *Homo heidelbergensis*, sometimes called Heidelberg man, a new hominin species that soon extended its range to Europe. Excavations at the Boxgrove site in southern England, dated to about 500,000 years ago, provide clear evidence that Heidelberg man hunted large mammals, including wild horses, red deer, and bear. While many of the animal bones found at Boxgrove display cut marks made by hand axes, some of the bones exhibit cut marks overlaid by tooth marks, indicating that Heidelberg man had killed and butchered the mammals before animal carnivores chewed the discarded bones.

Representing a new hominin species that descended from Heidelberg man, *Homo neanderthalensis*, commonly called Neanderthals, evolved between 300,000 and 200,000 years ago in southwestern Europe. Neanderthals settled in places where mean winter temperatures fell significantly below freezing, and they developed large bodies and short limbs that served to minimize heat loss and the chance of frostbite. During a warm interglacial period that began about 130,000 years ago, Neanderthals expanded their range into eastern Europe and Siberia. They sustained themselves in cold habitats by hunting big herbivores and consuming large quantities of meat. Their high caloric diet, heavy in fat and protein, gave them sufficient energy to engage in vigorous activity in frigid environments. To acquire large amounts of meat, Neanderthals moved their camps during different seasons of the year to intercept and kill animals that migrated in predictable patterns.

The Appearance of Modern Humans

While Neanderthals were emerging in Europe, Heidelberg man was evolving on a parallel but separate track in Africa and developing into a new species. Heidelberg man possessed brains that quickly expanded between 600,000 and 400,000 years ago from around 1,000 to about 1,200 cubic centimeters. Skulls found at several African sites reveal that brain enlargement continued at a rapid pace among the archaic human descendants of Heidelberg man. By 200,000 years ago, archaic humans had brains that were nearly 1,400 cubic centimeters in volume, or approximately the size of the average person living today. These archaic humans mark a transition along an evolutionary sequence beginning with the disappearance of Heidelberg man and the emergence of anatomically modern humans, known as *Homo sapiens*. Basing their calculations on a combination of fossil and genetic evidence, archaeologists estimate that anatomically modern humans made their appearance on the stage of world history sometime between 200,000 and 100,000 years ago somewhere in Africa south of the Sahara Desert.

The Beginning of Modern Behavior

Archaeologists have raised several key questions about the origins of modern behavior: When did *Homo sapiens* begin to act in modern ways? Where did various aspects of modern behavior first appear? Did modern behavior arise suddenly as a cohesive package or gradually in a piecemeal fashion?

Early archaeological excavations in Europe uncovered numerous examples of behavior considered to be modern, such as the spectacular paintings of animals on the walls of caves in southern France and northern Spain. The oldest of these realistic images of wild animals were painted more than 30,000 years ago by highly skilled artists, possibly **shamans**, who possessed an excellent sense of proportion. Investigations have shown that many other aspects of modern behavior, such as the use of bone tools and the production of symbolic objects, appeared in Europe at about the same time. Impressed by these findings, some scholars have suggested that a cultural revolution, perhaps rooted in a fundamental reorganization of the human brain, occurred in Europe around 40,000 years ago.

Recent archaeological studies, however, have shown that various aspects of modern behavior emerged much earlier in Africa than in Europe or anywhere else. *Homo sapiens* living near the Congo River were fishing with barbed points made from bone as early as 90,000 years ago. About 15,000 years later, anatomically modern humans living at Blombos Cave in South Africa were making bone tools and producing symbolic objects in the form of ochre pieces inscribed with crossing triangles and horizontal lines. Ostrich eggshell beads, found at widely scattered sites in Africa, provide evidence of personal adornment among different groups of modern people beginning around 60,000 years ago. Rather than appearing at the same time and in the same place, these and other examples of modern behavior emerged in a piecemeal fashion and then spread from one area in Africa to another. *Homo sapiens* carried these elements of their culture with them when they migrated from Africa to different parts of the world.

Language and Social Evolution

Both archaic humans and modern humans possessed significantly greater linguistic as well as mental abilities than all of their hominin ancestors. Although cranium fossils suggest that the voice box of *Homo ergaster* populations had already started to descend from a high position in the throat, it was not until about 200,000 years ago that the skull base of archaic humans show that the larynx had assumed a position as low in the throat as modern humans. This means that archaic humans and their modern descendants had the mechanical capacity to produce the vast array of different sounds needed to engage in fully articulate speech. As their fluency in speech increased, *Homo sapiens* were better able to engage in abstract thought, to communicate with each other, and to flourish in diverse environments.

The emergence of *Homo sapiens*, equipped with impressive cognitive abilities and communication skills, was accompanied by a fundamental transformation in the process of evolution. Prior to the arrival of modern humans, anatomy and behavior evolved slowly together in Africa for millions of years. Genetic inheritance and social learning were equally important mechanisms in the long process of evolution. Since the appearance of modern people, however, only minor changes in body form have occurred, while alterations in behavior have rapidly increased. The passage of genes from one generation to the next continued to determine superficial differences in human anatomy, such as skin color. But as the pace of cultural evolution accelerated dramatically, the social transmission of learned behavior played the predominant role in shaping patterns of human behavior.

Homo sapiens Colonize the World

Modern humans began radiating out of their African homeland around 100,000 years ago. At that time, at least three distinct human lineages existed: *Homo sapiens* in Africa, *Homo neanderthalensis* in Europe and eastern Asia, and *Homo erectus* in eastern Asia. As the competitively superior *Homo sapiens* swept across the Eurasian land mass, the remaining hominin species dwindled into extinction.

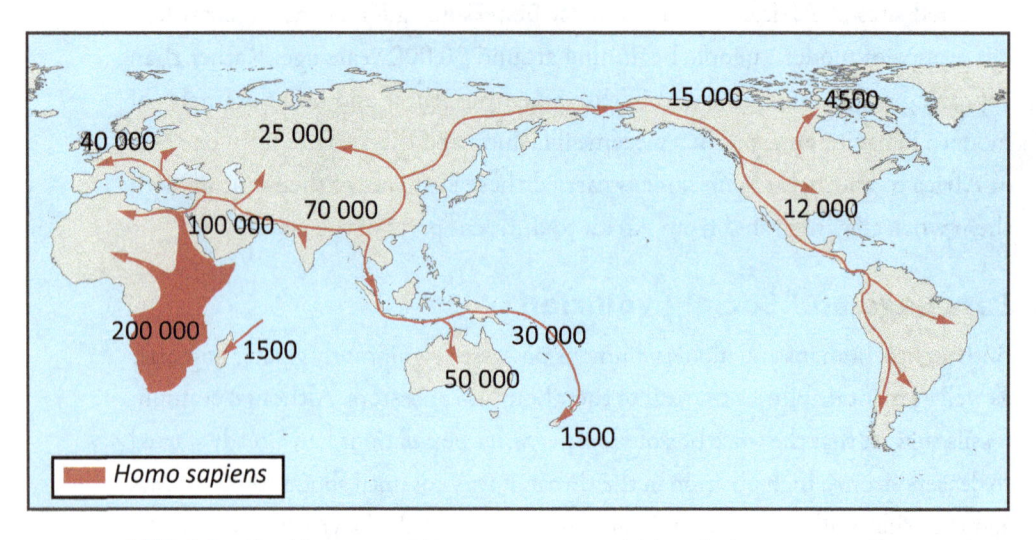

MAP 1.1 The Migration of *Homo sapiens* out of Africa before present. Groups of modern humans left Africa and traveled around the world.

Separate groups of *Homo sapiens* branched out in various directions and developed increasingly significant differences in their behavior while learning to cope in diverse environments. Distinct populations, held together by a common language and shared customs, embarked on different trajectories of cultural development. There is not, therefore, a universal world history with every society progressing in a uniform pattern through the same stages of cultural evolution.

The Great Human Diaspora

During the last Great Ice Age, dating roughly from 75,000 to 12,000 years ago, modern humans traveled over land and across water as they spread out from Africa and rapidly colonized almost every habitable part of the planet. These long-distance travelers carried their culture with them when they dispersed from their tropical homeland, and they developed new technologies that enabled them to exploit a whole array of maritime as well as terrestrial food resources. As they moved into new territories and replaced all other hominin species, *Homo sapiens* began to have a significant impact on the biosphere. The initial group of modern humans who migrated from Africa followed in the footsteps of earlier hominin pioneers. Trekking along a land route across the Sinai Peninsula during a wet climate interval around 100,000 years ago, a small number of people settled in the adjoining area of modern-day Israel. But their encampments left little trace on the landscape, and their genes may have perished or blended with those of later pioneers.

The great human **diaspora** probably got underway around 75,000 years ago when small groups of *Homo sapiens* living in eastern Africa began making a short passage over shallow water near the southern end of the Red Sea. After crossing from Ethiopia into the Arabian Peninsula, one stream of migrants traveled eastward across the southern edge of Asia all the way to Greater Australia. This huge land mass, composed of New Guinea, Australia, and Tasmania, was formed as expanding glaciers locked up vast quantities of water and oceans dropped several hundred feet below present levels. Although Sumatra, Java, Borneo, and Bali became extensions of mainland Southeast Asia, modern humans needed to construct water craft that could carry them across at least 60 miles of open sea in order to reach Greater Australia. Small groups began arriving in Greater Australia about 50,000 years ago, and within 15,000 years, sparse populations of modern people known as Aborigines were living in scattered communities stretching from New Guinea in the north to Tasmania in the south.

Meanwhile, a second stream of migrants began flowing northward into western Asia and eastern Europe. Excavations of a site occupied around 45,000 years ago and located about 250 miles south of Moscow have revealed stone blades along with tools and ornaments made by *Homo sapiens*. Despite having bodies adapted to a warm climate, reflecting their recent origins in tropical Africa, modern people were able to expand their range further to the north than any of the Neanderthals. They learned to survive in cold environments by developing innovative technologies, such as making warm clothes by using needles and thread to stitch animal hides together. Some became skilled at killing mammoths and other mammals in order to obtain large quantities of meat.

Mammoth Hunters in Eastern Europe

While doing fieldwork near the town of Dolni Vestonice in the Czech Republic, archaeologists discovered a site that was occupied by mammoth hunters between 27,000 and 25,000 years ago. The Dolni Vestonice site, located in the Dyje River valley, was not far below the limits of forest growth in northern Europe. In the surrounding steppe, broad expanses of grass, moss, and lichen provided food for herds of wild animals, including reindeer and horses as well as mammoths, which became extinct about 10,000 years ago. The European mammoth was a magnificent animal roughly one and a half times the size of the modern African elephant. Possessing huge domed heads and massive bodies covered with long fur, the mammoths that roamed the cold steppe must have been a formidable prey for those who hunted them.

To protect themselves from frigid winter temperatures, mammoth hunters built artificial shelters with interior hearths. Excavations at Dolni Vestonice have uncovered several huts, partially dug into the ground, with mammoth bone superstructures. Most of the huts were about 15 feet in diameter and had one or more fireplaces for heat, light, and cooking. The remains of more than 800 giant mammoths, which provided the major source of food for the inhabitants of Dolni Vestonice, were found near the village.

The dwellings at Dolni Vestonice contained a large array of tools, weapons, and jewelry. While about 30 percent of the stone tools in the village were made from local sources of flint, the rest were crafted from material that came from over 60 miles away in southern Poland. The residents of Dolni Vestonice used mammoth bone and ivory to make knives, spear points, and lances, as well as pendants and headbands. They also made ornaments for personal adornment from marine shells, which came from the Mediterranean Sea hundreds of miles to the south.

Furthermore, the inhabitants of the village built kilns to fire thousands of small clay figurines. These ceramic pieces of portable art were produced some 10,000 years before people in East Asia invented pottery.

Modern Humans Replace the Neanderthals

After establishing settlements in southeastern Europe about 43,000 years ago, modern humans, popularly known as Cro-Magnons, began sweeping westward and replacing Neanderthals who had been residing in the region for a long time. The Neanderthals disappeared from southwestern Europe about 40,000 years ago, and the last isolated Neanderthal group living on the southern tip of Spain vanished around 27,000 years ago. What happened to the Neanderthals? No one really knows. The Cro-Magnons may have occupied land that was rich in resources and pushed the Neanderthals into marginal areas where their numbers dwindled. Some Neanderthals may have been killed during violent attempts to defend their hunting grounds from the encroachment of the newcomers, while a small amount of interbreeding may have led to the assimilation of some Neanderthals into the growing Cro-Magnon population.

While the Cro-Magnons were colonizing Europe, other modern humans migrated northward from China to Siberia around 30,000 years ago and established a few settlements west of Lake Baikal. But these settlements were abandoned during the **last glacial maximum** between 24,000 and 20,000 years ago. As temperatures became milder during the next several thousand years, some groups of modern people reoccupied depopulated areas near Lake Baikal, while others moved into northeastern Siberia, probably in pursuit of large animals and sea mammals. Between 18,000 and 15,000 years ago, some people were living in Beringia, the land bridge that connected Siberia to Alaska during this period of low sea levels.

The Colonization of the Western Hemisphere

Although the evidence is limited because the Pacific Ocean now covers former coastal areas, some archaeologists have offered the following scenario as a possible explanation for colonization of the Western Hemisphere. The first modern groups of trans-Pacific migrants paddled canoes along the southern coast of Beringia, hopping from one shore refuge to another. Some of these travelers, after making their way down the western coast of North America, established a settlement in southern Chile as early as 14,500 years ago. During the next 2,000 years, people dispersed into diverse habitats in South America, such as the torrid rainforests of Brazil, the frigid landscapes of Patagonia, and the temperate highlands of Peru.

In the meantime, other groups of modern humans journeyed along land routes from Beringia into Alaska. Some of these migrants, after proceeding southward through an ice-free corridor around 13,000 years ago, established settlements in several areas of North America south of the melting ice sheets.

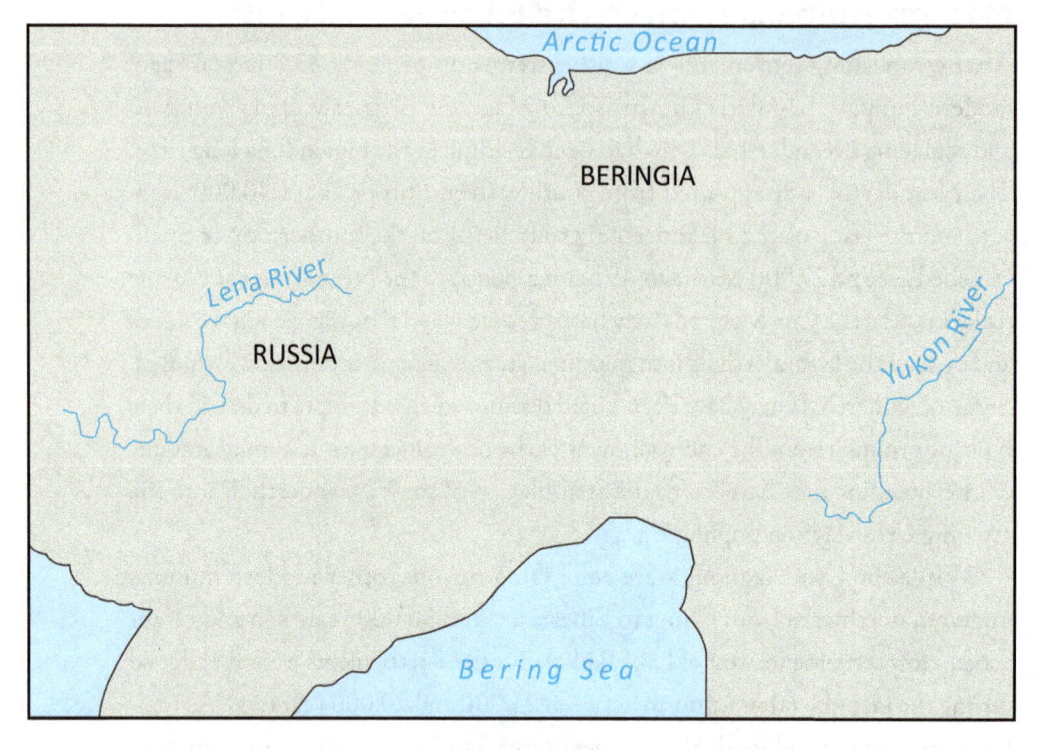

MAP 1.2   Beringia. Low sea levels during the last glacial maximum created a land bridge that allowed humans to travel from Siberia to Alaska.

By the time the Ice Age ended some 12,000 years ago, modern humans had colonized the entire planet save for the polar regions and various islands widely scattered across the oceans of the world. As rapid global warming and melting glaciers led to rising ocean levels, water flooded the Beringia land bridge that had temporarily connected Asia and America while surging seas separated New Guinea and Tasmania from Australia. By then, about half of the megafauna (animals weighing more than 100 pounds) that had inhabited the world during the Ice Age had disappeared. The extinctions included some 35 species in the Americas and about 50 species in Greater Australia. What caused the relatively sudden demise of the megafauna? Archeologists have suggested three possible answers. Some emphasize the effects of climate change, others stress human predation, and still others point to alterations in the environment due to fires that people ignited to clear broad swaths of land. Although none of these factors alone seem to offer an adequate explanation for the megafauna extinction, they may have worked together in subtle ways that left only a few large animals available for later domestication in the Americas and Australia.

Egalitarian Groups of Hunters and Gatherers

Most Ice Age people belonged to hunting and gathering bands that moved around frequently in search of food. These mobile foragers did not accumulate significant quantities of material goods or store large amounts of food for future consumption. Unlike more recent hunter-gatherer peoples, Ice Age foragers did not have any contact with agricultural or industrial societies. Anthropologists cannot therefore assume that all foragers throughout history behaved in the same way. Nevertheless, **ethnographic studies** of recent foragers can shed light on early hunter-gatherers. And these studies reveal that the distribution of food and other scarce resources is relatively equal in numerous foraging societies around the world.

The Sharing Ethic

Ethnographic studies show that meat is often shared among the members of foraging groups. While residing in areas of limited and uncertain animal resources, even a skilled hunter cannot always be sure of success. But a member of a male hunting party could create debts by sharing with others when he managed to kill a large animal even if his family received the biggest portion of the meat. And he could expect to be repaid in kind whenever one of his hunting partners succeeded in killing a large animal. The reciprocal sharing of fresh meat that is hard to procure, therefore, can provide a form of insurance that gives everyone in the group access to a portion of an animal that was too big for a single family to eat. From an evolutionary perspective, the sharing ethic reduced the risk of malnutrition and increased the chance of survival for each group member.

It requires considerable effort, however, to maintain a relatively equitable allocation of food and other resources. In any given collection of people, some ambitious individuals will seek to acquire more resources than others. Many ethnographic studies of recent hunter-gatherer populations show that people with acquisitive dispositions are prevented from violating the sharing ethic in various ways. Group members sometimes use humor to belittle successful hunters or make accusations of stinginess to keep anyone from hoarding. Exceedingly ambitious individuals are frequently expelled from the group or even killed if they persist in behavior that their peers regard as detrimental to the welfare of the community.

In foraging populations that anthropologists have examined, the two major food procurement tasks are almost always divided along gender lines: men hunt large animals, and women gather plant food. The pursuit of big game over long distances would be difficult and dangerous for pregnant women and nursing mothers with the primary responsibility for rearing children. And the resulting death of women of child-bearing age would be a serious blow to small hunter-gatherer bands. Whereas fruit and nuts collected by women are usually consumed only by their own family, the meat from a large animal killed by a male hunter is generally shared with everyone in the community. Hence, men have a greater opportunity to achieve a higher status than women even when living in foraging groups that obtain more calories from plants than animals. In **egalitarian societies**, however, successful male hunters do not have power over adults outside their families, nor do they possess significant amounts of wealth that their children can inherit.

Technology and Trade

During the Ice Age, different hunter-gatherer communities developed new technologies that spread with considerable speed through much of the world. People were using stone microblades and wood to make composite tools and weapons as early as 25,000 years ago in many parts of Africa, Europe, and Asia. At about the same time, foragers in Europe began making thread by twisting wild plant fibers and locking them together. They used the string for many purposes: to bind small blades to wooden shafts, to make fishing lines and nets, and to stitch hides together to form warm clothing. They also made needles out of antler, bone, and ivory to draw thread through small holes punched into beads that could be warn as necklaces or sewn into garments. Moreover, sometime before 20,000 years ago, European foragers invented devices that could deliver spears at high velocity and over a great distance. These spear-throwing implements, called atlatls, spread rapidly across Asia and Australia before finally reaching the Americas.

Ice Age hunter-gatherers flourished in many different environments not only by developing new technologies but also by establishing exchange networks that extended over vast areas. As early as 30,000 years ago, for example, communities along the Eastern shores of the Mediterranean acquired obsidian from a source that was more than 100 miles away in Anatolia (modern Turkey). They used the obsidian, a fine black volcanic glass, to make extremely sharp tools and weapons. Moreover, during a relatively brief period around 26,000 years ago, many communities in Europe were engaged in the long-distance exchange of a great number of small statues of women endowed with very large breasts. These so-called Venus figurines, usually carved from mammoth ivory and produced in a uniform style, have been discovered in archaeological sites widely scattered across Europe from the Pyrenees Mountains in the west to the Don River in the east. Some anthropologists have speculated that these pieces of portable art may have been distributed as gifts to help reduce the risk of hostility among highly mobile bands of foragers.

Ice Age Warfare

Despite the exchange of gifts and goods, however, small groups of male hunters sometimes formed war parties and attacked the members of other Ice Age communities. Archeologists have found evidence for violent death in the skeletal remains of people buried in many different parts of Europe between 34,000 and 12,000 years ago. Signs of violence include spear tips embedded in bones, smashed skulls, and forearms with fractures probably sustained during attempts to ward off aggressive blows. It is not easy to know if these victims of violence died as a result of homicide within their own communities or wars between rival communities. Nor is it possible to be sure if conflicts among different groups of foragers were frequent or infrequent.

The earliest clear evidence for warfare comes from a cemetery in North Africa. Located near the Nile River in an area possessing an abundant supply of food but surrounded by desert, the cemetery contains the remains of 58 men, women, and children buried around 14,000 years ago. Of these, 24 were killed by projectile points or severe blows to the head. Several adults suffered from multiple wounds caused by spears and arrows as well as defensive fractures caused by blows to their forearms. Although it is difficult to determine whether a single massacre or a series of attacks led to these deaths, the indiscriminate slaughter of men, women, and children suggests a deliberate attempt to wipe out an entire population and to acquire territory that was rich in wild food resources.

Affluent Ice Age Foragers

A small minority of Ice Age hunter-gatherers lived in environments that were especially rich in food resources. Exploiting a wide variety of fish, waterfowl, nuts, fruit, and mammals, these broad-spectrum foragers did not need to travel frequently to find enough food to satisfy their nutritional requirements. They therefore became less mobile and more sedentary. Taking advantage of exceptionally plentiful habitats, these groups began establishing semipermanent settlements where they resided for several months each year. They also stored food for future consumption and accumulated material goods that did not have to be carried from campsite to campsite. These surplus items often became the property of individual members of a community.

The Emergence of Self-Interested Households

In areas where most people faced little risk of starvation under normal conditions, a fundamental restructuring of social relations occurred. The motivation for sharing diminished, and families began functioning as autonomous economic units. Living in separate households, people started producing and storing food to be consumed by their own families or traded for materials possessed by other families. This led to growing differences in the accumulation of goods that children could inherit from their parents. Thus, the transition from sharing bands to self-interested households paved the way for the development of social and economic inequality.

During the Ice Age, foragers living in the most productive households in resource-rich locations sought to differentiate themselves from the less fortunate members of their communities. Wealthier individuals signaled their higher status by adorning themselves with finely crafted necklaces and bracelets. These fashionable pieces of wearable art were often made from exotic materials, such as mammoth ivory or seashells, that came from faraway places. Members of autonomous households therefore had an incentive to accumulate surplus food that could be exchanged for rare materials. By engaging in long-distance trade, ambitious individuals in hunter-gatherer communities could obtain prestige goods needed to display their elevated social position. These luxury goods, moreover, were often buried with elite individuals.

In addition to reflecting social and economic divisions among the living, Ice Age burials furnish tangible evidence for a belief in an afterlife and a desire to prepare the dead for the spirit world. The concept of a spiritual realm, which provided the common foundation for the rise of religion throughout the world, may have been rooted in visions that appeared in the mind of shamans during trances induced by rhythmic dancing, fasting, or hallucinogenic substances. Recent ethnographic studies have repeatedly demonstrated that shamans in foraging communities in many different regions of the world claim to possess an exclusive ability to communicate with supernatural entities and to obtain their aid in hunting animals, curing diseases, and destroying enemies. As these investigations show, ritual specialists generally enjoy a high status and have an ability to influence members of their community, and they may have played an important role in the development of differences in prestige and power in Ice Age communities around the globe.

A Remarkable Ice Age Burial

Although people living during the last Ice Age could effectively communicate with each other by engaging in fully articulate speech, they did not develop writing systems that would enable them to transmit their ideas to later generations in permanent records. But archaeology can shed considerable light on the lives of preliterate foragers. By studying the skeletal remains of people who died long ago, scholars can determine how long they lived, what kind of food they consumed, whether they were healthy or not, and if they were killed as the result of a violence. The goods buried with people can also reveal much about them, including the level of their wealth compared to their neighbors and the inherited status of their children.

The elaborate burials of affluent foragers who lived in Europe between 30,000 and 20,000 years ago provide strong evidence for the early appearance of social and economic inequality. While most people were interred in simple graves without any offerings, a few adults and children were buried with an impressive assortment of prestige goods, such as jewelry made from marine shells or other exotic materials that came from hundreds of miles away.

The spectacular graves discovered at Sungir, a settlement located about 95 miles northwest of Moscow, furnish dramatic examples of unusually luxurious Ice Age burials. The graves, which were dug more than 25,000 years ago, contain the remains of an older male and two adolescents. All three were buried with necklaces, bracelets, and thousands of beads, carved from mammoth ivory, that had been stitched into their clothing. While the man was dressed in garments holding about 3,000 ivory beads, the boy's and girl's clothes were each decorated with over 5,000 ivory beads sewn into the material. These grave goods, which probably took more than 9,000 hours of labor to produce, indicate not only the possession of an immense amount of wealth by

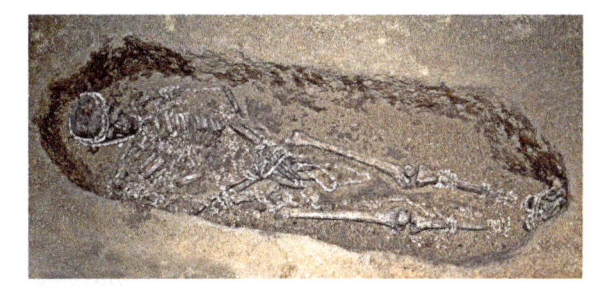

FIGURE 1.2 A Rich Burial at Sungir. Archaeologists discovered these skeletal remains of an elite individual who was buried in a settlement northwest of Moscow between 28,000 and 30,000 years ago.

a prominent man, perhaps a chief, but also the inheritance of an elevated social position by his children.

The Spread of Social and Economic Inequality

As global temperatures steadily rose between 20,000 and 13,000 years ago, several changes associated with the emergence of socioeconomic inequality became more pronounced in a few places. People living in areas of abundance consumed a broader range of food, built more substantial dwellings, established more permanent settlements, and acquired exotic materials from more distant sources. At Nelson's Bay on the coast of South Africa, for example, broad-spectrum foragers subsisted on a varied diet of wild foods, including eland, bush pigs, ocean fish, and sea birds.

As hunter-gatherers recolonized parts of the East European Plain that had been abandoned during the last glacial maximum, they established numerous settlements and used mammoth bones to construct large oval houses. One such settlement, established around 15,000 years ago, was located at Mezhirich, about 10 miles west of the Dnieper River in central Ukraine. This small village provided shelter for up to 50 people during the winter months. The foragers living at Mezhirich hunted large animals and rabbits, caught river fish, and stored food in deep pits. They also made ornaments from shells that had been carried over 400 miles from the shore of the Black Sea.

Around 14,500 years ago, foragers known as Natufians began establishing a far more affluent group of sedentary communities in southwestern Asia. Some of the larger Natufian villages housed as many as 150 people in permanent dwellings. Residing in rich habitats such as the Jordan River valley in Israel and the Euphrates River valley in Syria, the Natufians exploited a wide range of food resources. They hunted gazelle and deer, caught river fish and waterfowl, gathered almonds and pistachio nuts, and harvested wild stands of wheat and barley. These broad-spectrum foragers not only used mortars and pestles to grind seeds for storage but also obtained shells from both the Red Sea and the Mediterranean Sea to make beads for personal adornment.

While most Natufians were buried in simple graves without any luxury goods, a few adults and children were interred in elaborate graves and decorated with ornaments made from animal bones and marine shells. The significant differences in the treatment of the dead found in these burials mirror the unequal distribution of wealth and status that differentiated the people who lived in the flourishing Natufian villages.

Social Stratification and Warfare Before Agriculture

As global temperatures began a relatively steady upward movement around 12,000 years ago, the climate of the planet grew warmer and wetter except for a few periods of cooler and drier weather. Plants and animals became more plentiful under these conditions while melting glaciers created many rivers, lakes, and marshes that provided rich habitats for increasing numbers of migratory birds and freshwater fish. Living in areas where they could exploit an abundance of wild food resources, different groups of hunter-gatherers established permanent settlements with growing populations.

Affluent Foragers in Asia and Europe

After the Ice Age ended some 12,000 years ago, the transition from egalitarian bands of mobile hunter-gatherers to more complex societies of sedentary foragers occurred at a faster pace, especially in places with rich aquatic resources. The complex Jomon culture emerged in Japan about 11,500 years ago when nomadic foragers established a string of permanent settlements where they exploited a wide array of terrestrial animals, sea mammals, and saltwater fish. In the Ganges River valley of India, roving bands of hunter-gatherers began to settle into villages about 10,000 years ago and to subsist on abundant quantities of wild animals and freshwater fish. And sometime around 8,500 years ago, mobile foragers started building several villages at the Iron Gates, a long and deep gorge on the Danube River in Serbia, where they flourished on a nourishing diet of fish caught in the river and animals killed in the surrounding hills.

A more complex culture blossomed in the Baltic Sea region between 8,000 and 6,000 years ago as seasonal hunting and fishing camps evolved into permanent settlements. Located along the coasts of Denmark, southern Sweden, and northern Germany, the foragers in these Baltic communities thrived on a reliable and abundant supply of maritime resources. They built canoes to gain access to great numbers of cod, flounder, oysters, mussels, and seals. To supplement their nutritious marine diet, they hunted and trapped animals and gathered nuts and berries. These broad-spectrum foragers buried some of their dead with prestige goods, such as polished flint axes. In addition to revealing the existence of social inequality within individual villages, Scandinavian cemeteries provide evidence for warfare between different settlements. Skeletal remains indicate that large numbers of people buried in Sweden and Denmark suffered from traumatic blows to the head.

Stratification and Warfare in North America

In some regions of North America, the intensive exploitation of rich aquatic resources led to the emergence of complex foraging societies marked by warfare as well as social stratification. On the banks of the Illinois River about 50 miles northeast of St. Louis, for example, a seasonal camp developed around 7,000 years into the permanent settlement of Koster where approximately 100 people lived in a dozen houses. The inhabitants of the village subsisted on a diverse array of food resources, including fish, mussels, water fowl, nuts, and deer. Participating in a far-flung exchange network based on river-borne canoe traffic, the foragers residing in Koster acquired copper from deposits near Lake Superior, high quality flint from the Ohio River valley, and seashells from the Gulf of Mexico. Cemeteries that contain the remains of people interred between 7,000 and 4,000 years ago at Koster and other permanent settlements east of the Mississippi River and south of the Great Lakes provide evidence for social ranking and lethal fighting. While some were buried with exotic grave goods, many others were interred with projectile points embedded in their bones.

The most complex foraging societies in North America developed in a vast region stretching 1,400 miles along the Pacific coast from southern Alaska to northern California. After about 4,500 years ago, social and economic divisions became increasingly visible in permanent settlements located in areas with large and predictable runs of salmon. Prominent men and women started to distinguish themselves as privileged individuals by wearing lip plugs called labrets. They also began to bury their children with prestige goods that reflected high status ascribed at birth and not achieved during life. In their quest to accumulate wealth and expand their power, aggressive chiefs organized war parties to gain control of coveted territory with abundant supplies of salmon. Social inequality and warfare, therefore, made their appearance in two large areas of North America long before any of the foragers in these regions became farmers.

Review Questions

1. What role did the creation of tools play in the evolution of hominins?
2. How did modern humans manage to reach the Americas?
3. Why was sharing important in mobile bands of hunter-gatherers?

4. How did foragers behave in areas that were especially rich in wild food resources?
5. Under what conditions did social stratification and warfare appear among foragers?

Additional Readings

Ames, Kenneth M., and Herbert D. G. Maschner. *Peoples of the Northwest Coast: Their Archeology and Prehistory.* New York: Thames and Hudson, 1999.

Bellwood, Peter. *First Migrants: Ancient Migrants in Global Perspective.* Chichester, UK: Wiley-Blackwell, 2013.

Feinman, Gary M., and T. Douglas Price, eds. *Archeology at the Millennium: A Sourcebook.* New York: Kluwer Academic/Plenum Publishers, 2001.

Gat, Azar. *War in Human Civilization.* Oxford: Oxford University Press, 2006.

Guilaine, Jean, and Jean Zammit. *The Origins of War: Violence in Prehistory.* Oxford: Blackwell Publishers, 2005.

Hoffecker, John F. *A Prehistory of the North: Human Settlement of Higher Latitudes.* New Brunswick, NJ: Rutgers University Press, 2005.

Kelly, Robert L. *The Lifeways of Hunter-Gatherers: The Foraging Spectrum.* Cambridge: Cambridge University Press, 2013.

Klien, Richard G. *The Human Career: Human Biology and Cultural Origins.* 3rd ed. Chicago: University of Chicago Press, 2009.

Mithen, Steven. *After the Ice: A Global Human History, 20,000-5,000 B.C.* London: Orion Books, 2003.

Price, T. Douglas, and Gary M. Feinman, eds. *Pathways to Power: New Perspectives on the Emergence of Social Inequality.* New York: Springer, 2012.

Renfrew, Colin. *Prehistory: The Making of the Human Mind.* New York: Random House, 2007.

Scarre, Chris, ed. *The Human Past: World Prehistory and the Development of Human Societies.* 4th ed. London: Thames & Hudson, 2018.

Figure Credits

Fig. 1.1: Copyright © by Fidelis T. Masao (CC BY 4.0) at https://commons.wikimedia.org/wiki/File:Testpit_L8_at_Laetoli_Site_S.jpg.

Map 1.1: Source: https://commons.wikimedia.org/wiki/File:Spreading_homo_sapiens_la.svg.

Map 1.2: Source: https://www.nps.gov/articles/aps-v8-i2-c1.htm.

Fig. 1.2: Source: https://commons.wikimedia.org/wiki/File:Sunghir-tumba_paleol%C3%ADtica.jpg.

CHAPTER 2

The Agricultural Revolution, 9000 BCE–1 BCE

The Origins and Spread of Agriculture

The Agricultural Revolution was the first major turning point in world history since *Homo sapiens* began leaving their African homeland and migrating to different regions around the globe. Before modern humans started domesticating plants and animals, most people lived in small groups that moved as the seasons changed in search of wild sources of food. Recent **ethnographic studies** reveal that women in mobile hunter-gatherer bands usually give birth to only one child every three or four years. By maintaining a relatively long interval between pregnancies, they can travel from one habitat to another collecting wild fruit and vegetables without caring for several infants at the same time. Ethnographic accounts also show that mobile foraging groups do not store large quantities of food or accumulate bundles of goods that would be difficult to carry from place to place. In these societies, the rate of population growth is very slow, and the distribution of wealth and power is relatively equal.

As global temperatures warmed following the end of the last Ice Age around 10,000 BCE, foragers in several different regions began at different times domesticating local plant and animal species. Agriculture spread from these original centers of food production first to adjacent territories and then to distant lands. By 1 BCE, farmers or herders were living in almost every part of the world except for a few remote islands or marginal areas that were extremely frigid or arid. Sparse populations of foragers continued to survive in these cold and dry environments, but they often traded with nearby agricultural communities to obtain various goods.

In both the original and secondary areas of food production, the transition from hunting and gathering to farming and herding was a gradual process. The early agriculturalists relied for a considerable period of time on wild sources of food for the bulk of their diet. But as farming communities produced more and more food, they grew larger and larger, and as domesticated plants and animals eventually provided most of their nutritional requirements, they could not revert to foraging without risking starvation.

Although the shift from foraging to farming unfolded slowly over several generations, the emergence and spread of agriculture had two revolutionary consequences. First, the production of a growing supply of food sparked an explosion in human population. As farmers established permanent villages close to their fields and pastures, the number of people inhabiting the earth jumped from fewer than 5 million to more than 100 million in just eight millennia. Second, while paving the way for the beginning of urbanization and **environmental degradation**, the production of surplus food had a profound impact on the distribution of wealth and power in agricultural societies. Some ambitious individuals grasped the opportunity to extract from others food that could be exchanged for goods and services. Such acquisitive behavior resulted in a dramatic increase in social stratification, economic inequality, and warfare in many different parts of the world.

The Domestication of Plants and Animals and the Production of Surplus Food

The dramatic change in global climate following the Ice Age provided a necessary precondition for the Agricultural Revolution. As the weather became warmer and wetter beginning around 9600 BCE, foragers in at least seven different regions—Southwest Asia, East Asia, New Guinea, North Africa, Central America, South America, and North America—began domesticating at different times local plant and animal species. Each of these core areas, broadly dispersed across the middle latitudes of the earth, possessed a different pool of potential domesticates. While some places had few if any large mammals that were suitable for selective breeding, for example, others had several animals that were good candidates for **domestication** because of their gregarious nature, their willingness to follow a dominant leader, and their tolerance for confinement.

Agricultural societies evolved gradually in each of the original hearths of domestication. In the early stages of the transition from collecting to producing food, people in small villages established mixed economies that combined foraging with farming and herding. Domesticated plants and animals only supplemented

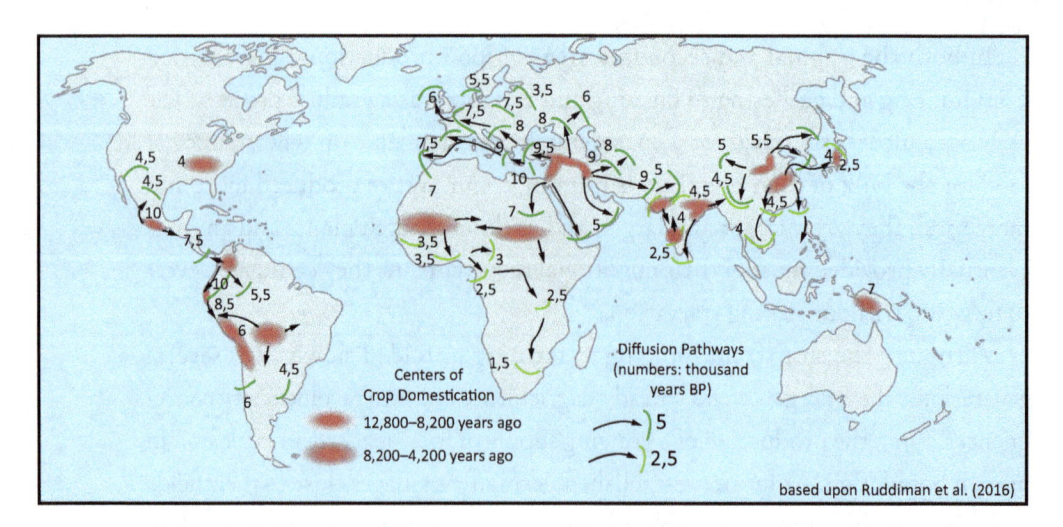

MAP 2.1 Original Centers of Plant Domestication. Presented are the approximate dates for the domestication of plants in different parts of the world.

wild species as sources of food for a considerable time, but eventually, domestics provided the bulk of the diet for growing farming populations. And after agricultural communities became dependent on plant cultivation and animal husbandry for their sustenance, they could not revert to foraging to obtain an adequate food supply needed to nourish their expanding populations.

The Spread of Farming Throughout the World

Agriculture did not become the dominant mode of subsistence, however, until farming spread from the initial centers of food production first to adjacent territory and then to more distant regions. While some mammals, such as cattle and pigs, were domesticated at different times and places, most plant and animal species were domesticated at only one time and place before they were taken to other locations. The expansion of agriculture involved two different processes: migrating farmers introduced domesticated species into new areas, and indigenous foragers adopted farming practices after establishing trade relations with agrarian communities.

As agriculture spread throughout the world, several technological innovations led to the production of greater quantities of food. Irrigation permitted farming in dry areas by channeling water to crops, terracing allowed for the cultivation of hilly terrain by preventing water from running down slopes, and new ways of exploiting animals for physical labor greatly increased agricultural productivity. At first, goats, sheep, and cattle were used primarily as sources of meat, but after years of breeding, they also became sources of milk, wool, and traction. The use of oxen and horses for plowing made it possible for farmers to till heavier soil and for families to cultivate more acres, and the dispersion of livestock dung made fields more fertile.

The Invention of Irrigation

The successful cultivation of plants and the breeding of animals depend on several conditions. In addition to fertile soil and a warm climate, farming and herding require an adequate supply of water. Some crops grow better than others in relatively dry areas. In many regions around the world, rainfall usually provides a sufficient amount of moisture for the cultivation of grains, fruit, and vegetables. If irrigation projects deliver enough water to nearby fields, however, agriculture can thrive in more arid environments.

Irrigation played an important role in the Agricultural Revolution. In prehistoric times, irrigation systems made farming possible in many dry areas ranging from southern Mesopotamia and the Indus River valley to the highlands of Peru and the Tucson basin in Arizona. Temples and palaces were responsible for the construction of a few large and complex irrigation works in the ancient world. But most early irrigation projects were built by local farming communities without any outside supervision. These were usually small works based on simple technological innovations, such as dams, dykes, and ditches that channeled water from rivers and streams to adjacent farm lands.

These ancient irrigation systems had two important consequences. In the short run, irrigation enabled farmers to grow crops in places with limited amounts of annual rainfall. Agriculture could therefore spread into many dry regions and greatly expand the supply of surplus food. Besides providing nourishment for a growing number of nonfarmers residing in urban centers, the production and storage of large quantities of food enabled some to live off the labor of others. And the accumulation of surplus food by ambitious and acquisitive individuals led to increasing economic inequality in agricultural societies around the world.

In the long run, however, the continued use of irrigation caused severe environmental damage in several areas. The heavily irrigated fields between the Tigris and Euphrates Rivers in southern Mesopotamia, for instance, gradually became less fertile as water-soluble salts increasingly accumulated in the soil. Farmers in southern Mesopotamia responded to the problem of environmental degradation first by cultivating less wheat and more barley, which tolerates salt better, and then by migrating to other areas in Southwest Asia.

Agriculture and Social Inequality

The emergence and spread of agriculture resulted in an unequal distribution of resources in a growing number of societies around the world. Prior to the beginning of farming and herding, significant socioeconomic inequities had appeared in only a few affluent foraging settlements located in areas that were especially rich in food resources. But the advent of agriculture permitted the accumulation of much larger food surpluses and allowed social and economic differences to develop to a far greater degree in many farming communities. In early agricultural societies, some households with ambitious heads were more successful than neighboring families in producing surplus food that could be exchanged for goods or services. And as children in affluent families inherited land, animals, and equipment from their parents, disparities in wealth and status became perpetuated over generations.

As agricultural communities became increasingly divided along class lines, powerful chiefs emerged in many parts of the world. Many recent ethnographic studies reveal that ambitious chiefs have employed several common strategies designed to enhance their economic position and political authority. In widely dispersed geographical areas, enterprising chiefs have persuaded farmers to contribute food to communal feasts. Then, after skimming off a portion of the collected food, these chiefs distribute some of it to others in order to create debts that have to be repaid in goods or services. Chiefs have often dispensed prestige goods to elite individuals in return for their loyalty, and they have frequently claimed exclusive spiritual powers to justify their privileges in the eyes of ordinary people. Finally, aggrandizing chiefs have repeatedly used military force to gain control over people and property in surrounding communities.

Southwest Asia, Europe, and Central Asia

The Agricultural Revolution commenced in Southwest Asia on the well-watered hilly flanks of the Fertile Crescent, an arc of territory stretching from Israel northward through Syria into southwestern Anatolia (modern Turkey) and then eastward across northern Iraq and finally southeastward through western Iran. Between 9600 and 8800 BCE, as the climate became increasingly favorable for agriculture, some affluent foragers, including the Natufians who were living in permanent villages and subsisting on a broad spectrum of wild foods, began domesticating a great variety of plants and animals.

Agriculture gradually expanded beyond the Fertile Crescent into large parts of both Europe and Central Asia between 6500 and 4000 BCE. After farmers migrated from Southwest Asia and established agricultural settlements in Greece, farming spread as far west as the Atlantic Ocean and as far north as the Baltic Sea. Meanwhile, farmers from Southwest Asia moved east of the Caspian Sea, and others migrated from Southeast Europe and established agricultural communities east of the Carpathian Mountains.

One Starting Point: The Fertile Crescent

The Fertile Crescent possessed a larger number of wild species that could be successfully domesticated than any other region in the world. The suite of species that were first domesticated in Southwest Asia provided a potent food package: four cereals (emmer wheat, einkorn wheat, barley, and rye) supplied ample quantities of carbohydrates; and four large mammals (goats, sheep, pigs, and cattle) furnished considerable amounts of protein. Although each of these species was probably domesticated only once in a specific place within its natural range, agriculture spread quickly into nearby upland areas that received sufficient rainfall as domesticated seeds and breeding stock were traded from settlement to settlement.

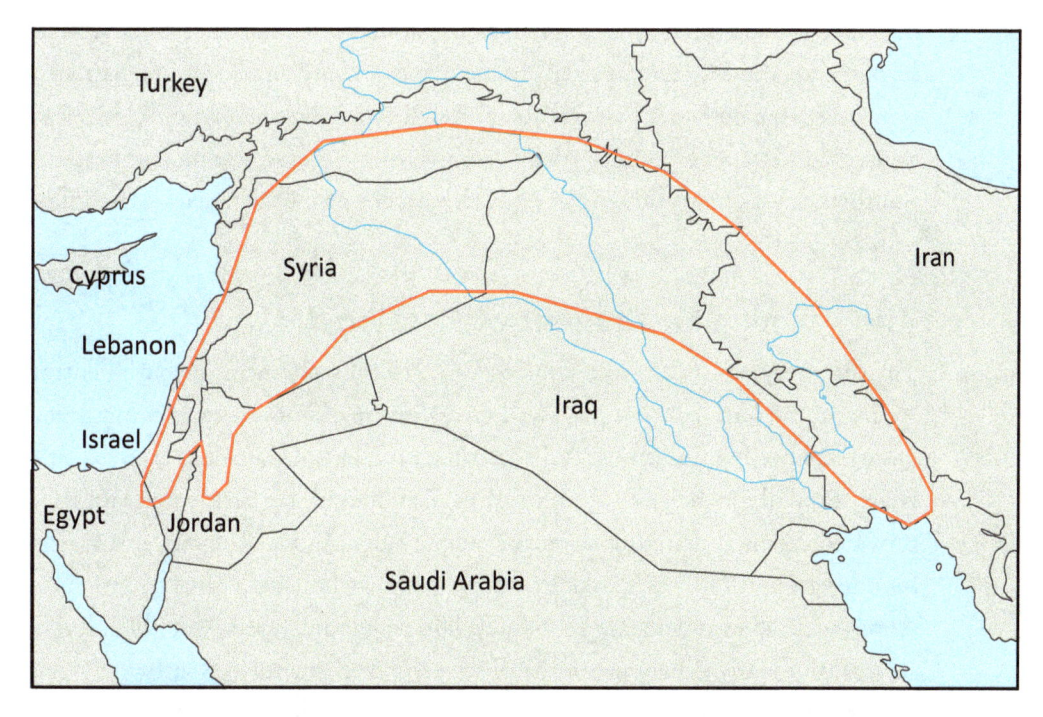

MAP 2.2 The Fertile Crescent. This was an early area of food production with a large number of domesticated plants and animals.

The transition from hunting and gathering to farming and herding occurred gradually over many centuries, and people in the Fertile Crescent became increasingly dependent on domesticated plants and animals for their nourishment. Indeed, between 8800 and 6900 BCE, most communities in Southwest Asia developed mixed agricultural economies based on the supervision of animals and the cultivation of cereals and legumes, such as peas, beans, and lentils. The production of large food surpluses permitted an increase in population throughout the region. In south-central Anatolia, the farmers in several small villages joined together and established the unusually large agricultural community of Catalhoyuk.

The rapid increase in population and the intensive exploitation of the land, however, soon led to severe environmental degradation in some areas of the Fertile Crescent. While tilling and grazing exposed the soil in fields to erosion, cutting trees to obtain wood for fires to cook food and heat dwellings caused extensive deforestation. As farmers in Southwest Asia and then in other parts of the world began clearing forests, which absorb large amounts of **carbon dioxide** from the atmosphere, they unintentionally laid the foundations for a growing accumulation of **greenhouse gases**.

As ecologically fragile areas in the Fertile Crescent became less productive, people began abandoning large agricultural communities, such as 'Ain Ghazal in Jordan and Abu Hureyra in Syria. Some dispersed into small farming hamlets, others became nomadic pastoralists, and still others colonized new territories that could sustain agriculture. While some farmers moved to different areas in Southwest Asia, many others migrated to adjacent regions where winter rainfall could water their crops.

The Farming Settlement of Catalhoyuk

The discovery of Catalhoyuk, a major agricultural settlement in south-central Anatolia (modern Turkey), has given us a glimpse of how an early community of farmers lived in Southwest Asia. Located on a fertile plain that received sufficient rainfall for the cultivation of crops, Catalhoyuk sat beside a stream that provided essential drinking water for people and animals. The settlement was founded around 7300 BCE and grew rapidly into an unusually large community. Covering 32 acres and housing almost 10,000 people at its peak, Catalhoyuk was several times larger than any of the other early settlements in Southwest Asia. The community disappeared about 6200 BCE for unknown reasons, but several small farming villages continued to flourish in the region.

The economy of Catalhoyuk was geared to the cultivation of cereals and legumes and the herding of large flocks of sheep that provided the community with meat and wool. Because the settlement was prone to seasonal flooding, farmers probably grazed their sheep and planted their crops in fields a few miles from their homes. The inhabitants of Catalhoyuk supplemented their diet, which was based primarily on the consumption of domesticated plants and animals, by hunting wild deer in the forested mountains to the south and west. They also obtained obsidian, used to make projectile points, from a volcanic area in these mountains.

Catalhoyuk was a densely packed community. The mud-brick houses looked like rectangular boxes pushed together with the sides of each one touching the walls of four others. Since almost no lanes separated the dwellings, people entered their home through a hatch on the flat roof and climbed down a ladder to their living quarters. Each one-story house consisted of a main room and a smaller room for storage; their floors and walls were covered with white plaster that was often painted red. A clay oven for heating and cooking was usually situated below the access ladder so that smoke could escape through the trapdoor on the roof.

Many people were buried under the floors of their homes at Catalhoyuk, and their graves show clear signs of social and economic inequality. While most people were buried without any grave goods, some individuals were interred with a few inexpensive goods. But a small handful of elite members of the community were buried with a number of valuable items, such as jewelry made from marine shells for women and flint weapons for men.

Expansion into Europe

Migrating farmers, probably sailing across the Aegean Sea from Anatolia, established the first agricultural settlements in mainland Europe around 6500 BCE on the fertile plains of Thessaly in eastern Greece. These pioneers brought the full complement of plants and animals, such as wheat, barley, sheep, and goats, that had been earlier domesticated in Southwest Asia. As the population in these villages grew to a level that could not be supported by the available land, groups of farmers began moving northward, leaping from one valley to the next and encountering indigenous foragers who sometimes became farmers themselves. Agriculture spread rapidly through the Balkan Peninsula and into the Hungarian plain.

By 5000 BCE, mines in the Balkan and Carpathian Mountains were supplying the copper and gold that metal smiths in southeastern Europe used to make ornaments. These pieces of wearable art were often buried with elite individuals to display their elevated status. In cemeteries located next to the agricultural towns dotting the lower Danube River valley, differences in the disposition of grave goods indicate the development of a sharp division between elites and commoners.

The spread of agriculture westward across Europe involved both colonizing farmers and indigenous foragers who either adopted farming or became absorbed by growing agricultural populations. The expansionist thrust proceeded swiftly along two main pathways between 6000 and 5200 BCE. On the first route, farming spread across southern Europe from Greece to Portugal. Farmers traveling in boats probably spearheaded this movement by establishing agricultural enclaves along the Mediterranean and Atlantic coasts where local populations were sparse. On the second route, agriculture spread across the temperate forests of central Europe from Hungary to France. Migrating farmers established scattered villages in river valleys containing fertile windblown **loess soil** that had been ground into fine particles by glaciers and could be easily tilled by using simple hoes.

Although there is little evidence for hostile relations between farmers and foragers in Europe, there are clear examples of warfare among neighboring agricultural communities. Farmers launched violent attacks against other farmers around 5000 BCE both at Talheim in Germany and at Schletz in Austria. The desire to seize land or livestock may have triggered the massacre at Talheim. In this small agricultural settlement, 34 men, women, and children were slaughtered. Most of them were killed by blows to the head inflicted by heavy stone axes that farmers in the area used as weapons to kill people as well as tools to clear forests.

Shortly after 4000 BCE, the agricultural frontier moved rapidly northward into the British Isles and southern Scandinavia. Affluent foragers living in sedentary communities in Denmark and Sweden had been trading with farmers in Germany and Poland for more than 1,000 years. Then they suddenly began adopting agriculture and building long earthen mounds where they buried elite individuals with prestige goods made from both amber and flint.

Hierarchical societies headed by chiefs emerged in many parts of Europe between 3000 and 1000 BCE as several agricultural innovations generated larger food surpluses. Together with the widespread use of oxen to plow heavier soils and larger fields, the breeding of wool-bearing sheep and milk-producing cows greatly expanded agricultural output and provided the foundation for increasing socioeconomic stratification.

The elaborate burials of elite individuals in farming communities dispersed across Europe indicate that wealth was concentrated in the hands of chiefs and their armed supporters. These men not only owned large parcels of land but they also acquired exotic materials from distant sources to display their exalted position. While high-status women were often buried with valuable jewelry, such as gold earrings or necklaces made with amber beads, prominent men were frequently buried with finely crafted weapons and vessels for consuming alcohol. These grave goods encapsulated the ideal male image of fighting and drinking, and they became universal prestige symbols that separated chiefs and warriors from ordinary people throughout Europe.

The most dramatic evidence for the early appearance of social stratification in a European farming community comes from a cemetery at Varna on the Black Sea coast of Bulgaria. In this cemetery, 211 burials reflect striking differences in the distribution of wealth among the people who lived in the area. Most of the graves contained only a few goods, and over 20 burials had no offerings. But 18 graves were richly endowed with a large number of valuable gold and copper pieces.

One elaborate grave contained the remains of a man buried with some 320 luxury goods made of gold. These glittering objects, which included beads, rings, bracelets, and a penis sheath, weighed 3.3 pounds and today would be worth about a million dollars. Before he died around 4500 BCE, the man probably had been a paramount chief in a region where clan leaders were frequently buried with similar but less ostentatious displays of wealth and position.

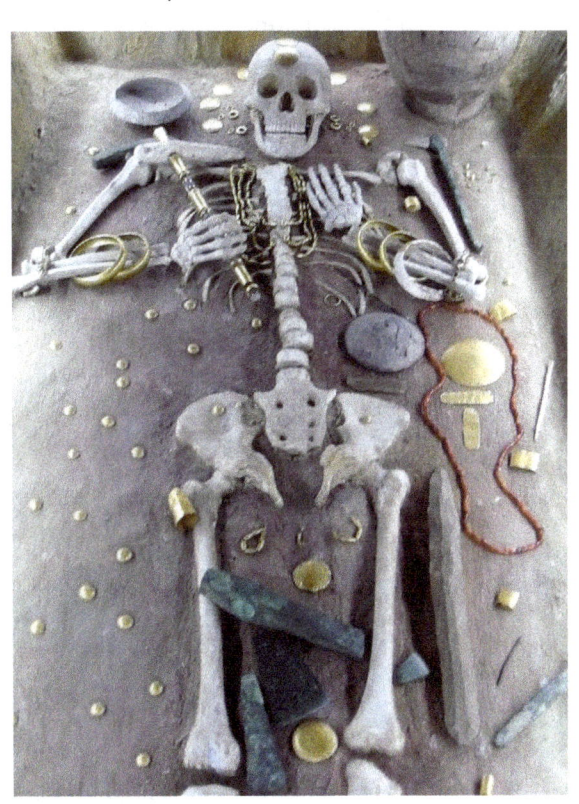

FIGURE 2.1 A Rich Burial at Varna. Archaeologists uncovered these remains of a man buried with hundreds of gold objects at the Varna cemetery in Bulgaria about 4500 BCE.

Expansion into Central Asia

Agriculture also spread eastward into Central Asia along two separate courses. Migrating along a southern line, farmers from Southwest Asia began around 6000 BCE establishing communities east of the Caspian Sea where rivers allowed them to irrigate their crops. Agriculture later spread into the river valleys further to the east. Moving along a northern line, farmers from Southeast Europe started around 5800 BCE settling east of the Carpathian Mountains with the full package of animals and plants that had originally been domesticated in Southwest Asia. When farmers pushed further east into the treeless **steppes** north of the Black Sea, they encountered dense populations of foragers who adopted farming and herding in river valleys where their cattle and sheep thrived.

Evidence for the emergence of wealthy families and powerful chiefs appear in elaborate burials on the steppes after 5000 BCE as herding spread eastward to the Ural Mountains. In settlements in the Dnieper River valley, for example, a few individuals and their children were buried with copper and gold ornaments, while chiefs were interred not only with many luxury goods but also with wild boar tusks, which symbolized their military strength.

Herders on the steppes first domesticated horses to provide an additional source of meat, and sometime before 3300 BCE, they began riding horses and using oxen to draw wheeled vehicles. This enabled them to practice a more mobile form of pastoralism. With wagons full of tents and supplies, herders could take their cattle, sheep, and horses far into the open steppes and exploit the vast grasslands between the major rivers. Herders riding horses, moreover, could drive bigger herds over more extensive pastures. After 2800 BCE, the ownership of larger herds led not only to conflicts over grazing land but also to the accumulation of greater wealth that was often deposited in graves sprinkled across the steppes.

East Asia, Southeast Asia, and the Pacific

Agriculture emerged independently in East Asia when two different areas in China became original centers of food production. In both the Yellow and Yangzi River valleys, native foragers began domesticating local species of wild plants and animals. Rice farming eventually spread from China into both Southeast Asia and the Pacific Basin. Meanwhile, agriculture developed independently in New Guinea when indigenous foragers began domesticating taro, yams, and other local plants. In all these areas, farming provided the economic foundation for the emergence of hierarchical societies.

Another Starting Point: East Asia

Agriculture emerged independently in East Asia, a huge region separated by mountains and deserts from the Fertile Crescent, when two different areas in

China developed into early centers of food production. Sometime around 7000 BCE, foragers in the Yangzi and Yellow River valleys started domesticating wild plants that had proliferated after the last Ice Age as temperatures rose and rainfall increased. The fertile loess soils in the Yellow River valley in northern China furnished an excellent environment for the cultivation of millet, while the lakes, marshes, and **floodplains** in the middle and lower Yangzi valley in southern China provided ideal habitats for the cultivation of rice.

Agricultural villages were flourishing by 6000 BCE in each of these areas where people were living in permanent houses, using querns or pestles to grind grain, and storing their surplus food in pits. In the Yellow River valley, farmers cultivated foxtail millet as their main crop. They also raised domesticated pigs and chickens as they continued to engage in their traditional hunting, fishing, and gathering activities. In the Yangzi valley, farmers cultivated rice as their primary staple. They also began keeping domesticated cattle and pigs while continuing to collect wild food. The mixed farming economies in each area produced increasing amounts of food that supported a growing number of town dwellers who by 5000 BCE had become dependent on domesticated plants and animals for most of their nutrition.

The thriving economies in these two agricultural centers provided the foundation for the development of highly stratified and militant chiefdoms. In both northern and southern China, many towns had defensive walls built to furnish protection from aggressive neighbors. They also had cemeteries that reveal a widening gap that separated elite individuals from common people. In a cemetery holding the remains of 700 people from a large fortified town established around 4000 BCE in the middle of the Yangzi basin, most of the dead were buried with few if any grave goods, but some people were interred with jade ornaments and fine pottery vessels.

Similarly, in a town established in the Yellow River basin about 2500 BCE, a cemetery contained 87 burials organized into three clusters with a few rich graves surrounded by many poor ones in each cluster. The societies that had evolved in the Yellow River valley were marked not only by pronounced social and economic differences but also by constant warfare between rival chiefs in power struggles that eventually culminated in the formation of a unified state in northern China.

Expansion into Southeast Asia

Rice farmers in the Yangzi valley, in the meantime, began migrating southward. They moved first down the Bei River into the region around Hong Kong on the south coast of China and then down the Red and Mekong Rivers into mainland Southeast Asia. While some pioneering rice farmers established settlements in the broad Red River delta in northern Vietnam between 2500 and 2000 BCE, others founded villages during the same period in the extensive lowlands of Thailand and Cambodia. These expanding populations soon encountered indigenous foragers who started cultivating rice in various locations. Consequently, by 1500 BCE, rice farming had spread into many areas of mainland Southeast Asia.

The Red River valley, blessed by a moist climate and fertile **alluvial soil**, was especially productive. By planting two crops each year and using water buffalo to plow their fields, many poor Vietnamese peasants could harvest enough rice to feed their families and to pay high rents to a few rich landowners. The prosperous and militant Dong Son society, which emerged in the Red River delta around 500 BCE, was dominated by wealthy landlords and powerful chiefs. The great Vietnamese landholders dressed in elegant clothing, adorned themselves with impressive ornaments, and carried splendid bronze daggers and swords. While frequently engaging in warfare, aggressive Dong Son chiefs commanded large boats propelled by crews of oarsman and equipped with fighting platforms that supported companies of plumed warriors.

Expansion into the Pacific Basin

Agriculture had already commenced spreading from the Asian mainland into the Pacific Basin. After learning about farming, probably through trade contacts with China, indigenous foragers in Korea began cultivating millet around 4500 BCE and then rice about 2000 BCE. The production of surplus rice soon led to the development of significant economic and social disparities, and by 1000 BCE, elite Koreans were often buried with jade ornaments in large tombs with massive capstones weighing more than 100 tons.

The subsequent spread of rice farming into Japan around 400 BCE involved both the migration of people from Korea and the adoption of agriculture by the native population of affluent foragers. As rice cultivation became widespread and villagers started keeping pigs, which had been domesticated on the mainland, Japanese society became increasingly stratified and belligerent. Some industrious families produced more food than their neighbors, and a few acquisitive individuals found ways to wrest food from others. Many Japanese farming settlements after 200 BCE developed into fortified bastions ruled by elites dressed in fancy silk garments, while commoners still wore simple clothing made from ramie, a tough vegetable fiber.

In contrast to the situation in Japan where immigrants played a major role in the spread of agriculture, farming had independent origins in the remote and isolated highlands of New Guinea. Indigenous foragers who had no contact with distant food producers began as early as 4000 BCE domesticating several local species of plants, such as taro, yams, sugarcane, and bananas. But like what had occurred in Japan and in many other parts of the world, the development of farming in the New Guinea highlands eventually led to the emergence of wealthy and powerful chiefs who regularly waged war against each other in hopes of expanding their domains.

Meanwhile, between 3500 and 3000 BCE, groups of farmers migrated in boats from China to Taiwan where they started cultivating foxtail millet and rice and keeping domesticated pigs. Farmers in Taiwan subsequently began moving southward, and by 2000 BCE, they established settlements in the Philippines. During the next 500 years, some farmers in the Philippines sailed eastward across more than 1,500 miles of open sea to the Mariana Islands, and others traveled southward before branching westward to Borneo and eastward to the Bismarck Archipelago adjacent to New Guinea. They encountered indigenous farmers in the Bismarck and Solomon Islands and learned to cultivate local crops, such as taro, yams, and bananas.

These farmers were expert navigators. After learning to determine latitude by observing the position of stars and to use the winds to reach distant landfalls and to return home safely, they launched voyages of exploration. They embarked on fast canoes equipped with sails and built with either double hulls or single hulls and outriggers that provided stability in rough seas. Their sailing vessels carried diverse cargoes sufficient to begin viable agricultural settlements: several men and women; germinating root plants, such as yams and taro; young trees that could produce a variety of fruit and nuts; and domesticated chickens or pigs to serve as breeding stock.

Migrating from the Solomons around 1200 BCE, some farmers sailed as far south as New Caledonia, while others sailed as far east as Fiji, Tonga, and Samoa where they founded settlements during the next two or three centuries. They also established long-distance trading networks and began shipping obsidian more than 2,000 miles from sources in the Bismarcks to settlements in Borneo and Fiji. Then, after a long pause in maritime colonization, Austronesian-speaking farmers commenced sailing across vast stretches of the Pacific Ocean, and between roughly 700 and 1200 CE, they established settlements in many far-flung Polynesian islands, including the Society Islands, the Marquesas, Easter Island, the Hawaiian Islands, and New Zealand.

The colonization of the Pacific islands led to environmental degradation as well as to the development of hierarchical societies. On many of these islands, intensive farming and rapid population growth resulted in deforestation, soil erosion, and the extinction of some bird species. Meanwhile, on several of the larger islands, the production of surplus food paved the way for the emergence of aggressive chiefs who frequently engaged in warfare in attempts to increase their wealth and power.

Africa, South Asia, and the Americas

The development of agriculture in North Africa was based on the domestication of local species of wild plants and animals as well as the diffusion of species that were originally domesticated in the Fertile Crescent. As farmers and herders migrated from northern Africa, agriculture spread across most of the African continent. The emergence of agriculture in South Asia also involved plant and animal species that had been domesticated both locally and in other places. Meanwhile, in the Americas, agriculture emerged independently in three separate centers of food production and then spread throughout most of the Western Hemisphere.

Africa: Farming and Pastoralism

Agriculture emerged in North Africa as increasing amounts of rainfall led not only to the proliferation of wild plants and animals across the region but also to the appearance of lakes and marshes in the Sahara, which only later became a vast desert. Around 7000 BCE, foragers in the eastern Sahara began independently domesticating an indigenous species of cattle. The subsequent development of herding and farming in the lower (northern) Nile River valley probably involved the migration of people and the diffusion of domesticated plants and animals from both the eastern Sahara and the Fertile Crescent. By 5000 BCE, people living at Merimde, a village of mud huts on the western side of the Nile delta, were cultivating emmer wheat and barley as well as tending cattle, sheep, goats, and pigs.

A similar economy based on farming and herding developed in numerous villages in the upper (southern) Nile valley. The transition from foraging to food production began not long after 5000 BCE with the introduction of cattle into the region. Sometime around 3000 BCE, farmers in the area started cultivating wheat and barley, crops that had spread from the lower Nile valley. Later, during the first millennium BCE, they began growing sorghum, a crop that had been domesticated in West Africa.

The unequal distribution of goods found in graves demonstrates the emergence of striking differences in wealth and status of those who lived in the upper Nile valley during the fifth millennium BCE. The emergence of social and economic differences can be illustrated by a cemetery at Kadero, a settlement where cattle, sheep, and goats were herded just to the north of modern Khartoum. While most people were buried without any offerings, a few individuals were interred with highly valuable items, such as bracelets made from elephant ivory. Moreover, the fact that some children were buried at the Kadero cemetery in richly furnished graves indicates that high status could be inherited as well as achieved.

Pastoralism had spread westward from northeastern Africa even before animal husbandry began in the upper Nile valley. Between 5000 and 4000 BCE, cattle herding became the primary means of subsistence in the central Sahara. As rainfall began declining around 3500 BCE and the Sahara gradually dried, some pastoralists migrated southward along major rivers into the **savanna** belt of grasslands and trees in West Africa. They brought domesticated cattle, sheep, and goats into the grasslands above the bend of the Niger River and below the shores of Lake Chad.

FIGURE 2.2 A Rock Painting of Cattle in Algeria. This petroglyph depicts a cattle herd in the central Sahara during a period when the local climate was moist.

By 1500 BCE, people in West Africa were also cultivating pearl millet, and after 1000 BCE, they started cultivating African rice and sorghum. All these indigenous African crops had been domesticated from wild ancestors somewhere north of the equator. Like their counterparts in the upper Nile valley, the residents of the mixed agricultural villages in West Africa differed greatly in their wealth and status. One burial chamber at Igbo-Ukwu in Nigeria, for instance, contained many bronze objects and thousands of glass beads.

After moving southward from West Africa into the Congo River basin, some farmers migrated eastward between 1000 and 300 BCE into the Great Lakes region of East Africa. These immigrant farmers mixed with local populations who cultivated grain and raised livestock, and some of their descendants soon dispersed across East Africa to the coasts of Kenya and Tanzania.

Between 300 BCE and 200 CE, scattered groups of agriculturalists moved into South Africa and encountered foragers who sometimes began cultivating plants and rearing animals.

Although farming and herding spread rapidly throughout the southern half of Africa, many early agricultural communities south of the equator continued hunting wild animals to augment their diet. And some people in this part of the continent, especially those living in tropical forests and temperate deserts, remained committed to their foraging way of life even if they engaged in mutually beneficial trade relations with nearby farmers.

Farming in South Asia

The first small agricultural villages in South Asia were established by either farmers migrating from Iran or indigenous foragers living in western Pakistan astride a trade route that ran between the Iranian plateau and the Indus River valley. In addition to cultivating wheat and barley, plants originally domesticated in the Fertile Crescent, the residents of these settlements herded zebu cattle, a locally domesticated species, and to a much lesser extent sheep or goats.

The settlement at Mehrgarh, founded around 6500 BCE, provides the earliest solid evidence in western Pakistan for the development of a mixed economy that combined farming and herding, and after 5000 BCE, many similar villages appeared in the region. The burials in these agricultural settlements reflect increasing differences in wealth and status. While some graves were devoid of goods, others contained a few personal ornaments, and still others were filled with many items, including valuable bronze pieces.

Agriculture soon extended southward first into the Indus valley by 4000 BCE and then into the Ganges River valley and the Deccan plateau in central India by 2000 BCE. In the Ganges valley, farmers cultivated not only cereals that had originated in Southwest Asia but also rice that may have been domesticated locally or may have been acquired from China or Southeast Asia. On the Deccan plateau, farmers cultivated native millet and legumes together with pearl millet and sorghum introduced from Africa and cereals from Southwest Asia. Some farmers also began herding cattle, sheep, or goats, and in parts of the Deccan, increasing differences in house sizes reflected growing disparities in the accumulation of wealth. Farming or herding spread into different regions of South Asia at different times, and by about 500 BCE, agriculture was firmly established throughout most of India.

The Americas: Independent Centers of Food Production

Central America gradually developed into one of the three independent centers of food production in the Western Hemisphere. Around 4300 BCE, mobile bands of indigenous foragers in southwestern Mexico domesticated maize from wild teosinte. But the cobs were quite small at first, and for a long time, people throughout Central America continued to depend primarily on hunting and gathering for their sustenance. As the cobs slowly became larger and the kernels were consumed with beans and squash, maize became the basis of a nutritious diet that could support more sedentary populations. By 1600 BCE, permanent agricultural villages became widespread in Mexico, and they soon exhibited clear signs of socioeconomic stratification.

Agricultural economies also developed gradually in South America. In the lowlands along the Pacific coast of Peru, indigenous foragers began cultivating beans and squash after 5000 BCE, although for more than 2,000 years farming took a back seat to fishing. But the intensification of agriculture after 2500 BCE led to the establishment of permanent farming villages, the construction of irrigation canals, and the emergence of hierarchical societies. In the political center of Caral, located near the Peruvian coast and occupied until about 2000 BCE, a small number of elite families resided in grand houses close to six large pyramids, while commoners lived in modest dwellings.

The Andean highlands of Peru exhibited a similar evolutionary trajectory. Between 5000 and 4000 BCE, foragers in the Peruvian highlands began domesticating llamas and alpacas primarily as sources of meat and hides. During the next 2,000 years, they started raising guinea pigs and cultivating native quinoa and potatoes as well as maize, which had been originally domesticated in Central America. Permanent settlements and irrigated fields appeared in the highlands near Lake Titicaca by 2000 BCE, and the intensification of farming and herding eventually led to the development of significant economic and social disparities. In graves that were lavishly provisioned about 400 BCE in the highland village of Kuntur Wasi, a few elite individuals were buried with gold ornaments and fine pottery, and one older woman was interred with nearly 7,000 beads that may have been stitched into her clothing.

The emergence of agriculture in North America involved both the spread of crops into the desert southwest and the domestication of native plants in the eastern woodlands. In the dry landscapes of Arizona and New Mexico, around 2100 BCE, people began cultivating maize and other crops that may have been introduced into the region by farmers migrating from central Mexico. Farmers constructed irrigation canals in the Tucson basin and in northwestern New Mexico between 1500 and 1000 BCE, and the intensive production of maize, beans, and squash eventually led to the development of hierarchal societies in several areas in the arid southwest.

Meanwhile, between approximately 2500 and 2000 BCE, indigenous foragers in the eastern woodlands of North America domesticated wild stands of marsh elder, goosefoot, and sunflowers that were growing in river floodplains. These native seed-bearing plants furnished many communities, such as Koster on the banks of the Illinois River, with storable food supplements as they continued for more than 1,000 years to rely on fishing, hunting, and gathering for most of their nourishment.

But settlements in the eastern woodlands became increasingly dependent on domesticated crops, and they developed marked socioeconomic differences. As farming became more intensive between 800 and 400 BCE, some communities built large earthen mounds over the remains of elite individuals who were interred with many prestige items, while common people were buried without any luxury goods. After 800 CE, maize, beans, and squash were introduced into the eastern woodlands. The widespread cultivation of these crops provided the foundation for the emergence of numerous hierarchal societies headed by wealthy families and powerful chiefs much like those that had evolved earlier in many other parts of the world.

Review Questions

1. What role did irrigation play in the Agricultural Revolution?
2. How did the domestication of plants and animals lead to population growth in agricultural societies throughout the world?
3. How did the transition from hunting and gathering to farming and herding impact people as they migrated from the Fertile Crescent to other parts of Asia and Europe?
4. How did farming spread from China to Southeast Asia and the Pacific?
5. What were the consequences of increased food production in Africa, South Asia, and the Americas?

Additional Readings

Adas, Michael, ed. *Agricultural and Pastoral Societies in Ancient and Classical History*. Philadelphia: Temple University Press, 2001.

Anthony, David W. *The Horse, the Wheel and Language: How Bronze-Age Raiders from the Eurasian Steppes Shaped the Modern World*. Princeton, NJ: Princeton University Press, 2007.

Barker, Graeme. *The Agricultural Revolution in Prehistory: Why Did Foragers Become Farmers?* Oxford: Oxford University Press, 2006.

Bellwood, Peter. *First Farmers: The Origins of Agricultural Societies*. Oxford: Blackwell Publishing, 2005.

Cunliffe, Barry. *Europe between the Oceans: 9000BCE–AD1000*. New Haven, CT: Yale University Press, 2008.

Diamond, Jared M. *Guns, Germs, and Steel: The Fates of Human Societies*. New York: W. W. Norton, 2006.

Feinmann, Gary M., and T. Douglas Price, eds. *Archaeology at the Millennium: A Sourcebook*. New York: Academic/Plenum Publishers, 2001.

Kirch, Patrick V. *On the Road of the Winds: An Archaeological History of the Pacific Islands Before European Contact*. Berkeley: University of California Press, 2000.

Kuzmina, E. E. *The Prehistory of the Silk Road*. Philadelphia: University of Pennsylvania Press, 2008.

Price, T. Douglas, ed. *Europe's First Farmers*. Cambridge: Cambridge University Press, 2000.

Scarre, Chris, ed. *The Human Past: World Prehistory and the Development of Human Societies*. 4th ed. London: Thames and Hudson, 2018.

Smith, Bruce D. *The Emergence of Agriculture*. New York: Scientific American Library, 1998.

Figure Credits

Map 2.1: Copyright © by Liam987 (CC BY-SA 3.0) at https://commons.wikimedia.org/wiki/File:Holocene-crop-domestication-en.svg.

Map 2.2: Source: https://commons.wikimedia.org/wiki/File:Fruchtbarer_Halbmond.JPG.

Fig. 2.1: Copyright © by Mark Ahsmann (CC BY-SA 4.0) at https://commons.wikimedia.org/wiki/File:20140611_Varna_08.jpg.

Fig. 2.2: Copyright © by Fondazione Passare (CC BY-SA 3.0) at https://commons.wikimedia.org/wiki/File:Fondazione_Passar%C3%A9_V31_192.jpg.

CHAPTER 3

The Urban Revolution and State Formation, 4000 BCE–1000 BCE

Mesopotamia: City-States and Empires

The first cities in the ancient world arose in southern Mesopotamia on the broad **floodplain** formed by the Tigris and Euphrates Rivers. In the early years, temples occupied a preeminent position in the region, but with the emergence of a group of neighboring city-states, power gradually shifted from priests to kings. The gap between the rich and the poor widened as a growing number of independent farmers lost their land to large palaces, temples, and private estates. Moreover, frequent wars between rival city-states resulted in significant transfers of wealth, and eventually, aggressive Mesopotamian kings established powerful but short-lived regional empires.

A Great Transformation: Urban Growth and Temple Development

As the snow melted each spring in the Taurus Mountains in eastern Anatolia (modern Turkey), water rushed down the Tigris and Euphrates to the Persian Gulf. Once every few years, floods deposited a fresh layer of rich **silt** across the broad plain of Mesopotamia, the land between the two rivers. Rainfall in southern Mesopotamia was insufficient for agriculture, but farmers could produce abundant yields by constructing simple irrigation works to divert water from the rivers and channel it onto the fertile alluvial soil in the adjacent fields.

During the sixth millennium BCE, small farming hamlets dotted southern Mesopotamia, traditionally called Sumer by archeologists. Sumerian farmers used their two principal crops, wheat and barley, to make bread and beer. Almost every village in Sumer had a small temple built with mud bricks, and farmers came to these houses of worship to pray to the gods and to donate food to the priests.

Between 4000 and 3000 BCE, southern Mesopotamia underwent a great transformation. As herders from the Arabian and Syrian deserts migrated into the region, the number of agricultural settlements increased rapidly, and some villages expanded into towns and cities. Uruk, the largest of the urban centers, grew from a city with less than 10,000 people into a metropolis with more than 40,000 residents. At the same time, large temples replaced small cult buildings, and religious institutions acquired a preeminent position in Mesopotamian society. Each city in Sumer constructed temples, usually atop stepped pyramids known as **ziggurats**, which towered over surrounding buildings and stood as physical expressions of the power of priests to command the labor of others. Scholars have estimated that the construction of a massive temple erected in Uruk required the labor of 15,000 people working 10 hours a day for five years.

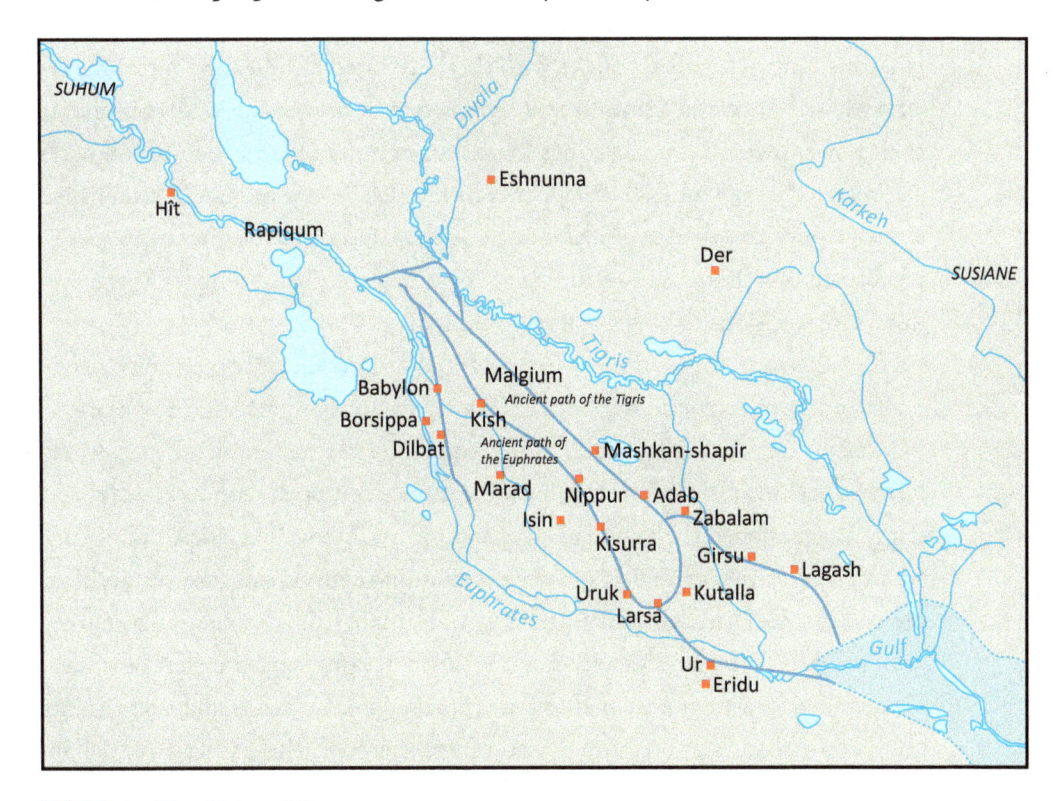

MAP 3.1 The Cities of Sumer

During the fourth millennium BCE, southern Mesopotamia developed a mixed economy. Most of the people, while residing in villages dispersed across the countryside, belonged to autonomous households and worked their own land.

Many other independent people worked as potters, stonecutters, metal smiths, and bricklayers in towns and cities. But some temples in Sumer evolved into major productive units that duplicated these economic activities. Besides persuading independent farmers and artisans to provide temples with labor services, priests relied on a large, highly specialized, and dependent work force to toil in their shops and to cultivate their extensive landholdings. Scribes recorded the food rations that workers who were attached to temples received. Managers of the large temple estates adopted techniques that dramatically increased agricultural productivity, and the resulting food surplus helped to elevate the priestly elite to the apex of power.

Intercity Warfare

During the third millennium BCE, more than 30 city-states, composed of large urban centers that directly controlled agricultural and pastoral hinterlands, emerged in southern Mesopotamia. Hereditary male kings ruled these city-states while residing in fortified palaces with their extended families and high officials who advised them and administered their extensive royal estates. To consolidate their power, Mesopotamian kings made large grants of land to loyal followers and married local women from upper-class families. These monarchs established strong armies and then assumed many religious duties that had previously been performed by priests. As a result, palaces gradually replaced temples as the predominant decision-making agencies in Sumer.

The city-states in southern Mesopotamia, situated in close proximity to one another, often fought as well as traded with each other. As their populations increased, competition for arable land frequently led to intercity warfare. Many farmers, seeking protection from invading armies equipped with battle-axes and daggers, abandoned their rural villages and moved into walled cities. While continuing to cultivate their fields in the surrounding countryside, they established orchards inside cities where fruit trees would be safe from destruction by enemy soldiers. Wars between rival city-states resulted in significant transfers of wealth. Vanquished kings not only had to cede disputed border lands and water rights but they also had to pay **tribute** to victorious neighbors. The extraction of tribute usually meant that commoners in defeated city-states were forced to pay more taxes in the form of goods or labor.

The Gap Between Rich and Poor

The gap between the rich and the poor widened in Sumer as more and more farmers became indebted to affluent creditors. Poor farmers who could not repay loans often lost their land to palace, temple, and private estates, which became larger and larger economic units. Because intensive irrigation caused increasing **salinization** of the soil, the great estates gradually produced less wheat and more barley, which tolerated salt much better. The big landholders used large gangs of dependent farmers to cultivate their extensive fields in return for subsistence rations of food. They also brought in temporary workers during reaping seasons to produce more grain than was needed to feed their permanent labor force.

In addition, the religious, private, and royal estates devoted considerable attention to the production of woolen cloth and luxury goods. They permitted the shepherds who supervised their flocks to keep a portion of the wool and newborn lambs. For the intensive work of spinning and weaving, the great estates used female slaves and their children, usually war captives, who were cheaper to feed than men. They also provided dependent artisans with raw materials used for the production of prestige goods and paid them with rations of barley or small plots of land so they could grow their own food.

While guards protected the workshops and storerooms of the great estates, scribes kept track of the output of goods and the distribution of rations by using a system of writing, devised in Sumer and known as **cuneiform**, in which a stylus with a triangular end was pressed into clay to form wedge-shaped characters. These characters could represent abstract ideas, like walking, as well as concrete items, such as sheep or barley, and could thus be used to write any word in the spoken language. Because cuneiform was a highly complex writing system that took years of training to master, however, it was mostly used by a small number of scribes working on Sumerian estates.

Functioning as integrated economic units, the royal, temple, and private estates played a major role in widening the gap between the rich and the poor in Sumer. The managers of the large estates paid workers practically nothing for producing surplus products that could be exchanged for raw materials and precious metals from different ecological regions. In other words, the kings, priests, and nobles in Sumer derived most of their wealth from the systematic exploitation of commoners toiling on their estates.

Regional Empires and Long-Distance Trade

During the final centuries of the third millennium BCE, aggressive Mesopotamian kings established short-lived regional empires. Sargon from Akkad, a city in northern Mesopotamia, conquered the city-states of southern Mesopotamia and created a unified empire that flourished between 2330 and 2150 BCE. The Akkadian Empire, like other polities in Mesopotamia, was a patriarchal society. But a few women from aristocratic or royal families enjoyed significant opportunities and privileges because of their wealth and status. Enheduanna, the daughter of King Sargon, provides a good example of a woman who exercised considerable influence in a male-dominated society.

Hoping to use religion as a means of maintaining control over conquered peoples, Sargon appointed Enheduanna to the position of high priestess of the most important temple in Sumer. She was an accomplished poet who composed a series of hymns dedicated to the deities residing in 42 major temples. Enheduanna aimed to help her father consolidate his power by blending the religious traditions of the different peoples living in the Akkadian Empire. Her hymns to different gods and goddesses were copied by scribes and recited for centuries. As the earliest known poet in the world, Enheduanna was the first of many women to play an important role in the history of literature.

Despite her efforts to use religion as a unifying force, rebellions soon weakened the authority of Sargon and his successors. Tribes sweeping down from the Zagros Mountains eventually destroyed the Akkadian Empire. After a coalition of city-states ejected these invaders, monarchs from the southern Mesopotamian city of Ur established another regional empire in 2112 BCE. Known as the Third Dynasty of Ur, this empire collapsed in 2004 BCE due to internal revolts and raids launched from southwestern Persia.

While enjoying a brief period of plenty before its demise, Ur accumulated great wealth not only by collecting taxes from defeated city-states and by demanding tribute from neighboring territories but also by trading with distant areas. Private merchants from Ur sailed down the Persian Gulf in boats filled with woolen textiles, barley, sesame oil, and silver. After reaching Bahrain, they exchanged these products for copper, carnelian beads, and other goods from Oman and the Indus valley.

In the 1700s BCE, King Hammurabi from the Sumerian city of Babylon established another short-lived empire in southern Mesopotamia. Hammurabi is best known for devising a law code that portrayed his rule as divinely sanctioned and specified his right to make decisions for three social classes: freemen, dependent people, and slaves. Reflecting the superior position of men in Mesopotamian society, the law code stipulated that a man could sell his wife if he was in debt, that he could take a concubine if his wife failed to give birth to a child, and that he could have his wife killed if she was caught sleeping with another man. The law code was displayed on a **stele** erected in Babylon.

During Hammurabi's reign between 1792 and 1750 BCE, economic life in Sumer became increasingly privatized. Wealthy people acquired more land while palaces and temples began using private individuals to operate their estates. Small plots of land were assigned to independent farm tenants who paid rent by relinquishing a share of their crops, and contracts were made with private entrepreneurs who collected dues, distributed resources, and sold produce.

Meanwhile, in northern Mesopotamia, private merchants in the city of Ashur, the ancient religious capital of Assyria, established a vast commercial network. They organized donkey caravans in Ashur and loaded each pack animal with Mesopotamian textiles and tin from southern Afghanistan. Then they embarked on a long trip, traveling some 1,000 miles in about 50 days, before reaching their trading settlements in central Anatolia. After exchanging their cargo for gold and silver, the Assyrian merchants returned home with these precious metals. Their profit margins were very high. By selling textiles and tin in Anatolia for more than double what they had paid for them in Ashur, these entrepreneurs could make a 50–100 percent return on their investment, even after paying several kings for permission to travel through their territories.

FIGURE 3.1 The Stele with the Code of Hammurabi. This stele shows King Hammurabi standing and receiving a rod and a ring, the symbols of royal authority, from Shamash, the god of justice.

This lucrative cross-cultural trade, which flourished between 1910 and 1830 BCE, stimulated economic development and social stratification in Anatolia as well as Assyria. By opening mines and exchanging metals for prestige goods from Ashur, headmen in Anatolia created work for local people while reinforcing their own elevated status.

Egypt: Unification and Disintegration

The production of vast quantities of surplus food on the fertile Nile floodplain provided the agricultural basis for urban development and state formation in ancient Egypt. Ruling over a highly stratified kingdom, pharaohs dominated the Egyptian economy and communicated with the gods to assure bountiful harvests of grain. Aggressive pharaohs employed military force to make Egypt a great empire. But the power of the pharaohs fluctuated as Egypt went through successive periods of political unification and fragmentation.

Gifts of the Nile: Plenty and Power

The wealth and power of ancient Egypt were gifts of the Nile, the longest river in the world. The Nile flows northward for more than 4,200 miles from the Ethiopian mountains down to the Mediterranean Sea. In several places along the way, boulders in shallow water cause rapids or **cataracts** that make navigation difficult and form natural boundaries. In Upper Egypt, the area between Cairo and the first cataract to the south at Aswan, the Nile snakes through a narrow valley only 5–10 miles wide and lined by cliffs separating the lush floodplain from the arid deserts on each side. The river spreads out in Lower Egypt with multiple branches forming a huge triangular delta measuring about 100 miles from Cairo to the Mediterranean and 150 miles along the coast.

Although Egypt did not receive enough precipitation to sustain agriculture, the Nile provided a very dependable kind of natural irrigation. Each summer, rains swelled the tributaries of the Nile in Ethiopia, sending silt-filled water rushing downstream and flooding Egypt between July and October. Every year in November, the reddish-brown water began receding to the main river channel, washing away salts that impede plant growth and leaving behind a thick layer of rich black silt. Following the annual inundation, farmers plowed their fields and scattered seeds over the waterlogged soil that remained moist throughout the winter months. Their two main staples, wheat and barley, were harvested each spring before the river began rising in the summer. In normal years, Egyptian farmers produced much more grain than their families needed, and the large food surplus could be used to feed many non-food producers.

Egyptian Rulers: The Pharaohs

As food surpluses and population grew during the fourth millennium BCE, Egyptian society became increasingly hierarchical, with elites residing in expanding urban centers supported by farmers in the surrounding countryside. Differences in the amount and value of grave goods buried with the dead reflected the growing differences of wealth and status among the living. Various competing power clusters gradually emerged in Upper Egypt, and after joining together around 3100 BCE, they extended their control over Lower Egypt.

During the Early Dynastic period, between about 3000 and 2686 BCE, a succession of single monarchs ruled the unified country from Memphis, the capital city, strategically located close to where Upper and Lower Egypt met. A **vizier** serving as second-in-command to Egyptian pharaohs, headed a large civil service, and oversaw all aspects of the government bureaucracy. For administrative purposes, Egypt was divided into several provinces. Lower officials residing in regional capitals supervised the collection of taxes and the conscription of labor.

As the Egyptian population spread beyond the floodplain of the Nile, farmers began raising crops on higher ground that required artificial irrigation. Most of the canals and dykes constructed in Egypt were simple installations built by a small number of workers operating under local supervision. The development of a unique form of writing, known as **hieroglyphics**, played an important role in the process of state formation in Egypt. Working for the government, scribes wrote on sheets of papyrus, a paper-like material made from reeds growing along the banks of the Nile. They kept track of tax payments as well as the production, storage, and distribution of grain and other commodities.

During the Old Kingdom period, from about 2686 to 2160 BCE, the central government in Memphis dominated the Egyptian economy. Male pharaohs, who had one or more wives and many concubines, maintained several large estates worked by bound agricultural laborers and dependent artisans. Commoners working on extensive temple and private estates provided the government with conscripted labor for various construction projects while these institutions used a portion of the crops that they collected from tenants as rents to pay taxes to the state. Although some temples grew wealthy from royal endowments, they did not challenge the power of pharaohs who appointed government officials to serve as the highest ranking priests on a rotating basis.

Egyptian rulers not only controlled major quarrying and mining operations but they also monopolized long-distance trade. Besides sending expeditions to quarry stone in the eastern and western deserts and to mine copper and turquoise in the Sinai Peninsula, they dispatched royal ships to sail along the Mediterranean coast to Lebanon to obtain cedar, cypress, and pine. Royal ships also sailed up the Nile against the current but with a prevailing wind at their back to reach Nubia, which acted as a corridor linking Egypt with sub-Saharan Africa. Egyptian manufactured goods, such as linen cloth and copper tools, were exchanged in Nubia for slaves and a range of exotic commodities, such as elephant ivory, ebony, ostrich feathers, and leopard skins. By procuring raw materials from distant sources and manufacturing luxury articles in royal workshops, Egyptian rulers could restrict access to prestige goods and thereby enhance their own power.

Egyptian officials asserted that pharaohs were the embodiment of the god Horus as well as the offspring of the sun god Ra. During their lives, these autocratic rulers claimed that they communicated with the gods to assure the regular changes of the seasons, the annual flooding of the Nile, and abundant harvests of grain. Pharaohs thus used religion to legitimize their rule. When pharaohs died, embalmers preserved their bodies so they would be prepared to join the gods and enjoy eternal life. The mummified bodies were placed in pyramids, and these tombs were stocked with both utilitarian and luxury goods that would accompany the rulers on their journey to the next world.

The massive pyramids constructed in the Old Kingdom stand as enduring symbols of the supreme position of the pharaohs in Egyptian society. To build these gigantic monuments glorifying and sanctifying the pharaohs, state officials conscripted vast numbers of peasants to do heavy labor, probably during the slow winter months before the busy spring harvest. Huge blocks of stone needed to be carved from quarries, transported on the Nile in boats, carried overland in carts, chiseled into varying sizes at the construction site, and then placed in layers reaching toward the heavens.

Erected for Pharaoh Khufu around 2500 BCE, the largest of the famous pyramids built at Giza measures 755 feet per side at the base, stands 481 feet high, and contains approximately 2.3 million stone blocks weighing 2.5 tons on average. Scholars have estimated that the construction of this awesome monument, attesting to the godlike status of Khufu, required an enormous labor force equivalent to about 84,000 people working 80 days a year for 20 years.

FIGURE 3.2 The Pyramids at Giza. The pyramid at Giza erected for Pharaoh Khufu (center) was the largest monument built in ancient Egypt.

Cycles of Centralization and Fragmentation

The power of the pharaohs fluctuated as Egypt went through successive periods of centralized authority and political fragmentation. By 2160 BCE, agricultural prosperity made local leaders in several regions wealthy and powerful. Provincial officials, rather than obeying the commands of the pharaohs, began acting like small kings and often warred among themselves. This first period of political division ended in 2055 BCE, however, when a prince from one of the rival dynasties launched a military campaign and succeeded in reuniting Egypt under a single ruler with a capital at Thebes.

During the Middle Kingdom period, from 2055 to 1700 BCE, pharaohs once again sponsored maritime expeditions to Lebanon to obtain timber for shipbuilding and resin for embalming, and they began sending Egyptian ships down the Red Sea to acquire exotic goods from East Africa. Furthermore, Pharaoh Senusret III launched a series of military campaigns into Nubia and succeeded in annexing the territory between the first and second cataract where he erected steles taunting his victims. "I have plundered their women," one of his steles declared, "and carried off their underlings, gone to their wells, driven off their bulls, torn up their corn, and put fire to it."[1]

Egypt soon entered a second period of political disintegration. While a series of rulers held power in Thebes, Hyksos immigrants from western Asia settled in the eastern delta and developed a rival dynasty with a capital at Avaris. The Hyksos soon extended their authority beyond the delta and compelled the small kings in the middle of the Nile valley to become their vassals. After the Hyksos were gradually driven out of Egypt, central authority was restored and Egypt was reunified once more.

During the New Kingdom period, which began in 1550 BCE and lasted almost 500 years, Egypt was ruled by some of its most famous pharaohs: Amenhotep III, Akhenaten, Tutankhamun, and Rameses II. These rulers used military force to make Egypt a great imperial power. While commoners were drafted for individual campaigns, professional soldiers made up the core of the Egyptian army. The Egyptians used large squadrons of mobile chariots drawn by fast horses to pursue fleeing adversaries with devastating effect. Pharaohs sent military expeditions to take control of Syria, Palestine, and Nubia as far south as the fourth cataract.

---

[1] Richard B. Parkinson, *Voices from Ancient Egypt: An Anthology of Middle Kingdom Writings* (London: British Museum Press, 1991), 45. (All texts in this anthology were translated by R. B. Parkinson.)

Although the territory north of the third cataract was governed as an Egyptian province and administered by viceroys, Egyptian rule was less direct in the rest of Nubia and other areas where local leaders governed in the shadow of small garrisons of Egyptian troops.

A Prosperous and Patriarchal Society

Egypt remained a patriarchal society that vested authority in men. They governed the country, served as scribes, headed their households, and dressed in fine linen garments spun from flax by lower class women. However, in one exceptional case, a woman named Hatshepsut ruled Egypt after her husband died. While Hatshepsut was acting as regent for her young stepson, statues and sculptures portrayed her as a woman.

But after Hatshepsut was crowned king around 1473 BCE, she began dressing like a man and erecting statues that represented her as a man. Hatshepsut ruled as the pharaoh of Egypt for 15 years. But after her stepson Thutmorse III became pharaoh, he had her name removed from numerous monuments and had statues of her smashed.

Despite the unconventional reign of Hatshepsut, the empire continued to bring tremendous wealth into Egypt. Syria and Palestine paid tribute mainly in the form of agricultural products, while Nubia was forced to relinquish large quantities of gold that helped set elites in Egypt apart from the lower class. Pharaohs used the tribute collected annually from conquered territories to enrich government officials and religious leaders, and the New Kingdom became a time of extravagant building projects. Grand palaces and royal tombs packed with valuable grave goods were constructed while many temples were renovated and enlarged. But the long period of prosperity and political stability came to a close in 1069 as the state fragmented once again and the empire disintegrated.

The Urban Revolution in South Asia

The first cities in South Asia emerged on the broad floodplains of the Indus and Ghaggar-Harkra Rivers and their tributaries. Intensive agricultural production provided the surplus needed to support a growing urban population, and skilled artisans manufactured luxury goods that local merchants shipped throughout the region and to distant markets. While archaeological evidence shows a widening gap in distribution of wealth among the inhabitants of these cities, the political

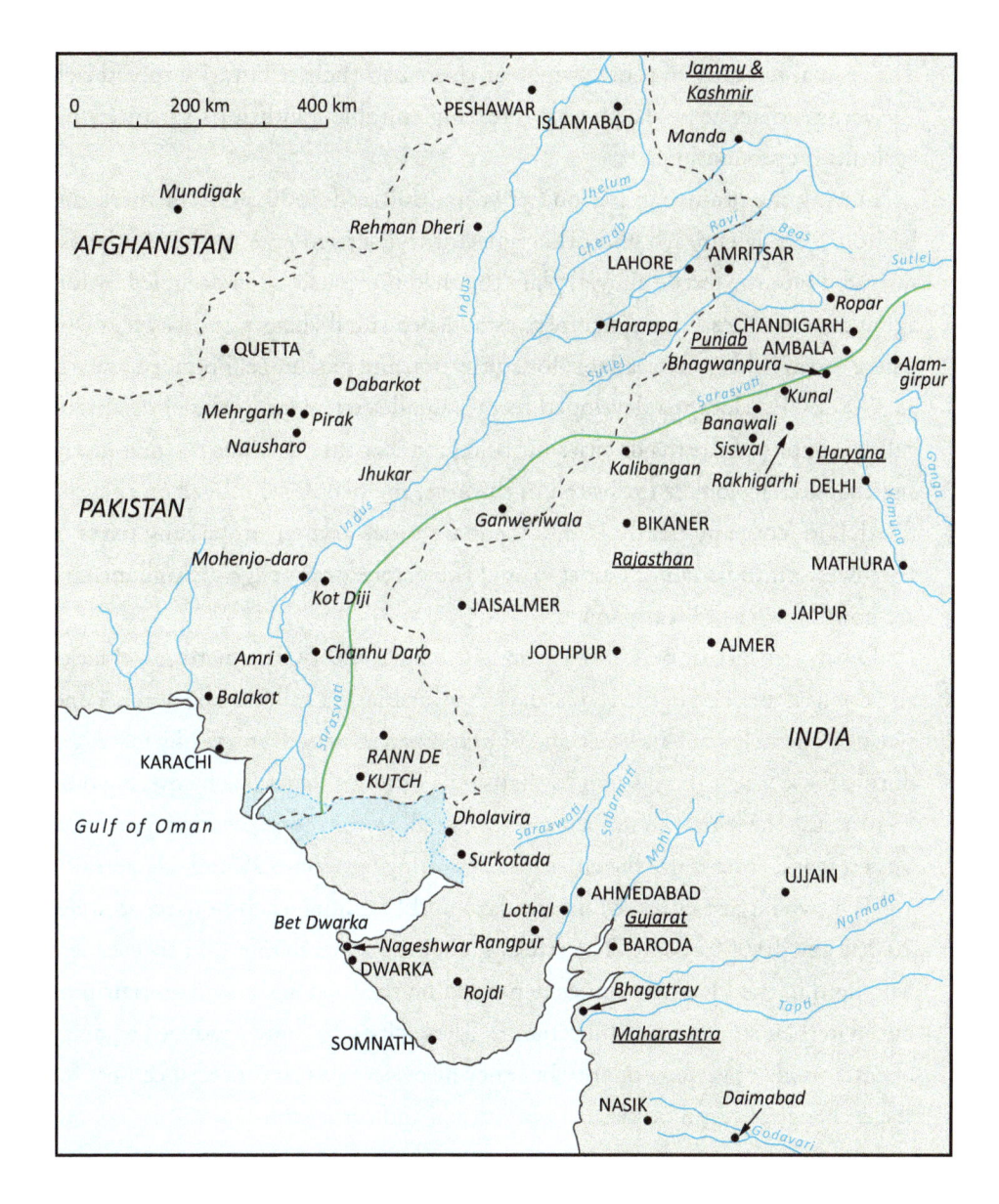

MAP 3.2 The Cities in the Indus Valley. The green line represents a river that is now dry.

organization and power relations in the region continue to be controversial topics because their system of writing has not been deciphered.

Urban Growth in the Indus Valley

As the snow melted in the Karakorum and Himalayan Mountains each spring, large quantities of water rushed down the Indus and Ghaggar-Harkra Rivers for almost 1,900 miles in a southwesterly direction before emptying into the Arabian Sea.

The annual flooding of these two great rivers and their tributaries spread rich silt across adjacent fields, thereby creating suitable conditions for intensive agricultural production.

During the pre-urban period between 4000 and 2600 BCE, farmers and herders from Mehrgarh and other agricultural settlements to the northwest migrated into the fertile alluvial plain that had previously been occupied by foraging communities. The newcomers established small villages and larger towns where broad fields were available for cultivation and pasturage. Founded as early as 3300 BCE, Harappa developed from a small settlement in the upper Indus valley into one of the major cities in the region. Because this was the first urban site that archaeologists excavated in the area, the people who lived on the vast floodplain (covering nearly 200,000 square miles and encompassing parts of northwestern India, all of Pakistan, and the northeastern edge of Afghanistan) are now known as **Harappans.**

During the urban period between 2600 and 1900 BCE, a network of cities and towns flourished in the Indus and Ghaggar-Harkra valleys. The number and size of settlements in this heartland of Harappan society dramatically increased during these years. In addition to thousands of tiny villages (each covering only 2–10 acres), the region contained some 32 small towns (none covering more than 50 acres) and at least five big cities (each covering between 198 and 247 acres).

The two largest cities, Mohenjo-daro and Harappa, each housed between 20,000 and 40,000 people. The artisans, engineers, merchants, and civic leaders who lived in the Harappan cities depended on the food and raw materials produced in their surrounding hinterlands. These cities not only produced an array of craft goods of varying quality but they also served as commercial centers for the exchange of commodities between urban and rural areas.

Agricultural Intensification and Craft Production

The farmers and pastoralists, who made up the bulk of the Harappan population, developed new ways to increase their output needed to feed the non-food-producing residents of the towns and cities. By employing a multicrop strategy, farmers in the river valleys could grow plant food throughout the year in a two-season pattern. Their winter crops included wheat, barley, lentils, chickpeas, and flax, while their summer crops included millets, grapes, dates, sesame, and hemp.

Although farmers primarily depended on the annual flooding cycles of rivers to water their fields, they did construct some dams and reservoirs used to irrigate their crops in areas outside the alluvial plain. The pastoralists, who lived in higher locations between the rivers, likewise developed new methods to increase their production. In addition to raising sheep, goats, and cattle for meat, herders started breeding these animals to produce milk, cheese, and wool. They also began to breed cattle to pull carts and plows.

Meanwhile, the craft specialists in Harappan towns and cities developed new techniques to produce high-quality goods for both local and distant markets. Artisans fashioned a diverse array of goods from stones (e.g., lapis lazuli, turquoise, chert, agate, and carnelian) and metals (e.g., copper, gold, silver, and tin) mostly obtained in the surrounding highlands. They also produced goods from marine shells obtained from nearby seas. Skilled artisans produced exquisite ornaments for personal adornment, standardized weights used for measuring quantities, distinctive seals to serve as markers of identification, and a variety of ceramic containers for cooking food, storing products, and transporting goods over long distances.

Harappan merchants transported many of these craft goods throughout their homeland and into neighboring regions. Besides using carts to carry goods over relatively flat land, they used small boats to move products up and down navigable rivers and larger vessels to ship commodities across the Arabian Sea and into the Persian Gulf. Harappan traders sent carnelian beads and other products via overland routes and mountain passes into Afghanistan, Iran, and Central Asia.

At the same time, maritime routes provided the main corridors for the shipment of Harappan goods to settlements along the Arabian coast and further up the Persian Gulf to Mesopotamian cities. While excavating sites in Oman and the United Arab Emirates, archaeologists have uncovered large black jars that were made in Harappan cities for transporting products. Mesopotamian texts, moreover, confirm that imports of copper, tin, ebony, lapis lazuli, carnelian, gold, and pearls came from Harappan sources.

Urban Plans and Public Works

Archeological investigations have revealed much about the major Harappan cities. Located about 250 miles apart, Mohenjo-daro and Harappa were constructed according to similar but slightly different urban plans with streets laid out in a grid pattern. Residential areas made up the largest part of these cities. While most houses contained a few rooms and a courtyard, some had additional rooms and more amenities. Commercial areas had streets lined with stores and workshops, and imposing nonresidential buildings were located in separate areas. However, excavations have not produced any contextual evidence to indicate that specific buildings were used as temples, religious shrines, or administrative centers.

The Harappan cities featured impressive systems of public works designed by engineers to control water and waste. While vertical shaft wells were constructed to bring drinking and bathing water into homes, toilet and bathing areas were positioned on an outside wall and sloped toward an outlet so that waste could flow into a drain or cesspit. Individual house drains were connected to an elaborate network of street drains that channeled water and waste out of the cities. Moreover, in many Harappan cities, massive platforms were constructed to raise the level of buildings, thereby preventing damage from the periodic encroachment of floodwaters.

Political Organization and Urban Decline

Interpretations concerning the distribution of wealth and the exercise of power among the Harappans rest on archaeological evidence because their system of writing has not yet been deciphered. Although the remains of Harappan cities do not show any spectacular differentials in the accumulation of wealth, excavations of their houses and cemeteries reveal that significant economic and social differences did exist. The larger houses in the Harappan cities contained more valuable items than the smaller dwellings. Further indications of disparities in wealth and status come from two Harappan cemeteries in which two older men were buried with prestige goods not found in other graves. But there is no way to determine what kind of people lived in the larger houses or were interred with more expensive goods. Were they wealthy merchants, highly skilled artisans, religious leaders, or civic authorities? We don't know.

The political organization of Harappan society continues to be controversial in scholarly circles. Struck by the uniformity and standardization of many aspects of Harappan culture, such as pottery styles and written script, some archaeologists have asserted that a central political authority, located in Mohenjo-daro or one of the other big cities, governed the whole region. Others have argued that differences in urban plans suggest that local authorities had power to command the massive human labor required to build the Harappan cities. In attempting to make sense out of the puzzling evidence, some archaeologists have concluded that Harappan society was ruled by several independent city-states that traded with each other and shared many cultural traits. Archaeologists will continue to debate how the Harappans were governed as long as their written language remains undeciphered.

During the post-urban period between 1900 and 1300 BCE, Harappan society underwent a general decline. People abandoned the large cities and dispersed into small towns and villages that were scattered throughout the countryside, and Harappan material culture became less uniform and more localized. As the cities diminished in population, their elaborate waste disposal systems deteriorated, and squatters moved into formerly well-ordered neighborhoods.

What caused the urban collapse? Since the old hypothesis of Aryan invasions into Harappan territory has been discredited, archaeologists with different areas of expertise have pointed to different ecological disasters as possible explanations for what happened in different places. These include deforestation in the highlands and salinization in the lowlands as well as a shift in the course of the Indus River and the drying up of the Ghaggar-Harkra River. Many archaeologists now believe that all or some combination of these factors delivered a series of severe blows that disrupted the Harappan economy and undermined the authority of city leaders.

Cities and States in East Asia

Originating in the mountains of western China, the Yellow River flows eastward for nearly 3,400 miles across northern China before emptying into the Pacific Ocean. Occasional summer rains in the central plains of North China eroded the extremely fine **loess soil** deposited by retreating glaciers at the end of the Ice Age. Every year vast quantities of silt washed into the Yellow River, giving the water a much higher content of silt than any other river in the world. Possessing a yellowish color that explains its name, the river periodically unleashed tremendous floods that devastated large areas. But each inundation left behind a thick residue of rich silt on broad floodplains that produced ample harvests of millet, barley, and wheat.

The Yangzi River, much like the Yellow River, flows eastward from the highlands of Tibet and carries an enormous volume of water more than 3,900 miles across southern China before reaching the Pacific Ocean. On the broad fields adjacent to the Yangzi and its tributaries, the construction of irrigation works allowed for the intensive cultivation of rice, the principal crop in the region. The agricultural production in the fertile valleys of these two great rivers provided the economic foundation for the emergence of the first cities and first states in China.

The First Chinese State

The process of urbanization and state formation in China began in the Yellow River valley in the midst of expanding populations and warring chiefdoms. During the latter part of the third millennium BCE, people in northern China built rammed-earth walls around a growing number of towns. The earliest Chinese state emerged around 1800 BCE with a capital at Erlitou, located in a fertile alluvial basin. While high agricultural yields in the surrounding countryside permitted Erlitou to develop into a densely populated city of some 20,000 inhabitants, a small ruling class exercised political authority from a palace complex built in the center of the capital.

Erlitou rapidly expanded into a territorial state that dominated a large region containing many highly desired natural resources. In addition to acquiring salt for cooking and preserving food, the ruling elite in Erlitou gained access to timber for constructing buildings, clay for making white pottery, and metal ores (copper, tin, and lead) for casting bronze daggers and drinking vessels. Nomadic pastoralists who had migrated from the steppes of Central Asia introduced the technology used to produce bronze into Northwest China. Several medium-sized urban centers established on rivers, which served as key routes of communication, procured and transported these valuable resources to Erlitou.

The elites in Erlitou controlled the production of bronze weapons and vessels that were used in rituals to honor their ancestors. Craft specialists developed a sophisticated technique employed in the production of multipiece bronze ritual vessels. Using clay molds for casting, skilled craft specialists manufactured these bronze vessels that served as important symbols of wealth and status. Mortuary practices, moreover, reveal that Erlitou quickly became a highly stratified urban center. While commoners were buried in ash pits without any grave offerings, elites were interred in impressive tombs containing prestige goods.

The Rise of the Shang Kingdom

The powerful Shang state, which emerged in the middle reaches of the Yangzi River around 1600 BCE, was ruled by hereditary male kings living in heavily fortified capital cities and wealthy aristocrats residing in a number of walled towns. As owners of large estates, both kings and aristocrats extracted surplus food from tenants who received small allotments of land to raise crops but were obligated to surrender a portion of the harvest in return. These peasants were also required to fight in the army and to help construct buildings in the towns and cities.

The city of Zhengzhou served as one of the early Shang capitals. The royal palace and ritual area in the center of the city was protected by a surrounding wall over 30 feet high with a base more than 60 feet wide. Enclosing an area of two square miles, the wall consisted of layer upon layer of earth packed between wooden frames. This project, which would have taken some 10,000 workers almost 20 years to complete, illustrates the power of Shang monarchs to command heavy labor service from their subjects. Living outside the imposing city wall, highly skilled craft specialists manufactured luxury goods for the royal court.

Shang kings claimed to have an exclusive ability to communicate with the spirit world. These rulers approached Shangdi, the principal Shang god, through the mediation of their dead ancestors. Believing that supernatural powers animated the physical world, Shang kings made offerings to the gods in the form of food, beverages, and sacrificed animals and humans. By nourishing and pleasing the gods, they hoped to ensure good weather, abundant harvests, and successful military campaigns.

Aggressive Shang kings used military force to conquer new territories, to suppress provincial rebellions, and to defend their northern frontier against raids by pastoralists. These nomads, who had migrated from the central Asian steppes, introduced horse-drawn chariots into the East Asian grasslands. Sometime around 1300 BCE, Shang artisans in royal workshops began producing large numbers of chariots with spoke wheels. Aristocrats in chariots lead foot soldiers into battle. Each chariot carried three men: a driver who directed the horses, an archer firing arrows with a compound bow, and a warrior equipped with a long-handled axe that had a dagger blade fastened to it. In addition to providing a mobile firing platform, chariots served as command centers and shock forces.

Agricultural laborers, conscripted and equipped by nobles subservient to the royal dynasty, made up the bulk of the Shang army. Besides maintaining an armed force numbering around 1,000 troops that he personally led into battle, the Shang king could mobilize about 13,000 soldiers, if necessary, to counter a serious threat, such as an insurrection or an invasion. Shang infantrymen were armed with an assortment of bronze weapons, such as daggers, battle-axes, and spears, that were far superior to the stone, wood, and bone weapons used by their enemies. To produce these weapons, a great many people were required for mining, refining, and transporting the copper, tin, and lead needed to make bronze. Thus, in addition to strengthening the Shang army, the production of large quantities of bronze stimulated the Shang economy.

A Strong and Stratified Kingdom

Formidable Shang armies extended their control over much of the Yellow River valley. Presiding over a loosely consolidated state, Shang monarchs appointed officials to administer their newly acquired territories. Tax collectors in the conquered provinces sent huge amounts of food and raw materials to Anyang, the last Shang capital, which covered more than nine square miles.

A royal cemetery on the outskirts of Anyang reflected the great affluence and status of the Shang kings. Along with the remains of the dead rulers, the 11 large tombs in the cemetery were filled with exquisitely crafted grave goods, including chariots, bronze weapons and drinking vessels, and jade and ivory ornaments. In addition to these valuable items, the tombs contained the decapitated bodies of hundreds of humans to serve the monarchs in the next world.

The Shang kingdom, like most if not all early states, was patriarchal as well as hierarchal. Constituting only a small proportion of the Shang population, members of the upper class possessed beautiful jade ornaments and bronze vessels that set them apart from commoners. Unable to obtain prestige goods, peasants drank from ceramic vessels and worked in their fields with wooden digging sticks. Men dominated family life as well as public affairs in Shang society. As heads of their households, older males exercised authority over their wives and children. Most lower-class men and women were monogamous, but upper-class men often took secondary wives in order to ensure the birth of sons needed to perpetuate their lineage.

Emperor Wu Ding, while ruling Shang China from about 1250 to 1192 BCE, cultivated the allegiance of neighboring tribes by marrying a woman from each of them. As a result, he had 60 wives, including Fu Hao who entered the royal household through such a marriage. Fu Hao eventually became the favorite wife of the emperor and attained an exceptionally high status for a Chinese woman. Wu Ding repeatedly instructed her to conduct rituals and offer sacrifices. Besides acting as a high priestess, Fu Hao led several successful military campaigns against enemies of the Shang state. Two important generals and as many as 13,000 soldiers served under her command.

When Fu Hao died around 1200 BCE, the emperor had a tomb constructed for her on the edge of the royal cemetery at Anyang. She was buried in a wooden chamber that held a lacquered coffin that has since rotted away. Reflecting the high status that Fu Hao enjoyed while alive, her tomb contained 6,900 cowry shells, 755 jade carvings, and 468 bronze items (the bronze alone weighed about 3,500 pounds). Also, 16 sacrificed humans were buried around the perimeter of the tomb so that they would be ready to serve Fu Hao in her after life.

The Changjiang State

Studies of the first kingdoms in the Yellow River valley have long shaped interpretations of early Chinese states. But the recent archaeological discovery of Sanxingdui, a large city located in the upper Yangzi valley, has altered current views of ancient Chinese history by drawing attention to developments in southern China. Flourishing simultaneously with the last Shang capital at Anyang, this city served as the capital of a regional state that Chinese scholars call Changjiang. Massive walls that were as wide as 154 feet at their base enclosed a special zone covering 112 acres in the heart of Sanxingdui. Working in a six-square-mile area beyond these walls, craft specialists manufactured splendid bronzes, ceramics, and jades.

In recent excavations further down the Yangzi valley from Sanxingdui, archaeologists have unearthed a large royal tomb at Xin'gen. This burial in southern China contained 150 jades and 475 bronzes (about half of the bronzes were weapons). Dating to the late Shang period, these grave offerings are almost as impressive as the goods buried with Fu Hao in northern China. The discovery of the royal tomb at Xin'gen, like the revealing excavations at Sanxingdui, provides striking evidence for the early rise of a prosperous and powerful kingdom in the Yangzi valley. As was the case in other parts of the ancient world, Xin'gen and Sanxingdui arose on the floodplain of a great soil-bearing river that allowed for intensive agricultural production.

Review Questions

1. What role did temples play in the economy of southern Mesopotamia?
2. Why did Egypt go through successive periods of centralization and fragmentation?
3. How did artisans and merchants contribute to the prosperity of the Harappan cities?
4. How did the Shang state gain control of much of the Yellow River valley?
5. What set Fu Hao apart from the other wives of the Chinese emperor?

Additional Readings

Crawford, Harriet. *Sumer and the Samarians*. 2nd ed. Cambridge: Cambridge University Press, 2004.

Kenoyer, Jonathon. *Ancient Cities of the Indus Valley Civilization*. Oxford: Oxford University Press, 1998.

Liu, Li, and Xingcan Chen. *State Formation in Early China*. London: Gerald Duckworth, 2003.

Liverani, Mario. *Uruk: The First City*. London: Equinox Publishing, 2006.

Possehl, Gregory L. *The Indus Civilization: A Contemporary Perspective*. New York: Alta Mira Press, 2002.

Rothman, Mitchell, ed. *Uruk Mesopotamia and Its Neighbors: Cross-Cultural Interactions in an Era of State Formation*. Santa Fe, NM: School of American Research Press, 2001.

Scarre, Chris, ed. *The Human Past: World Prehistory and the Development of Human Societies*. 4th ed. London: Thames and Hudson, 2018.

Trigger, Bruce G. *Understanding Early Civilizations*. Cambridge: Cambridge University Press, 2003.

Van De Mieroop, Marc. *A History of the Ancient Near East: ca 3000–323 BCE*. 2nd ed. Oxford: Blackwell Publishing, 2007.

Van De Mieroop, Marc. *A History of Ancient Egypt*. Oxford: Wiley-Blackwell, 2011.

Wright, Rita P. *The Ancient Indus: Urbanization, Economy, and Society*. Cambridge: Cambridge University Press, 2010.

Yoffee, Norman. *Myths of the Archaic State: Evolution of the Earliest Cities, States, and Civilizations*. Cambridge: Cambridge University Press, 2005.

Figure Credits

Map 3.1: Copyright © by Sémhur (CC BY-SA 3.0) at https://commons.wikimedia.org/wiki/File:Map_of_Southern_Mesopotamia.png.

Fig. 3.1: Copyright © by Rama (CC BY-SA 3.0 FR) at https://commons.wikimedia.org/wiki/File:Code_of_Hammurabi-Sb_8-IMG_7753-gradient.jpg.

Fig. 3.2: Copyright © by Hanc Tomasz (CC BY-SA 3.0) at https://commons.wikimedia.org/wiki/File:Pyramids_of_Giza_-_panoramio.jpg.

Map 3.2: Copyright © 2004 by Nataraja. Reprinted with permission.

CHAPTER 4

Early Empires in Asia, Africa, and Mesoamerica, 1200 BCE–1 BCE

The Unification of China

Warfare played a major role in shaping the early history of China. After employing a strong military force to defeat the Shang kingdom, the powerful Zhou state incorporated the territory of its vanquished foe into an enlarged domain that encompassed most of the Yellow River valley. The Zhou kings relied on members of the royal clan to administer different regions of their huge realm. But these provincial officials became aggressive warlords who fought against each other in attempts to gain control of more territory.

As several large Chinese states expanded northward, they came into contact with pastoral tribes that exploited the extensive grassland that stretched along the frontier of China. The militant Chinese states dispatched soldiers that defeated the nomadic tribes and assumed control of their land. Zhao Zheng, the ruler of the powerful Qin state eventually conquered all of the smaller Chinese kingdoms in both the Yellow and Yangtze valleys. Then he incorporated the former territory of defeated states into the enormous Qin Empire, which unified China for a brief period.

The Zhou State and the Rise of Regional Warlords

The powerful state of Zhou emerged in the fertile Wei River valley to the south and west of the neighboring Shang kingdom. In 1045 BCE, an ambitious Zhou king employed a strong military force, composed of chariots and foot soldiers, to attack and defeat the Shang army. The victorious Zhou monarch promptly incorporated the former Shang territories into a greatly enlarged domain, which encompassed most of the Yellow River valley. In justifying their conquest, the Zhou kings claimed that the heavenly powers had withdrawn the mandate to govern from the irresponsible Shang dynasty and had given them the right to rule. The Zhou kings asserted, furthermore, that they would retain the **Mandate of Heaven** as long as they exercised power in a conscientious manner.

Zhou monarchs shared their authority with royal kinsmen who received large grants of land and commanded the labor of farmers and artisans working on their estates. While residing in their capital at Zongzhou, the Zhou kings relied on members of the royal clan to rule different regions of their extensive realm. These aristocratic subordinates in the provinces sent tax revenue in the form of grain to Zongzhou and provided military forces that the Zhou kings used to defend their domain. However, as provincial lords developed a taste for power, they established their own armies and stopped delivering tax proceeds to the royal court. They also took a considerable portion of the grain produced by servile peasants who toiled on their estates. Archaeology excavations of rich burials in several regional capitals reveal that some of the provincial rulers became extremely wealthy.

The Zhou state received a powerful blow in 771 BCE when nomadic pastoralists from the west assaulted the capital at Zongzhou. After the regional nobles refused to send troops to support the besieged king, the Zhou army suffered a humiliating defeat. The royal court fled to the east and established a new capital at Luoyang. But the Zhou kings in Luoyang were too weak to control the regional warlords, who lived in walled cities and began fighting with each other in hopes of extending their territorial reach.

The Chinese philosopher Confucius lived between 551 and 479 BCE at a time of weakening central authority and growing friction among provincial warlords. Raised in the Shandong Province in northeastern China, Confucius showed an early interest in scholarship and eventually became a prominent teacher and political thinker. He denounced militarism and advocated civility and enlightened leadership. Confucius argued that the best way to restore order in China was to fill government posts with well-educated and virtuous individuals determined to promote the public good. Although his ideas would have a profound impact on later generations, they had little immediate effect in China.

The Warring States and the Northern Tribes

As central authority continued to decline, several large and potent states emerged in the Yellow River valley where aggressive kings employed strong armies to defeat their weaker neighbors and to expand the territory under their control. The aptly

MAP 4.1 The Warring States of China, ca. 260 BCE

named **Warring States period**, between 481 and 221 BCE, was a time of almost constant military conflict in China.

The invention and spread of a new metallurgical technology fueled wars of increasing intensity among the aggressive Chinese states. Around 500 BCE, Chinese metalworkers developed furnaces that were hot enough to melt iron, producing the first **cast iron** in the world. At a temperature of 1130 degree Celsius, iron combines with carbon and turns into liquid that can be cast into molds. By adding small amounts of carbon, metalworkers could transform the iron into steel, which was lighter and stronger than bronze. These technical achievements were not matched in Europe for 1,000 years, but by 300 BCE, the use of iron had become widespread in China for making agricultural implements and lethal weapons.

As the warring states expanded northward in the middle of the fifth century BCE, they came into increasing contact with pastoral tribes that moved with their herds according to a fixed seasonal pattern, thereby exploiting the extensive grasslands along the Chinese frontier. These nomads bred large horses for sustained riding, made short but strong bows, and trained to become mounted archers skilled at shooting arrows in any direction. Led by aristocratic warriors, the mobile tribes acquired luxury goods by either raiding sedentary farming communities or trading with them. Archaeological excavations of graves found on the **steppes** that stretched across the northern frontier of China reveal that these pastoral societies became increasingly stratified. While most tribal members were buried with only a few offerings, the graves of some aristocratic warriors were filled with hundreds of valuable gold and silver ornaments.

The aggressive Chinese states intended to incorporate the northern pastoralists and their resources into their expanding domains. Realizing that archers riding fast horses could outmaneuver chariots on the battlefield, the Chinese states traded with the nomadic tribes to obtain large horses to create their own cavalry units. The Chinese then dispatched their mounted warriors to seize grazing land from the pastoral tribes. To defend the territory that they had taken from the nomads, the rulers of the expanding Chinese states began around 300 BCE to construct long walls across large expanses of grassland that was inhabited exclusively by non-Chinese people. The walls were built to facilitate the Chinese colonization of the newly acquired territory.

The Rise of the Qin Empire

As the rival Chinese kingdoms continued to fight one another, the rulers of the Qin state decided in the middle of the fourth century BCE to institute agrarian policies that greatly increased their power. Qin monarchs encouraged the breakup of large agricultural estates and made land grants to individual peasant households. Their goal was not only to give cultivators an incentive to work harder but also to maximize the number of households obligated to provide military service to the state and to pay taxes in grain, usually amounting to 10 percent of their crop. Furthermore, the Qin rulers decided that land taken from aristocrats in conquered states would be distributed to peasants who in return would be required to pay taxes and serve in the army. These agrarian reforms had three important consequences for the Qin state: agricultural production increased, tax collections swelled, and the armed forces grew.

As agricultural output and tax revenue increased in their realm, Qin rulers used their growing wealth to build formidable armies equipped with iron weapons produced in royal workshops. Rather than depending on small military forces led by nobles riding in chariots, Qin monarchs fielded much larger infantry units composed of peasant conscripts. They also rewarded soldiers who performed with distinction on distant battlefields with grants of land and promotions to higher military ranks. While establishing the family farm as the mainstay of agricultural production and foundation of military strength, the Qin monarchs reduced the authority of provincial officials and concentrated power in the central government.

The First Emperor of China

Born in 259 BCE, Zhao Zheng established the first unified Chinese empire. His father, Zhuangxiang, became the king of the Qin state in 250 BCE with the help of Lu Buwei, a rich Chinese merchant. When King Zhuangxiang died in 246 BCE after a short reign of just three years, he was succeeded by Zheng, his 13-year-old son. But Lu Buwei served as the acting head of the Qin government until 235 BCE when Zheng came of age and assumed full royal powers. In 230 BCE, King Zheng unleashed the final campaigns of the Warring States period, and during the next nine years, he succeeded in conquering the remaining six independent Chinese kingdoms.

After incorporating all the conquered states into a unified Chinese empire in 221 BCE, King Zheng assumed the title Qin Shi Huangdi. The self-proclaimed first emperor of China announced with unbounded confidence that his dynasty would last for 10,000 generations. Determined to make good on his prediction, Qin Shi Huangdi took a series of steps aimed at consolidating his power and unifying his vast domain. He mandated the use of a common script, minted bronze coins to create a uniform measure of value, and started building a network of roads that radiated from the capital city of Xianyang. Hoping to bring the wealthy provincial aristocrats under his authority, he demanded that their families reside in the Chinese capital.

Qin Shi Huangdi, while claiming that his rise to power was part of the divine plan, sought to impose his will on his subjects. After banning Confucianism and all other philosophies, he endorsed legalism as the official ideology of the Qin state. Legalist scholars believed that humans were inherently evil and that the job of the king was to force the naturally flawed masses to behave in a correct manner. From the legalist perspective, the Chinese people must abide by the laws of the state or be punished for any transgressions. Qin Shi Huangdi used legalism to justify his despotic rule. The harsh punishments that he imposed on dissidents reflected his determination to perpetuate his dynasty.

In 215 BCE, Qin Shi Huangdi launched a military expedition to drive the nomads farther north. Then he started connecting the already existing fortifications along the northern frontier, creating a defensive system that eventually became the Great Wall of China. The northern tribes responded to Chinese imperialism by forming large political federations. In 209 BCE, one of the nomadic tribes, the Xiongnu, organized the first great steppe empire in world history. The Xiongnu Empire, in fact, lasted much longer than the Qin Empire.

The Collapse of the Qin Empire

The Qin Empire, ruled from the capital at Xianyang, flourished for only a brief period. Emperor Qin Shi Huangdi died in 210 BCE and was buried in a sumptuous underground palace along with many valuable goods and sacrificed human servants. An entire army of more than 15,000 life-size terracotta replicas of soldiers, including cavalry and infantry units, were buried nearby to guard the emperor in his next life.

Before he died, Qin Shi Huangdi had drafted hundreds of thousands of workers from all over China to construct not only his massive burial complex but also many roads, defensive walls, and irrigation works. These major building projects generated unrest among the conscripted workers compelled to leave their families and to labor far from home. A few years after the death of the first Chinese emperor, ambitious aristocrats in the former warring states led a rebellion against the central government. Angry rebels sacked Xianyang in 207 BCE, and the Qin dynasty quickly dissolved.

FIGURE 4.1   The Tomb of Qin Shi Huangdi. This photo shows only a small number of the statues in the huge terracotta army that was buried with the first emperor of China. Each life-size replica of a soldier has a distinct face.

Empire Building in South Asia

About 1,000 years after people abandoned the large cities in the Indus valley, small cities began to emerge far to the east in the Ganges River valley. Originating in the Himalayas, the Ganges flows southeastward for over 1,500 miles across northern India before forming a fertile delta and emptying into the Bay of Bengal. The Ganges is the second greatest silt-carrying river in the world, and farmers living on its flood plain were blessed by rich soil, a warm climate, and **monsoon** rains. In large areas in the middle and eastern Ganges plain, farmers cultivated wet rice, which provided a considerably higher yield than any other cereal. They produced enough rice and other crops to feed both their own families and a growing population of nonfarmers. The agricultural surplus provided the economic foundation not only for the emergence of cities and states in the Ganges plain but also the formation of a prosperous and powerful empire that embraced most of the Indian subcontinent.

Chiefs and Brahmans

During the period between 1200 and 600 BCE, farmers and herders in the central portion of the Ganges valley formed clan-based societies, which were both patriarchal and hierarchal. Women were subordinate to men who headed individual households and dominated the political and religious life of the agricultural villages. While military leaders became chiefs who protected their followers from neighboring communities, priests called **Brahmans** performed ritual sacrifices in hopes of pleasing the gods and assuring the well-being of the entire clan. Some of the wealth that clan members voluntarily offered their chiefs was consumed in ritual sacrifices, but the rest was distributed as gifts to other chiefs and to the Brahmans. In addition to increasing the wealth of the priests, these religious ceremonies legitimized the power of the chiefs.

The chiefs and Brahmans occupied the highest social positions in an evolving **caste system**, which ranked different categories of people according to the purity of their occupations. Comprising only a small minority of the Indian population, the Brahmans eventually came to be regarded as members of the highest and purist social class. Cultivators, traders, and others were ranked in descending order down to the despised outcasts, or **untouchables**, who were viewed as belonging to the lowest and least pure group in the status hierarchy. As the caste system developed, the social position of every member of Indian society was fixed at birth, and the Brahmans continued to be treated as members of a privileged class.

The Second Urbanization

In the years between 600 and 400 BCE, South Asia experienced a second period of urbanization as a growing number of towns and cities arose in the middle reaches of the Ganges plain. Small towns usually began as commercial or political centers, but the inhabitants of larger cities engaged in many different activities.

For example, the city of Kaushambi not only served as a regional capital but it also controlled river traffic on the Ganges and hosted religious institutions. The artisans and merchants who resided in the towns and cities depended on farmers in the surrounding countryside for much of their food. As agricultural output increased in the Ganges valley, artisans in the urban centers produced a wide range of iron objects, including hoes, sickles, knives, hooks, nails, and arrowheads. These craft specialists also manufactured various trade goods, such as beads, pottery, glassware, and ivory ornaments. As merchants shipped luxury goods on roads and rivers, the volume of commerce and the circulation of silver coins increased substantially.

The flourishing urban centers on the Ganges plain were relatively tolerant of unorthodox beliefs. As the prevailing religion of the Indian elite, Brahmanism emphasized the importance of deities, ritual sacrifices, and caste distinctions. Many wandering ascetics rejected the views of the Brahmans and objected to their control over religious and social affairs. These dissidents began preaching to audiences gathered in parks and groves on the outskirts of towns, which attracted many competing religious sects. Founded by two unorthodox preachers, **Buddhism** and **Jainism** gradually developed into major religions.

Siddhartha Gautama was born into an aristocratic family in the town of Kapilavastu about 563 BCE, and he eventually came to be known as the Buddha (the Enlightened One). After leaving home as a young man and wandering for many weeks, Gautama believed that he had become enlightened through meditation and understood that human desire was the cause of suffering in the world. The Buddha started preaching around 530 BCE as he traveled from town to town in the middle part of the Ganges plain. Rather than regarding his teachings as divine revelation, he viewed them as apparent truths. The Buddha called for ethical behavior and a concern for the welfare of all humanity, and he did not make caste a barrier to those wishing to become monks or lay followers. In the early stages of its development, Buddhism was largely supported by merchants and traders who were growing in economic importance but were regarded as socially inferior to the Brahmans.

Chiefdoms and Kingdoms

The chiefdoms and kingdoms that emerged in the Ganges valley during the sixth century BCE were political entities that controlled territories that varied in size. Headed by successful military leaders, chiefdoms consisted of a single clan or a confederacy of clans. Chiefs presided over assemblies composed of the male heads of families, but they did not inherit their authority and could not pass their power onto their sons. Over time, some of the chiefdoms slowly evolved into kingdoms in which ruling families established hereditary dynasties. Loyalty to clans eventually gave way to loyalty to kings. As the kingdoms expanded in size, the power of the assemblies weakened. Monarchs appointed ministers to serve as advisors and to assist them in extracting wealth from peasants, artisans, and traders who had no kin ties with their rulers.

While chiefdoms tended to occupy less fertile and hilly areas on their periphery, three large kingdoms competed for control of the central Ganges plain. Magadha was the strongest of these kingdoms, and during the second half of the sixth century BCE, its rulers embarked on an aggressive program of military conquest. By 460 BCE, Magadha had succeeded in defeating and annexing its two major rivals, the neighboring kingdoms of Kash and Kosala. The victorious kingdom remained the dominant power in northern India for more than 100 years. In addition to possessing rich soil needed for the production of surplus rice, Magadha had two other advantages. The kingdom controlled key points on the Ganges river system as well as neighboring forests that provided timber for the construction of buildings and elephants for its army. Around 362 BCE, Mahapadma Nanda usurped the throne and established a dynasty that ruled Magadha for the next three decades. The Nanda dynasty extended the frontiers of Magadha, but its attempt at empire building soon came to an abrupt end.

The Rise of the Mauryan Empire

Chandragupta Maurya usurped the Nanda throne in Magadha around 321 BCE and started building a vast empire that soon stretched across northern India from the Ganges delta to the Indus valley. After Chandragupta died around 297 BCE, his son Bindusara succeeded him and continued the Mauryan campaign of military conquest. Both Chandragupta and Bindusara maintained a large number of permanent troops in a standing army composed of four branches: infantry, cavalry, chariots, and elephants. They also employed soldiers on a temporary basis when needed to conquer additional territory. To obtain duties on imports and exports, toll houses were established at city gates throughout the expanding Mauryan Empire. By the time Bindusara died around 272 BCE, large parts of the Indian subcontinent had come under Mauryan domination.

The Mauryan Empire was centrally administered from the capital of Pataliputra, a city with monumental architecture revealing the presence of imperial power. Located at a strategic point on the Ganges River and on the main highway running across northern India, Pataliputra stood at the center of the most important trade routes in the realm. The kings who resided in grand style in Pataliputra exercised supreme authority in the flourishing empire. While an appointed council of ministers served as an advisory body, the kings made all the important decisions. The Mauryan state employed a great many officials who were primarily concerned with financial matters. These bureaucrats collected taxes, stored income in the royal treasury, and supervised the expenditure of state funds. Tax revenue was used to pay the salaries of public officials, to build roads, to maintain the army, to make grants to religious institutions, and to support the royal family.

A variety of taxes provided the financial resources that buttressed the Mauryan state. Generated by regular assessments, the land tax supplied the largest source of revenue for the central government. The amount of taxes collected from private landowners was based on the extent of the area under cultivation and the size of the harvest. After collecting rent from their tenants, large landowners paid taxes to the state. The farmers who worked under state supervision on small parcels of the extensive crown lands also paid taxes. While the owners of cattle paid taxes according to the number and productivity of their animals, artisans working as individuals or as members of guilds paid taxes in the form of labor service to the state.

Mauryan kings presided over a mixed economy, with private enterprise and state-owned business existing side by side. The state employed craft specialists and manual laborers in its mines, agricultural estates, and workshops, which manufactured arms, ships, and cotton textiles. In addition, the state paid high salaries to officials who supervised the sale of merchandise in order to prevent merchants from charging excessive prices that would harm the general population. The state kept cultivators unarmed to reduce the likelihood of peasant uprisings. Rather than rebelling, discontented peasants often migrated to neighboring kingdoms. Artisan guilds sometimes used slaves to aid in the production of craft goods, and prosperous households were commonly served by domestic slaves. Merchants profited from financial as well as commercial transactions. While the average interest rate on borrowed money was 15 percent a year, merchants charged as much as 60 percent on loans involving risky sea voyages.

Following the death of Bindusara, his ambitious sons engaged in a four-year struggle for succession. Prince Ashoka eventually outmaneuvered his brothers, and around 269 BCE, he became the third monarch of the Mauryan Empire. In the ninth year of his reign, Ashoka ordered his armies southward, and they succeeded in conquering the state of Kalinga, which sat astride the east coast trade route to south India and Ceylon. But the victorious king was filled with remorse about the suffering that his armies had inflicted on the people of Kalinga.

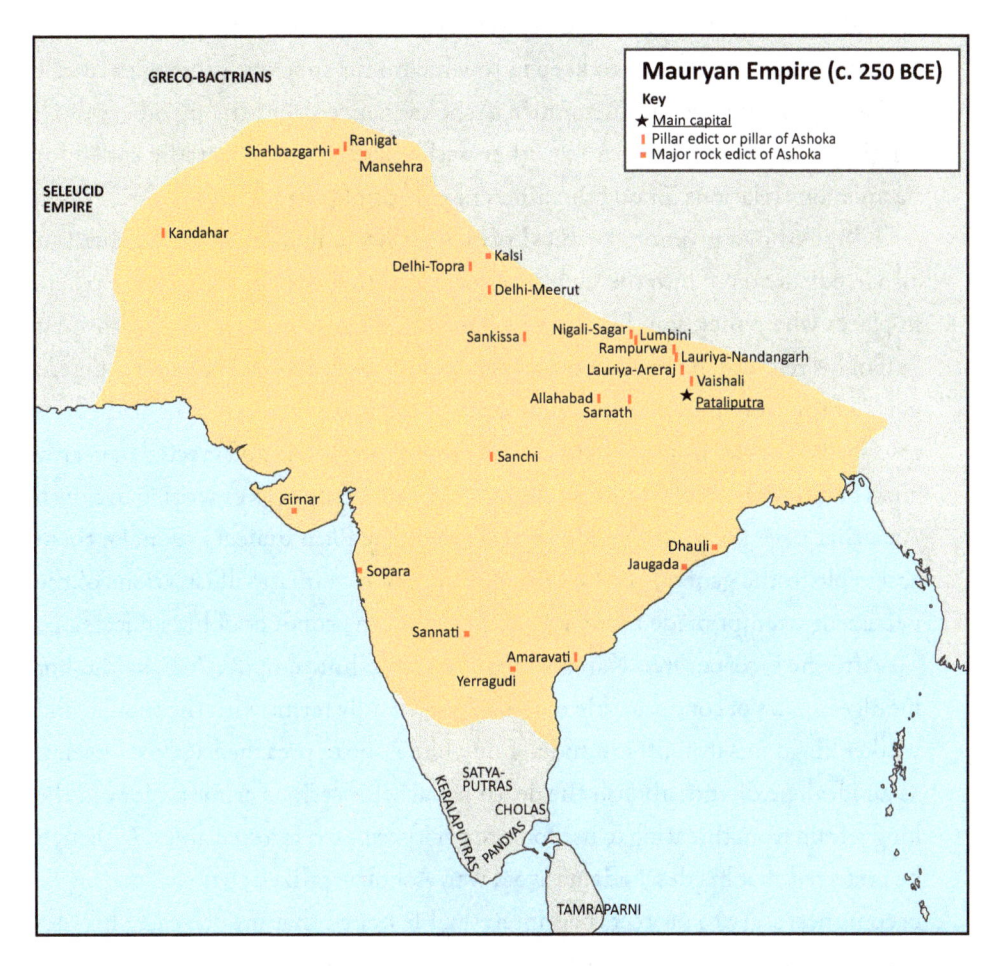

MAP 4.2 The Mauryan Empire

King Ashoka and His Quest for Social Harmony

About two and a half years after his conquest of Kalinga, the repentant King Ashoka became personally devoted to Buddhism as a way of life. But he did not want to make Buddhism the officially sanctioned religion of the state. Rather than compelling his subjects to become members of the Buddhist religion, Ashoka sought to persuade others to behave in a way that would help consolidate his enormous domain. He intended to use the Buddhist emphasis on ethical principles as a binding factor that would help keep his geographically vast and culturally diverse empire intact.

A paternalistic monarch who regarded everyone in his kingdom as his children, Ashoka challenged the caste system by advocating equal treatment for all people regardless of their status. Ashoka traveled extensively throughout the Mauryan Empire because he wanted to keep in touch with his subjects. Hoping to reduce social tension and sectarian conflict, Ashoka insisted that the members of all religious sects should treat each other with respect. He repeatedly called for harmonious relations among the different groups of people in his realm.

King Ashoka promoted ethical principles not only in public speeches but also in edicts carved into the surface of rocks and well-polished sandstone pillars in places where they could be seen by large numbers of people. During the first half of his reign, Ashoka had edicts inscribed on rocks located in many different parts of the Indian subcontinent. In the second half of his reign, he had edicts inscribed on tall stone pillars that were transported by river and erected in nearby areas on the Ganges plain. These edicts are the earliest pieces of writing in South Asia that have been deciphered. Inscribed in the local dialects to make them accessible to the general public, the edicts provide dramatic illustrations of the persistent attempt made by Ashoka to influence the conduct of his subjects.

After he incorporated Kalinga into his multiethnic empire, Ashoka did not indulge in wars of conquest. He remained on friendly terms with the smaller and weaker kingdoms in southern India. But while Ashoka preached against violence as an ideal, he did not abolish the death penalty for serious crimes. Nor did the king refrain from threating to use force to pacify tribes in forested areas. Although he preferred that his descendants avoid war, Ashoka realized that violence might become necessary to protect their interests. He hoped that in such cases his successors would treat conquered people with mercy and clemency.

When Ashoka died around 232 BCE, the Mauryan Empire began to break apart. Ashoka had managed to maintain a firm grip for 37 years over different regions inhabited by people clinging to different customs and speaking different languages. But he was followed by a succession of weak kings who were unable to hold the vast and diverse empire together. After the assassination of the last of these monarchs around 185 BCE, the Mauryan Empire rapidly disintegrated. The larger cities became the nuclei for the emergence of many smaller kingdoms that engaged in intense rivalry with each other. Thus, the relatively brief period of centralized political control that the Mauryan dynasty had exercised over most of South Asia came to a close.

Early Urbanization and States Formation in Tropical Africa

When Egypt was unified during the New Kingdom period, Egyptian pharaohs extended their control of Nubia into the area south of the third cataract on the Nile River. Egyptian forces promptly attacked Kerma, the capital of the earliest state in sub-Saharan Africa. After conquering the kingdom of Kerma around 1500 BCE, the Egyptians established a fortified settlement at Napata downstream from the fourth cataract. They also built a temple dedicated to the god Amun at the foot of a rock outcrop—the Gebel Barkal—across the Nile from Napata.

But when the New Kingdom fragmented around 1069 BCE, Egyptian domination of Nubia declined. The area south of the second cataract was subsequently governed by multiple chiefs who controlled small territories adjacent to the Nile. During the ninth century BCE, a chiefdom in the fertile region along the Nile between the third and fourth cataracts grew into a powerful Nubian kingdom with its capital at Napata. The settlements around Napata flourished until the fourth century BCE when the capital of the Nubian state, which the Egyptians called Kush, was moved south to Meroë, a city located in a fertile area on the Nile floodplain between the fifth and sixth cataracts.

The Rise of the Napatan Empire

The early kings in Napata restored the temple that the Egyptians had built for the worship of Amun at Gebel Barkal. Using the temple to provide a religious justification for their authority, the Nubian monarchs claimed that Amun had granted them the right to rule. The heartland of the Napatan state was located on the floodplain of the Nile between the third and fourth cataracts. But Napatan kings established their authority over a string of settlements that extended along the bank of river both upstream to the south and downstream to the north.

King Piye organized a strong Nubian army, and in 728 BCE, he invaded politically fragmented Egypt. After his soldiers captured several fortified towns in Egypt as far to the north as Memphis, Piye returned to Napata and erected a victory **stele** topped with a relief of him accepting the submission of the Egyptian rulers. "Then Memphis was seized as if by a cloudburst," an inscription on the stele boasted. "Many people were slain in it, or brought as captives to where his majesty [King Piye] was."[1] While residing in Napata, Piye allied with the high priests of Amun in Thebes and established Nubian rule over southern Egypt.

King Shabaqo, a grandson of Piye, soon extended Nubian control over northern Egypt. After setting himself up as a new pharaoh in Memphis in 711 BCE, Shabaqo formally annexed Egypt. As a result of his actions, the extent of the Nubian empire was enormous, with some 1,000 miles separating Napata and Memphis by river. For a relatively brief period of 50 years, Shabaqo and his successors ruled Egypt as pharaohs. But after competing with the Assyrians for control of their weak Egyptian neighbor, the Nubians were eventually driven out of Egypt.

While displaying many distinctive Nubian features, the culture of Napata was strongly influenced by Egyptian practices. Napatan scribes used Egyptian hieroglyphics to record the proclamations and accomplishments of their rulers. When Napatan kings died, they were interred in tombs covered by small pyramids made of stone that were like those built over the nonroyal tombs of prominent Egyptians in Thebes. The construction of these impressive burial monuments demonstrates the power of Nubian monarchs to command the labor of many manual workers. The Egyptian luxury goods excavated from these royal graves, moreover, reveal the great wealth and high status of Napatan kings who possessed exotic commodities acquired from distant places.

The Napatan state had a diversified economy based on agriculture, manufacturing, and commerce. The peasants who provided food for the urban population living in Napata engaged in mixed farming. While many peasants cultivated barley and other crops on land covered in rich silt deposited by the annual flooding of the Nile, others grew vegetables and grain on irrigated land that did not benefit by the seasonal rise of the river. The Nubian farmers also raised cattle, sheep, and goats, which provided meat and milk that added protein to the diet, as well as wool and hides that were used to make clothing.

While farmers produced surplus food in the countryside, craft specialists in Napata cut stone, made bricks, and produced remarkably fine pottery. But the prosperity of Napata depended more on its middleman role as a shipper of commodities than as a manufacturer of goods. Strategically located on the banks of the Nile, Napata served as an important commercial center in a long-distance trading network based on the exchange of slaves, ivory, and other commodities for a variety of Egyptian manufactured goods.

---

1 Miriam Lichtheim, ed. and trans., *Ancient Egyptian Literature, Vol. III: The Late Period* (Berkeley: University of California Press, 1980), 76. (Copyright in 1980 by the Regents of the University of California)

The Formation of the Meroitic State

During the fourth century BCE, the seat of Nubian power shifted to the south and east from Napata to Meroë. The new capital at Meroë, laying downstream from modern Khartoum, had a more favorable geographical location than Napata with respect to both agriculture and commerce. In the drier area surrounding Napata, the cultivation of crops was restricted to a narrow belt of naturally inundated or mechanically irrigated farmland near the Nile. But the wetter region around Meroë received sufficient rainfall for growing crops and herding animals on grasslands that extended far away from the river. Nourished by a broader agricultural hinterland, the urban settlements in the Meroitic kingdom grew larger than those in the Napatan state.

Sitting astride the east banks of the Nile, Meroë profited from its strategic location. By using a road, which ran overland from Meroë across the great bend in the river, traders in the royal capital could bypass the fifth and fourth cataracts when shipping goods to Egypt. Meroë and some of its sister towns along the Nile also benefited from their access to suitable ports on the Red Sea, a waterway that served as an important route for the shipment of products between the interior of Africa and the eastern coast of the Mediterranean Sea.

Meroë grew into a large political center. The capital city, which housed as many as 20,000 residents by 1 BCE, flourished until the Meroitic Empire perished 300 years later. Protected by a stone wall, a royal precinct in the heart of Meroë contained several monumental buildings made of mud bricks and often with an exterior facing of fired bricks. These buildings included palaces, storage facilities, and a temple dedicated to the god Amun. Like the earlier kings of Napata, the monarchs of Meroë sponsored the cult of Amun as a religious ideology that legitimized their supreme political authority. Scribes in Meroë developed their own Nubian language during the second century BCE, but modern scholars have not yet been able to decipher their writings.

Archeological investigations indicate that many ordinary people lived in Meroë outside the central enclosure reserved for members of the royal family and government officials. The population included many skilled artisans, including iron smiths, bricklayers, and weavers who made cloth from cotton grown in the surrounding countryside. The discovery of large mounds of iron slag in the immediate vicinity of the city make it clear that Meroe was the site of a substantial iron-working industry. Besides producing simple agricultural implements, such as hoes, the iron smiths in Meroe crafted a wide array of weapons, including spears, arrowheads, swords, and battle-axes.

Archeological excavations of six cemeteries located on the eastern outskirts of Meroë show that Meroitic society was stratified, with a wide gap separating elite individuals from common people. Reflecting the lower strata of the social order, hundreds of simple burials contained the remains of commoners accompanied by no more than a ceramic jar or cup. Mirroring the upper level of the social structure, a small number of richly furnished graves held the remains of monarchs and members of their immediate families.

The most impressive of these royal burials were covered by small stone pyramids. Although men dominated Nubian society, a few exceptional women did manage to assume a position of supreme authority in Meroë. Queen Shanakdakhete, for example, ruled the Meroitic state in the middle of the second century BCE, and archeological evidence indicates that she was buried under one of the stone pyramids for which Meroë has become famous.

Archaeologists have excavated several other large settlements in the Meroitic heartland between the fifth and sixth cataracts. Excavations at Hamadab, a site located less than two miles south of Meroe, have revealed a settlement containing a temple and large residential area of mud-brick houses. Excavations at Naqa, an inland site located on a tributary some 30 miles east of the Nile, have uncovered an extensive settlement of mud-brick and fired-brick buildings, including several temples, as well as a nearby cemetery to the northeast. The earliest inscriptions found at Naqa were written during the reign of Queen Shanakdakhete in the second century BCE.

A small chain of Meroitic settlements dispersed along the Nile in a sparsely populated region north of the third cataract served as waystations for controlling trade and communications with Egypt. Reflecting the demands of river-borne transportation, many of these outposts were located at strategic positions where rapids made navigation difficult. The monarchs of Meroë, like their predecessors at Napata, probably maintained a monopoly over long-distance trade with Egypt so that they could retain their political power by distributing foreign luxury goods, such as fine glassware and bronze vessels, to reward their elite supporters. In line with their elevated status, elite individuals were often buried with Egyptian imports in the Meroitic kingdom, the greatest state yet to emerge in sub-Saharan Africa.

Early Urbanization and State Formation in Mesoamerica

The earliest cities and states in the Western Hemisphere appeared in Mesoamerica, a large region stretching from central Mexico southward to Nicaragua. As was the case in Asia and Africa, agricultural intensification in ancient Mesoamerica provided the economic foundation that supported some very impressive cities and states. The cultivation of maize, beans, and squash—the principal staples in most of Mesoamerica—supplied abundant food surpluses that fed growing populations of nonfarmers living in urban centers. Frequently grown together, these three crops furnished a nutritionally balanced diet, which was supplemented by other locally domesticated plants, such as chili peppers and avocados.

The process of early urbanization and state formation in Mesoamerica, however, differed in significant ways from similar developments in the Eastern Hemisphere. Unlike the situation in Mesopotamia, Egypt, South Asia, and China, the first cities and states in Mesoamerica did not arise on the broad floodplains of major soil-bearing rivers. The ancient Mesoamerican societies, moreover, were characterized by technological simplicity compared to their Asian and African counterparts. Although the people in Mesoamerica used gold, silver, and copper to make objects for religious ceremonies or personal adornment, they seldom used metals to manufacture tools or weapons. Not only did the early Mesoamericans lack wheeled vehicles but they also did not have any large domesticated animals, such as horses, mules, oxen, or water buffalo, that could be used to pull plows or transport goods. Nevertheless, the ancient Mesoamericans did establish prosperous cities and powerful states that flourished for more than 1,000 years.

Agricultural Villages and Long-Distance Exchange

In the period between 1600 and 1200 BCE, sedentary farming communities emerged in several different regions of Mesoamerica. Large areas in both the highlands and lowlands of Mexico were blessed with fresh water and fertile soil, which provided excellent habitats for the establishment of agricultural settlements. During these years, farmers colonized the Basin of Mexico in the central highlands, and soon about 10,000 people were living in the region, which possessed rich volcanic soil as well as an extensive lake system. Many small farming communities also arose in the coastal lowlands along the Gulf of Mexico, on the rich alluvial soil near river channels in the Valley of Oaxaca located in the heart of the southern highlands, and on the coastal plain adjacent to the Pacific Ocean.

Some of these settlements rapidly grew into large villages. By 1400 BCE, about 200 people were living in San Jose Mogote, a thriving agricultural community in the Valley of Oaxaca.

During the period between 1200 and 900 BCE, the volume of long-distance exchange significantly increased across much of Mesoamerica. Human carriers transported a wide variety of goods within a large trading area, which encompassed the Basin of Mexico, the gulf coastal lowlands, the Valley of Oaxaca, and the Pacific coastal plain. For example, obsidian was mined in only two areas in Mesoamerica, and this volcanic glass with sharp edges became an important item of interregional trade. Elite households in all the major regions of Mesoamerica gained access to exotic goods, such as brightly colored bird feathers, oyster shells, and jade pieces, that often came from sources more than 100 miles away.

The extensive trading area in Mesoamerica gave elite individuals an opportunity to display their elevated status by using luxury goods as personal ornaments or as grave offerings for family members. By 1000 BCE, sharp distinctions between the nobility and common people had not yet developed in the agricultural communities in Mesoamerica, but social and economic differences were beginning to appear. Mortuary practices in San Jose Mogote provide clear evidence for the emergence of status differences in the Valley of Oaxaca. While some people were buried without any grave offerings, others were interred with prestige goods, such as jade earspools, well-made ceramic vessels, and marine shell ornaments. But neither San Jose Mogote nor the other important nodes of long-distance trade had more than 1,000 residents at this time, and no single region dominated the large Mesoamerican exchange system.

The Rise and Fall of Olmec Chiefdoms

The gulf costal lowlands formed the heartland of hierarchal **Olmec** societies, which were ruled by powerful chiefs. Around 1200 BCE, San Lorenzo emerged as the first political capital and ritual center in the Olmec region where meandering rivers flowed through dense tropical forests. San Lorenzo stood on the top of an artificially flattened natural plateau over 100 feet above the surrounding countryside. Thousands of farmers lived in nearby hamlets and small villages located on fertile alluvial soil. Inscribed on a serpentine block near San Lorenzo around 1000 BCE, a set of 62 signs might be the oldest fragments of writing yet found in Mesoamerica. The signs are arranged in a manner consistent with later texts, but they are not readable.

San Lorenzo was an important node in the extensive Mesoamerican exchange network. Using raw materials imported from distant sources, artisans in San Lorenzo made luxury goods that served as symbols of elite social status. Some craft specialists produced mirrors by polishing metals acquired in the Mexican highlands, while others manufactured ornaments carved from blue-green jade that came from Guatemala. By obtaining and displaying these exotic items, wealthy individuals were able to set themselves apart from their poorer neighbors.

Along with civic buildings and elite houses containing many luxury goods, San Lorenzo featured 10 colossal stone heads. These gigantic monuments, the larger ones weighing between 25 and 50 tons, were carved from boulders of basalt quarried in the Tuxlas Mountains dozens of miles from San Lorenzo. Representing different rulers, the colossal stone heads illustrate the power of Olmec chiefs to command the labor of large numbers of people who were needed to mine and transport these awe-inspiring monuments. Although no one knows why San Lorenzo was abandoned about 900 BCE, many archaeologists now think that a shift in river courses may have induced people to migrate.

FIGURE 4.2   A Colossal Stone Head from San Lorenzo. This gigantic statue was produced by Olmec artisans and placed in the political and ritual center of San Lorenzo.

The decline of San Lorenzo coincided with the rise of La Venta, which quickly became the second prominent Olmec political and ritual center. Located about 55 miles to the northeast of the former Olmec capital, La Venta featured a massive earthen pyramid, over 100 feet high, which was surrounded by platforms, courtyards, and four colossal stone heads. Some wealthy individuals in La Venta were interred in impressive tombs. The burial of two infants in an elaborate tomb filled with rich mortuary offerings provides one of the earliest pieces of archeological evidence for the emergence of inherited social position in Mesoamerica. Many scholars believe that the abandonment of La Venta around 400 BCE was probably caused by serious environmental changes that rendered the region unsuitable for intensive agriculture, as was the case in San Lorenzo.

A Great Transformation in the Valley of Oaxaca

The Valley of Oaxaca was agriculturally more productive than any other area in the rugged southern highlands of Mexico. Besides having narrower floodplains and less farmland, the neighboring valleys were higher and colder. The Valley of Oaxaca not only had the largest expanse of relatively flat land in the mountainous region but it also possessed water sources that supplemented rainfall and permitted the planting of more than one crop of maize each year. Farmers exploited the high water table in the valley by digging shallow wells and carrying pots filled with water that they poured on their plants. Moreover, farmers tapped the many streams in the valley by constructing simple canals and diverting water to their crops.

The Valley of Oaxaca underwent a dramatic transformation marked by the emergence of the first city in Mesoamerica. In 600 BCE, the entire valley contained only about 2,000 inhabitants. More than half of these people resided in the town of San Jose Mogote, while most of the rest lived in tiny hamlets. Inscriptions found on a rock at a site near San Jose Mogote reveal that some people in the valley had begun to write. Around 500 BCE, people abandoned San Jose Mogote, and Monte Alban suddenly arose on a previously unoccupied mesa in the central part of the valley. The population of the new settlement, located where the three arms of the Y-shaped valley join, burgeoned from zero to over 5,000 in fewer than 200 years. By 150 BCE, Monte Alban was packed with 17,000 residents, and the valley contained more than 50,000 people, including many living in towns with over 1,000 inhabitants. The spectacular 6 percent annual growth rate of the Monte Alban population was made possible by the migration of large numbers of people into the city.

Monte Alban was the fortified capital of a powerful state that dominated the entire Valley of Oaxaca for over a millennium. Compared to other parts of the valley, the farmland in the immediate vicinity of the capital was only marginally productive. The rapid expansion of its urban population, therefore, depended on surplus food grown in rural areas, especially by farmers who lived in villages within a day's walk from the city. Residing in Monte Alban, the rulers of the state extracted **tribute** in the form of labor as well as maize from villages that were scattered throughout the valley. Conscripted workers built the main plaza of the capital into a vast civic-ceremonial area, which was surrounded by massive pyramids. While most people in Monte Alban lived in small dwellings, wealthy families resided in larger houses elevated on stone and mud-brick platforms. Burials in the capital, moreover, revealed a widening gap that separated the nobility from the common people.

Sometime after 200 BCE, the kings of Monte Alban embarked on a series of imperial ventures outside the Valley of Oaxaca. Their program of territorial conquest brought increasing amounts of tribute into the city. While monumental construction at the capital continued, people moved out of the valley as neighboring territories were colonized. As a result, between 100 BCE and 300 CE, the population of both Monte Alban and the rest of the Valley of Oaxaca declined by more than 15 percent. But the monarchs of Monte Alban remained in power until 750 CE when their greatly enlarged state mysteriously collapsed. Archeologists have not yet found any evidence for an external attack, an internal revolt, or an ecological change that could explain why entire buildings in Monte Alban began to crumble and why people gradually abandoned the main plaza.

State Formation in the Basin of Mexico

The population of the Basin of Mexico gradually increased as farmers exploited the extensive aquatic resources and the abundant stretches of fertile soil in this area in the central highlands. In 1200 BCE, about 10,000 people were living in many small villages scattered throughout the basin, and by 400 BCE, around 80,000 people resided in the region. Most of these inhabitants lived in five or six large communities that relied on the surplus maize, beans, and squash produced by farmers in the surrounding countryside. Hardly any of these cultivators resided in the Teotihuacan valley located in the northern part of the basin.

Then, between 300 and 100 BCE, large numbers of farmers colonized this fertile valley in the Basin of Mexico, and Teotihuacan suddenly emerged as the largest city not only in Mesoamerica but in all of the Western Hemisphere. The population of Teotihuacan had reached nearly 40,000 by 100 BCE, and a century later, around 60,000 people resided in the city, which had expanded to cover over six square miles. Such a remarkable demographic growth was made possible because 80–90 percent of the entire population of the basin was concentrated in Teotihuacan. Most of the people who lived in this huge urban center were part-time farmers and part-time artisans. These city-dwelling agrarians cultivated fields located within a day's walk of Teotihuacan, and they irrigated their crops with water drawn from local springs and streams.

Teotihuacan had become the political capital of a powerful and prosperous state that dominated the whole Basin of Mexico. But the archaeological evidence does not indicate that its authority extended beyond the basin into neighboring regions. Sometime before 600 CE, the population of Teotihuacan began to shrink, and new urban centers emerged throughout the Basin of Mexico. Due to the scarcity of written records in ancient Mesoamerica, archaeologists do not know any more about the factors that led to the decline of Teotihuacan than those involved in the collapse of Monte Alban, the first great states in the Western Hemisphere.

Review Questions

1. How did the Qin rulers manage to establish the first Chinese empire?
2. How was Ashoka able to consolidate his ethnically diverse empire?
3. How did the kings of Napata and Meroë seek to legitimize their supreme political authority?
4. How did the expansion of long-distance exchange lead to growing differences in social prestige in Mesoamerica?

Additional Readings

Allchin, F. R. *The Archaeology of Early Historic South Asia: The Emergence of Cities and States*. Cambridge: Cambridge University Press, 1995.

Blanton, Richard E., Stephen A. Kowalewski, Gary M. Feinman, and Laura M. Finsten. *Ancient Mesoamerica: A Comparison of Change in Three Regions*. 2nd ed. Cambridge: Cambridge University Press, 1993.

Blanton, Richard E., Gary M. Feinman, Stephen A. Kowaleski, and Linda M. Nicholas. *Ancient Oaxaca: The Monte Alban State*. Cambridge: Cambridge University Press, 1999.

Connah, Graham. *African Civilizations: An Archaeological Perspective*. 3rd ed. Cambridge: Cambridge University Press, 2015.

Di Comos, Nicholas. *Ancient China and Its Enemies: The Rise of Nomadic Powers in East Asia*. Cambridge: Cambridge University Press, 2002.

Evans, Susan Toby. *Ancient Mexico and Central America*. 3rd ed. London: Thames & Hudson, 2013.

Lewis, Mark E. *The Early Chinese Empires: Qin and Han*. Cambridge, MA: Harvard University Press, 2002.

Loewe, Michael, and Edward Shaughnessy, eds. *The Cambridge History of Ancient China*. Cambridge: Cambridge University Press, 1999.

Marcus, Joyce, and Kent Flannery. *Zapotec Civilization*. London: Thames & Hudson, 1996.

Scarre, Cris, ed. *The Human Past: World Prehistory and the Development of Human Societies*. 4th ed. London: Thames & Hudson, 2018.

Thapar, Romila. *Early India: From the Origins to AD 1300*. Berkeley: University of California Press, 2002.

Thapar, Romila. *Asoka and the Decline of the Mauryas*. 3rd ed. New Delhi: Oxford University Press, 2012.

Van De Mieroop, Mark. *A History of Ancient Egypt*. Malden, MA: Wiley-Blackwell, 2011.

Wolpert, Stanley. *A New History of India*. 7th ed. Oxford: Oxford University Press, 2004.

Figure Credits

Map 4.1: Copyright © by Philg88 (CC BY-SA 3.0) at https://commons.wikimedia.org/wiki/File:EN-WarringStatesAll260BCE.jpg.

Fig. 4.1: Copyright © by David Stanley (CC BY 2.0) at https://commons.wikimedia.org/wiki/File:Terracotta_Warriors_(48814752157).jpg.

Map 4.2: Copyright © by Avantiputra7 (CC BY-SA 3.0) at https://commons.wikimedia.org/wiki/File:Maurya_Empire,_c.250_BCE_2.png.

Fig. 4.2: Source: https://commons.wikimedia.org/wiki/File:Sanlorenzohead6.jpg.

CHAPTER 5

The Mediterranean World, 2000 BCE–500 BCE

The Eastern Mediterranean Exchange Network

The Mediterranean, the largest inland sea in the world, was a vital conduit for cross-cultural trade. For thousands of years, the Mediterranean served as a commercial highway that facilitated the exchange of goods among distant peoples. Mariners sailed the Mediterranean on ships that carried large cargoes at low costs. While engaging in long-distance trade, merchants hoped that the financial rewards would outweigh the economic risks posed by pirates and shipwrecks.

The eastern Mediterranean became the center of a thriving exchange system. The small Minoan states on the island of Crete took the lead in establishing trading circuits in the Aegean Sea and the eastern Mediterranean, but most of their palaces were destroyed and their prominent commercial position was usurped by the aggressive Mycenaean kingdoms on the Greek mainland.

Eventually, a group of large and powerful states—Egypt, Babylonia, Mitanni, and Hatti—became active participants in the eastern Mediterranean exchange network. The members of the small upper class in all these kingdoms enjoyed the blessings of prosperity until a general political and economic collapse resulted in a sharp decline in the volume of long-distance trade in the eastern Mediterranean.

Minoans and Mycenaeans

The small Minoan states that emerged on the island of Crete around 2000 BCE played a prominent role in establishing the eastern Mediterranean trading circuits. A series of regional administrative centers without defensive walls, usually referred to as palaces, developed along the Cretan coast at places such as Knossos, Malia, Zakros, and Phaistos. These regional centers developed into flourishing urban settlements. By 1500 BCE, Knossos, the largest city on Crete, had around 15,000 residents.

Each Minoan palace contained residential quarters, storage facilities, and workshops where craft specialists converted raw materials into finished articles of enhanced value. Palace administrators kept written records of the production of various goods, the provision of rations to different categories of male and female workers, and the volume of maritime commerce. But these administrators did not maintain exclusive control over economic affairs in Crete as can be seen by the fact that several grand houses located outside the palace at Knossos contained craft workshops and prestige goods.

Minoan merchants skillfully sailed their ships throughout the southern Aegean and eastern Mediterranean Seas. They exchanged wine, olive oil, woolen textiles, and beautifully decorated pottery produced in Crete for elephant ivory from Egypt as well as copper, tin, silver, and gold from many distant regions. As early as 1900 BCE, wealthy Minoans were buried with many luxury goods imported from Egypt, the Cycladic islands in the Aegean, and the cities along the Levantine coast.

By 1600 BCE, enterprising Minoan traders began shipping an array of Mediterranean products to the emerging Mycenaean states on the Greek mainland. The prosperous Minoan states flourished until 1425 BCE, when all their palaces except for the one at Knossos were burned to the ground. The Minoan palaces were most likely destroyed by Mycenaean invaders who quickly usurped the important trading position that Crete had occupied in the eastern Mediterranean.

In contrast to the highly vulnerable Minoan administrative centers, most of the palaces and attached urban settlements in Mycenaean Greece were strongly fortified by massive stone walls, some as thick as 50 feet. The citadels at Mycenae, Pylos, Thebes, Athens, and several other locations on the Greek mainland served as the capitals of militant kingdoms. While royal families resided in these fortresses, aristocratic warriors rode chariots

FIGURE 5.1 The Entrance to the Citadel of Mycenae. Mycenaean citadels were fortified by massive walls of large stone blocks.

into battle, and government officials supervised the construction of roads, bridges, and port facilities. The Mycenaean citadels, which were surrounded by fertile lowlands, sat astride major routes of communication and transportation.

The Mycenaean kingdoms participated in extensive and overlapping exchange circuits. Writing on clay tablets, government scribes kept track of economic activities, such as the production and exportation of craft goods. Mycenaean pottery made its way to Italy, Sicily, and Sardinia as well as Egypt, the **Levant**, Cyprus, Crete, and many Aegean islands. Mycenaean traders probably conducted private business while acting as government agents, and these enterprising individuals helped link distant communities living near the Aegean, Mediterranean, and Tyrrhenian Seas.

Ruled by monarchs and their loyal warriors, the Mycenaean states were highly stratified. Mycenaean kings maintained control over the importation of exotic materials needed for the production of luxury articles in royal workshops. They used these luxury goods to symbolize their sovereignty and to secure the support of aristocrats who helped them govern. While commoners were interred in simple graves with few or no offerings, Mycenaean kings were buried in huge chamber tombs shaped like beehives. These burial chambers were filled with exquisite goods, including finely crafted gold face masks, bronze armor, and bronze weapons sometimes inlaid with imported silver and gold.

Trade and Diplomacy in the Eastern Mediterranean

Utilizing the prevailing winds and currents, seafarers typically sailed in a counterclockwise pattern along the eastern shores of the Mediterranean, often stopping at safe harbors during each trip to buy and sell merchandise. A merchant vessel, which was probably sailing from Egypt when it encountered a violent storm, sank around 1310 BCE off the southern coast of Anatolia near the town of Uluburun. Underwater investigations have revealed that the 50-foot vessel carried a wide range of goods before it sank to the bottom of the sea. Besides 10 tons of copper and one ton of tin, both transported in the form of **ingots**, the cargo included ebony logs, elephant tusks, hippopotamus teeth, ostrich eggshells, glass beads, cedar logs, and resin for making perfume. The discovery of these commodities, which came from many different areas, vividly illustrates the cosmopolitan nature of Mediterranean commerce.

The city of Ugarit, strategically located on the coast of northern Syria, served as a hub in the eastern Mediterranean exchange network. Taking advantage of the good harbor possessed by Ugarit and the overland trade routes that reached into Mesopotamia and Anatolia, many local and foreign merchants who resided in the city made large profits by shipping metals from places where they were abundant and cheap to areas where they were rare and expensive.

Trade and diplomacy were closely linked in Ugarit. Operating within the framework of treaties that their kings negotiated with the rulers of neighboring states, private merchants in Ugarit acted both as royal agents and as independent entrepreneurs. Merchants received land in return for their service when trading goods produced in royal workshops on behalf of Ugarit kings. But these enterprising merchants had to pay taxes on their profits when they traded their own goods in private transactions.

Beginning around 1500 BCE, a group of large and powerful states became active participants in a thriving eastern Mediterranean exchange system. These kingdoms—Egypt, Babylonia, Assyria, Mitanni, and Hatti—formed a club of great powers that interacted with each other as equals and rivals: exchanging gifts, making alliances, fighting wars, and negotiating peace treaties. By offering gifts with the expectation of receiving presents of a similar value in return, kings could acquire luxury goods not locally available and pave the way for merchants to trade on a regular basis. The great powers, while limiting the freedom of action of private merchants, competed to control the key trade routes in the small states lying in their shadow along the Levantine coast.

Around 1450 BCE, the Egyptians launched a military campaign in northern Syria where the rulers of several weak states had sworn allegiance to the monarchs of Mitanni. The Egyptians, while seeking to acquire tribute-paying vassals, succeeded in gaining control of the Eleutheros River valley, which served as a main corridor for transporting goods between the Mediterranean coast and eastern Syria. The weak rulers in the area remained vassals of Egypt until about 1330 BCE when some of them switched their allegiance to the Hittites who lived in the powerful kingdom of Hatti.

The Hittites, after having reduced the Mitanni kings to their vassals, expanded into northern Syria against Egyptian resistance. The Hittites, whose capital lay far from the sea, wanted to gain access to trunk routes leading to the Mediterranean. By 1295 BCE, the Hittites had asserted their dominance as far south as Kadesh, a city that controlled two key highways in northern Syria: the east-west road that ran along the Eleutheros River and the north-south road that ran along the Orontes River. An ensuing struggle to control this strategic city culminated in the Battle of Kadesh in 1274 when Egyptian and Hittite armies, each with thousands of charioteers leading some 40,000 foot soldiers, fought to a draw that marked the end of Egyptian influence in northern Syria.

Social Stratification in the Eastern Mediterranean

An international upper class, living in small city-states as well as large territorial states, basked in the sunshine of a prosperity generated by trade in the eastern Mediterranean. Behaving in a similar fashion to distinguish themselves from commoners, the members of this cosmopolitan elite class signaled their socioeconomic superiority by dressing in elegant garments, adorning their bodies with glittering jewelry, and burying their dead in elaborate tombs filled with lavish goods. They also resided in splendid houses in grand cities, such as Ugarit and Hattusa (the Hittite capital in central Anatolia). The spread of wine consumption across the eastern Mediterranean revealed the growing convergence of cultural practices at the top of the social order.

The prosperity of the upper class, however, depended not only on the expansion of commerce but also on the exploitation of the lower class. While enjoying their wealth and indulging in conspicuous consumption, the nobles living in Ugarit and other cities in the region demanded tax payments and labor services from farmers struggling to eke out a living in the countryside. Farmers often had to borrow funds to meet their tax obligations, and many fell into **debt slavery** because they could not repay their creditors.

Flight was a common response by distressed rural people in almost all of the powerful kingdoms in the eastern Mediterranean. Many impoverished farmers abandoned their fields and fled into marginal areas to escape exploitation. These refugees often joined groups of social outcasts who lived in territories that were beyond the control of states like Mitanni, Hatti, and Egypt. Diplomatic exchanges between rival kings often demanded the return of refugees so they could be forced to work for wealthy landowners. "If Idrimi seizes a fugitive of Pilliya, he will return him to Pilliya," a treaty stated in typical fashion, "and if Pilliya seizes a fugitive of Idrimi, he will return him to Idrimi."[1]

Abruptly, during a relatively brief period between 1250 and 1150 BCE, a general political and economic collapse in the eastern Mediterranean brought the era of prosperity to an end. Several Mycenaean palaces were destroyed or abandoned, Ugarit was devastated, the royal citadel in Hattusa was burned down, the Hittite empire disintegrated, and both Egypt and Assyria declined from their position as great powers.

---

1   James B. Pritchard, ed., *The Ancient Near East: Supplementary Texts and Pictures Relating to the Old Testament* (Princeton: Princeton University Press, 1968), 96.

A combination of factors probably caused the widespread collapse: internecine warfare, peasant unrest, crop failure, the migration of vast throngs of people in search of food, piracy at sea, caravan raids on land by nomadic tribes, and a growing tension between the interests of wealthy merchants and the constraints imposed by powerful monarchs. A potent mixture of such factors, occurring almost simultaneously in different places and interacting in ways that amplified their total effect, resulted in a dramatic contraction in the volume of long-distance trade.

The commercial disruption marked the beginning of a new social and economic order in the eastern Mediterranean. As the monarchs in the region lost their power, the centrally organized command economies of the royal palaces were replaced by less restrictive commercial practices and more flexible employment opportunities. Private merchants engaged in freelance trade in pursuit of profit, while many skilled craft workers became mobile and escaped from the confines of royal control.

The Phoenician Commercial Empire

The Phoenician city-states, headed by strong kings and rich merchants, played a key role in the restoration of flourishing commercial relations throughout the eastern Mediterranean. As Tyre and the other Phoenician cities in the Levant became increasingly prosperous, the gap separating the elite from the common people widened. But the determination of Assyrian kings to extract tribute from the Phoenician cities threatened their prosperity.

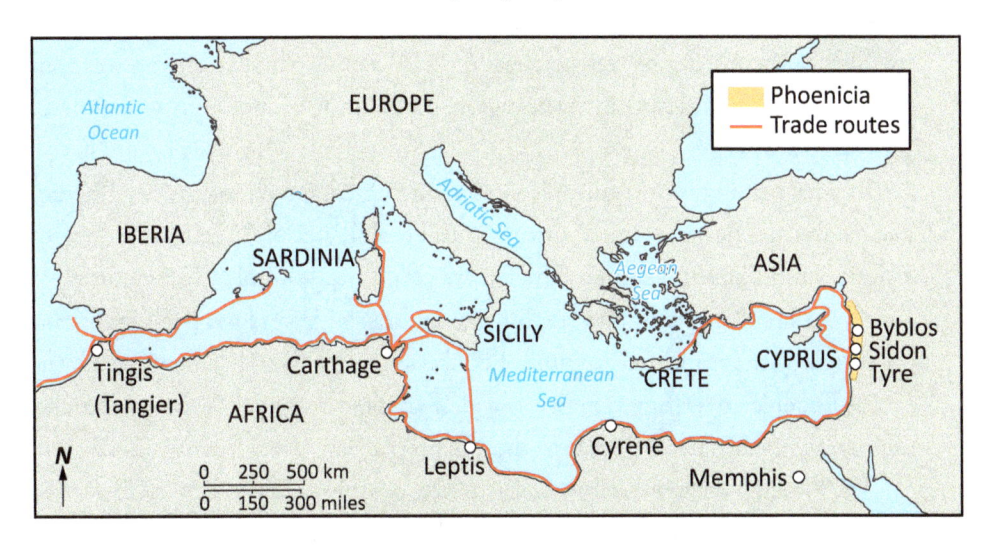

MAP 5.1 The Phoenician Commercial Empire

To satisfy Assyrian demands for precious metals, the Phoenicians established a vast commercial empire that stretched from one end of the Mediterranean to the other. The Phoenicians reaped large profits from their overseas operations until they fell victim to the expansionist policies of the Assyrians and the Babylonians. After the Phoenician cities in the eastern Mediterranean lost their independence, Carthage, a settlement that had been established in North Africa by merchants from Tyre, became the seat of a new empire in the western Mediterranean.

The Phoenicians and the Israelites

The Phoenician city-states, stretching along a narrow coastal strip roughly coinciding with the boundaries of modern Lebanon, took the lead in reestablishing trade in the eastern Mediterranean. Separated by mountain spurs and river valleys, the Phoenician cities developed as independent kingdoms and never coalesced into a unified state. Each city had a small hinterland, sandwiched between the mountains and the sea, without enough farmland to feed its growing population. But each city was located on a bay or island and had an excellent harbor that protected anchored ships from winds and storms. Although the main Phoenician cities—Award, Byblos, Sidon, and Tyre—survived the general collapse during the decades around 1200 BCE, they did experience a decline in prosperity caused by the decrease in international trade.

Adapting to what the environment provided, the Phoenicians and others living in the eastern Mediterranean began exploiting local supplies of iron when it became difficult to gain access to distant sources of copper and tin needed to make bronze. Because they learned how to mix iron with carbon to produce a metal that was harder as well as cheaper than bronze, the use of iron weapons and tools became widespread in the region, supplanting bronze even as commerce picked up again.

Besides helping to introduce iron as a cutting-edge technology, the Phoenicians devised a new system of writing with an alphabet of 22 letters, each with a designated phonetic sound. The letters could be assembled in any order to sound out spoken words, and the limited number of letters were relatively easy for people with a minimal amount of education to learn and remember. As the simple Phoenician writing system was widely adopted by neighboring populations, an increasing number of people in the Mediterranean world became literate.

The Phoenicians gradually increased their prosperity after 1150 BCE as they slowly expanded their trade both on land and at sea. Again, capitalizing on what the environment offered, the merchants of Byblos exploited the dense stands of cedar, pine, and cypress in the nearby mountains and exported large shipments of logs to Egypt. Tyre soon became the most important port in the eastern Mediterranean, and its merchants developed a flourishing business exchanging manufactured goods for agricultural produce from Palestine.

Although to a lesser extent than the Phoenicians, the Israelites participated in the eastern Mediterranean trading network. Much of our information about the Israelites comes from Hebrew scriptures describing many events that have not been confirmed by separate archaeological or literary evidence. According to the Hebrew Bible, 12 tribes, known as the Israelites, had migrated from Egypt to Palestine around 1300 BCE under the leadership of Moses. The early scriptures claim that the highest ranking Hebrew god, called Yahweh, gave Moses 10 commandments that warned against worshiping false gods or engaging in unethical behavior, such as lying and stealing.

The early Israelites, like their neighbors in the eastern Mediterranean, had been **polytheists** who believed in the existence of various deities. However, they gradually began to view Yahweh as not simply the greatest among many deities but as the one and only God, the all-powerful Creator of the universe. This **monotheistic** concept provided the core intellectual foundation for the later rise of both Christianity and Islam as major world religions.

The Israelites eventually abandoned their tribal structure and established a unified kingdom in Palestine. Thriving under the rule of King David and King Solomon from 1000 to 930 BCE, the Israelites dominated much of the territory between the Phoenician city-states and the Sinai Peninsula. They built a lavish temple for worshiping Yahweh in their capital at Jerusalem. They also engaged in diplomatic and commercial relations with the Mesopotamians, Egyptians, and Phoenicians. However, following the reign of Solomon, growing tribal antagonism led to the division of the monarchy into two separate kingdoms: Israel to the north and Judah in the area called Judea to the south.

Royal Authority and Merchant Oligarchy

Meanwhile, as Israel and Judah were headed by monarchs, each Phoenician city was ruled by a strong king together with a council of elders representing the wealthiest merchants. Governing in the name of the patron god of their city, monarchs assumed the position of chief priest and acted as an intermediary between his subjects and the spiritual realm. Phoenician kings were therefore able to use religion to gain and maintain popular support, to legitimize their authority, and to justify their demands for revenue.

Although they inherited their crowns from their fathers, Phoenician monarchs sought the advice of the leading merchants and allowed them ample room to engage in private enterprise. Royal merchants and private traders often worked hand in hand in their quest for profits, and Phoenician naval vessels helped guard both those working for the palace and those dealing on their own account. The power of the state thus helped the merchants become increasingly prosperous.

As the merchant **oligarchy** acquired more wealth and prestige, the Phoenician cities became increasingly divided along class lines. Skilled craft specialists stood below rich merchants with respect to status while slaves who formed a significant component of the work force occupied the lowest rung on the social ladder. While some slaves labored as urban artisans, many others worked in state-owned mines and naval shipyards or on large private estates as agricultural field hands and household servants.

Phoenician mortuary practices clearly reflected the growing socioeconomic differences among the living, a general if not universal cultural pattern among societies that possessed abundant material resources. Common people in the Phoenician cities were buried in modest graves with only a few inexpensive offerings, mostly utilitarian items such as ceramic bowls, to accompany them in the next world. But the merchant aristocrats and members of the royal family were put to rest in elaborate chamber tombs filled with an array of prestige goods, including gold and silver jewelry.

While the Phoenician oligarchs were enjoying their affluence, the Assyrians were busy rebuilding and enlarging their empire. Assyrian kings, living in splendor in their capital at Kalhu on the Tigris River in northern Mesopotamia, unleashed ruthless military campaigns to conquer neighboring territories. Like other empire builders in the ancient world, the Assyrians espoused a religious ideology designed to legitimize their economic exploitation of subjugated peoples. Assyrians demanded that all people acknowledge the sovereignty of their king as the representative of Ashur, the supreme deity who ruled over all other gods. And they intimidated the rulers of smaller states into swearing oaths of obedience that included promises to pay tribute to the Assyrian king.

The Phoenician Commercial Empire

As the Assyrians expanded westward, they demanded that Tyre and the other Phoenician cities pay tribute in the form of iron, silver, copper, and tin or else suffer military conquest. In no position to resist the Assyrians, the merchants of Tyre spearheaded a Phoenician drive to establish a chain of colonies throughout the Mediterranean. They sought to acquire new sources of metals needed to satisfy Assyrian demands for tribute. Following a deliberate plan that would guide Phoenician colonization for hundreds of years, these energetic merchants began establishing settlements in sheltered harbors that were close to rich mineral deposits.

The technological superiority of their ships enabled the Phoenicians to establish a far-flung commercial empire and to maintain their sea power advantage for several centuries. In fact, their ships were so advanced that after the Phoenicians lost their empire, both the Greeks and the Romans built their own fleets by using designs similar to those first introduced by their Phoenician rivals.

Phoenician merchant ships were designed to transport large cargoes over long distances. Having rounded hulls, these vessels were almost 20 feet wide and were able to carry bulky commodities throughout the Mediterranean. Although merchant ships were equipped with both sails and oars, they depended mainly on the wind for power. Each cargo vessel had a single mast supporting a rectangular sail that only performed well if the wind was blowing from behind. As long as the breeze was favorable, the captain used the sail to propel his ship. But when the wind died down or became adverse, he dropped the sail to the deck and ordered his crew to man the oars.

Phoenician war galleys were designed to protect merchant ships from enemy attacks and pirate raids. Narrower and longer than cargo vessels, military ships carried many oarsmen and warriors. A bronze beak extending from the bow of Phoenician war galleys was used to ram and sink enemy ships. A forecastle at the bow of these ships provided a platform for archers and catapults. Phoenician warships had two masts, one in the center with a mainsail and one in the front with a small sail that could catch crosswinds.

A key innovation made Phoenician war galleys even more lethal. Around 700 BCE, Phoenician shipbuilders started installing oars on two different levels, thereby doubling the number of rowers for vessels of the same length. These so-called biremes, which were guided by two rudders attached to each side of the stern, could travel at high speeds and ram enemy vessels with their powerful beaks. Sometime before 500 BCE, the Phoenicians began sailing triremes that had three banks of oars and even greater rowing power.

Sometime around 820 BCE, merchants from Tyre founded a settlement at Kition on Cyprus, and they rapidly annexed areas with copper mines in the southwestern part of the island. In 814 BCE, with the blessings of the royal family in Tyre, they established a colony at Carthage on a peninsula in the Bay of Tunis on the North African coast. Carthage not only had a fertile hinterland that produced large quantities of grain, olive oil, and wine but it also straddled the main shipping lanes in the central Mediterranean. Then, around 720 BCE, Phoenicians sailing from Carthage founded a colony at Motya in northwestern Sicily, providing easy access to mineral-rich Sardinia in the Tyrrhenian Sea. They soon established a series of settlements along the southern and western shores of Sardinia to mine copper, iron, and silver-bearing lead ores.

In both their home cities and their overseas colonies, the Phoenicians specialized in the production of luxury goods that they exported to pay for imports of agricultural commodities and raw materials, especially metal ores. Highly skilled Phoenician artisans earned widespread praise for crafting exquisite ivory ornaments, bronze containers, and gold and silver jewelry. They also became famous for manufacturing beautiful woolen textiles dyed to a deep purple. To obtain a single ounce of the special purple dye, the Phoenicians had to catch and kill thousands of murex, a small shellfish, and then extract and heat the glands of the dead snails in salt water for 10 days. The liquid dye was literally worth more than its weight in gold, and the wool was double dipped in the dye to produce the coveted purple cloth used to make garments for kings.

After manufacturing expensive goods using purple wool and precious metals, the Phoenicians sold these prestige items to affluent customers throughout the Mediterranean world. Many of their luxury goods that ended up in Assyrian palaces or royal tombs were the products of commercial exchanges stimulated by tributary relations. In their business transactions, the Phoenicians used silver as a standard of value measured by weight. A shekel of silver, for example, was equivalent in value to 200 shekels of copper. Thus, silver circulated as a form of money from one end of the Mediterranean to the other.

The Colonization of the Western Mediterranean

Phoenician colonization in the western Mediterranean began on the **Iberian Peninsula** around 800 BCE when merchants from Tyre founded Gadir (modern Cadiz) on an island off the Atlantic coast of Spain. They hoped to gain access to silver and other metals in the area. Gadir fulfilled all the requisites the Phoenicians sought when establishing overseas colonies. In addition to having an excellent harbor, Gadir was close to three main rivers that provided easy access to interior sources of gold, iron, copper, and silver.

The Phoenician merchants in Gadir promptly built a temple where they could pray to Melqart, the patron god of Tyre, and where local Iberian leaders could trade with them without being attacked or robbed. After mobilizing native workers to mine and smelt ores in mountainous areas in southwestern Spain, indigenous elites supervised the transportation of ingots downstream to the Atlantic coast. Then they exchanged the metals for luxury goods made in Phoenician workshops in Gadir or for olive oil, fine wine, and other valuable products imported from the east. While native Iberian leaders gained prestige by acquiring these exotic goods, Phoenician merchants made large profits by obtaining metals from Spain where they were abundant and cheap and then shipping them to places in the eastern Mediterranean where they were rare and expensive.

Between 770 and 550 BCE, Phoenicians based in Gadir expanded their colonial activity northward and southward along the Atlantic coast. They established trading settlements both on the coast of Portugal to exploit inland mineral resources and on the coast of Morocco to gain access to iron, copper, and gold in the Atlas Mountains. At the same time, the Phoenicians established several agricultural communities along the Mediterranean coast of Spain where fertile soil enabled them to produce surplus crops and rivers allowed them to trade with people living in the interior.

The Demise of the Israelites and the Phoenicians

The expansionist policies of Assyria and Babylonia had a profound effect on the kingdoms in the eastern Mediterranean. After Tiglath-pileser III became the Assyrian king in 745 BCE, he waged war against Tyre, Byblos, and Sidon and reduced their rulers to his vassals. These Phoenician cities continued to function autonomously, but they were forced to pay Assyria huge amounts of tribute in the form of iron, gold, ivory, and purple cloth. In 722 BCE, after gaining control of the Phoenician cities, the Assyrian forces conquered the kingdom of Israel and deported many of its vanquished inhabitants to other areas in the region.

During the next 100 years, Assyrian kings conquered additional territory until their empire stretched from the Persian Gulf to the Mediterranean Sea. Imperial expansion, however, resulted in increasing costs. In fact, expenditures on military campaigns, provincial administration, and public buildings grew faster than revenues from war booty, tribute collection, and provincial taxation. The Assyrians therefore tightened their grip on conquered territories, but the mounting exploitation provoked widespread unrest among subject populations.

The overextended Assyrian Empire collapsed in 612 BCE when it was attacked by the Babylonians and their allies in southern Mesopotamia and western Persia. After defeating the Assyrians, the Babylonians conquered the kingdom of Judah in 586 BCE and destroyed Jerusalem. Many of the residents who were deported by the victorious Babylonians eventually returned to Judea and became known as Jews. As the Hebrew Bible fostered a deep sense of ethnic solidarity, the Jewish people remained committed to monotheism and built one of the major religions in the world.

Meanwhile, the Babylonians started to bring the Phoenician cities under their domination, and in 572 BCE, King Nebuchadnezzar II began a 23-year-long siege of Tyre. The formerly great Phoenician city was finally subdued, its king was deported to Babylon, and its overseas empire began to fragment. After Tyre was subjugated, some of its colonial enclaves in the central Mediterranean Basin fell under the political hegemony of Carthage, which had been founded by merchants from the once prosperous city. Carthage then began its own expansionist policies and soon became the seat of the rising **Punic** Empire.

The Greek Agrarian Governments

The Greek city-state, or polis, consisted of an urban center surrounded by a rural hinterland that was filled with farmers who owned relatively small plots of land. Comprising roughly 80 percent of the Greek population, these middling farmers served as soldiers who fought in the infrequent but violent clashes involving borderlands between antagonistic cities. The soldiers, known as **hoplites**, wore expensive bronze armor needed for protection during hand-to-hand combat. The Greek farmers who could afford to buy their own body armor and fight in the bloody military contests gained political representation in their cities. Although more and more middling farmers became members of polis governing councils, the distribution of wealth continued to be unequal in every Greek city-state.

Dark Age Chieftains

After the destruction of the Mycenaean palaces and the decline in the eastern Mediterranean trading circuits around 1200 BCE, power became decentralized in Greece. Many impoverished Greeks died at a young age, and the population of Greece in 1000 BCE was probably less than half of what it had been two centuries earlier.

During the so-called Greek Dark Age, which lasted until 800 BCE, the Greek mainland and islands remained highly stratified. Greek society was dominated by a rural aristocracy that raised livestock and bred horses on large estates in a sparsely populated countryside. Riding large horses that only aristocrats could afford to feed, local chiefs and their retainers formed war parties that intimidated peasants and conducted raids to acquire cattle and slaves.

These aristocratic warriors stood on the top rung of the socioeconomic ladder in Greece, and some were buried in rich graves containing exotic goods imported from overseas. For instance, at Lefkandi, a flourishing settlement on the island of Euboea across a narrow channel from the mainland, a local Greek leader was buried around 950 BCE with a team of four horses (suggesting that he rode a chariot into battle) and his wife who was bedecked in imported gold.

The Polis

Between 800 and 700 BCE, a dramatic change occurred in Greece. A shift in emphasis from pastoralism to mixed farming coincided with the emergence of the Greek city-state, or polis, consisting of an urban center and a rural hinterland with hundreds or even thousands of independent agricultural households. The intensive cultivation of grains, olives, and grapes, along with the rearing of some animals, provided food for a growing population. A few rich landowners specialized in raising large herds of livestock or producing large quantities of grain for export.

Although there were some large estates with 50–70 acres, most Greek farms were relatively small, ranging from 10–20 acres. These middling farmers sought self-sufficiency by planting orchards and vineyards, cultivating several different crops, and raising a few goats or sheep. To reduce the risk of starvation during years of poor harvests, the independent Greek farmers routinely stored a portion of their output. At the same time, they aimed to produce surplus food and fiber that could be hauled to a nearby town and exchanged in the market area, or **agora**, for local goods, such as shoes, pottery, and tools, that their families needed.

Slavery became widespread in Greek society. Although grapevines and olive trees could be grown on thin soil, the production of wine and olive oil required long periods of hard work grafting, pruning, fertilizing, harvesting, crushing, pressing, and storing. Adult male slaves, often war captives purchased at auctions, helped satisfy the demand for heavy labor in the Greek countryside. While aristocrats avoided manual labor themselves and depended on many slaves to work on their large estates, middling farmers who owned small plots of land usually purchased one or two slaves to work side by side with them in their fields.

Though farmers constituted roughly 80 percent of the population during the Archaic Period between 800 and 500 BCE, a growing number of people living in Greece participated in mining, manufacturing, and commerce. Foreign residents could not own land, and rather than toiling in the countryside as tenants or as paid farm laborers, most lived in urban centers and worked in craft industries or mercantile businesses. While most Greek workshops were small operations that produced utilitarian articles for local customers, some large enterprises produced luxury goods for distant as well as domestic markets. Craft specialists in Athens, for example, produced high-quality painted ceramics with shapes and patterns that were designed to satisfy the tastes of customers in Italy.

To obtain revenue for polis expenditures on such things as public buildings or food relief during famines, city governments in Greece levied taxes on commerce but not on land or income. All imported or exported commodities were subject to customs duties, usually at a rate of 2 percent of their price. In the early city-state years, before coins were minted, the Greeks, like the Phoenicians, used weighted silver as a standard of value to facilitate their commercial transactions both at home and abroad.

The Greeks had access to a local source of silver in the rich Laurion mines, located only about 25 miles from Athens, where many slaves worked in miserable conditions. Slaves also performed a variety of tasks in towns and cities throughout Greece. While a few worked for their masters in commercial undertakings, many others were apprentices in craft industries, laborers on construction projects, or servants in wealthy households.

The Hoplites and City-State Governance

Wars between Greek city-states were infrequent but violent contests fought by farmers who owned their own land and usually a few slaves. Since horsemen riding vulnerable animals could not defeat massed infantry units armed with spears or pikes, relatively prosperous farmers who fought on foot replaced mounted aristocrats as the dominant force in Greek warfare. These hoplite soldiers, while carrying round shields made of bronze, used short swords and long spears, weapons largely made from less costly iron. But they wore expensive cast bronze armor as standard equipment, which included helmets, body corselets, and greaves to protect their knees and shins.

Most wars between Greek city-states were brief and bloody clashes involving disputes over borderlands. After slaves helped them carry their heavy armor to an agreed-upon field of battle, disciplined hoplite soldiers formed opposing **phalanxes** and engaged in hand-to-hand combat. Highly motivated hoplite soldiers fought resolutely to defend immovable property, especially grapevines and olive trees that took many years to mature. After inheriting orchards and vineyards from their parents and cultivating them for decades, these agrarian warriors were determined to protect their valuable trees and vines and pass them down to their children and grandchildren.

Unlike the Dark Age chiefs who fought to acquire cattle and slaves, the hoplite soldier engaged in warfare for the benefit of his polis. Greek lyric poems asserted that the most important virtue for hoplite combatants was courage and that victory would bring glory to their communities. Writing in the seventh century BCE, the Spartan poet Tyrtaeus noted that a valiant soldier killed in battle would be remembered forever. "Never has fame forgotten a brave man or his name," Tyrtaeus declared. "But though he is under the earth he becomes immortal."[2]

Between 700 and 600 BCE, the Greek farmers who possessed enough wealth to buy their own armor and fight in hoplite armies gained political representation. Thus, hoplite soldiers, comprising a third to a half of the adult male population in Greece, acquired political standing that matched their economic and military position. The transition from narrowly based aristocratic governments to more broadly controlled agrarian polities was a gradual process that occurred sporadically in different places and at different times.

In many Greek city-states, ambitious war heroes, like Cypselsus of Corinth or Pheidon of Argos, overthrew aristocratic governments and established systems of one-man rule, typically with the support of hoplite soldiers. But these tyrannies were usually short-lived, and after their collapse, a growing number of the middling farmers became members of polis governing councils. This happened in Athens as the result of legislation drafted by Solon.

Solon and His Reforms in Athens

During the seventh century BCE, Athens remained under aristocratic rule, and many unsuccessful peasants in the surrounding countryside fell into debt. Some lost their land to aristocrats and ended up as slaves or bound sharecroppers. Impoverished peasants soon demanded that the large aristocratic estates be confiscated, divided into small plots, and distributed to the landless. The aristocrats who sat on the Athenian governing council hoped to protect their property and to avoid an agrarian insurrection.

Solon first gained fame around 600 BCE when the Athenians and their neighbors from Megara were fighting for possession of the island of Salamis. Solon grew up in an aristocratic family of moderate wealth, but he made his fortune in commerce. As the commander of the Athenian forces, Solon wrote a poem

---

2   Oswyn Murray, *Early Greece* (Cambridge: Harvard University Press, 1993), 135.

urging his troops to fight hard as a patriotic duty. The Athenians eventually defeated their enemies from Megara, and Solon was credited with gaining control of Salamis for his city.

The governing council of Athens chose Solon in 594 BCE to be the chief magistrate. As the tensions between rich and poor reached a crisis point, Solon was authorized to reform the laws of the polis. He promptly drafted economic and political legislation aimed at balancing the interests of rich and poor in order to prevent a revolution.

Although he allowed the aristocrats to keep their large landholdings, Solon abolished debt slavery and cancelled existing debts to prevent more peasants from losing their land. He also helped the poor at the expense of the wealthy landowners by prohibiting the export of grain to avert food shortages in Athens.

By lowering the requirements for holding public office in Athens, Solon promoted the political interests of middle-class farmers, artisans, and merchants. He reserved the highest government offices for the wealthiest citizens, but members of the middle classes were eligible to be elected to lesser posts. Only the poorest were excluded from all government positions. After completing his task, Solon wrote poems that defended his reforms by asserting that he sought to be fair to everyone.

A Stratified Society

Although the aristocracy lost its political monopoly in Athens and elsewhere, property and voting rights continued to be distributed unequally in every Greek city-state. Citizenship was a privilege limited to less than half of the native adult males (aristocrats and hoplites) who owned enough property to qualify for participation in polis governing councils. The rest of the Greek population—women, foreigners, slaves, and poor men—were excluded from citizenship and denied political representation.

In general, even if they belonged to a wealthy family, women were treated like children and lived under the guardianship of a father, husband, son, or some other male relative. A typical gendered division of labor, common to rural households throughout the Mediterranean world, prevailed in the Greek countryside. While men did most of the outdoor work in the fields, vineyards, and orchards, women devoted most of their attention to indoor chores, such as cooking, cleaning, spinning, weaving, and sewing.

But while most women in ancient Greece spent much of their time performing routine household tasks, a few highly educated female members of elite families became accomplished literary figures. Sappho was a celebrated Greek poetess. Born into an aristocratic family on the island of Lesbos in the late seventh century BCE, Sappho sometimes expressed in lyric poems her intense feelings of attraction for other women. Based on surviving fragments of her verse, many scholars have portrayed Sappho as a homosexual, and the term "lesbian" is derived from the name of her home island.

Greek society remained hierarchical as well as patriarchal. With hard work and good luck, middling farmers could feed their families, produce surplus crops, and live in relative comfort. But there was an extreme disparity in wealth and status between the rich aristocrats who owned much of the best land and the impoverished peasants who struggled to pay their debts. As a few graves filled with imported luxury goods reveal, social and economic inequality was a constant feature of all the Greek city-states.

The Greeks Overseas

Because less than 15 percent of the mountainous Greek mainland can sustain agriculture, food production eventually failed to keep pace with population growth. Greek city-states responded to the problem of excess population in three ways: by going to war and expropriating farmland from neighboring communities, by exporting people to overseas colonies, and by trading goods manufactured at home for food produced in distant regions.

Prompted by a desire to find new economic opportunities, a growing number of Greeks sailed from their homeland and established a string of settlements along the shores of both the Mediterranean and the Black Seas. Most of the Greek colonies became involved in commerce as well as agriculture. As they founded overseas settlements, the Greeks developed profitable trading relationships with many foreign communities. These colonies, moreover, provided food for growing Greek cities and new homes for farmers struggling to survive on small plots of land in Greece.

Greek Colonization

During the Archaic period between 800 and 500 BCE, tens of thousands of Greeks sailed from their homeland and founded hundreds of colonies around the Mediterranean Sea and the Black Sea. Continued demographic growth in Greece and a widespread desire to find new economic opportunities abroad produced a strong wave of emigration that lasted more than six generations. After forming separate colonizing parties in different Greek city-states, groups of 100–200 men, often the younger sons of farmers, established overseas settlements and then quickly asserted their independence from their home polis.

The motives for Greek colonization were mixed. While some pioneers intended to establish trading posts and profit by acquiring resources, such as metals, grain, or fish, others aimed to found agricultural settlements and prosper by raising various crops on good farmland. The Greek colonies all had urban centers and rural hinterlands, and sooner or later, most became involved in both agriculture and commerce. Trading posts usually attracted immigrant farmers, while many settlement colonies eventually became large exporters of surplus crops. As colonization stimulated long-distance trade, many cities in Greece began importing grain on a regular basis in order to feed their growing populations. Professional merchants, including foreign residents, handled most of the merchandise traded in Greek ports.

Greek colonization began in the central Mediterranean around 770 BCE when merchants from Euboea founded a permanent settlement at Pithekoussai on the small island of Ischia just off the northern tip of the Bay of Naples. The Euboean settlers promptly started acquiring metal ores from the native peoples on the Italian mainland and shipping processed ingots to the eastern Mediterranean where they were in heavy demand, especially to produce weapons, and fetched high prices. Within a generation, the Euboeans residing in Pithekoussai had established a profitable commercial business, and around 740 BCE, they founded a new trading post at Cumae on the adjacent Italian coast.

Greek colonization in the central Mediterranean proceeded apace. On the island of Sicily, colonists from Euboea founded Naxos around 734 BCE, and others from Corinth established Syracuse a year later. Achaeans from the northwestern Peloponnese founded several colonies a short time thereafter along the instep of the boot of Italy. By 600 BCE, flourishing Greek settlements dotted the shores of eastern Sicily and southern Italy.

These colonies possessed fertile agricultural fields, and they were located close to deposits of copper, tin, and iron in central Italy. Taking advantage of the available resources, most quickly became prosperous farming or trading settlements. Some of these thriving Greek communities, such as Syracuse, soon outstripped their home cities in wealth and splendor. In addition to building magnificent houses and temples, some rich aristocrats in Sicily and Italy traveled to Olympia to compete in chariot races, the forerunners of the modern Olympics.

Competition with the Etruscans

The Greeks developed friendly commercial relations with the Etruscans who inhabited the western side of central Italy between the Arno and Tiber Rivers. Similar to the Greeks, the Etruscans belonged to independent city-states that often fought each other. Etruscan merchants obtained manufactured goods from Greek and Phoenician traders in exchange for copper, tin, and lead from local mines near the Italian coast and iron from mines on the island of Elba. The Etruscans were strongly influenced by the Greeks. Etruscan worshipers adopted Greek gods, Etruscan soldiers emulated the hoplite style of warfare, and Etruscan artisans learned from Greek immigrants how to make exquisite ivory, gold, and silver items.

Lavish graves containing prestige goods imported from Greece and more distant areas in the eastern Mediterranean reveal the emergence of an affluent Etruscan aristocracy. The wealthiest Etruscans were buried in huge chamber tombs filled with luxury goods, such as gold and silver jewelry, bronze armor and chariots, and painted ceramics made in Phoenician or Greek workshops. Built in isolated splendor away from the main cemeteries, these chamber tombs stood as enduring monuments that displayed the elevated status of Etruscan aristocrats for the wonderment of future generations.

FIGURE 5.2 An Etruscan Tomb in the City of Tarquinia. Tarquinia had 60 tombs with elaborate wall paintings.

As Etruscans and Greeks expanded along the northern shores of the Mediterranean, they began trading with the **Celtic** peoples living farther to the north. The Etruscans founded settlements in the Rhone delta and quickly began distributing large amounts of wine to people living in southern France. Their commercial activity rapidly declined around 600 BCE, however, when Greeks from Phocaea, a city on the west coast of Anatolia, founded a settlement at Massalia (modern Marseille) near the mouth of the Rhone River. Soon, the entire Mediterranean coast from the Alps to the Pyrenees was ringed with Greek ports. Merchants in Massalia, which developed into a bustling city with as many as 15,000 inhabitants, began sending large quantities of wine and drinking cups up the Rhone in exchange for timber, hides, grain, honey, and slaves.

Several fortified hilltop settlements that housed Celtic rulers in eastern France and southern Germany became actively involved in trading with the Greeks. At the foot of many of these hilltop settlements, such as Heuneburg situated above the Danube River in Bavaria, archaeologists have excavated massive circular mounds containing one or two wealthy individuals buried in central chambers with imported Greek luxury goods. The grave of an elite woman buried at Vix, a cemetery in Burgundy just below a major Celtic settlement, contained among its treasures a huge bronze krater used for mixing and storing wine. This extremely valuable item, weighing 450 pounds, was probably made in a Greek workshop around 530 BCE and presented as a diplomatic gift intended to promote commercial exchanges with the stratified Celtic settlement in Burgundy.

About 60 years after Greek pioneers from Phocaea founded Massalia, others from Phocaea established a settlement at the port of Alalia on the east coast of Corsica. This Greek initiative, which threatened long-established Etruscan commercial interests in the Tyrrhenian Sea, led in 535 BCE to a naval battle near Sardinia between the Greek and Etruscan fleets. Although the Etruscans succeeded in getting the Greek immigrants to abandon their settlement on Corsica, they failed a decade later to expel the Greeks from their trading post at Cumae on the Italian coast just north of the Bay of Naples.

The Etruscans then realized that their commercial activities in the Tyrrhenian Sea would be increasingly restricted. Around 500 BCE, they shifted their attention eastward to the Po valley and quickly gained control of the trade routes that ran northward through the main Alpine passes into the heart of central Europe. Etruscan merchants soon began sending large quantities of luxury goods, including bronze vessels used in wine-drinking rituals, to the Celtic peoples living north of the Alps. Many of these prestige goods flowing northward from the Po valley ended up in rich Celtic burials located along the major European trade routes that linked the Mediterranean, Baltic, and Black Seas.

Into the Black Sea

Long before the Etruscans moved into the Po valley, the Greeks began establishing colonies around the Black Sea. The Greeks gained control of the entrance to the Black Sea around 660 BCE when they founded a settlement at Byzantium (the future Constantinople and Istanbul) on the **Bosporus Strait**. While establishing settlements along the northern shores of the Black Sea during the next 160 years, the Greeks used rivers, such as the Dniester, Bug, and Dnieper, to conduct trade with the Scythians who lived on the Ukrainian steppes. Greek artisans working in Black Sea colonies made luxury goods designed to suit the tastes of wealthy Scythians. After presenting Scythian chieftains with prestige goods as diplomatic gifts to pave the way for regular commerce, Greek merchants began exchanging wine, olive oil, pottery, jewelry, and metal vessels for grain, fur, leather, and fish as well as slaves who came from southern Russia.

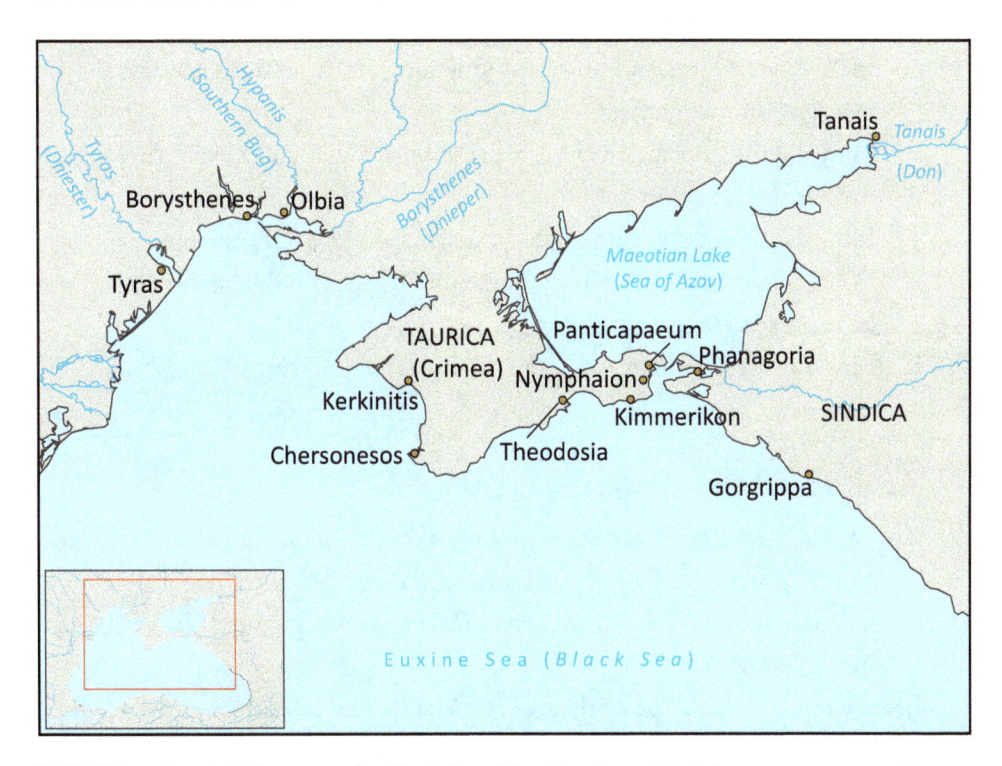

MAP 5.2   Greek Colonies in the Black Sea. The Greek and English names appear side by side.

Scythian chiefs in the Ukraine, like their Celtic counterparts in France and Germany, not only adopted Greek customs, such as wine drinking, but they also displayed their wealth in lavish burials. Covered by large mounds known as kurgans, rich Scythian graves were filled with many Greek luxury goods, including exquisite pottery, expensive jewelry, and elaborate sets of gold and silver drinking vessels.

The mutually beneficial commercial relations between the Greek merchants and the Scythian rulers, like those between the Phoenician traders and the Iberian elites, dramatize two overriding trajectories that characterized the Mediterranean world since the Minoans and Mycenaeans began venturing overseas: increasing commercial and social integration and growing socioeconomic differentiation. Merchants spread cultural practices as well as various commodities throughout the Mediterranean world. The almost universal adoption of wine drinking among elites in different regions dramatizes the gradual emergence of a pan-Mediterranean way of life.

Review Questions

1. How did the large and powerful kingdoms in the eastern Mediterranean interact with each other?
2. Why did the Phoenician city-states establish a chain of colonies throughout the Mediterranean?
3. How did Greeks become eligible to participate in polis governing councils?
4. What might have been the outcome for Athens if Solon's reforms had not been implemented?
5. How did Greek colonization spur overseas commerce?

Additional Readings

Aubet, Maria E. *The Phoenicians and the West: Politics, Colonies, and Trade.* 2nd ed. Cambridge: Cambridge University Press, 2001.

Barker, Graeme, and Tom Rasmussen. *The Etruscans.* Oxford: Blackwell Publishing, 2000.

Broodbank, Cyprian. *The Making of the Middle Sea: A History of the Mediterranean from the Beginning to the Emergence of the Classical World.* Oxford: Oxford University Press, 2013.

Cornell, T. J. *The Beginnings of Rome: Italy and Rome from the Bronze Age to the Punic Wars (c. 1000–264 BCE).* New York: Routledge, 1995.

Cunliffe, Barry. *Europe Between the Oceans: 9000 BCE–AD 1000.* New Haven: Yale University Press, 2008.

Freeman, Charles. *Egypt, Greece, and Rome: Civilizations of the Ancient Mediterranean.* 2nd ed. Oxford: Oxford University Press, 2004.

Hanson, Victor D. *The Other Greeks: The Family Farm and the Agrarian Roots of Western Civilization.* 2nd ed. Berkeley: University of California Press, 1999.

Markoe, Glenn E. *Phoenicians.* Berkeley: University of California Press, 2000.

Migoette, Leopold. *The Economy of the Greek Cities: From the Archaic Period to the Early Roman Empire.* Berkeley: University of California Press, 2009.

Parkinson, William A., and Michael L. Galaty, eds. *Archaic State Interaction: The Eastern Mediterranean in the Bronze Age*. Santa Fe, NM: School for Advanced Research Press, 2009.

Price, T. Douglas. *Europe Before Rome: A Site-by-Site Tour of the Stone, Bronze, and Iron Ages*. Oxford: Oxford University Press, 2013.

Scarre, Chris, ed. *The Human Past: World Prehistory and the Development of Human Society*. 4th ed. London: Thames and Hudson, 2018.

Van De Mieroop, Marc. *A History of the Ancient Near East, ca. 3000–323 BCE*. 2nd ed. Oxford: Blackwell Publishing, 2007.

Figure Credits

Fig. 5.1: Copyright © by Zda (CC BY-SA 4.0) at https://commons.wikimedia.org/wiki/File:Lion_Gate,_Mycenae,_201507.jpg.

Map 5.1: Source: https://commons.wikimedia.org/wiki/File:PhoenicianTrade_EN.svg.

Fig. 5.2: Source: https://commons.wikimedia.org/wiki/File:Tarquinia_Tomb_of_the_Leopards.jpg.

Map 5.2: Copyright © by Amitchell125 (CC BY-SA 3.0) at https://commons.wikimedia.org/wiki/File:Map_ancient_Greek_colonies_in_northern_Black_Sea-en.svg.

CHAPTER 6

The Clash of Empires in the Ancient World, 550 BCE–1 BCE

The Persians and the Greeks

Starting in southwestern Iran, the kings who belonged to the Achaemenid family built the enormous Persian Empire. But the imposition of heavy tax levies sparked numerous uprisings among the newly conquered peoples, including the oppressed Greeks living the **Ionian cities** along the coast of Anatolia. When the Athenians sent warships to aid their rebellious kinsmen across the Aegean, the Persians launched an assault on the Greek mainland. The independent Greek city-states cooperated with each other and defeated the Persian forces.

Growing antagonism between Athens and Sparta, however, resulted in a war for domination of Greece. Although Athens lost the war, the city remained independent and prosperous. Some Athenian citizens became increasingly rich and powerful by engaging in highly profitable commercial and financial transactions. These elite Athenians not only delivered most of the speeches in the polis assembly but also set themselves apart from their poorer neighbors with their fine clothing and luxurious homes.

The Achaemenids Forge a Vast Empire

Shortly after becoming the king of the Persian tribes in 559 BCE, Cyrus II, a member of the Achaemenid clan, created a strong military force and embarked on a spectacular program of territorial conquest. Cyrus began by defeating the Medes in 550 BCE and acquiring the lands under their control in northern Iran and eastern Anatolia. After conquering the kingdom of Lydia in western Anatolia three years later, he bullied the Greeks living in Ionia along the eastern shores

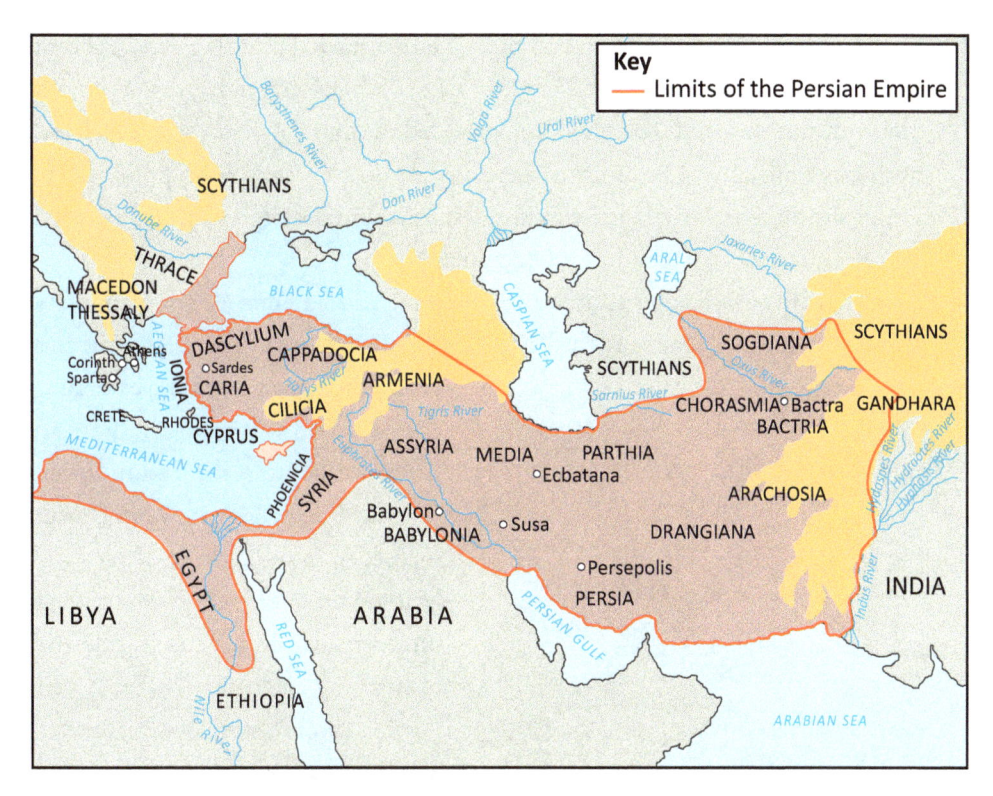

MAP 6.1   The Persian Empire in 490 BCE

of the Aegean into submitting to Persian rule. Cyrus conquered the Babylonian Empire in 539 BCE and incorporated Mesopotamia, Syria, and Palestine into his rapidly expanding realm. After gaining control of the Phoenician cities on the eastern shore of the Mediterranean, he marched his army eastward and extended his authority as far as Bactria in central Asia.

After Cyrus died in 530 BCE, his successors continued expanding the dimensions of the Persian Empire. Cyrus was buried at his grand palace in Pasargadae, and his son Cambyses II became king. In 525 BCE, Cambyses and his military forces succeeded in conquering both Egypt and Cyprus. Cambyses died three years later, and after some turmoil, one of his bodyguards, Darius I, usurped the throne with the help of six nobles.

Darius, the son of a provincial governor and a member of the ruling Achaemenid family, had to use military force to impose his rule. His assumption of power in 522 BCE was followed by a series of revolts in the Persian Empire. In several provinces, men who claimed to be descendants of former rulers set up independent governments. But these uprisings were spontaneous and uncoordinated, and with the support of loyal generals, Darius succeeded in suppressing them one by one.

After order was restored in 518 BCE, Darius started building a magnificent new capital at Persepolis about 25 miles to the south of Pasargadae. An enormous platform, measuring 900 by 1,350 feet, provided the foundation for several palaces, audience halls, and a treasury constructed at the center of Persepolis. These impressive buildings had massive mud-brick walls, and the largest one had sculpted stone columns standing almost 60 feet high.

While his new capital was under construction, Darius launched several military campaigns designed to expand the Persian Empire. He began by conquering the area east of the Caspian Sea and extending the eastern frontier of the Persian Empire as far as the Indus River. Turning his armies westward, Darius succeeded in subjugating Thrace and Macedonia, but his efforts to conquer Greece ended in failure. By the end of his long reign in 486 BCE, the Persian Empire stretched more than 2,500 miles from the Aegean Sea to the Indus River and contained an estimated 30–50 million inhabitants.

FIGURE 6.1 Bas Relief of Tribute Bearers at Persepolis. This image depicts tribute bearers ascending the stairs of a palace built at Persepolis by Darius I.

Ruling the Multiethnic Empire

The perpetuation of the Persian Empire depended on the maintenance of a formidable military force. While native Persians served in a large personal bodyguard that protected the Achaemenid kings, the imperial army drew upon an enormous pool of conscripts who came from various ethnic groups. Soldiers from different provinces sometimes had special military skills, making it possible for army commanders to utilize the talents of diverse groups, such as Arabian camel drivers and Libyan charioteers. Soldiers received modest parcels of land in return for military service, but their descendants were expected to pay taxes to the state if they were not needed in the army. Moreover, soldiers were stationed at garrisons throughout the empire so they would be ready to suppress rebellions, which remained a continuing threat to Achaemenid rule.

Darius I and his successors who belonged to the Achaemenid family managed to keep the Persian Empire together for 200 years. They realized that the inhabitants of their vast empire spoke different languages, held different religious beliefs, and had different political traditions. Determined to win their allegiance and maintain their obedience, the Achaemenid kings adopted the customs and protected the cults of the newly conquered peoples. They showed their respect for local scripts by inscribing Persian monuments with several languages.

Like many other monarchs in the ancient world, the Achaemenid kings used religion to legitimize their rule and to discourage rebellions in their multiethnic empire. They claimed that the supreme god Ahura Mazda, who created the earth and the sky, had not only selected them to rule Persia but also helped them conquer many other countries. Furthermore, they maintained that Ahura Mazda had given them the ability to distinguish right from wrong and the responsibility to promote justice and to preserve order among the diverse communities that were scattered across their realm.

The Persian kings presided over a highly stratified society. Possessing supreme authority in the imperial system, they personally appointed provisional governors and made all the important political, economic, and military decisions. The kings and other members of the royal family maintained huge agricultural estates across the width and length of the empire. When Persian kings made large grants of land to provincial governors, the recipient would receive the income produced by property that would remain under royal ownership. These estates, located in different parts of the empire, were administered by local agents and worked by tenant farmers. The provincial governors were almost always Persian nobles, and these aristocrats often lived in palaces that had earlier housed indigenous rulers.

The Persian kings needed to maintain the support and to curb the political ambition of the powerful group of nobles who held all the top posts in the imperial government. Roving inspectors and spies, dispatched to the provinces, reported directly to the kings. As a reward for loyal service, provincial governors received grants of land that provided them with a regular source of income from rents. They also received gifts of prestige goods, such as gold necklaces and bracelets, which were displayed as marks of royal esteem. Persian monarchs punished corrupt officials by stripping them of court ornaments and thus signaling the withdrawal of royal favor. Rebellious officials could expect a public execution or a slow death by torture.

As was the case with other imperial polities in the ancient world, the Persian Empire was a tribute-taking entity. The Achaemenid kings, who monetized the Persian economy by minting silver and gold coins, compelled all their provinces to pay a set amount of taxes to the state each year. Provincial governors collected taxes in the form of food or coins from the local population. While some of the tribute was used to support officials and soldiers in the provinces, the rest was sent to the central government on the network of roads that crisscrossed the immense empire.

Economic exploitation by the central government, however, provoked serious discontent in several provinces of the Persian Empire. In response to burdensome tax levies, the oppressed people in some of the newly conquered territories grew increasingly defiant. The Greeks living in the Ionian cities along the coast of Anatolia harbored a deep desire to regain their independence. In reaction to heavy tax assessments, the Ionian Greeks revolted in 499 BCE and expelled their Persian rulers who had been appointed by Darius I. The Athenians sent a fleet of 20 warships across the Aegean to aid their Greek kinsmen and commercial partners. But Darius deployed additional forces, and by 493 BCE, the Persians succeeded in subduing the Ionian cities.

The Persian and Peloponnesian Wars

Following the subjection of the Ionian cities, Darius mobilized his forces for a conflict that the Greeks now call the Persian War. Darius assembled a large army made up of many different ethnic groups and a strong navy led by Phoenicians who hoped to destroy their Greek commercial rivals. Then he launched a punitive attack on Athens. When a Greek army defeated Persian ground troops at Marathon in 490 BCE, Darius quickly withdrew both his soldiers and sailors from the Greek mainland.

Darius died a few years later, but his son and successor Xerxes I decided to dispatch another large military expedition to conquer Greece. Despite their animosity toward each other, the Greek city-states joined forces to resist what they viewed as a **barbarian** invasion of their homeland. The Athenians possessed a large navy because they had used huge amounts of silver extracted from a recently discovered rich layer of minerals at the Laurion mines to finance the construction of some 200 warships. In a great sea battle in the Bay of Salamis in 480 BCE, the Athenians with help from some of their neighbors defeated the Persian fleet. The war ended in the following year when the Spartans, who possessed the strongest land force in Greece, took the lead in routing the Persian army at Plataea.

In the aftermath of the Persian War, Athens established a powerful and prosperous seaborne empire. The imperial city maintained a large fleet of 300 warships propelled by thousands of paid oarsmen who, unlike hoplite soldiers, had no need for expensive armor. As many landless rowers began playing a key role in naval warfare, Athens dropped the property qualification for political representation and allowed all native-born males to vote in the assembly, the central organ of governance in the city.

Many small city-states scattered around the Aegean came together under Athenian leadership in 478 BCE and created the **Delian League**, an alliance intended to stymie any future Persian attacks and to plunder Persian territory. In return for naval protection, the members of the confederation paid tribute to Athens. The city, acting as an imperial power even after the military threat from Persia subsided, continued to exact tribute from about 150 subject states in the Delian League. Most of the tribute was used to build warships and to pay many Athenians serving in the navy. But some of the money was used to construct the Parthenon, a magnificent temple dedicated to Athena, the patron goddess of Athens.

FIGURE 6.2 The Parthenon in Athens. This building stands as an enduring example of the relationship between accumulated wealth and monumental architecture.

In 431 BCE, growing antagonism among the Greek city-states culminated in a long and destructive conflict, known as the Peloponnesian War. Two rival camps, one headed by Athens and the other by Sparta, located on the **Peloponnese**, contended for hegemony on the Greek Peninsula. The Athenians used every means at their disposal, including intimidation, to persuade the smaller city-states in the Aegean to help them defeat the Spartans.

With a population of more than 200,000 residents, Athens had become dependent on regular commercial imports of grain from overseas. The Athenians used their fleet to patrol vital trade routes, especially the narrow **Hellespont** and Bosporus passages linking the Aegean to large grain supplies along the Black Sea coast. But the Spartan fleet defeated the Athenian navy in the Hellespont in the summer of 405 BCE before the grain ships were ready to sail to Greece. Facing starvation, Athens surrendered in the next year, and the Peloponnesian War finally ended.

The Recovery of Athens: A Stratified Society

Despite suffering a humiliating defeat, Athens remained independent and continued to prosper as a passion for profit spread throughout the city. Many wealthy Athenian landowners became heavily involved in marketing surplus crops in order to obtain large sums of cash that they were expected to donate to the city for the maintenance of warships or the construction of public buildings. While many Greek intellectuals denounced small shopkeepers as greedy traders lusting for profits, aristocrats in Athens often made large interest-bearing loans. They also invested funds with discreet bankers who concealed their identity and protected them from public criticism.

Private banking developed in Athens as the Greek economy became increasingly monetized. Many Greek cities minted their own coins, and money changers in Athens began accepting deposits that had to be repaid but could be loaned or invested in activities that might result in a profit or loss. Besides extending credit to individuals who desired liquid funds for personal consumption, Athenian banks also made loans to finance various business ventures.

Maritime loans allowed creditors to spread their risks over many transactions. If the vessel or cargo were lost at sea, borrowers were not obligated to repay the loan. Creditors therefore demanded high interest rates to offset the high risk of shipwrecks or pirate attacks. Since banking was open to noncitizens in Athens, it provided an opportunity for former slaves and foreign residents, known as metics, to acquire large fortunes and to gain prestige by making generous donations to the city.

Athens remained politically, economically, and socially divided. A few of the metics in Athens made enough money in banking, manufacturing, or commerce to mingle with large landholders and buy citizenship in the city-state. But the vast majority of metics, who constituted about half of the free population of Athens, had no chance to socialize with aristocrats or to become citizens and thereby gain the right to vote in the assembly. Outnumbering freemen in Athens by about two to one, slaves, like women, were also excluded from participation in the political life of the polis. Therefore, even though landless male natives had gained political representation, only about a quarter of the adult men in Athens could vote in the assembly where aristocrats delivered most of the speeches and dominated the proceedings.

As a growing number of people engaged in commercial or financial transactions, rich Athenians increasingly set themselves apart from the poorer classes. They had traditionally avoided any kind of personal displays of their wealth and had spent large sums on communal projects, such as the construction of magnificent temples. Before the Peloponnesian War, lavish burials and luxurious homes were virtually nonexistent in Athens, and clothing styles remained quite restrained. During the century following the conflict, however, Athenian elites began dressing in more sumptuous clothes, building expensive houses with mosaic floors and double courtyards, and burying family members in huge tombs. Conspicuous consumption in a flourishing market economy in Athens was thus making a mockery of the old agrarian ideal of a Greek community of equals.

The Hellenistic World

After his father conquered the Greek city-states, Alexander the Great of Macedon led a large army in a series of successful military campaigns across the extensive Persian Empire. Alexander died from battle wounds, but his generals divided the vanquished Persian Empire into three separate kingdoms that were ruled by Macedonians who promoted the Greek language and culture. While heavily engaged in long-distance trade, these kingdoms became increasingly prosperous and socially stratified. But all these kingdoms eventually lost their independence and ended up as conquered provinces in the expanding Roman Empire.

The Macedonians: Philip II and Alexander the Great

In 359 BCE, when Philip II became the king of Macedon in the northern reaches of the Greek Peninsula, he aimed to pursue an ambitious policy of territorial conquest. Philip began by establishing a powerful military force composed of infantry units drawn from the ranks of small landowners and elite cavalry units staffed by aristocrats with large estates. After consolidating his hold on Macedon, he extended his authority first eastward across Thrace and then southward into Thessaly. A coalition of Greek cities, headed by Athens and Thebes, attempted to stop the advancing Macedonian army. However, the coalition forces were defeated in 338 BCE at Chaeronea in a battle that ended the era of independent city-states in Greece. After subduing the Greeks, Philip intended to conquer Persia, but he was assassinated two years later before he could embark on his next imperial venture.

His son, later known as Alexander the Great, was only 20 years old when he became the Macedonian king. He immediately started preparing for an invasion of Persia. During a spectacular military adventure that commenced in 334 BCE and continued for a decade, Alexander led his large army, which included many

Greek mercenaries, in a series of successful battles. His cavalry and infantry forces campaigned throughout the vast stretches of the Persian Empire and conquered one province after another. After driving his army into the Indus valley, Alexander was determined to press ahead in hopes of subjugating all of India. But he was forced to retreat because his exhausted troops were on the verge of mutiny.

During the last years of his life, Alexander became increasingly egocentric. He frequently associated himself with symbols of an eastern divinity, clearly departing from Greek traditions. Appropriating many of the trappings of a Persian king, Alexander married the daughter of a conquered Achaemenid monarch. Many of his troops and officers viewed these developments with alarm. Alexander died in 323 BCE at the age of 33 while he was residing in Babylon. His death was probably caused by infections stemming from wounds he had received while leading his troops in battle.

Seleucus, Antigonus, and Ptolemy

After Alexander died, his generals divided his conquests into three separate **Hellenistic** empires governed by Macedonian dynasties that used Greek for their official language. Seleucus took the huge area extending from Anatolia to Bactria; Antigonus took Macedon and Greece; and Ptolemy took Egypt, Libya, Palestine, and Cyprus. While seeking legitimacy in the eyes of their subjects, the rulers of these large territorial states all linked themselves to Alexander who was widely worshiped as a god. Many Greek and Macedonian colonists flocked to the numerous cities founded by Alexander and his successors. However, the Hellenistic kings depended increasingly on local elites who learned the Greek language and helped them exploit the indigenous rural peoples who continued to speak their native languages and practice their traditional customs.

These islands of Greek culture prospered as long-distance trade flourished in the Hellenistic world. Established at the mouth of the Nile around 331 BCE by Alexander the Great, the city of Alexandria became a grand commercial port that attracted many foreign merchants, both Greek and non-Greek. Its enormous harbor could accommodate more than 1,000 ships, and its renowned lighthouse, completed around 280 BCE, was a technical marvel. Built from large stone blocks sealed with molten lead to withstand the pounding of waves, the lighthouse stood over 300 feet high and could be seen by mariners 35 miles out at sea. Regarded as one of the seven wonders of the ancient world, the lighthouse helped sailors navigate the Mediterranean for more than 1,000 years.

The island of Rhodes, located near the center of the eastern Mediterranean trade routes, also developed into a thriving emporium. Rhodes produced vast amounts of wine that was exported to customers living as far apart as Sicily and the northern shores of the Black Sea. At the same time, Rhodesian vessels sailed to Alexandria and brought large cargoes of Egyptian grain back to their home port for transshipment to many other Mediterranean destinations.

The Antigonid Kingdom

In the Antigonid kingdom, embracing Macedon together with the Greek mainland and offshore islands, the gap between rich and poor significantly widened. A growing number of merchants in Athens and Corinth prospered as an expanding volume of goods passed through their hands while manufacturers in many Greek cities became wealthy as their workshops expanded and employed an increasing number of slaves. To pay for their lavish palaces and large armies, the Macedonian rulers imposed high tax levies on the land and the agricultural products in their realm. Many small farmers fell into debt and lost their land to wealthy aristocrats.

While some wealthy landowners in the Antigonid kingdom focused on growing olive trees or grapevines, others concentrated on grazing flocks of sheep or herds of cattle on vast tracts of land. The rich owners of great estates, some with over 1,000 acres, hired managers to supervise the tenants and slaves working in their vineyards, orchards, and pastures. As large estates replaced small farms, the rural population declined in many parts of Greece. Many impoverished peasants who did not want to toil as tenants paying high rents on aristocratic estates sought their fortunes as mercenary soldiers guarding the Macedonian frontier against northern tribes. Nonetheless, after a Roman army sacked Corinth in 146 BCE, the Antigonid Empire came to an end.

The Seleucid Kingdom

The huge Seleucid kingdom, occupying the heartland of the former Persian Empire, suffered a similar fate. After settling in the newly founded cities throughout the Seleucid realm, Greek and Macedonian traders established lucrative commercial relations with merchants in Tyre and Sidon, thereby gaining access to markets in the Mediterranean. But these immigrants constituted only a small portion of the population living under Seleucid domination, and the indigenous peoples residing in the countryside struggled to make tax payments required to support the central government. Resenting Seleucid rule, some native Persians serving as provincial governors revolted and established their own independent kingdoms.

The Parthians, who had migrated from central Asia and settled in eastern Iran, presented a greater threat to the Seleucids. After 163 BCE, the Parthians seized much of the Seleucid territory between the Tigris and Indus Rivers. The Parthians allowed Greek, Persian, Babylonian, and other merchants to travel across the broad expanse of land they controlled. These entrepreneurs soon began carrying luxury goods in caravans traveling between the Mediterranean and China. Transporting products high in value but low in weight, the merchants could feed themselves and their animals during long overland trips and still make large profits. The Seleucids, in the meantime, continued to rule their truncated empire until 83 BCE when Roman conquerors put an end to their regime.

The Ptolemy Kingdom

The Ptolemies ruled Egypt even longer, exploiting its resources for almost 300 years. Acting like traditional pharaohs, these Greek-speaking foreigners made large contributions to Egyptian temples to win the support of native priests. And they rewarded provincial officials who helped them dominate key aspects of the Egyptian economy. Royal agents extracted huge amounts of grain from peasants who were left with barely enough food to sustain their families. After storing the grain in silos in Alexandria, the Ptolemies sold it all over the Mediterranean and pocketed the proceeds.

In addition to developing the port facilities at Alexandria, the Ptolemies built harbors on the Red Sea and constructed overland routes that linked them to the Nile. Greek merchants from Alexandria soon began sailing down the Red Sea to the Horn of Africa to acquire ivory, cinnamon, and slaves. Then, after learning the seasonal pattern of the **monsoons** from an Indian mariner in 120 BCE, merchants from Alexandria began sailing directly across the ocean to obtain pepper, gems, and other products in India. These valuable commodities were transported to Alexandria and then transshipped to many different Mediterranean ports. The prosperity of the Ptolemies ended abruptly in 31 BCE, however, when Roman forces expelled them from Egypt and the last of the Hellenistic empires, now ruled by Cleopatra, fell into the grasping hands of Rome.

The Rise of Rome

As Rome grew from a group of hamlets into a thriving urban center, kings ruled the city. But the Roman nobility eventually seized power and established a **republican** form of government. From the outset, the aristocrats who governed Rome pursued a policy of territorial expansion. The conquered Italian countryside was divided along class lines as poor farmers cultivated small parcels of land and rich aristocrats owned large agricultural estates worked by slaves. As tribute extracted from the defeated Italian states flowed into Rome, the rulers of the imperial city used war profits to help finance the construction of aqueducts, roads, and temples.

From Monarchy to Republic

Rome was founded on the banks of the Tiber River in central Italy. Between 625 and 570 BCE, Rome developed rapidly from a group of small hilltop settlements with simple huts into a growing urban center that contained stone houses with tile roofs. The city soon featured public squares with communal sanctuaries and elegant buildings. Residing in Rome and in the surrounding communities, wealthy aristocrats who had succeeded in appropriating the surplus products of the region were buried in lavish tombs. Patricians formed a clearly defined elite group within the Roman nobility. Their exalted status derived from the fact that they could trace their ancestry back to the most ancient aristocratic clans in the city.

Rome was ruled in the beginning by kings who were chosen by patricians and who governed with their advice and consent. Soon, however, warlords began competing for power, and some eventually became monarchs and won the support of the lower classes. In 509 BCE, patricians led a coup against a king known as Tarquin and, despite his popularity among the lower classes, deposed him and took control of the government. The leaders of this aristocratic revolution justified their actions by asserting that they had destroyed tyranny and restored liberty. After seizing power, the Roman nobility quickly replaced the monarchy with a republican form of government that represented the rich.

A republican constitution gave supreme civil and military power in Rome to two magistrates, called consuls, elected by an assembly dominated by wealthy aristocrats. The consuls jointly held office for just a year, and each had the authority to check the actions of the other. In the event of emergency, a single dictator would be granted absolute power, but his term of office would last for only a half year or even less if the crisis ended before then. The assembly elected lesser magistrates as the city grew and gave them responsibility for handling financial and judicial affairs and taking the census.

In the middle of the fifth century BCE, the plebeians, all members of the community who were not patricians, established their own assembly and elected tribunes to protect them from the rich and powerful. The members of this popular assembly swore a sacred oath to guarantee the safety of their leaders. Fearing restive plebeians and the threat of rebellion, patricians allowed the tribunes to acquire the authority to intervene in all executive and legislative undertakings and to veto any measure that they deemed unfair to the plebeians.

During the second half of the fifth century BCE, the patricians tried to prevent wealthy aristocrats who were not patricians from attaining high office. The patrician attempt to monopolize political authority in Rome drove some affluent non-patricians into the plebeian camp. These ambitious aristocrats found the prospect of wielding power as leaders of the plebeians more appealing than remaining subservient to patricians who offered to protect their economic interests in return for receiving their continued political support. Despite the division among members of the aristocracy, however, the republic survived and continued to be dominated by the wealthy.

Early Roman Expansion

The aristocrats who governed the Roman Republic pursued an expansionist policy from the very outset. In 493 BCE, they defeated a coalition of small **Latin states** that had formed to resist the growing threat from Rome. The Romans and the subjugated Latin states then entered into a military alliance that bound both parties to aid one another in any future conflict and to share the spoils of war. Around 406 BCE, Rome began paying wages to soldiers while they were away from their farms during long military campaigns. This innovation enabled the heavily armed Roman legions to enlist all citizens who possessed a modest amount of property rather than just those who had enough money to buy their own equipment.

The Romans then continued their aggressive program of territorial conquest on the Italian Peninsula. In 390 BCE, Roman armies defeated the once wealthy Etruscan city-state of Veii. The victors promptly annexed the Etruscan territory just to the north of the Tiber River, thereby greatly increasing the size of the Roman Republic. While its armies were away subduing the Etruscans, however, a band of Celtic raiders from the Po valley advanced on Rome, sacked the defenseless city, and left with whatever plunder they could carry. But the Romans quickly recovered from this humiliating setback, and they began demanding indemnities from vanquished enemies in order to obtain food, clothing, and equipment for their troops.

During the first half of the fourth century BCE, plebeians became increasingly concerned about the disposition of public land that the Roman state had acquired as the spoils of warfare. Many peasants needed access to public land to raise crops and graze animals in order to supplement the meager income generated by their small plots. In the wake of territorial conquests, however, aristocrats occupied large blocs of public land and treated them as part of their own private estates. Moreover, the rich landholders drove peasants off these lands and then granted loans to their poor neighbors who needed them for survival. Those independent peasants who could not repay their debts often lost their land and ended up as bondsmen working for aristocrats on their large estates.

As the gap between the rich and the poor widened in the Roman countryside, plebeian leaders attempted to protect their peasant constituents. They made three basic demands: (1) debt bondage must be outlawed; (2) newly acquired land must be distributed in allotments that would become the private property of the recipients instead of remaining state property open to possession by the wealthy; and (3) a limit must be placed on the amount of public land that any household could occupy.

In response to plebeian agitation, a law enacted in 367 BCE imposed fines on those holding public land in excess of a prescribed limit. Many Romans who worked small farms soon began receiving parcels of land taken from vanquished peoples, and by the time debt bondage was formally abolished in 326 BCE, the settlement of conquered territory had already made it possible for most peasants to avoid falling into servitude. In any case, by then a growing number of war captives had already begun to provide Romans who owned large areas of land with an abundant supply of slaves to work on their estates.

While many poor Romans were receiving land taken from defeated people who had been killed, driven away, or enslaved, a power-sharing arrangement within the ranks of the aristocracy helped perpetuate the rule of the rich. A small number of wealthy and politically ambitious plebeian leaders succeeded in breaking the patrician monopoly on high office and entering the ruling class. The first plebeian consul was elected in 366 BCE, and it soon became an established custom that a plebeian should always serve as one of the two consuls. Once wealthy plebeian landowners became senior magistrates, they stopped protecting the poor and began promoting the economic interests of the wealthy. The position of tribune became the preserve of affluent young plebeians who sought the support of patricians in an endeavor to climb to the top of the power structure.

The Roman Senate, originally serving only as an ad hoc body of advisers to the consuls, evolved into an important organ of government. The Senate was composed mostly of former magistrates who remained members as long as they lived. Like the consuls and tribunes, the senators in Rome were all drawn from the nobility, and high-office holding rotated among a relatively small number of wealthy aristocrats. Popular assemblies did not develop into effective democratic institutions that could check the power of the elite, because they met only when summoned by a magistrate, and they could not initiate any legislation. As a result, the Roman Republic continued to be governed by a self-serving and self-perpetuating aristocratic oligarchy.

New Period of Military Conquest

After agreeing to share power in Rome, the wealthy plebeians and patricians were determined to extend their authority over the entire Italian Peninsula. A period of more intensive military campaigning began in 343 BCE with a successful war against the Samnites, a mountain people living in the interior of Italy. Then, after defeating a coalition of Italian states in 338 BCE, Rome created a commonwealth of subjugated peoples who accepted its domination. Some defeated people became Roman citizens with the right to vote and hold office, while others became Roman allies without these privileges. Although their political status differed, citizens and allies were all obligated to serve in the Roman army. As Rome either annexed or concluded alliances with a growing number of Italian communities, its military power therefore became greater and greater.

The allied states were essential to Roman military success. In many of the major battles fought during the conquest of Italy, allied contingents made up more than half of the Roman forces. And because the allies paid for these contingents, Rome could draw on a large reserve of allied manpower at little cost to itself. The wealthy landowners who ruled the allied states supported the Roman wars of conquest for two reasons. First, on numerous occasions, local aristocrats depended on Roman troops to defend them against peasant insurrections. Second, as military partners, local elites received a share of the loot confiscated from defeated enemies.

Rome became much larger and richer as people and property from the defeated Italian states flowed into the imperial city. The population of Rome grew from about 30,000 residents in 343 BCE when the war against the Samnites began to more than 90,000 by 264 BCE when the conquest of all the land south of the Po valley was completed. In 312 BCE, Romans began constructing the Agua Appia, the first aqueduct that supplied water to their rapidly expanding city, and in the same year, they started building the Via Appia, their first great military road, which ran from Rome to Capua. War profits in the form of booty and indemnities extracted from conquered states helped finance these huge and expensive projects as well as the magnificent temples and public buildings erected in Rome and standing as expressions of its wealth and power.

After migrating to Rome from many different areas of Italy, some wealthy landowners began investing in commercial, industrial, and financial enterprises. Acting as agents for profit-seeking aristocrats, slaves and freedmen set up banks that accepted deposits and made interest-bearing loans. They also manufactured a wide assortment of goods, including high-quality pottery exported to many customers around the Mediterranean. And while serving aristocrats in Rome, slaves and freedmen imported large quantities of grain, olive oil, and wine to satisfy the increasing appetite of the city. Thus, a small but growing number of ambitious Roman aristocrats invested some of the money that they had made in agriculture in urban businesses to augment their fortune.

The Imperial Republic

Motivated by a strong desire to achieve fame and fortune, aristocrats were the driving force behind Roman warfare and imperial expansion. Military service for 10 years provided the surest path for a young aristocrat with political ambitions to distinguish themselves and to compete successfully for public office. As they climbed the ladder to the highest positions of authority in Rome, aristocrats could expect to become supreme military commanders. Conquering generals were able to add to their wealth as well as bask in the glory of victory. Roman armies plundered enormous quantities of silver and gold plus millions of slaves in conquered territories, and military commanders took a substantial share of the booty for themselves.

But aristocrats were not alone in reaping the economic benefits of Roman warfare. After returning to Rome and leading a victory parade displaying the spoils of war to cheering crowds, the triumphant general often used part of his share of the loot to construct temples or other monuments, thereby gaining additional prestige for himself. And as a reward for fighting in victorious Roman legions, ordinary soldiers could expect to acquire land and booty in conquered territories. The Roman state also benefited economically from successful wars by extracting tribute and taxes from defeated peoples.

Carthage and the Three Punic Wars

After extending its dominion in Italy as far north as the Po valley, Rome clashed with the city-state of Carthage, the former Phoenician colony, which had established the prosperous **Punic** Empire in the central and western Mediterranean. Carthage possessed a vast hinterland in North Africa with huge estates owned by aristocrats and worked by slaves who produced large amounts of wheat, olive oil, and wine. Carthage also had a flourishing overseas commerce based on the export of agricultural produce, textiles, and fish and the importation of metals from Sardinia, Spain, and Portugal. Using revenue generated by trade, Carthage maintained a powerful navy largely manned by its own citizens but also drawing conscripts from Libya and other subject states to fill the ranks of its army.

Growing antagonism between Carthage and Rome led to three military conflicts known as the Punic Wars. When the First Punic War began in 264 BCE, the Romans lacked a navy, but they used a grounded Carthaginian galley as a model to build a fleet of warships with one significant modification—a gangway that could be dropped onto the decks of enemy vessels so that their soldiers could board them and turn the contest into a duel between floating armies. The Romans won several great sea battles that ended Carthaginian naval supremacy, and in the ensuing peace settlement in 241 BCE, Carthage was forced to pay large war reparations and cede Sicily, a major grain producer, to Rome. Within three years, the victorious Romans seized Corsica and Sardinia, an important source of metals, from Carthage.

Having been pushed out of the central Mediterranean after the First Punic War, the Carthaginians focused their attention on the western Mediterranean. They turned the rich Iberian Peninsula into a strong military base and prepared for an attack on Rome. The Second Punic War commenced in 217 BCE when General Hannibal left Spain with a powerful army, crossed the Alps with his soldiers and elephants, and invaded Italy from the north. As he advanced southward, Hannibal won a series of battles. But he could not take Rome, and a stalemate ensued. With his supply lines overstretched, Hannibal was forced to retreat, and the tide of war turned in favor of Rome. Eventually, Roman forces defeated Carthaginian armies in both Spain and North Africa. When the war ended in 202 BCE, Carthage was forced to destroy its fleet, pay heavy indemnities to Rome, and relinquish its hold on the Iberian Peninsula.

The triumphant Romans continued their campaign for political and economic hegemony in the Mediterranean. They gradually extended their control throughout the Iberian Peninsula, thereby gaining access to new sources of grain, olive oil, and wine as well as iron, copper, tin, silver, and gold. After losing their maritime empire, the Carthaginians developed their fertile North African hinterland. But the Romans launched the Third Punic War in 149 BCE to defeat Carthage once and for all. The war ended in 146 BCE with the complete destruction of Carthage.

Its buildings were burned to the ground, its citizens were slaughtered or enslaved, and its North African territories were converted into a valuable Roman province.

While subduing Carthage, the Romans also conducted successful military operations in the eastern Mediterranean. Rome capitalized on the victories of its armies by annexing both Macedonia in 148 BCE and Greece two years later. By then, almost the entire Mediterranean had become a preserve of Rome, and for good reason, the Romans began referring to the huge inland body of salt water as mare nostrum (our sea).

The Polarization of Wealth and Social Unrest

These military campaigns and territorial acquisitions had an enormous economic impact on Rome. During the Punic Wars, the number of Roman legions increased fivefold, and in the years that followed, Rome maintained a standing army of 50,000 men with many troops stationed in distant lands. The opportunity to make enormous profits by supplying soldiers with food, clothing, and arms led to the formation of private firms, known as publican companies, which bid on the open market to obtain military contracts from the Roman government. Functioning like modern corporations, the publican companies sold shares of their stock to wealthy individuals to raise operating capital in Rome for their far-flung transactions.

Many aristocrats became silent partners in these business ventures to avoid being viewed as greedy money-grubbers. Because Roman senators were legally prohibited from owning non-agrarian enterprises, they often purchased unregistered and nonvoting shares in publican companies to preserve the appearance of propriety. In addition to acquiring and transporting shields, helmets, swords, and other essentials to legions deployed abroad, the publican companies contracted with the Roman state to collect taxes on agricultural produce and commercial activity in the overseas provinces. Tax payments in the form of grain provided food needed to feed the population of Rome, which had grown by 130 BCE to about 375,000 residents. Moreover, the Romans used some of the silver extracted annually as tribute from subjugated peoples to fund the construction of new aqueducts and public buildings.

Besides sucking resources out of conquered territories and providing lucrative opportunities for Roman investors, frequent overseas military campaigns transformed the Italian countryside and produced social unrest in Rome. Peasant recruits provided the bulk of the Roman armies, and the prolonged absence of large numbers of able-bodied young men undermined the ability of many small farms to survive. Those soldiers who were fortunate enough to return from distant battlefields in a fit condition often found that their farms had been abandoned. Many impoverished veterans drifted into Rome, which became a hotbed of social discontent.

Slaves who were mostly war captives began to constitute an increasingly significant proportion of the Italian population. Between 225 and 30 BCE, well over one million slaves were imported from conquered provinces into Italy. Many slaves served as skilled artisans or estate managers, but most slaves toiled as unskilled laborers in manufacturing, construction, or farming. As wealthy aristocrats bought up peasant holdings and public lands, huge estates worked by large numbers of slaves replaced small farms, especially in central Italy. Consequently, fewer and fewer Romans could meet the minimum property qualification for military service.

Tiberius Gracchus, a tribune from a noble family, drafted a land reform measure designed not only to create more farmers who would be eligible for recruitment into the Roman army but also to alleviate the distress of the growing landless population in Rome. In 133 BCE, he sponsored legislation that required individuals to surrender any public land that they held in excess of 310 acres to a commission that would distribute small plots to the poor. Unable to gain the support of a majority in the Senate, Tiberius asked the popular assembly to approve his proposal. But his opponents reacted violently. Tiberius and many of his supporters were bludgeoned to death.

A decade later, his brother Gaius Gracchus became a tribune and revived the commission to redistribute land. However, like Tiberius, he also encountered bitter opposition in the Senate. Gaius won broad support from the large mass of urban plebeians by linking his land reform program with a proposal to provide grain to citizens of Rome at a subsidized price. But Gaius along with many of his supporters were murdered, and Rome continued to be ruled by a relatively small number of aristocrats who lived in luxury amid an increasingly volatile mob.

Civil Wars in Rome

The Senate, composed of some 600 permanent members, played a central role in the ensuing struggles for power and wealth in imperial Rome. Only senators could hold military commands, which enabled them to pillage the resources of conquered territories. And only the most prominent senators could obtain frequent or prolonged overseas military commands, which offered them great opportunities to acquire plunder and accumulate private fortunes.

While serving as a political and military leader between 107 and 100 BCE, Gaius Marius showed a readiness to break the rules of the Senate in order to advance his career. He secured a series of six consulships and thereby subverted the precedent that prohibited any individual from holding a consulship for more than a single term. Moreover, while leading successful military campaigns in North Africa and Gaul (modern France), Marius ignored the traditional property requirement for enlistment into Roman armies. He recruited the urban poor who were willing to fight as professional soldiers for long periods in anticipation of receiving land, in addition to loot, as a reward.

Ambitious Roman generals, following in the footsteps of Marius, soon began mobilizing personal armies of intensely loyal soldiers. Between 88 and 82 BCE, rival military commanders led their troops into Rome for the first time in the history of the republic. After enduring a violent period of intermittent civil war, Rome was rocked once again in 73 BCE by a massive slave rebellion led by Spartacus, the famed gladiator. The Senate asked Pompey, an energetic and ruthless general, to crush the revolt. The insurrection ended with 6,000 crucified slaves lining the road from Rome to Capua as a warning against future uprisings.

After rewarding Pompey with a consulship for his brutal suppression of the slave rebellion, the Senate appointed him to command an enormous naval force of 500 ships to eliminate the pirate menace throughout the Mediterranean. Pompey promptly accomplished this task in 67 BCE, and he soon gained more glory by conquering Judaea and Cyprus.

Competition for fame and fortune among rival generals created political turmoil in Rome. In 59 BCE, the Senate awarded Julius Caesar with a consulship after he led a successful and profitable military campaign in Spain. Caesar secured a more lucrative military command a year later and embarked on a successful conquest of Gaul, thereby extending the Roman frontier to the Rhine-Danube line. Flush with booty from their military conquests, Caesar and Pompey soon began competing for popular support by funding huge public building programs in Rome.

Their struggle for power ultimately resulted in violence. Caesar used his legions in 48 BCE to defeat Pompey and his loyal soldiers in a bloody confrontation in Greece. After returning to Rome with great wealth and popularity, Caesar declared himself dictator for life, and like an old Roman monarch, he adorned himself with a purple robe and a golden wreath. Caesar also began confiscating the land of his wealthy opponents and distributing parcels to the veterans of his armies. Many senators regarded Caesar as a tyrant who had elevated himself above his peers by pandering to the lower classes to win their political support. In 44 BCE, a group of wealthy conspirators assassinated him in hopes of restoring a republican government based on the rotation of high offices within the ranks of the aristocracy.

The End of the Roman Republic

Rome soon plunged into another period of civil strife, which ended when an emperor with supreme authority replaced the aristocratic oligarchy, which had ruled the imperial Republic from the Senate floor. After Caesar was murdered, his nephew and adopted son Octavian competed for power with Mark Antony who soon joined forces with his mistress Cleopatra, the last Ptolemaic ruler of Egypt. Octavian defeated their combined navies in a sea battle off the coast of Greece in 31 BCE, and when Antony and Cleopatra committed suicide the following year, Egypt became a Roman province. After Octavian returned to Rome as a popular war hero, the aristocrats in the Senate could not stop him from destroying what was left of the republic.

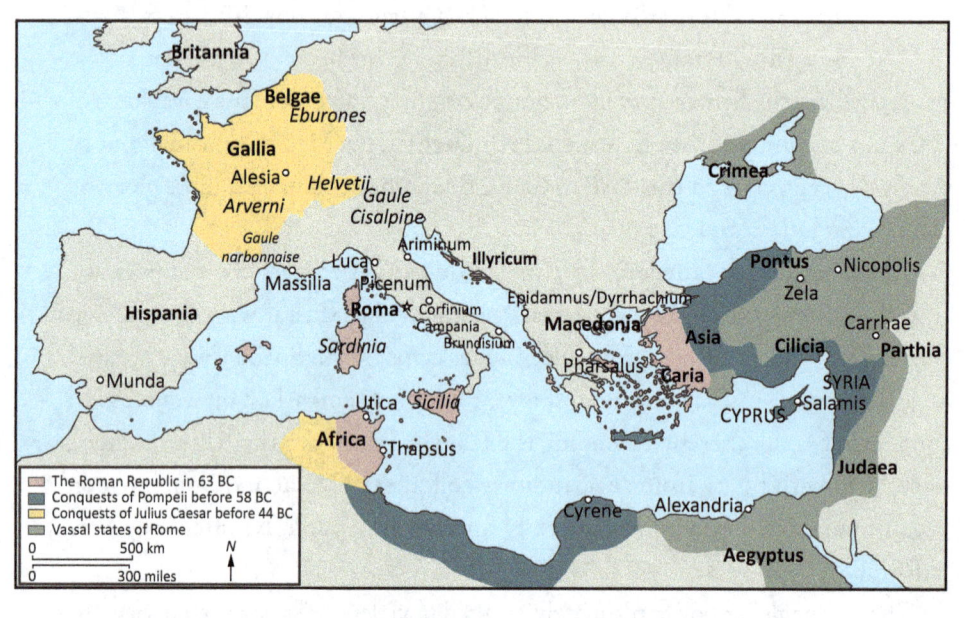

MAP 6.2   The Roman Empire When Octavian Came to Power

In 27 BCE, Octavian assumed the title of Augustus, a term suggesting divine powers, and became the first Roman emperor. Augustus promptly created a new standing army with commanders who were directly responsible to him, thereby ending the destructive struggle for power among rival generals. Moreover, rather than continuing the disruptive practice of confiscating land and distributing plots to army veterans, he established a pension system that provided financial support to soldiers who had completed their military service. Augustus succeeded in restoring order to Rome, which had grown into a thriving metropolis of around a million residents. At the same time, he also presided successfully over the enormous Roman Empire, which contained more than 50 million people, or about 20 percent of the entire population of the world. His stable reign of 41 years inaugurated a peaceful and prosperous era, known as the Pax Romana, which would last for several centuries.

Review Questions

1. What circumstances led to the rise and fall of Athens as a preeminent city-state?
2. What role did long-distance trade play in the Hellenistic world?
3. How did the way Rome was governed evolve between 509 and 312 BCE?
4. Why did the gap between the rich and the poor widen as the Roman Republic expanded?
5. Why did a group of Roman aristocrats assassinate Julius Caesar?

Additional Readings

Alcock, Susan, Terence N. D'Altroy, Kathleen D. Morrison, and Carla M. Sinopoli, eds. *Empires: Perspectives from Archaeology and History*. Cambridge: Cambridge University Press, 2001.

Andreau, Jean. *Banking and Business in the Roman World*. Cambridge: Cambridge University Press, 1999.

Cohen, Edward E. *Athenian Economy and Society: A Banking Perspective*. Princeton: Princeton University Press, 1992.

Cornell, T. J. *The Beginnings of Rome: Italy and Rome from the Bronze Age to the Punic Wars (c. 1000–264 BCE)*. New York: Routledge, 1995.

Cunliffe, Barry. *Europe between the Oceans: 9000 BCE–AD 1000*. New Haven: Yale University Press, 2008.

Freeman, Charles. *Egypt, Greece, and Rome: Civilizations of the Ancient Mediterranean*. 2nd ed. Oxford: Oxford University Press, 2004.

Hanson, Victor D. *The Other Greeks: The Family Farm and the Agrarian Roots of Western Civilization*. 2nd ed. Berkeley: University of California Press, 1999.

Harris, W. V. *Roman Power: A Thousand Years of Empire*. Cambridge: Cambridge University Press, 2016.

Markoe, Glenn E. *Phoenicians*. Berkeley: University of California Press, 2000.

Migoette, Leopold. *The Economy of the Greek Cities: From the Archaic Period to the Early Roman Empire.* Berkeley: University of California Press, 2009.

Moore, Karl, and David Lewis. *The Origins of Globalism.* New York: Routledge, 2009.

Morris, Ian, and Walter Scheildel, eds. *The Dynamics of Ancient Empires: State Power from Assyria to Byzantium.* Oxford: Oxford university Press, 2009.

Scarre, Chris, ed. *The Human Past: World Prehistory and the Development of Human Society.* 4th ed. London: Thames and Hudson, 2018.

Figure Credits

Map 6.1: Copyright © by Amizzoni~commonswiki (CC BY-SA 3.0) at https://commons.wikimedia.org/wiki/File:Persian_empire_490bc_Bactria.gif.

Fig. 6.1: Copyright © by A. Davey (CC BY 2.0) at https://commons.wikimedia.org/wiki/File:Bas_Reliefs_of_Tribute_Bearers,_Persepolis,_Iran_(4693735854).jpg.

Fig. 6.2: Source: https://commons.wikimedia.org/wiki/File:Parthenon_from_west.jpg.

Map 6.2: Copyright © by Historicair (CC BY-SA 3.0) at https://commons.wikimedia.org/wiki/File:-Map_of_the_Ancient_Rome_at_Caesar_time_(with_conquests)-fr.svg.

CHAPTER 7

Conquest, Crisis, and Recovery: The Roman World, 27 BCE–400 CE

The Countryside and the City

The Roman Empire was overwhelmingly agrarian. This is not to deny the importance of cities, but the productive base of Rome's economy was rooted deeply in the land. Until about 400 CE, the Roman aristocracy expanded and consolidated its hold over the land—and the surpluses it rendered—while the land itself was worked by peasants and slaves. Life in the city offered dramatic contrasts from country life and reflected the stark inequality among the Roman Empire's inhabitants.

Landed Aristocrats

Already, during the second half of the last century BCE, thousands of Italian citizens had emigrated to the recently conquered provinces to obtain larger farms than they had in Italy. Military conquest brought land to the empire, and many emperors simply turned the conquered lands over to private ownership. Upperclass Romans moved swiftly to occupy important and often enormous tracts of provincial land. By the reign of the emperor Nero (54–68 CE), for example, six men who sat in the **Roman Senate**, a privileged preserve of the wealthiest aristocrats, were said to own half of the province of Africa. Not surprisingly, as families of senatorial rank invested increasingly in provincial land under the empire, they became increasingly wealthy.

The richest aristocrats had estates scattered across the whole Roman world. They benefited from—and remained dependent upon—the Mediterranean-wide unity of the empire. Aristocratic fortunes increased two- to threefold from the late Republic to 100 CE, and then five- to eightfold between 100 and 400. Landed wealth afforded the men of these families positions in local, provincial and imperial governance and, for men and women alike, allowed a luxuriant lifestyle.

Many of these landed aristocrats simply enjoyed the fruits of their ownership through the collection of rents from their peasant tenants. No doubt, most agriculture was produced for local consumption, but the fact that many great and middle-range landowners kept a keen eye on the products their land rendered and the value they fetched in the marketplace points to an economy that reached far beyond the local environment.

Many estates specialized production to meet market demands, quite evident in the regions clearly oriented toward export: Africa (Tunisia and Egypt produced the largest agrarian surpluses in the Empire), southern Italy, Sicily, southeastern Spain, southern Gaul, Syria, and Palestine. There is clear evidence that many estates were organized for efficiency and profit. Intense land management made sense in a system geared to profit, and many landowners employed systems of accounting to record production and income.

In many parts of the empire, this commercial agrarian economy was highly monetized, where not only coin coursed through its arteries, but systems of leasing, credit, and marketing were well-developed.

Peasants and Slaves

The mass of the agricultural workers in the ancient world were peasants. We do not know how many were independent farmers, but even if they were, they scratched out a meager living, finding much of whatever surplus they might produce going in taxes to the state. Soldiers cashiered after a career in the army were allotted small plots of land, usually in frontier regions on land that was marginal or formerly uncultivated. Their holding often not large or fertile enough to sustain independence, many of these farmers were forced to seek supplementary employment, perhaps working on estates of great landowners. The numbers of peasants either renting land or working on the estates of others increased under the empire. In either case, their wealth was a tiny fraction of that commanded by the great landowners.

As long as Roman legions conquered new lands, slaves as captives from war were numerous. Those with skills could be found mostly in cities and in domestic service, but the unskilled often toiled on large farms or, more unfortunately, under brutal conditions in mines. Roman agricultural writers observed that most of the workers on a farm were slaves, as was their overseer, but they were likely referring to large estates. Whether this was generally true is unknown. As conquests diminished, however, so did the numbers of captives, and so the percentage of slaves in the population gradually declined.

City Dwellers

Wealth and poverty existed side by side in the Roman city, and the dwellings they inhabited are a stark indicator of the gaping inequality that marked the Roman Empire. The wealthy lived in spacious villas with indoor plumbing, piping fresh water from nearby public fountains for drinking, heated baths, and toilets. The rich were tended by staffs of slaves. Aristocratic homes were usually a single-story structure, and one entered from the front into an open-air atrium with a pool in the center. Here, guests or clients were greeted, and private business was sometimes conducted. Flanking the atrium were small rooms used as bedrooms, libraries, or offices. Dining rooms were separate and usually in the rear, and behind them was the kitchen. Most villas had a private garden in the back.

The cities of the Roman Empire, above all Rome, drew migrants from smaller towns and the countryside seeking work that often was not available, becoming teeming hives of entire families poised on the brink of starvation. The poor, in sharp contrast to the rich, crowded into dilapidated, multistory tenement buildings called **insulae**. In Rome alone there were tens of thousands of these buildings in the early years of the empire. Many were overcrowded and poorly built, with inhabitants living in constant fear of fire or collapse. The floor on which a person lived depended on one's income. The apartments on the ground or first floor typically had windows for fresh air, several rooms, and indoor toilets. The poorer the resident, the higher the floor he and his family inhabited. In these upper floors, rent was paid daily or weekly as opposed to the lower floors where rent was paid monthly or annually, and so families moved in and out frequently. The upper apartments were cramped, with entire families squeezing into a single room. Few had access to light or fresh air, and none had indoor toilets. Human waste was dumped along with household refuse into the streets, creating not only a horrific stench but also a breeding ground for disease. Not surprisingly, the poor relied upon the free bread provided by the state and the water that flowed in public fountains. The nearly destitute urban populace was always restive, and the public dole of basic necessities as well as the free entertainment of chariot races and gladiatorial combat in the public arenas, like the Coliseum in Rome, were provided by the state to placate them.

The Power of the State

The power of the Roman state rested fundamentally on the army. To pay for it, the Roman bureaucracy assessed and collected taxes in coin, built roads to facilitate the movement of troops, and maintained harbors and shipping lanes to regularly supply the army with food, drink, and supplies. There were unintended consequences to such actions, however. Taxing in coin accelerated its circulation and so facilitated the ease and speed of business transactions (it is easier, faster, and more efficient to move coinage than bulk items in barter), and private merchants availed themselves of road and seaway.

The dominance of the army in imperial matters could also undermine the stability of the state, as the crisis of the third century demonstrates. Troops acclaiming their own commanders as emperor caused debilitating civil wars at a time when disease and economic dislocation were ravaging the empire and causing a general decline in the size of the population. Order and prosperity returned in the fourth century, but the empire was fundamentally reorganized to accomplish that.

Roman rulers were keen on projecting and maintaining their authority, so they invested heavily in public building projects closely identified with them and on the administration of law to secure public order. Religion, too, became closely associated with power, especially when Christianity became the official religion of the empire in the fourth century and emperors claimed the grace of the Christian God as justification for their unquestioned authority.

The Emperor and the Army

Warfare was a defining characteristic of the Roman Empire, and its needs are of immeasurable historical significance. The army was necessary to maintain power and exerted economic influence as an enormous consumer of food and supplies. Augustus, the first emperor who reigned from 27 BCE to 14 CE, came to dominate the Roman polity by gaining the loyalty of the armies. The grant of power in the Roman Republic was formally given by the Senate that acted theoretically for the people of Rome, but by the time of Augustus, everyone knew real power rested with the man who commanded the army. Augustus began a practice subsequent emperors would follow by substituting professional soldiers for conscripts and securing their loyalty to him by requiring personal oaths of allegiance and by granting them a substantial bonus when they left the service.

The power of the emperor rested on the army, and it was used to project the state's awesome power. A vivid example of this was the fate of the rebellious Jews of Judea. In 66 CE, they rebelled against Roman rule, and in the late summer of 70, a Roman army under the command of Titus, the son of the emperor Vespasian, besieged and captured Jerusalem, the capital of Judea. The Roman Jewish historian Flavius Josephus reports the fury of Roman destruction in his *History of the Jewish Wars*: "Here was to be seen a once prosperous countryside devastated … entire enemy war bands slaughtered … an army streaming within the walls [of the city], the whole place swimming in blood."[1] The sacred temple was sacked, its inner sanctum defiled, and its holy objects seized and carted off to Rome.

Back in Rome, the suppression of the revolt was celebrated by Vespasian and Titus, and a mopping-up operation was dispatched to eradicate about 1,000 rebels who continued to hold out in a fortress called Masada that stood on a rocky, narrow, sheer-sided plateau not far from Jerusalem in the desert near the Dead Sea. An enormous Roman army soon appeared, surrounded the plateau, and began a lengthy siege. The trapped Jews could only look on in terror as Roman engineers, day after day, built a large assault ramp up which, when completed, Roman legionnaires would march and take the fortress by storm. In 74, the fortress fell to Roman troops, and the rebels were slaughtered. It was a shuddering demonstration of the overwhelming power of an empire that would concentrate such resources, far from Rome on its eastern frontier, to suppress the remnants of a revolt that was already crushed with the destruction of Jerusalem.

FIGURE 7.1 Masada Fortress. After the destruction of Jerusalem by the Romans, Masada was the last stronghold of the Jewish rebels. The large ramp on the right was built by the Romans and was used to storm the fortress.

Trajan's Column in Rome, erected by the Emperor Trajan (r. 98–117), is another bold and stark illustration of the invasion, conquest, and pacification of enemy territory by the army. It is a 30-meter-high column commemorating the conquest of Dacia, but the themes of Roman supremacy and the futility of resistance are universal. It spirals 24 times, depicting 2,500 figures in 154 different scenes, many focusing on the commanding presence of the emperor.

---

1 Christopher Kelly, *The Roman Empire* (Oxford: Oxford University Press, 2006), 12.

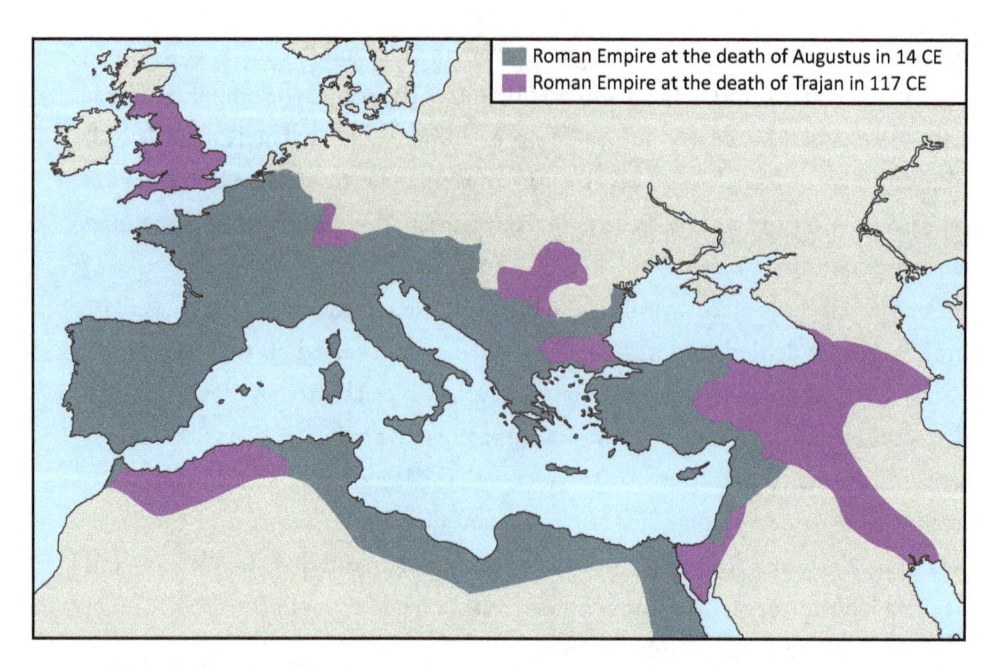

MAP 7.1   The Expansion of the Roman Empire from Augustus to Trajan

Trajan's immediate successor Hadrian (r. 117–138) erected an arch in a conquered Athens in 131 or 132 with a similar reminder of power and subjugation. The arch made it visibly clear who now unquestionably ruled this city. One side of the arch bears the inscription "This is Athens, the former city of Theseus," the legendary founder of the city. On the opposite side is inscribed "This is the city of Hadrian, not Theseus."

Roman rule in the provinces relied heavily upon a local aristocracy staffing the city councils throughout the empire. It was a lucrative business. As long as they maintained public order and made sure that most of the tax revenues that they were charged with collecting made their way to imperial coffers, the provincial governors appointed by the emperor left them alone. These local notables recognized clearly, however, as the famous writer Plutarch warned, that they conducted the affairs of their city with "the boots of the Roman governor just above [their] head."[2]

Still, Roman emperors were first and foremost commanders in chief, and for the first two centuries of the empire, they were able to keep their armies in check. In the third century, however, this changed, the result of a military, economic, and demographic crisis. A succession of emperors was placed on the throne by

---

2   Kelly, *The Roman Empire*, 60.

military factions temporarily victorious in the civil wars that tore at the fabric of the empire. Over a 50-year period, 26 generals claimed the title of emperor, and of these tellingly dubbed barracks emperors, almost none died peacefully.

The dire military situation was worsened by a collapse of some frontier defenses. For example, Germanic tribes drove the Romans from their province of Dacia in the middle of the third century. Other tribes penetrated the empire elsewhere, and though they were eventually held in check by a Roman counterattack led by Emperor Aurelian in 270, barbarian invasions would return a century later and would contribute significantly to the final collapse of the Roman Empire.

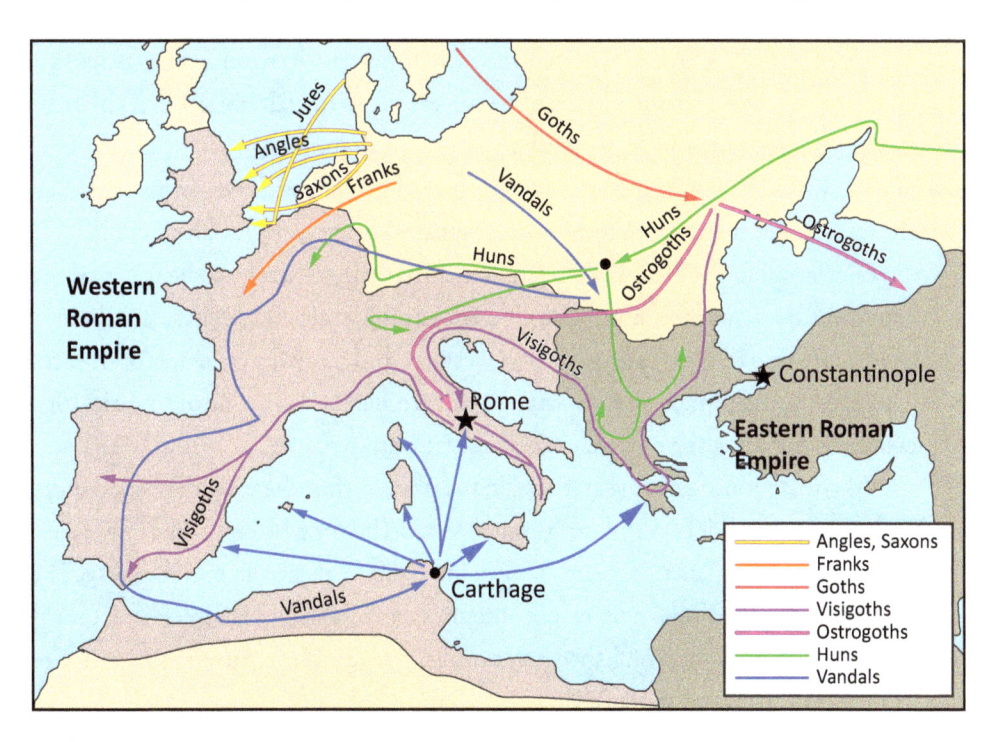

MAP 7.2 Barbarian Invasions of the Roman Empire, 100–500 CE

Crisis and instability during the late second and third centuries wrought by military challenges were compounded by economic factors. To gain or retain the loyalty of troops, emperors increased their pay but with **debased coinage**. There was less silver available for an expanded currency in part because a long-term unfavorable balance of trade was bleeding silver out of the empire, as Romans imported more goods from beyond the empire than they exported. Inflation followed.

The empire also was struck by waves of epidemic diseases, and the army was far from spared their effects. Plague, smallpox, and measles caused great mortality during these centuries, with smallpox killing about 10 percent of the population, or about six million people, in 25 years after it first arrived in 165. And epidemics like these joined other deadly illnesses that were ever-present. Dysentery, cholera, typhoid, malaria, pneumonia, and tuberculosis were constant companions of a malnourished population, many of whom lived in crowded, unsanitary conditions. Only half of babies throughout the empire lived to the age of five, and those that survived could expect to live perhaps another 35 or 40 years. The result was a long-term decline in the overall population, a decline that struck at potential recruitment into the army and the ability to pay for it.

Taxes and Money

The main cost of the empire was the army, something every emperor from Augustus on plainly knew. Augustus extended the **census** to provincial subjects in addition to Roman citizenry in order to establish the ability of all subjects to pay taxes. The land tax remained the dominant levy of the imperial period, and the census remained the instrument that recorded the amount of land in agricultural production.

Diocletian (r. 284–306) was convinced that the solution to the crisis of the third century was better and more efficient administration. He therefore divided the empire into two parts, eastern and western, and named a co-emperor in each. This split would remain permanent, the eastern half surviving until the mid-15th century, long after the empire in the west had disappeared.

To govern more effectively, Diocletian believed that the empire needed more officials, more soldiers, and more revenue to pay them, so he instituted new taxes. He refined the census to determine agricultural production in each region of the empire, basing the assessment on the amount of farmland and laborers it contained and assessing a tax on established and uniform values. His reform made tax levies more predictable and more reliable.

The civil administration expanded during the imperial period, especially under Diocletian, from a skeletal bureaucracy to one of 30,000 salaried officials staffing 1,500–2,000 administrative districts by the fourth and fifth centuries. Much of this growth was driven by the expanding tax system, and emperors drew men from the upper classes into their administration. To get its taxes collected, the state was forced to turn a blind eye to a massive skimming of tax revenues into aristocratic coffers so long as sufficient revenues reached the imperial treasury. The peasantry was saddled with the tax payments. Such collaboration in imperial rule raised the social status of this elite as it enriched it. An already wealthy aristocracy became more so, as it added the revenue stream generated by taxes to its possession of most of the agricultural surplus.

During the imperial period, tax collection increasingly shifted to a cash basis, coins being more easily collected than produce and then distributed as salaries to soldiers. Consequently, imperial mints continued to produce more and more coins. Between 50 BCE and 200 CE, gold entered the monetary system in very large quantities, accounting for about 60 percent of overall coin value, while silver represented about 30–35 percent and base metals like bronze the rest. Gold coins escaped debasement in the third century, but so severe was the debasement of silver coins that they were scarcely distinguishable from bronze ones.

Emperors minted coins mostly to pay for the army, but the unintended consequences were far-reaching, as the Roman economy became widely monetized. More and more, money became the dominant medium of exchange. As money always does, it increased liquidity and greased the wheels of business transactions. In hoards it also became a store of wealth.

Infrastructure

Just as military demands dictated monetary policy, so, too, did they deeply influence the state's investment in infrastructure—roads, ports, canals, bridges, fortifications, and even a standardized system of weights and measures. Add to that the necessity of keeping the empire pacified, especially its cities with teeming crowds, and the result was the impressive and well-known Roman contributions to public building, feats of engineering, and law. As with monetization, the development of infrastructure had a wide-ranging and profound impact on the Roman economy and its generation of wealth.

The rulers of the Roman imperial state had no elaborate, planned economic policy, but many emperors did recognize that taxes and custom duties on trade were a lucrative source of income. Roman officials diligently collected the *tetarte*, a 25 percent tax on all imports and exports across Roman borders. Roman road-building in most parts of the empire was first and foremost a means to move troops quickly and efficiently, but they also provided effective means of short-haul overland transport.

The Romans built the most extensive networks of roads in Eurasia—50,000 miles throughout the empire. Roman roads were four feet thick and slightly crowned so water would drain off. They were constructed of stone, sand, and concrete, the last being a waterproof composite discovered by Romans when a particular volcanic earth was mixed with lime and water.

Similarly, ports and canals were built to move necessary supplies to the army, but they also provided private commerce with expanded and well-maintained facilities for trade. Clearly, easing the movement of commercial goods and protecting them from bandits and pirates would be in the state's fiscal interest. The emperor Trajan, for example, reopened a canal in Egypt that had been built centuries before to move goods from the northern end of the Red Sea to the Nile River. The next emperor, Hadrian, built an extensive and fortified desert road system connecting the Red Sea ports of Myos Hormos and Berenike to the overland caravan routes that transported goods to the Mediterranean.

Concrete and sophisticated engineering also made possible the construction of elaborate water supply systems by Roman imperial engineers on a vastly larger scale than their predecessors. To supply the city of Rome with fresh water, for example, the state built nine canals with a total length of 300 miles along a gentle gradient of two to three inches per mile, erecting aqueducts to cross valleys. The water was then dumped into reservoirs or cisterns in the city and from there piped to fountains, public baths, and the houses of the rich. Aqueducts and cisterns were constructed in many parts of the empire, many of which survive today.

FIGURE 7.2 A Roman Aqueduct. This aqueduct, known as the Pont du Gard in southern France, was constructed of stacked arches in the first century CE and carried fresh water to the city of Nîmes.

FIGURE 7.3 Roman Cistern in Nîmes. Fresh water flowing across the aqueduct of the Pont du Gard was collected in cisterns like this. Hydraulic pressure from gravity pushed the water through the holes at the base of the cistern pictured here, and it was distributed through pipes to public fountains and some private homes of wealthy Romans.

As the imperial state standardized and expanded the monetary system, so, too, did it create and maintain an official system of weights and measures—and for much the same reasons. Such a regular system made it easier and more accurate to tax goods by standard units of quantity and cash value. And as with standardized coinage, merchants benefited from the imperial system of weights and measures by being able to measure a quantity of goods accurately, to agree on a price on a unit basis, and to know that the same measures would apply everywhere they traded within the empire.

Investment in infrastructure, though not a part of a thought-out economic policy by emperors or their officials, did clearly occur and had significant influence on the generation of wealth in the empire. The state's imposition of law and a legal system did as well. The state used law for its own interests—to keep the peace and to maintain a monopoly on violence—but Roman law's emphasis on property rights facilitated commercial exchange by providing greater security of transactions and thus a reduction in risk (of utmost importance to every merchant, here and everywhere, seeking a profit). We must not overstate the extent or application of law, however; for the development of Roman law was piecemeal and reactive, with magistrates devising new rules and principles as particular situations required. Indeed, Roman law would not be codified into a system until the sixth century CE. Moreover, rulers and imperial officials were far from immune to turning the legal system to their own interest or to that of their friends, families, or political allies.

Still, amid the development of Roman law was a clear growth in contract law, a recognition that each party to a transaction, more and more verified in writing attended by witness statements, had binding obligations. In 212 CE, citizenship was extended to all free inhabitants of the empire, and because Roman law applied to citizens, contract law spread widely across the Mediterranean, further facilitating, as with all developments in infrastructure, the development of commerce and the creation of wealth.

Religion and the Power of the State

The vast conquests of Roman armies before 200 CE brought into the empire a multitude of different ethnic groups, cultural traditions, and religious practices. The figure of the emperor stood above them all as a symbol of unity, proclaimed endlessly in statuary, public buildings, and monuments. Before the fourth century, civic officials administered and enforced a public religion that comprised offerings, rituals, prayers, and sacrifices to deities. Their correct performance was deemed required to make them effective, to win the favor of the gods, and bring their power into the everyday world. This "pagan" religion was **polytheistic** and local, with no unified system of beliefs and practices across the empire. What mattered to the state was the maintenance of public order and loyalty to the emperor.

Before 200, Christians for the most part were largely ignored by Roman society and the state. After that they were persecuted most often when they publicly refused to participate in public and civic cults. Beginning in 249, several imperial edicts intensified the persecution of Christians. The emperors presumably noticed that their numbers had increased and that they were now more visibly organized in churches. They suspected that Christians were gradually transforming into a separate society with their own loyalties and so feared political conspiracies against the state. Diocletian capped the persecution of Christians by an edict in 303 that ordered the destruction of Christian meeting places and sacred texts, confiscation of church property, and an order to offer traditional pagan sacrifices under pain of death.

The relationship between Christianity and the state changed dramatically with the next emperor, Constantine (r. 306–337). After the death of Diocletian, a civil war broke out over the succession to the imperial throne. Constantine was one of the claimants, and he enlisted Christians as a source of support. By 324, he had eliminated his rivals and consolidated his power to become sole emperor. He had already recognized Christianity as a legal religion by the Edict of Milan in 313, and he henceforth pursued policies that favored it. He convened the Council of Nicaea in 325, during which the doctrine of the **Trinity** was established for the Christian Church. The power and wealth of the Christian Church expanded mightily, Constantine and most of his successors asking in return that the Christians recognize them as unquestioned monarchs whose authority was sanctioned and legitimated by the Christian God. The emperor was now the Christian God's representative on earth.

Constantine outlawed sacrifices and closed pagan temples. The emperor Theodosius in 391 then outlawed all forms and practices of polytheism. By the end of the fourth century, the Christian faith and the Christian Church were well-integrated into the imperial power structure. It was enriched by innumerable private, pious donations. Its membership reflected the sharp divisions within Roman society, its administration in the hands of **bishops** who were mostly drawn from the class of urban aristocrats. The vast majority of Christians were the urban poor, a potentially restive class that the emperor relied upon the bishops to pacify. The bishops therefore assumed the duties of disseminating charitable donations—notably the distribution of bread—that the state gradually relinquished.

The Economy of the Roman Empire

There can be little doubt that the economy of Rome grew from the late Republic period to at least 200 CE. The third-century crisis caused a broad economic contraction, while the fourth century witnessed a stabilization before the empire became politically and economically fragmented in the fifth century and after, especially in the west.

Many aristocrats were investing heavily in specialized agricultural production for market, notably grain for bread, olives for oil, and grapes for wine. Intensive investment in grain was an empire-wide phenomenon, but certain areas, like North Africa and above all Egypt, led the way and geared their crop growing to feeding an export market, especially the army and the cities. Prosperous estate owners also invested their profits in trading ventures. The existence of diverse markets for the varieties of products that coursed through the regional and long-distance commercial networks of the empire provided the demand for those with capital available to invest and to seek profitable returns.

Conditions of Economic Growth

Because we have no precise population figures, little can be said concerning per capita growth, but clearly, many of Rome's elites saw their fortunes grow, even during the turbulent third century. What were the conditions for economic growth before the third century? We should not overestimate the level of economic integration that was achieved in the ancient economy, for uncertainty and insecurity ruled everywhere. Yet even amid such circumstances, evidence abounds that surplus was created and moved. How, where, and why? And who benefited most?

Consider the role of the state in economic growth. Rome's military conquests, while they lasted, channeled a tributary flow of goods into the empire, diverse resources entering an ever-widening sphere of circulation. An increasingly professional military defended the frontiers and secured peace within them. Amid such favorable conditions, trade expanded, especially from the east with the conquest of Egypt and Syria early in the imperial period. No wars were fought for explicitly economic reasons that we know of, but economic ramifications of conquest and imperialism were nonetheless profound.

As we have seen, the Roman state did consciously build and maintain infrastructure, the rulers not only recognizing its military value but also grasping that enhanced trade would improve its own collection of dues and taxes. Roads, ports, warehouses, drainage projects, and canals—all received state funds. Economic viability was improved in the process and transaction costs for traders reduced.

The state also minted money for the payment of troops and the collection of taxes, but it also contributed to economic growth by stimulating trade. An increased supply of coinage and a consistent valuation of it (at least before the third century) across the entire Mediterranean integrated markets by easing payment and accelerating exchange. No inflation followed the increased volume of coinage in circulation before 200 CE, suggesting that productivity increased with the money supply. Rome's growing surplus was being increasingly commercialized.

State taxes and aristocratic rents were more frequently demanded in cash, further stimulating the monetization of the economy, as tax- and rent-paying peasants were thrown onto the market to sell their produce for the needed cash. How burdensome state land taxes were is not well known (they were instituted to replace booty from conquests in war), but there is evidence before the third century that they were likely less than 10 percent and therefore far from crippling to economic growth. True, they were unfairly assessed, with the poor and powerless paying a disproportionate share, but in terms of overall economic growth, the impact of taxation was probably greater in terms of state spending (most tax monies were spent to supply the army, a huge demand sector of the economy) than as a drag on growth.

Agricultural production supplied the lion's share of the surplus that was in such demand in the empire. The army and large cities, above all the capitals Rome in the western sector of the empire and Constantinople in the eastern sector, as well as large cities like Alexandria, had enormous appetites for grain (bread), olive oil, and wine, the three fundamental agricultural products. To supply the army and the cities, the state created a system within which it bought the necessary goods at state-determined but market-based prices and employed private traders to ship the supplies to their destinations. A vast network emerged, with most grain coming from Sicily, Egypt, and above all North Africa and most oil and wine coming from Syria, Greece, Italy, Spain, and southern Gaul. Because private commerce moved along the same channels, the state purchase-and-distribution system contributed to a generalized commercialization of the economy.

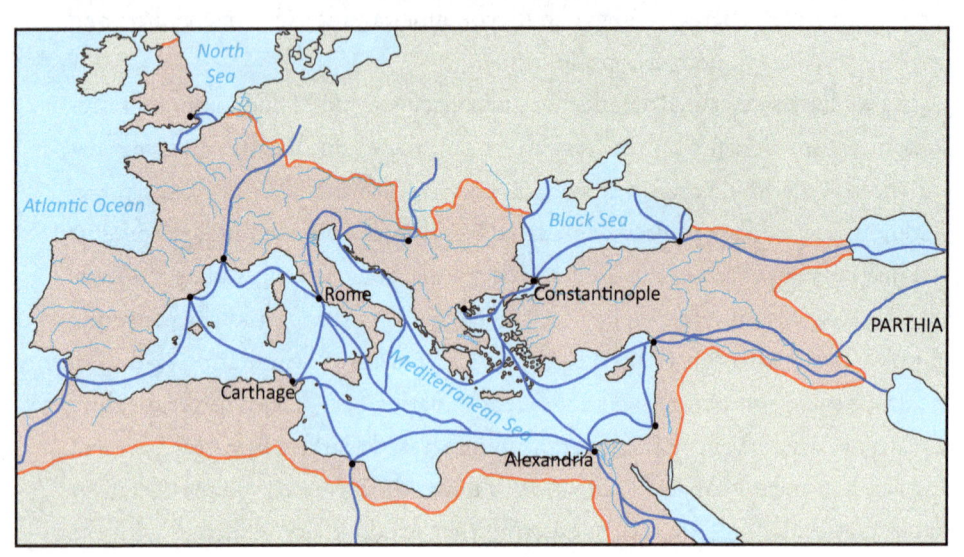

MAP 7.3   Trade Routes of the Roman Empire in 180 CE

Specialization, Export, and Investment

Conquest brought vast tracts of land into the empire, and it was greedily acquired by an elite class alive to the profitable opportunity of agricultural production. Recent archeological finds demonstrate that many aristocrats were investing heavily in specialized agricultural production for market. Vast storehouses with vats, presses, and cellars point to large-scale wine production in some areas, and similar evidence exists for olives. In Syria, an important center of agricultural production for the entire empire, olives were clearly being grown for export, and huge surpluses were shipped to cities and, after olive oil was added to the state distribution system in the third century, to the army.

Archeological research shows that Spain and North Africa were major centers of olive production, with many of the groves of trees being planted on previously undeveloped land. Olive presses have been found in large masonry buildings, a factory-like industrial organization suggesting a mentality seeking increased efficiency and maximum yields. Roman elites were clearly involved in the production and manufacturing of this product, but so were some small-scale farmers, testified by archeological discoveries of one or two presses. Further evidence that this was an export-oriented business, remains of concentrated ceramic manufactures have been found in areas of olive production, **amphorae** being the essential shipping container of the ancient economy. Archeological remains of significant construction activity have been discovered in towns (notably in Africa) around olive-pressing and ceramic operations, alerting us to the availability of capital for expenditure on buildings.

As important as grape and olive growing was, by far the most important agricultural product in the empire was grain. Here, too, we find much production for export and economic activities geared explicitly for profit. Romans used vertical waterwheels, both undershot and overshot, to grind grain, a design adapted from an earlier Persian wheel. Such waterwheels could be found everywhere in the empire, sometimes grouped in as much as 16 wheels in a row, capable of grinding three tons of grain an hour, enough to feed 80,000 people.

Intensive investment in grain production was not an isolated practice, but the best evidence comes from Egypt. Here, the rural economy was deeply monetized, and the wealthy elite certainly practiced land management that calculated profitability in cash terms. Estates, like the well-documented one of the Egyptian aristocrat Aurelius Appianus in the third century, were highly centralized, efficient, and profit-conscious.

Production of vast surpluses poured increasing wealth into the coffers of aristocrats. What did they do with it? Much was spent on luxurious consumption, but much also was channeled into various forms of investment beyond the agricultural sector. Vast sums of money financed trade, largely supplied by the landholding elite and managed by slaves or freedmen. Throughout antiquity, some rich elites (at first just senators but later provincial notables and even the emperor and members of his entourage) loaned money at interest, and during the imperial period, the practice was so widespread that many wealthy people came to depend on the income from finance as well as land.

Women of this class, too, were involved in finance, advancing interest-bearing loans drawn from their own patrimonies. This was a cash-based economy. Bills of exchange (like modern checks) did not exist in antiquity, nor did any system of public debt. Interest rates rose, therefore, when and where cash was scarce and declined when and where it was abundant. The emperor's response to credit crises was to mint more coins, not to borrow against future revenues. Status-conscious elite men and women felt intense pressure to maintain social rank that was pegged to an ostentatious consumption lifestyle of sumptuous clothing, personal adornment, and opulent housing that required vast wealth. This social pressure drove many of them in search of increasing profits. The widespread practice of financial investment is partly a reflection of this, as is the increased commercialization of the agricultural economy.

Markets and Profits

Ample evidence suggests that regional as well as long-distance trade became increasingly important during the time of the Roman Empire. A wide range of commodities—both foodstuffs as well as manufactured items, like pottery, glass, mosaics, and metalware—were loaded onto cargo ships that sailed everywhere across the Mediterranean. Both state distribution and private commercial exchange held the empire together, and responsiveness to demand was the key. Supplying the army, of course, was fundamental, but demand from cities was enormous as well, for they were the sites of basic demand for necessities exerted by their millions of inhabitants and of demand for luxury goods driven by the wealthy aristocracy who also counted the cities their primary home. Describing Rome, the second-century Greek writer Aelius Aristides wrote, "So many merchant ships arrive here, conveying every kind of goods from every people every hour, every day, so that the city is like a marketplace common to the whole earth."[3]

---

3   Fik Meijer and Onno van Nijf, eds., *Trade, Transport and Society in the Ancient World: A Sourcebook* (London: Routledge, 1992), 83.

Of the estimated 60 million inhabitants of the Roman Empire in the second century CE, for example, 9 million were town dwellers. Rome alone held a million people at the time of Augustus, but places like Egypt were well-known for their urban density too. Every city had its agora or forum, a center of religious, civic, and commercial activity. Cities like Rome were large enough for specialized wholesale and retail markets. It had one for cattle, one for vegetables, one for wine, one for pigs, and one for fish. Cities created demand that could only be met through trade.

Markets in the Roman world most likely resembled the bazaar, trading places akin to spot markets today and, as such, only loosely integrated. Merchants responded to such market fragmentation and the uncertainty and risk it brought by establishing trustworthy personal relations with other merchants, often family members.

Profits were to be made from trade, and wealthy entrepreneurs—wholesalers, ship owners, private financiers—joined merchants and rich aristocrats in trading ventures. As the early second century Roman poet Juvenal put it in verse,

> Ship on ship the dangerous ocean braves,
>
> And half the human race is on the waves.
>
> Wherever gain or hope of gain is found,
>
> Thither the adventurous fleet is quickly bound.[4]

Cities and, at times (given the vagaries of climate and uneven agricultural production), entire regions were dependent upon the arrival of merchant ships.

Profit seeking brought risk, and in the case of maritime commerce, these risks could be high. Already, in the second century BCE, Cato the Elder wrote in *De agricultura* that "the trader is an energetic man and someone who is dedicated to accumulating money, but ... he is also someone who lives dangerously and is always on the verge of disaster."[5] Unpredictable winds (notorious in the Mediterranean from November to March), shipwreck, and piracy made venturing onto the seas a dangerous proposition. Merchants throughout time have sought to reduce exposure to risk and have devised varieties of ways to accomplish this. One was the maritime loan, in existence at least since the fourth century BCE

---

4   Juvenal, *The Satires*, trans. Charles Badham (New York: Harper Brothers, 1855), Satire 14, lines 359–362.

5   Neville Morley, *Trade in Classical Antiquity* (Cambridge: Cambridge University Press, 2007), 82–83.

and in wide use during the imperial period. Wealthy individuals would advance the capital to a trader to fund a particular voyage and establish a rate of interest to be collected with the principal at the end of it. If the venture were lost through no fault of the trader, the principal was forfeited. Naturally, rates of interest were high, but enough voyages must have been successful; otherwise, maritime loans would not have been offered at all.

Long-Distance Trade with the East

The emperor's entourage and the aristocracy were both prodigious consumers of luxury goods from exotic origins. Rarity conferred high social and economic value on such products as fine silks, lacquerware, spices, and aromatics, goods that came from eastern regions—China, India, Arabia. When the Roman Empire established control over Cilicia, Syria, Judea, and Egypt in the eastern Mediterranean in the mid-first century BCE, an avenue to the east (where well-established trade routes were already in existence) was opened. Imperial and aristocratic demand for luxury eastern goods accelerated dramatically. Henceforth, the eastern part of the empire would be the greatest source of wealth for Rome, and conquering legions expanded the boundaries of the empire eastward until the mid-third century CE. Although we cannot quantify the volume, the eastern trade was large and highly risky, but undoubtedly immensely profitable.

Trade routes beyond the empire channeled these exotic goods westward toward Rome. They came overland from the Arabian Peninsula and along the Silk Road through central Asia from China and by sea from India across the Arabian Sea and up the Persian Gulf or the Red Sea into the Mediterranean basin. Roman traders carried eastward glass, red coral, fine wines, and other commodities rare in Asia, but above all, they shipped gold and silver. The effects of this bleeding the empire of bullion was felt by the third century.

To the East

There were three basic routes that connected the empire with India and China. First, goods moved overland in both directions. From the west, they travelled through the Parthian and later Sassanian Empires onto the Silk Road of central Asia, passing caravans laden with Chinese goods heading in the other direction. Second, Roman trade was shipped down the Euphrates River to the Persian Gulf where it was loaded onto ships that sailed down the gulf and across the Arabian Sea to ports in India. And third, goods were shipped up the Nile River

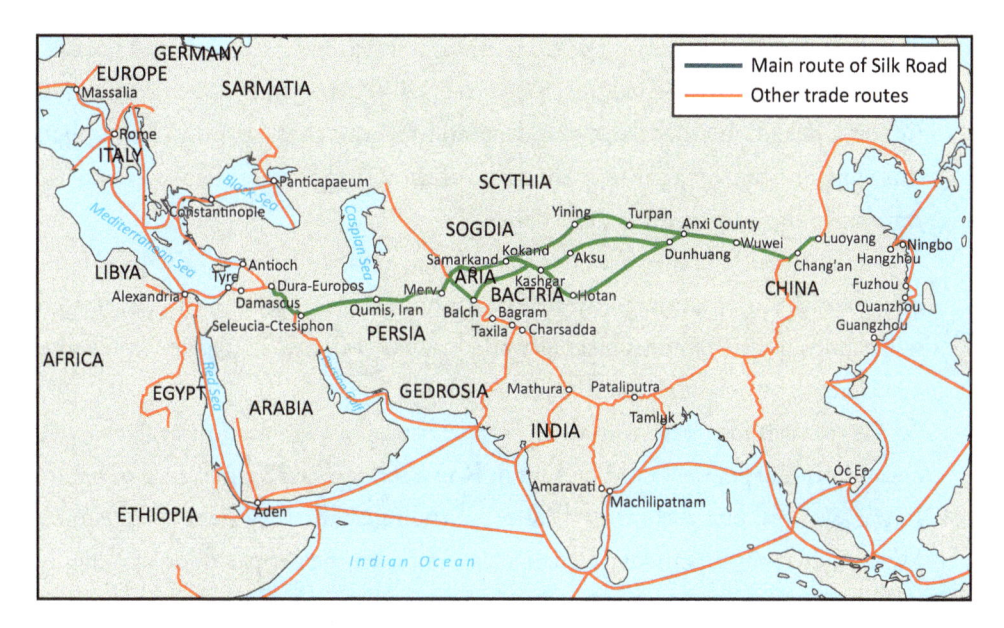

MAP 7.4 The Silk Road During the Roman Empire

from Alexandria, carried overland to the ports on the Red Sea, and from there into the Indian Ocean.

All three routes connected Rome with India and ultimately with China. The overland route from the Chinese capital of Chang'an to the Mediterranean coast was about 4,200 miles. Although the Romans apparently tried to establish a direct sea link to China (in 166 Chinese accounts report that an envoy of men from the Roman Empire had arrived in the Han capital), nothing came of it.

Overland trade passed through many hands. No single merchant made the entire journey from India or China himself. Still, the fact that goods and coins traversed these trade routes at all is a testimony to the level of demand exerted at each end of the transactions. Vintage Roman wine was greatly desired in the courts of Indian princes, as were glass, red coral, Arabian frankincense, metals, and, above all, gold coinage. Indian cotton textiles, cinnamon, cardamom, pepper, pearls, and precious stones and woods were brought west. Chinese silks were also prized in the west. At least until 400 CE, the Chinese had a world monopoly on silk production.

India, the Indian Ocean, and the Red Sea

Roman scale of trade with India, in both bulk and luxury goods, was surprisingly large. One documented consignment from Muziris in India to Alexandria gives a sense of the volume of trade from India. This single ship carried 1,700 pounds of nard (an aromatic balsam), 4,700 pounds of ivory, and 790 pounds of textiles, all worth a value great enough to purchase 2,400 acres of the best farmland in Egypt! Considering that there were Roman freighters that were even larger than this ship, one can get a sense of the value of these cargoes and the income to the state from the 25 percent tax on them.

Much evidence of the volume of the bulk trade comes from archeological finds of standardized amphorae. These clay containers, mass produced in clustered workshops, point to considerable trade in wine, oil, and fish sauce (a favored condiment), as well as rice and pepper.

Pepper was imported into the Roman Empire in large quantities. Relatively cheap in India, pepper could be sold in Rome for a price 32 times that of bread. Expensive, yes, but within reach of more than just the very richest consumer. With such a markup and with such a large market, the pepper trade was highly profitable.

Around the time of this burgeoning trade in the first century CE, sailors on the Indian Ocean learned how to manage the **monsoon** winds, charting their regular patterns and seasonal directions and thus making sailing more safe and predictable. This knowledge permitted for the first time direct, blue-water sailing between the Red Sea and the ports of India. A ship riding the monsoon winds as it cleared the Red Sea could reach India in about 20 days.

An anonymous Greco-Egyptian merchant living in Alexandria in the mid-first century CE wrote the *Periplus maris Erythraei* (*Periplus of the Erythraean Sea*). This is an extraordinary book that provides information about navigation routes, ports, markets, and products from the Red Sea and from the east coast of Africa to the shores of India. The accuracy of its descriptions has been increasingly upheld by archeology. It was a guidebook for Roman traders who, always seeking to reduce their exposure to risk, found the information provided here invaluable.

The *Periplus* identifies key Indian ports for Roman traders: Barbaricum at the mouth of the Indus River and Barygaza (mentioned more than any other port in the *Periplus*) on the northern bank of the Narmada River on the Gulf of Cambay. India was already well-integrated by exchange and trade when the Romans arrived, with established channels from the hinterland to coastal cities, such as Barbaricum and Barygaza. Barygaza, especially, was a thriving market and manufacturing center, connected to three different trade routes within and beyond India: the famous Silk Road north to Bactria and thence to central Asia and China; the Ganges valley; and the lower Krishna valley. Roman traders plied the western coast of India and even sailed southward around the tip and up the eastern Coromandel Coast, the heartland of Indian pepper production. From there they went no further, although they knew of Sri Lanka.

Roman traders sailed the busy sea-lanes of the Indian Ocean alongside, and in competition with, Indians, Persians, Africans, and Arabs. The third-century crisis and the consequent economic contraction created a sag in the Indian Ocean commerce, but the fourth century witnessed a revival. Nestorian Christians became more prominent in the trade after 400, persecuted as they were by Orthodox Christians in Constantinople for their differing views on the nature of Christ and forced to flee eastward. They established communities in India and along the Persian Gulf, situating themselves on both overland and maritime routes.

Just as Romans sailed to India, so, too, did Indians come west seeking to penetrate the Roman market for eastern goods. There is ample evidence of trading colonies of Indian merchants on the Red Sea and Persian Gulf coasts, and even in Alexandria. They came in great numbers to the annual trade fair at Batnae on the Euphrates River from the second century to the sixth.

On the Red Sea, the key Roman ports were Myos Hormos and Berenike on the western coast (the Roman Empire did not reach the eastern coast), with Roman roads connecting them to Coptos where the cargoes were loaded onto the many freighters plying the Nile River. Alexandria was the primary destination, and here the cargoes were unloaded in public warehouses where imperial officials assessed the 25 percent *tetarte* tax.

The general decline of Red Sea trade in the late third century signaled a withdrawal of Roman traders from the commerce. The reestablishment of order by the emperors Diocletian and Constantine brought recovery in the fourth century, but when Roman traders returned, they found increased competition from Persian and African traders in the Red Sea and Indian Ocean who had taken the place of the Romans who had retreated during the third-century crisis. The Aksumite Africans in particular remained a powerful international force from the third century to the seventh, centered on the west coast of the Red Sea at the port of Adulis, exporting valuable ivory and tortoise shell.

The Overland Trade to Arabia and Central Asia

Goods moved eastward overland through Syria and the Parthian and later the Sassanian Empires. Routes to central Asia were well-established, as were routes through Mesopotamia, up and down the Euphrates River, and in and out of the

Persian Gulf where Indian and Arabian products flowed. The city of Antioch in Syria thrived as a Mediterranean port, and Dura Europos, a Parthian border city until the Romans conquered it in 165 CE, likewise prospered from the east-west transit trade. Indeed, Syria was a crucial transit region of long-distance trade during the imperial period, and Syrian merchants and aristocrats profited handsomely.

The Romans never conquered territory on the eastern shores of the Red Sea, nor did they ever militarily command the Persian Gulf. They did, however, exert a great demand for the aromatic products harvested from the landmass in between these bodies of water, Arabia. The trade in aromatics, above all frankincense and myrrh, had existed for a long time before the imperial period, but spiking Roman demand (much of it for religious ceremonies) stimulated its growth and multiplied the profits accruing to the Arab Nabataean kingdom.

The crops were grown in the southwestern part of the Arabian peninsula. To reach Roman markets, however, the products had to traverse the "incense road" that was controlled by the Nabataeans who patrolled it with military forces, maintained watering and provisioning points, and, of course, collected taxes and customs on the commerce. Perhaps the prosperity of the Nabataeans contributed to their downfall, for the Romans under the emperor Trajan conquered and annexed the Nabataean kingdom in 106 CE, creating a new Roman province and building a new road that stretched northward from the Red Sea port of Petra toward Palmyra and Antioch, an action that stimulated the trade even further.

Trajan's annexation of northern Arabia was part of a grand plan to exert Roman power in the east. He had no discernible economic motives, but Roman presence in the area certainly had economic ramifications. Infrastructure (e.g., roads, ports, cities) and military security were boons to trade, and cities that sat astride the trade routes benefited enormously. Palmyra is a prominent example of this. An oasis city, Palmyra grew in size in the first century, thriving as a vital caravan city for travelers crossing the Syrian Desert from Mediterranean port cities to the west and from the Euphrates River to the east. It became a part of the Roman province of Syria during the reign of Tiberius (14–37 CE) and steadily grew in importance as a key city in Rome's eastern trade.

Palmyrene merchants joined with the landowning aristocracy to develop the trade routes that allowed them to prosper. The city provided military security on these highways, and merchants established ports of call in both directions to better organize a trade network that channeled merchandise through their city. Wars between Sassanian Persia and Rome in the third century disrupted commerce and weakened Palmyra, and a late-third-century rebellion allowed Palmyra to break away from Rome briefly before Emperor Aurelian reconquered and destroyed it. We find no more caravan trade there after 272. The eastern trade will revive in the fourth century, but the trade routes had shifted north, and the Palmyrenes were no longer a part of them.

Review Questions

1. What are the most important indicators of the distribution of wealth in the Roman Empire?
2. What were the most important elements of Roman imperial power?
3. Why did the economy of the Roman Empire grow during the first 200 years CE and contract after that?
4. Why did the Romans establish trading relations to the east, and what were the main commodities and trade routes?

Further Readings

Andreau, Jean. *Banking and Business in the Roman World*. Translated by Janet Lloyd. Cambridge: Cambridge University Press, 1999.

Ball, Warwick. *Rome in the East: The Transformation of an Empire*. London: Routledge, 2000.

Bang, Peter. *The Roman Bazaar: A Comparative Study of Trade and Markets in a Tributary Empire*. Cambridge: Cambridge University Press, 2008.

Begley, Vimala, and Richard Daniel De Puma. *Rome and India, The Ancient Sea Trade*. Oxford: Oxford University Press, 1992.

Harris, W.V., ed. *The Monetary Systems of the Greeks and Romans*. Oxford: Oxford University Press, 2008.

Liversidge, Joan. *Everyday Life in the Roman Empire*. London: Batsford, 1976.

Manning, J. G., and Ian Morris, eds. *The Ancient Economy: Evidence and Models*. Stanford: Stanford University Press, 2005.

Morley, Neville. *Trade in Classical Antiquity*. Cambridge: Cambridge University Press, 2007.

Rives, James B. *Religion in the Roman Empire*. Oxford: Blackwell, 2007.

Sartre, Maurice. *The Middle East Under Rome*. Translated by Catherine Porter and Elizabeth Rawlings. Cambridge, MA: Harvard University Press, 2005.

Scheidel, Walter, Ian Morris, and Richard Saller, eds. *Cambridge Economic History of the Greco-Roman World*. Cambridge: Cambridge University Press, 2008.

Scheidel, Walter, and Sitta von Reden, eds. *The Ancient Economy*. London: Routledge, 2002.

Scheidel, Walter, ed. *Rome and China: Comparative Perspectives on Ancient World Empires*. Oxford: Oxford University Press, 2009.

Tomber, Roberta. *Indo-Roman Trade: From Pots to Pepper*. London: Duckworth, 2008.

Young, Gary K. *Rome's Eastern Trade: International Commerce and Imperial Policy 31 BC–305 AD*. London: Routledge, 2001.

Figure Credits

Fig. 7.1: Copyright © 2018 Depositphotos/Keith Levit Photography.

Map 7.1: Copyright © by Varana (CC BY-SA 3.0) at https://commons.wikimedia.org/wiki/File:Extent_of_the_Roman_Republic_and_the_Roman_Empire_between_218_BC_and_117_AD.png.

Map 7.2: Copyright © by MapMaster (CC BY-SA 2.5) at https://commons.wikimedia.org/wiki/File:Invasions_of_the_Roman_Empire_1.png.

Fig. 7.2: Copyright © 2014 Depositphotos/razvanphoto.

Fig. 7.3: Copyright © by Krzysztof Golik (CC BY-SA 4.0) at https://commons.wikimedia.org/wiki/File:Castellum_Divisorium_in_Nimes_01.jpg.

Map 7.3: Copyright © by Adhavoc (CC BY-SA 3.0) at https://commons.wikimedia.org/wiki/File:Europe_180ad_roman_trade_map.png.

Map 7.4: Copyright © by Kaidor (CC BY-SA 4.0) at https://commons.wikimedia.org/wiki/File:Silk_Road_in_the_I_century_AD_-_en.svg.

CHAPTER 8

The Unification of China: The Qin and Han Dynasties, 221 BCE–220 CE

Imperial Unification in Classical China

The Qin and Han dynasties were the first to unify China. True, dynasties existed long before—recall the Zhou and Shang rulers from a previous chapter—but a politically unified empire with a relatively efficient administration across vast distances was new to China with the Qin dynasty that was established in 221 BCE. The system of central, bureaucratic government was the creation of the Qin and Han dynasties and, remarkably, persisted in its broad outlines through the whole imperial history of China until its disappearance in the early 20th century.

From Qin to Han: Central Control and the Warlord

As we have seen in an earlier chapter, only beginning with the Qin Empire were regional peoples brought under one governing system, an unlikely accomplishment given the hilly and mountainous terrain of China and, during the Warring States period (403–221 BCE), considering how politically fragmented it was. Among the patches of the quilt that was China was the Qin state. Small and remote, it was an unlikely candidate to be the unifier of China, but its rulers embarked down the road of increased accumulation of state power by administrative organization as early as the late fifth century BCE. By 221 BCE, the Qin conquest of Central China was complete.

The first Qin emperor, Shi Huangdi (r. 221–210 BCE), fashioned imperial institutions that were largely adopted by the later Han dynasties (Western or Former Han, 206 BCE–9 CE; Eastern or Later Han, 25–220 CE). The Qin Empire was administered by 36 commanderies, each under a civil governor, a

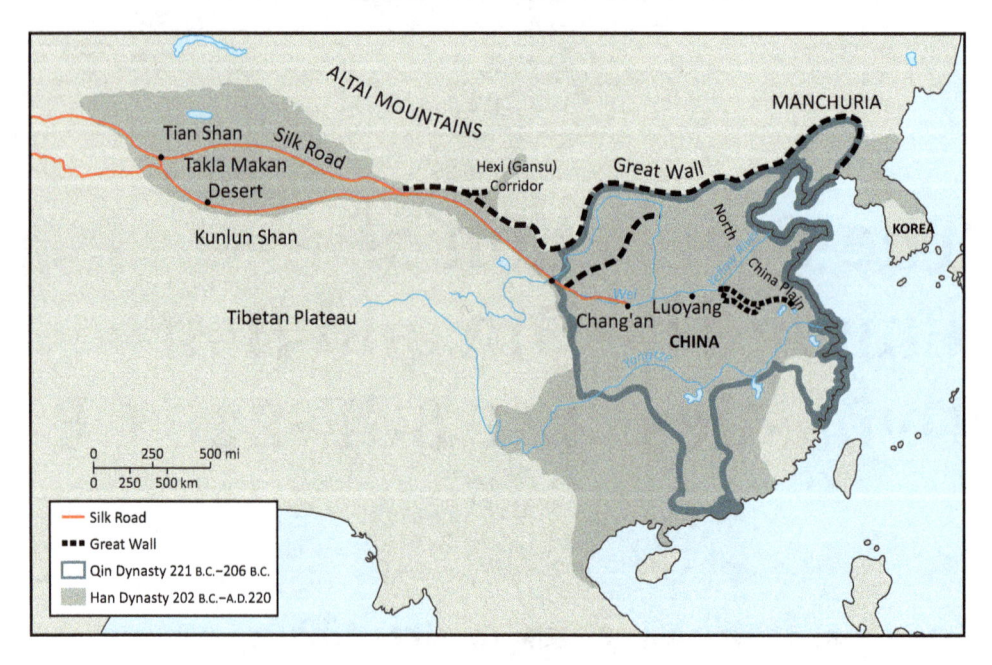

MAP 8.1   The Territorial Boundaries of the Qin and Han Dynasties

military commander, and an imperial inspector, the last being the immediate representative of the emperor. All three were appointed by the emperor.

In practice, especially under the Han, the governmental system was a mixture of feudal structures and a central bureaucracy, all of it in theory under the control of the emperor. The first Han emperor was dependent on military allies that made him victorious in a struggle for dynastic succession upon the death of Shi Huangdi. He rewarded his major followers with small kingdoms that initially were largely independent of imperial control.

For the first several decades of the Western Han dynasty, these semi-independent rulers controlled half the empire. The other half was administered by commanderies continued from the Qin dynasty and more closely under the emperor's control. Gradually, the kingdoms were reduced in number as emperors replaced heirless or rebellious kings with men bound to the emperor by family ties. The success of this systematic assault on the kingdoms brought the interior of China firmly under imperial control by 141 BCE, at least for a time.

The reign of Emperor Wu di (r. 141–87 BCE) was the high point of Han imperial power, but the conflict between wealthy and powerful subjects and the emperor never entirely disappeared. In fact, the Western Han dynasty fell as a result of it in 9 CE. A succession of child emperors had weakened the imperial structure and created a power vacuum at the center. Severe flooding and agricultural crisis drove many disgruntled peasants toward banditry and into rebel armies as military strongmen and warlords reasserted their power. When the Han emperor died without heirs in 5 CE, his mother appointed Wang Mang as regent. He soon installed himself as emperor and declared the Xin dynasty in 9 CE. He tried to institute radical land reform programs but was resisted by the great landlords. After over a decade of civil war, Wang Mang was dethroned in 23 CE and the Eastern or Later Han dynasty was established in 25 CE. Not surprisingly, it was dependent on the powerful landed families that supported it.

Powerful regional clans competed with one another for imperial influence and placement in the official bureaucracy, and the successful ones were those whose daughters became empresses and whose sons married imperial princesses. Ruthless factionalism marked imperial government as clans jockeyed for control of the empire's administration and the wealth that could be acquired from it.

At the same time, more and more tribes were moving inside the frontiers of the empire, tribes whose loyalty the emperor could not command. The imperial court gradually discovered that it could not mobilize an army to protect the frontiers or enforce imperial rule in distant provinces. Ultimately, the Eastern Han court concentrated on securing the eastern part of China and left the west and northwest defenseless. Provincial governors there were left to their own devices and by the late second century had become effectively autonomous, with armies answering only to them. Great families also created private armies, and the result was the dissolution of imperial power and the triumph of **warlordism** as the empire fragmented into local power bases that provided for their own self-defense. In 220, the last Han emperor abdicated, beginning the period of the Three Kingdoms.

Ideology and Legitimacy: Heaven's Mandate, Law, and Confucianism

Despite the sometimes-fragmented political order, the distinct regional cultures of China were transcended and unified by an imperial idea. Whatever the reality of power on the ground, there is no question that under the Qin and Han the political structure was centered on the person of the emperor. He was recognized by all as the embodiment of the state, which radiated out from his person. This meant that whoever was close to the emperor wielded enormous power.

Shi Huangdi, the first Qin emperor, actively asserted his godlike power, and the subsequent Han rulers elaborated on the old Zhou doctrine that the emperor ruled as the Son of Heaven with a mandate received from the highest celestial power. The emperor was thus the agent of that deity on earth, the possessor of a sacred legitimacy that theoretically commanded unquestioned obedience.

As an order was perceived in the cosmos, the Son of Heaven was charged with replicating it on earth. To visualize and reinforce his cosmic claims to authority, Shi Huangdi even launched a major building program to transform his capital city into a microcosm of the universe, complete with a new palace compound patterned on the North Star and the Big Dipper.

Religion in classical China had no systematic mythology about origins of the universe or the deeds of gods. There was a general belief that two realms existed in parallel, the visible world of mortals and the invisible one of spirits, and that there were shared points of contact between them, notably at shrines and sacrificial altars. The Qin emperor promoted a state cult to worship natural deities with sacrifices on outdoor altars on mountain peaks or hills in the territories he had brought under his rule. The purpose of the ritual was to mark the emperor's territorial sovereignty and to enlist the invisible world of the spirits in his claim to power. During the last years of the Western Han and especially under Wang Mang, the state cult of worship became a sacrifice more generally to "Heaven," justifying the emperor's claim to power as a dispensation from Heaven.

The emperor was also the supreme judge and source of all law, and again, Shi Huangdi was the initiator of a system that would last for 2,000 years. He oversaw the creation of a written legal code based on his decrees. Qin legalism was aimed at coercing subjects to obey the dictates of the state and thereby preserve social order. It was not intended to protect individual rights. Imperial legislation under the Han promoted a model of a hierarchical social system resting on a set of rules of behavior inspired by the teachings of Confucius, who lived in the sixth and fifth century BCE.

The Han promoted Confucian ideals that favored a well-ordered, hierarchical, and unified state managed by scholarly civilian officials. Rooted in the idea that the social order was upheld through prescribed laws and rituals that guided individual behavior, Confucianism became formal orthodoxy under the Han. This ethic drew upon the earlier Confucian texts, which by the late Western Han had evolved into a written canon. Though politically unified, the Qin and Han Empires were divided linguistically by a multiplicity of mutually unintelligible spoken languages. A more standardized system of writing, which was deliberately developed during the Qin dynasty, was a potent unifying force, for through it was expressed a state-sponsored common body of Confucian literature that sanctioned the state's existence and was conveyed by a dominant elite.

The Confucian canon taught that the purpose of government, and thus the moral duty of the emperor, was to teach the Confucian ideals to the people through education. The valuing of education was rooted in the Confucian assumption that humans carried within them a creative potential for improvement. Indeed, the concept of the educated gentleman was an example of the realization of this potential, and it blended seamlessly into the Confucian emphasis on social status and hierarchy.

The Confucian precept that behavior can be transformed through teaching and education inspired the creation of the Imperial University, first established under the Western Han emperor Wu di in 124 BCE. At first, this institution was designed to produce a cadre of scholars who would study Confucian texts and disseminate them throughout the empire. This was a task made easier by the increasing availability of books written on the newly invented paper.

By the end of the Western Han, 30,000 students attended the university. By then, it was recognized as a school for civic scholar-officials and one of the primary routes to imperial office and government administration. A network of official schools had been established by then as well, reaching all the way to local communities. These official schools became an important channel for the spreading of Confucian ideals, and they continued to fulfill this function into subsequent dynasties.

Social distinction and elite status increasingly were acquired through education and officialdom. Aspiring students were funneled through schools, some gaining entrance to the university and, after successfully passing state exams, likely found appointment to the imperial bureaucracy. The ideal of a meritocracy took hold, although we should guard against overestimating its sweep, for many students were admitted to the university and into officialdom through recommendations from influential and powerful patrons. Nonetheless, the ideal of the cultured, educated gentleman and government official remained long after the Han dynasties had disappeared.

Taxes and Infrastructure

Like Roman emperors, Qin rulers even before Shi Huangdi viewed agricultural productivity as crucial to a strong military and sought ways to extract for warfare as many resources as possible from their subjects. As in Rome, funding of the military and other administrative costs was primarily accomplished by taxation. The Qin emperor continued earlier Qin practices by imposing a property tax and a poll tax. The amount of the property tax was determined by the expected agricultural yield of a plot of land while the poll tax was levied on individuals. The Han continued these taxes (as well as taxes on merchants for their commerce), and though the land tax rate was reduced, the poll taxes were often increased, granting little benefit to the peasantry.

The rivers of the central plain of North China were prone to flooding, demanding from the state or landlords some form of flood control to protect the land's productivity and the taxes and rents squeezed from it. Supplying the capital cities of Qin Xianyang, Western Han Chang'an, and Eastern Han Luoyang with adequate food supplies was another imperative for emperors. Consequently, rulers and wealthy families alike built dikes and sluices to mitigate flooding and to channel water for irrigation.

Canal building also became a prime concern of the state and one that would remain so for subsequent dynasties. The Qin emperor constructed an extensive system of canals that made possible the uninterrupted transport of grain and other goods for over 1,000 miles. It stretched from the Yangtze River to the south, eventually connecting with the West River and reaching all the way to Guangzhou. In the 60s CE, the Eastern Han emperor organized a huge project to repair the system, again to control flooding and to irrigate fields but also to power watermills. Shortly thereafter, there is evidence for a significant rise in agricultural output in the regions where the canals were repaired, suggesting the measures had a notable impact.

The Qin emperor was a tireless builder of infrastructure, for he also built a network of earthen roads radiating from the capital, Xianyang. Intended for troop deployment and administrative communication, the network extended over 4,200 miles, with a special lane reserved for official couriers.

The network was extended even more by the Western Han rulers, who paved the roads with gravel, built bridges, and constructed rest houses for travelers and relay stations for government messengers. The government certainly recognized that such roads were useful for trade, for they also set up government checkpoints on them and assessed taxes on goods in transit.

Historical documents leave little doubt that Qin and Han officials pursued policies with an eye toward the economy. The Qin emperor imposed a standard scale of weights and measures to be used by all merchants in all transactions, a system continued under the Han. He also created a monetary system based in bronze coins of standard value.

The Han inherited the Qin monetary system, but the new dynasty's initial weakness made it impossible for the emperor to enforce a state monopoly on mints. For a time, other coinages circulated alongside the imperial stamp. By 112 BCE, however, the imperial government under Wu di was able to uphold a state monopoly on coin production, one that was maintained until 170 CE. Silver and gold coin joined bronze. Silver coins increased in quantity and importance relative to gold, but bronze coinage continued to be the most prevalent, especially in local market transactions. During the last century of the Western Han dynasty, perhaps as many as 28 billion coins were struck, and though that number may be inferior to the Roman issue in its first two imperial centuries, it is clear evidence that the Chinese economy was extensively monetized.

It is impossible to measure economic growth in antiquity with any degree of accuracy, but as with the Roman experience, classical China reveals varieties of policies and developments that point to growth. A closer inspection of the land seems to confirm this conclusion.

The State, the Peasant, and the Landlord

Carbohydrates from grain were the primary food source for everyone in antiquity everywhere in the world, one legacy of the Agricultural Revolution. Among the many ramifications of this revolution was creating value in land, the primary producer of surplus and, therefore, wealth. In classical China, the peasantry, who comprised 90 percent of the population, lived and worked on the land and was concentrated on the central plain of North China where the **loess soil** was very fertile, light, and therefore easily plowed. Because the topsoil was blown onto the plain from the west, the land was regularly replenished with nutrients and so required minimal crop rotation. Millet and wheat were the main crops grown. The land here, therefore, was highly productive and supported a growing population, in the countryside as well in cities.

Land and Taxes

Since 350 BCE, the Qin rulers had legally permitted the private ownership of land and the right of individuals to buy or sell it. In exchange for this right, peasants were required to pay taxes to the state and to provide labor and military service for its needs. By the time of the Qin and Han dynasties, many Chinese farmers possessed their own land registered in their own names and could dispose of it freely. The government endorsed the ideal that the independent peasant family farm was the foundation of social stability, an ideal that would be echoed by subsequent dynasties for centuries.

Behind this ideal image of the stable family farm is a reality of peasant life that was far from idyllic. Many peasants, in fact, lived on the brink of ruin. Chao Cuo, an imperial official, left an account in the mid-second century BCE that paints a grim picture:

> In a farming family of five members ... their arable land is no more than one hundred *mu* [11.3 acres]. ... Farmers plow in spring, weed in summer, reap in autumn, and store in winter. They cut undergrowth and wood for fuel and render labor services to the government. They cannot avoid wind and dust in spring, sultry heat in summer, dampness and rain in autumn, and cold and ice in winter. Thus all year round they cannot afford to take even a day's rest. ... Although they work as hard as this they still have to bear calamities of flood and drought.[1]

The Qin and Han imperial governments shared a theoretical commitment to protect landowning peasant farmers to secure the tax base, but taxes, as Chao Cuo observed, could have the opposite effect of the agrarian stability than the government desired. "Sometime taxes," Chao continues in the same account, "are collected quite unexpectedly. ... To meet this demand farmers have to sell their possessions at half-price, and those who are destitute have to borrow money at two-hundred percent interest. Eventually they have to sell fields and dwellings, sometimes even sell children and grandchildren into slavery in order to pay back the loan."[2]

Everyone in the government shared the assumption about the importance of agriculture and its contribution through taxes to the imperial treasury, but during the Western Han dynasty and continuing into the Eastern dynasty, two political camps emerged who differed sharply in how this fiscal objective could be best achieved. One group urged free enterprise in the countryside, assuming that this would encourage cultivators to develop unworked plots and so produce new wealth and increase state revenues. They accepted the growth of large, landed estates, which they assumed would accompany free enterprise, as a necessary consequence so long as they could be taxed effectively. The other group took an opposing position, asserting that the growth of large estates would widen the gap

---

1 Mark Edward Lewis, *The Early Chinese Empires: Qin and Han* (Cambridge, MA: Harvard University Press, 2007), 110–111.

2 Lewis, *Early Chinese Empires*, 111.

between rich and poor and swell the class of an impoverished, landless peasantry. This, in turn, would reduce the revenue stream of taxes for the government.

The Growth of Landed Estates

In reality, little could stop the growth of estates in the hands of wealthy landowners and the accelerating social and economic inequality that came with it. Indeed, emperors themselves were partly responsible for this. All new land brought into the empire by conquest was theoretically owned by the emperor, who could dispose of it as he saw fit. In practice, he usually distributed much of it to loyal aristocrats. The early Western Han emperors were notable in this regard. These aristocrats in turn put peasants to work on the land and extracted a percentage of its production in rents or shared crops. Deference and dependency accompanied these developments, supported by the Confucian ideal of hierarchical social relations.

Private land ownership and a free market in land sales allowed for the further concentration of wealth and an ever-growing gap between rich and poor. Under the Han, a clear, widening gulf between wealthy landlords and the peasantry occurred. The wealthy increasingly bought up land from an increasingly distressed peasantry.

Wars of the Han emperors, especially against the Xiongnu on the northern frontier, were a powerful catalyst for this development because the emperors increasingly required that taxes be paid in cash so they could quickly supply and pay their troops. Peasants were forced onto the market to sell their produce for money, or, as Chao Cuo pointed out, they were forced to borrow. Imperial taxation in cash was relentless, and when poor harvests stared peasants who were already poised on the edge of subsistence in the face, indebtedness to large landowners at ruinous interest rates was often the only recourse. Many peasants became entrapped in a spiral of debt and ultimately lost their land through foreclosure to wealthy landlords and aspiring merchants. This contributed to the growth of landed estates. These unfortunate peasants became rent-paying tenants or sharecroppers, or they drifted to cities.

The commercial tax on merchants was double the land tax, so merchants invested their profits from trade in lower taxed land, contributing further to the alienation of peasant land as merchants became ready buyers of it. Over time, many merchants merged into the landlord elite. Even technological developments (e.g., iron tools, oxen-pulled plows with iron plowshares, the new and expensive combined plow-seeder, brick-lined wells for irrigation, fertilizers, etc.) favored the wealthy. Not only were they costly and thus available only to the rich but they also increased productivity, thereby generating even greater surplus and wealth for their owners. The overall result was galloping inequities on a vast scale.

The Classical period was a time of flourishing wealthy families who maintained local order and were well-connected with the center of power, as they combined the ownership of land with office holding in the imperial bureaucracy. These families invested in land, but the law of **partible inheritance** whereby a father's patrimony had to be divided equally among surviving sons kept estates relatively small (less than one tenth the size of some great Roman estates). Daughters received none of the patrimony but were married into other families.

As a result of the divided inheritances and marriage alliances, enormous networks of kin and clients were built up. Again, the Confucian ideal of unquestioned obedience toward elders, especially the patriarch, supported the system, and heads of these networks could command broad loyalties. Some of these lineages came to dominate their districts or commanderies. At times, major lineages came to dominate entire regions, posing a challenge to central authority, a challenge so great during the later Eastern Han that imperial power disappeared.

Peasant Unrest and the Fall of the Eastern Han Dynasty

Peasant discontent also contributed greatly to the fall of the Eastern Han dynasty. The most serious challenge to Han rule came in the Yellow Turban Rebellion in eastern and central China. Conditions in the countryside were deteriorating in the 170s CE, and many peasants were in the grip of an agrarian crisis marked by drought, flood, famine, and epidemics of disease. Many were displaced from their farms.

Zhang Jue, a charismatic adherent of a Daoist messianic religious sect that had emerged in midcentury, predicted the Han dynasty would soon be replaced. Zhang was a popular healer who taught that illness resulted from sin and could be healed by confession and faith in the Daoist vision. He rallied a peasant army to his banner, thousands of them convinced that the drought, famines, flood, and disease were indicators that the Han emperor had lost his mandate of heaven and would soon fall from power. Zhang, called the "General of Heaven" by his followers who wore yellow turbans or scarves to identify themselves, vowed that his movement had the blessing of Heaven and would supplant the Han.

Initially, his army had success on the battlefield, but when Zhang died in the summer of 184, ironically from an illness, the Han armies turned the tide. By early 185, the emperor proclaimed that the rebellion had been crushed, but at great cost. Homeless peasants were left destitute by the wars, and bands of bandits roamed the countryside. The Han forces were in no position to do anything about them. Local military leaders, landlords, and administrators with private armies of their own stepped into the breach, securing power for themselves but hastening the collapse of the Han dynasty in 220.

The Economy of Classical China

During the Han dynasties, despite the inequalities of land distribution and peasant distress, evidence points to significant agricultural growth. Innovations in farming technology certainly contributed to it. Growth also occurred in manufacturing—paper, iron, porcelain, and, above all, silk. And equally certain, the growing populations of cities, especially in the capitals, stimulated demand among consumers for an agricultural surplus and a diversifying range of manufactured goods. Although the government remained wary of the effect of commerce on society and tried to regulate economic transactions, especially within the walls of the cities, much economic activity escaped its purview.

Technology and Production

The inequities of land ownership did not seem to hinder agricultural growth during the Han dynasty, at least until 184 CE when the peasant-led Yellow Turban Rebellion staggered the empire. Improvement in farm technology was certainly a contributing factor. The introduction of iron implements and the use of oxen-pulled plows appeared in the seventh century BCE and spread to more areas during the Warring States period, but it was under the Han when these techniques became widespread as plows with iron-tipped plowshares became common on the large estates. When joined with the employment of a combined plow-seeder, a new system of alternating fields, wider use of fertilizers, and the promotion of irrigation and flood control that brought tens of thousands of more productive acres into cultivation, the volume of agricultural production increased significantly.

Changes in technology beyond the agricultural sector also had an impact on economic growth. During the Han period, Chinese craftsmen learned how to make paper out of silk and later out of rice straw and bamboo wood pulp. Papermaking was driven by the mounting demand from the government's outpouring of official documents, from literary works, and from books used in proliferating schools.

There is evidence for iron smelting in China by 700 BCE. During the Han period, the quality of cast iron improved, as water-powered bellows were used in a rudimentary blast furnace where the metal was melted and the carbon blown away. Removing the carbon hardened the finished product and in some cases produced steel. The Eastern Han dynasty also witnessed the manufacturing of an early form of porcelain. Other luxury goods, like lacquerware, also appear even more widespread and of higher quality than during the Western Han dynasty.

Manufacturing fell into two categories: private enterprises and state-controlled manufactories. Han rulers seem to have controlled the salt and especially the iron industry. Evidence exists for large, state-run iron foundries with thousands of workers turning out enormous quantities of identical objects. This is the first known instance of mass production in history. Large-scale private operations can be found under the Han too. Brewing, for example, was widespread and profitable.

As significant as the iron, salt, or brewing industries were, they were dwarfed by silk production. The silk industry was already widely developed in China during the Warring States period where, along with hemp, it was a common and ordinary textile. Its production and use expanded considerably during the Qin and Han dynasties and, importantly, made its first journeys westward.

Silk thread comes from the cocoon of the silk worm that feeds on mulberry leaves. The cocoon, comprised of filaments secreted by the worm, was boiled and the worms killed before they hatched. The cocoons were then unraveled and the filaments spooled. One cocoon could have a continuous thread 1,000–2,000 feet long. The filaments were then twisted, and the resulting thread was not only lustrous and smooth but also strong. To get some idea of the scale of this industry, consider that a square yard of woven silk cloth required the filaments from 3,000 cocoons, and a roll or "bolt" of the fabric was typically 50 yards in length. And millions of rolls were produced annually throughout China.

As demand for the textile grew, especially for the luxurious items like brocades, **sericulture** and textile manufacturing spread across North China and even crept southwards (although southern silk was for a long time of lesser quality). Women did most of the textile manufacturing. In countless peasant homes, women wove as men worked the fields. Most silk cloth was produced by peasants in a decentralized cottage industry, but large-scale production also took place in workshops owned by the state or great families. These enterprises employed some men, but most of the workers were women. Some great families employed up to 700 women to tend the cocoons, produce the thread, and weave the silk cloth, with the wives of the landlord organizing the production operations and the sale.

The Importance of Cities

Although Classical China remained an overwhelmingly rural society, it did experience a dramatic growth in its urban populations. Many cities, especially the Han capitals of Chang'an and later Luoyang, were now completely different in terms of size and complexity from earlier Chinese cities. Under the Eastern Han, Luoyang likely reached a half million inhabitants. Cities now presented a dramatically greater array of consumption opportunities, and Han China's growing class of wealthy consumers were ready and eager customers.

Because the historical records only inform us about capital cities in any detail, we must confine our discussion to them. We do know that during the Warring States period, capital cities became physically divided between economic and political functions. Craft and commerce buzzed in one part, while the business of government was carried on in another. The two sectors eyed one another with mutual suspicion. Artisans and merchants were wary of government regulations that would curtail their profits. Rulers, protectors of a social ideal that prized closed, stable relations, were fearful of the instability and potential subversion that commercial activity could cause.

Such spatial organization and mutual distrust continued into the imperial period. Under the Qin and Han, the inner city of the capital comprised the imperial palace compound and was the site of state functions and the home of the political elite. The outer city contained the residential areas that clustered around the marketplaces.

In the Western Han capital of Chang'an, the outer city had two enormous marketplaces, the western and eastern. The western market, the larger of the two, spanned a half million square meters. Both markets were laid out on a grid, with each of four quadrants divided in rows containing shops grouped by product. At the center of it all was a two-story government observation tower.

The centrality and prominence of the government tower reflects the state's unease with commerce and the perceived necessity to control it. Indeed, both Qin and Han rulers assumed that every aspect of the economy should be closely controlled by the government, and supervision of the market was a clear reflection of that assumption. Qin law, for example, decreed that objects for sale in the market must have price tags attached to them. Moreover, shopkeepers and merchants had to keep written records of all transactions and make them available to government inspection at end of the day so that fraud could be detected and, of course, so that taxes could be collected.

Trade and Tribute

As trade grew, merchants benefited. The government's suspicion of commerce extended to the merchant class, but despite this official wariness, many merchant families thrived. Some of the more successful were involved in the movement of goods from China to its hostile, nomadic neighbor to the north, the Xiongnu. As a concession for peace, the Xiongnu demanded the payment of tribute from China, a tribute paid largely in silk. But as silk moved westward, following the demand for it as far away as Rome, products from the west and coveted horses from central Asia moved toward China, and the famous trade route called the Silk Road came into being.

The Role of Merchants

The Han inherited from the Qin the belief that the government had a duty to manage the economy and harbored fears of the market because of the ease with which it seemed to escape government regulation. The rulers also knew, however, that a monetized economy channeled surplus goods to market and through taxation to the imperial treasury. Merchants benefited from the monetized economy as well, and they thrived under the Han despite being taxed heavily, prohibited from holding office, and relegated to the bottom of the Confucian social hierarchy.

Despite this antimercantile ethos, large-scale operators made vast fortunes by speculative buying of commodities from all over China (e.g., bamboo, gemstones, fish, rhinoceros horn, horses, rugs, etc.), which were often protected from regulation by powerful families and even government officials. It was far from rare, then, for a merchant to live a life of luxury that exceeded even that of his social superiors. Some merchants even accumulated enough wealth to acquire landed estates.

Merchants were involved in trade of a vast array of agricultural and manufactured products and moved goods along the elaborate network of rivers, canals, and roads. They also benefited from the movement of goods across the Chinese frontier, a result of the bellicose relationship between the Han and their nomadic neighbors to the northwest, the Xiongnu.

The Xiongnu, Silk, and Horses

In 200 BCE, Han forces suffered a devastating defeat by the Xiongnu, and the peace arrangement demanded an annual payment to the victors of gold, grain, and, most importantly, rolls of silk cloth. Silk had long been the most common and ordinary textile in China, but now vast quantities of it (recall that each roll, or bolt, of silk cloth measured up to 50 yards in length) were passed to the Xiongnu. Some of it the nomads kept as symbols of power and authority, but most of it they traded west toward Iran and the Mediterranean. For the silk, they received in return other cherished goods, like wine, spices, woolens, red coral, and glass. Much of this trade was then channeled on to China. For the first time, therefore, the eastern and western ends of the Eurasian landmass were linked by trade. The famous Silk Road was born.

The Chinese sent silk to the Xiongnu as concessions for peace, but they also traded with the nomads for something they desperately needed but could not produce in sufficient quantity in China—horses. The Chinese emperor had an insatiable demand for horses for his cavalry to counter the horse-mounted armies of the Xiongnu, and he looked westward for the prized animals. The Chinese cherished a particular breed of horse from far-off Ferghana in central Asia, one with short legs, a stout chest, and great stamina. Thousands of the "heavenly horses" of Ferghana (present day Uzbekistan) were herded eastward and absorbed into the imperial cavalry.

The Chinese called the exchange of silk for horses "tribute," the symbolic submission of the Xiongnu to the Son of Heaven, the Chinese emperor. According to the Chinese, the emperor was the center of the world and the father of his subjects through the Mandate of Heaven, and tribute was required to recognize this supremacy. In exchange for the tribute, the emperor graciously offered gifts of equal or greater value. The nomads had no interest in conquering China (they numbered only about 1 million compared to the over 50 million Chinese). Their raids of Chinese settlements along the frontier were provocations to force the Chinese to offer concessions and to open their markets to trade with the nomads in exchange for peace.

The Xiongnu problem was the dominant foreign policy issue under the Han, and emperors shifted between launching military expeditions of conquest and assuming a defensive posture behind fortifications along the frontier. Under the Emperor Wu di, the Great Wall was extended northwest into the **Hexi Corridor** (present-day Gansu province) to the Jade Gate at the eastern reaches of the **Takla Makan Desert**, and garrisons of soldiers were stationed there to protect trade routes and newly established agricultural settlements.

Seeking allies to the west of the Xiongnu to outflank them, Wu di sent an expedition led by Zhang Qian in 138 BCE. An intrepid traveler, Zhang crossed thousands of miles through central Asia for 13 years and was the first official diplomat to bring back reliable information about the peoples of central and western Asia to the Chinese imperial court. His numerous and detailed reports were copied into the *Records of the Grand Historian*, a chronicle compiled by Sima Qian sometime before his death in 86 BCE. The information provided by Zhang Qian played an important pioneering role in the extension of the Han Empire westward as well as the emergence of the Silk Road. Zhang returned 13 years later with no allies, but the emperor still launched a military expedition against the Xiongnu in 120 BCE. Han armies won decisive battles against the nomads, moved into western regions, and reached Ferghana in 101 BCE.

Zhang provided Wu di a vast storehouse of new information, so diligently and thoroughly recorded by Zhang, about the cultures and economies of peoples to the west who were only vaguely known to the Chinese before Zhang Qian's expedition. Following Zhang Qian's embassy and report and Han control of the Tarim Basin, trade between China and central and western Asia began to flourish. After the success of Zhang Qian, and relying upon information contained in his reports, many more Chinese missions were sent westward, paving the way for the further development of the Silk Road.

The Silk Road

Whatever Wu di's political and military objectives, both the securing of the Hexi Corridor and the military ventures westward had important trade results, as they increased the security of goods moving along the Silk Road just when Roman demand for eastern goods was increasing. Recall that the Romans had conquered Egypt in the first century BCE and so gained access to eastern trade and developed a taste for eastern products like silk. Not surprisingly, the volume of goods, especially silk, moving along this trade route increased. As Bān Zhāo and Ban Gu, the authors of the *History of the Han Dynasty*, wrote, "Foreign traders and merchants knock on the gates of the Great Wall every day."[3]

Han armies eventually withdrew from the western regions beyond the Jade Gate. When merchants moved their caravans of luxury goods beyond this point, they were confronted by the Takla Makan Desert. The Silk Road, or more accurately roads, branched into northern and southern routes (see Map 7.4).

Chinese silk continued to ply its way westward along these routes for centuries, but in addition to this land route, a sea route was opened. In the 200s CE,

---

3   Xinru Liu, *Ancient India and Ancient China: Trade and Religious Exchanges, AD 1–600* (Delhi: Oxford University Press, 1988), 18.

Chinese sources refer to Indian ships in the South China Sea capable of carrying up to 700 people and 260 tons of cargo. The evidence is scanty, but it seems likely that maritime trade in the early centuries of the Common Era was substantial. Eastern goods, such as silk, were arriving in Roman markets in such quantities that eventually in Rome silk ceased to be a rare luxury item and came within the budget of many consumers. By the end of the fourth century CE, the Roman author Ammianus Marcellinus could write that all classes of Romans were wearing it. Further testimony to the vibrant trade between east and west are Roman coins from 14–275 CE uncovered in Shanxi province, as well as Alexandrian glass, Arabian frankincense and myrrh, Mediterranean red coral, and Alexandrian linen.

The collapse of the Roman and Han Empires and the diseases and population contraction that accompanied it dampened this long-distance trade but did not extinguish it. During the post-Han period, trade would still flourish in some places, as evidenced by the existence of prosperous merchants like Liu Pao. He had a house built in every provincial capital, and he employed messengers and stabled horses to keep himself informed of markets, prices, and politics. It was said that his business expanded wherever a cart or ship could reach, and his luxurious lifestyle was equal to many a prince.

Silk continued as the dominant Chinese commodity going west well after the demise of the Eastern Han Empire in 220 CE. Although the emergence of a silk industry in Byzantium and Persia in the fourth century CE gradually shifted the demand from cloth to raw silk, the surge in Indian demand for Chinese silk fabrics increased at this time. Buddhist monasteries and stupas, structures usually housing the ashes of Buddhist monks and serving as sites of meditation, were decorated in silk. The market for silk grew as the number of Buddhist stupas and monasteries increased along the southern route of the Silk Road.

Review Questions

1. How did the Qin and Han emperors unify and consolidate their rule in China between 221 BCE and 220 CE?
2. How did the changes in Chinese agriculture during the Qin and Han dynasties affect the state, the aristocratic landlords, and the peasantry?
3. What role did technology and urbanization play in the changes in the Chinese economy during the Qin and Han dynasties?
4. What was the "Silk Road," and why did it appear when it did?

Further Readings

Adshead, S.A.M. *China in World History*. New York: St. Martin's Press, 2000.

Barfield, Thomas J. *The Perilous Frontier: Nomadic Empires and China, 221 BC to AD 1757*. Oxford: Blackwell, 1989.

Bentley, Jerry H. *Old World Encounters: Cross-Cultural Contacts and Exchanges in Pre-Modern Times*. Oxford: Oxford University Press, 1993.

Boulnois, Luce. *Silk Road: Monks, Warriors and Merchants*. Translated by Helen Loveday. Hong Kong: Odyssey Books, 2008.

Chang, Chun-shu. *The Rise of the Chinese Empire: Frontier, Immigration, and Empire in Han China, 130 BC–AD 157*. Ann Arbor: University of Michigan Press, 2007.

Di Cosmo, Nicola. *Ancient China and Its Enemies: The Rise of Nomadic Power in East Asian History*. Cambridge: Cambridge University Press, 2002.

Holcombe, Charles. *The Genesis of East Asia, 221 BC–AD 907*. Honolulu: Association of Asian Studies and University of Hawaii Press, 2001.

Hsu, Cho-yun. *Han Agriculture: The Formation of Early Chinese Agrarian Economy (206 BC–AD 220)*. Edited by Jack L. Dull. Seattle: University of Washington Press, 1980.

Lewis, Mark Edward. *The Early Chinese Empires: Qin and Han*. Cambridge, MA: Harvard University Press, 2007.

Liu, Xinru. *Ancient India and Ancient China: Trade and Religious Exchanges, AD 1-600*. Delhi: Oxford University Press, 1988.

Scheidel, Walter, ed. *Rome and China: Comparative Perspectives on Ancient World Empires*. Oxford: Oxford University Press, 2009.

Twitchett, Denis, and Michael Lowe, eds. *The Cambridge History of China, Volume 1: The Ch'in and Han Empires, 221 BC–AD 220*. Cambridge: Cambridge University Press, 1986.

Figure Credit

Map 8.1: Adapted from: https://www.freeman-pedia.com/classicalchina.

CHAPTER 9

Empires and the Silk Road in Asia, ca. 200 BCE–ca. 850 CE

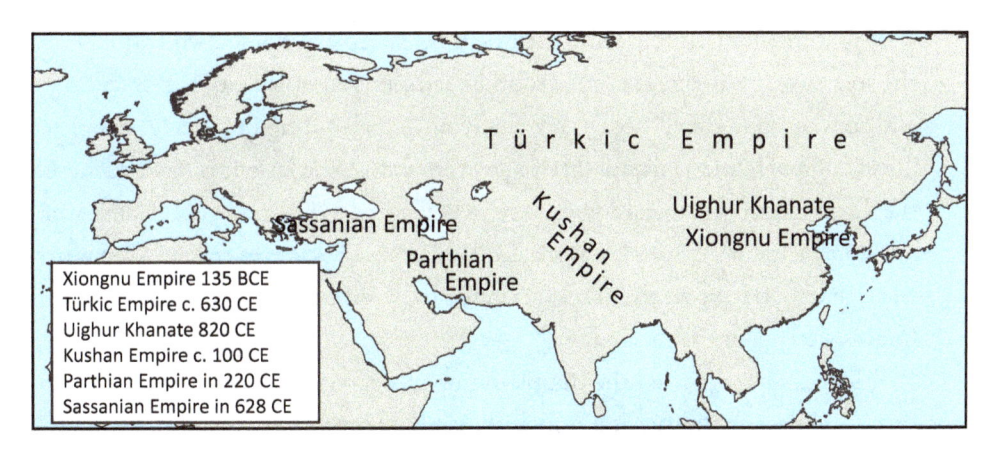

MAP 9.1   Empires of the Silk Road

The Ecosystem of Central Asia

Central and Southwest Asia's diverse environment—its physical topography, climate, and ecosystem—shaped, but did not determine, the course of historical events. Topographical formations of grassy **steppes**, towering mountains, high nearly barren plateaus, and scorching desert punctuated by occasional oases directed and hindered movement of both people and things, but humans found ways to overcome often daunting physical conditions as they pursued wealth and power by raiding, invading, or trading.

From north to south, central Asia sits between the subarctic forest zone and the soaring Himalaya Mountains. These mountains were thrust upward by a primordial geological event, the crashing of the Indian subcontinent into Asia. South of the northern forests is a sweeping horizontal belt of grassy steppe.

Further south, in the center of central Asia, soar more mountains, the Tian Shan range. As we plunge down their southern slopes, we reach the Tarim Basin with its forbidding desert that stretches south to the foothills of the Kunlun Mountain range. Indeed, it is this desert, the Takla Makan, that will loom large in our story about the process that connected the East and the West. This desert's arid climate and shifting sands made its center humanly impassable, but dotting its northern and southern rims were oases, replenished by mountain snowmelt. Further east in southwestern Asia, high nearly barren plateaus and more mountains rise, covering the landmass nearly all the way to the shores of the Mediterranean Sea. Dotted here and there we find some land suitable for agriculture, but not much, because not enough rain falls in these parts of Asia to sustain it.

The environment may shape the course of historical events, but humans adapt to it. Inhabitants of the grassy steppe, finding widespread agriculture impossible, were pastoral nomads following their herds of sheep and horses, while further to the southwest, some populations found conditions right for cultivation of crops and so were more likely sedentary, many of them residing in cities. As another illustration of human adaptability to environment, consider how people rendered the Tarim Basin passable. Horses were well-adapted to the grassy steppe but were not suitable for hauling goods in the Takla Makan. Packhorses required too much water and food to cross the desert stretches between oases. Moreover, their small hooves were ill-suited to sand.

Hence, voyagers used the double-humped Bactrian camel. This animal can go several days without water and with minimal food (it stores fat in its humps and draws energy from them and so has greater endurance than horses), and hot sand proved no obstacle, as this camel has broad hooves with thick pads.

Although goods from China may have trickled west before 200 BCE, it was during the early years of the Han dynasty that we find Chinese goods, above all silk, moving west in greater volume than ever before. The concessions demanded of the Chinese by the Xiongnu (see Chapter 8), were paid in silk and fed this growing current of trade at this time. As traders trekked westward, they were channeled by topography through the Hexi Corridor (in present-day Gansu Province) and, emerging from its western terminus at the Jade Gate, were plunged into the Takla Makan. Following either the northern or southern routes, their caravans emerged from the desert's western end at Kashgar and linked up with trade routes that were already crisscrossing western and southwestern Asia, linking Egypt, Mesopotamia, and the subcontinent India. A trans-Asia connection to China, the Silk Road, had opened.

People of the Steppe

Human habitation in the steppe environment was generally nomadic. The economies of the people of the steppe were largely pastoral, although there were some small pockets of agriculture where wheat, barley, and millet were grown. Nonetheless, the topography of the habitat encouraged pastoralism because the steppe was grassland ideal for herding domesticated animals—sheep and especially horses—but with insufficient rainfall to support crop cultivation on a large scale. The various tribes of the steppe wandered far and wide grazing their animals, one reason the empires that some of these tribes, such as Xiongnu, Türks, and Uighurs established, were so vast.

Horse-Riding Nomads

Chinese sources first mention horse-riding nomads on the steppe around 900 BCE. These nomads will continue to play a fundamental historical role for another 2,500 years.

For the two and a half millennia of their historical prominence, these dominant tribes of the steppe—Xiongnu, Türk, Uighur, and Mongol (see Chapter 13), to name the most important—shared some basic characteristics.

Most of the time, these tribes were on the move, living in temporary, felt huts as they followed their herds across the grasslands. Their daughters became wives in other clans, forging important bonds that held these tribes together through marriage alliances and kinship groups. They raised their sons to be hunters, and in times of war, which were frequent, all young men were enlisted in the army. These tribes were deeply militarized, comprising tens of thousands of fierce, horse-mounted warriors highly adept with the bow and arrow.

They shared a political and military organization that centered upon a supreme chief who usually claimed a divine mandate or blessing to rule and commanded a confederation of clans within the tribe. Arrayed beneath the chief were kings or lesser chieftains, then commanders and subcommanders of the armies. Significantly, these imperial confederacies had limited bureaucracies—the imperial government only handled warfare and foreign affairs—and so with no system of centralized government to speak of, rulers could not levy formal and regular taxation. The essential resources to maintain the power structure, we need to emphasize, had to come from outside, primarily from neighboring sedentary peoples, which is why these people of the steppe were raiders, invaders, and traders.

From the moment nomad cavalry appeared on the Chinese frontier, a particular relationship between the pastoral nomads and the sedentary Chinese emerged. In effect, each had goods the other desired, and for over two millennia, nomads and the Chinese moved such quantities of these goods between them that the famous Silk Road became a highway linking the East and West of Asia. Nomads had horses, meat, and animal fiber to offer, while the Chinese countered with metals, grain, and silk.

Chinese historians of the time bewailed the predatory actions of the nomads, vilifying their "barbaric" militarism and devastating raids along the frontier, but these are biased sources. Nomads were no more vicious in battle than the Chinese, nor more predatory upon their enemies.

The nomads, at least before the Mongols, however, had no territorial designs upon China. The well-documented frontier raids by the nomads were common and did result in plunder for them, but their motive was to coerce the Chinese to a payment of tribute to forestall more raids and, very importantly, to open the Chinese frontier market towns to nomadic trade. Throughout their history, trading was the lifeblood of the nomadic peoples, and access to Chinese markets was essential for their survival. Violence was a means to gain this access.

The Xiongnu Empire

The Xiongnu Empire, the result of an imperial confederacy formed in 209 BCE, eventually stretched from northwestern China to Bactria and lasted nearly four centuries. In the second century BCE, their empire underwent significant expansion, notably by attacking the Yuezhi people in western Gansu. The Yuezhi were defeated in battle in 177 BCE, their chief killed and his skull made into a drinking cup by the victor. They were driven west by the relentless Xiongnu, so far that we soon begin to hear of them in Greek sources. These refugees also reemerge in history as the founders of the Kushan Empire in India and will play a crucial role in the increasing linkage of the East and the West.

Xiongnu raiding and demands for tribute in concession for peace from the Chinese partly explain the imperialistic ambitions of the Han emperors, notably Wu di. In Chapter 8, we noted that Wu di launched several military campaigns against the Xiongnu and extended Han territorial power as far as Ferghana on the other side of the Tarim Basin by 101 BCE.

Given unstable succession procedures among nomads where sons did not automatically succeed fathers, civil war over accession to the title of **shanyu**, or chieftain, was a regular occurrence. During one of these civils wars, in 48–50 CE, the Han emperor drove a wedge between the warring northern and southern branches of the Xiongnu, and so began the eventual collapse of the Xiongnu Empire. In 216, Han armies definitively defeated the southern Xiongnu, and many of its soldiers were absorbed into the Chinese military. Many settled inside the Great Wall, a fortification begun under Wu di as a means to secure territory seized by the Han armies and settled by Chinese farmers as much as it was intended to keep the nomads out.

From the late first century to the mid-second century CE, the weakened northern Xiongnu were attacked and eventually crushed in 156 CE by the Xianbei tribes from the Mongolian-Manchurian border regions. Although the northern Xiongnu tribes would continue to exist in a scattered and decentralized state, their imperial confederacy dissolved and their empire disappeared. For several centuries, the political map of central Asia then fragmented into smaller states of bands of warriors following a chief.

The Türkic and Uighur Empires

One such band, however, will grow to become the First Türkic Empire (552–630). Nomadic like the Xiongnu, the Türks rose against their overlords in Mongolia and eventually formed an empire in central Asia. Like all nomadic empires, this one was an imperial confederacy of linked tribes, each with its own rulers but under the authority of the **khaghan**. This empire across the steppe was so vast that at its greatest extent it touched China in the east and the Roman Byzantine and Persian Sassanian Empires in the west.

The single empire quickly broke into eastern and western khanates (territories ruled by a khaghan) as a result of civil wars over succession. Nonetheless, under Türkic overlords, cities like Samarkand became commercial hubs in central Eurasia and linchpins of the Eurasian long-distance economy. As with all nomads, trade was essential for the Türks, and their military power allowed the Silk Road to flourish. Trade between the Türks and Chinese thrived, especially horses for silk. Indeed, the silk trade helped bind the nomadic empire together. Already in 550 the Türks sent 50,000 horses to the Chinese frontier to trade, and beginning in 553 and for 20 years thereafter, they extracted a concessionary annual "gift" of 100,000 rolls of silk from the Chinese Western Wei ruler.

All was not peaceful in central Asia, however, in either east or west. In the east, as we will see in Chapter 10, the Tang dynasty unified China in the early seventh century CE. Military action against the Türks, the Chinese reasoned, would not only end costly appeasement arrangements but also, by interrupting the flow of goods to the khaghan, incite civil war among the Türks whose warriors expected their khaghan to reward them with goods. The invasion by the Tang emperor Taizong in 629 had just such an effect. He threw an enormous army into the steppe and routed the Türks, signaling the demise of the eastern khanate of the First Türkic Empire and expanding China's borders deep into central Asia.

A Türkic inscription from the seventh century captures the fate of the Türks:

> The sons of Türkic nobles became slaves to the Chinese people, and their innocent daughters were reduced to serfdom. The nobles, discarding their Türkic titles, accepted those of China and made submission to the Chinese khag[h]an, devoting their labor and their strength to his service for fifty years. For him, both toward the rising sun and westward to the Iron Gates, they launched their expeditions. But to the Chinese khag[h]an they surrendered their empire and their institutions.[1]

By the middle of the next century, yet another nomadic tribal confederacy had arisen, that of the Uighurs. Their steppe empire controlled the lucrative trade routes west of the Hexi Corridor in Gansu and, like countless nomads before them, traded horses for silk. So desperate were the Tang rulers for horses that the Uighurs could extract 50 rolls of silk per horse, resulting in an enormous flow of silk westward considering that thousands of horses were sent to China annually.

In order to control the trade along the Silk Road, the Uighurs established a close relationship with the Sogdian merchants who handled much of the commerce along the trade routes of central Asia. Indeed, perhaps to secure this alliance, in 762 the Uighur khaghan Tengri Bögü converted to the Sogdian religion of **Manichaeism**, cementing a mutually beneficial relationship. The Uighurs profited from the trade, and the Sogdians gained military protection for their caravans.

The wealth coming to the Uighurs from the Silk Road prompted them to depart from previous steppe empires, like the Xiongnu, by establishing a permanent capital city, Ordu Baliq. This city served as a vast storehouse for an enormous inflow of goods and as a transit point for their export, a central place for traders to concentrate, and a political court to coordinate the ruler's role in this burgeoning commerce.

Ordu Baliq proved a tempting target for the Kirghiz, a confederate tribe to the north, who attacked it, sacked it, and killed the Uighur khaghan in 840. The empire collapsed, and the remnants of the Uighur tribes scattered.

---

1 René Grousset, *The Empire of the Steppes: A History of Central Asia*. Trans. Naomi Wahlford. (New Brunswick: Rutgers University Press, 1997), 92–93.

Empires of Southwestern Asia

The empires of Southwest Asia were both similar and noticeably different from their nomadic counterparts of central Asia. The Asian empires were similar, however, in that all were frequently engaged in warfare, and all facilitated and benefited from the commerce that traversed their lands along the Silk Road. Moreover, all rulers—shanyu, khaghan, or king—needed the loyalty of their warriors and aristocrats to remain in power. The biggest differences are that the Kushan, Parthian, and Sassanian Empires of South and Southwest Asia were not states comprised of pastoral nomads. Rather, their inhabitants were largely sedentary, many living in cities.

The Kushan Empire (ca. 124 BCE–ca. 230 CE)

The conquering Xiongnu defeated the Yuezhi in 177 BCE. Some Yuezhi fled south, but the great body of them were driven west. By 130 BCE, the dispersed Yuezhi reached Sogdiana, then pushed into Bactria, conquering and subduing as they went. In 124 BCE, they encountered the Parthians on the northeastern edge of their dominions, even killing the Parthian king in battle. The Yuezhi then settled in Bactria and established a strong kingdom. They allowed the Sogdians and Greek Bactrians to continue to handle trade, preferring to settle on the pasturelands of the area and extract tribute from their subjects in recognition of their overlordship.

Initially, the Yuezhi, reflecting their nomadic roots, comprised a confederation of five tribal groups, but in 50 CE, a tribal chief consolidated his power by defeating other Yuezhi chiefdoms and establishing the Kushan Empire. He expanded his realm southwards across the Hindu Kush Mountains and occupied the Jalalabad valley and Peshawar area all the way to the mouth of the Indus River.

The Kushan ruler thereby controlled the land routes from the central Asian Silk Road to the maritime trade routes that connected India with Roman Egypt at a time (see Chapter 7) when Roman demand for eastern products was accelerating. At the Kushan capital of Khorezm, archeologists have found European bronze statues and glassware as well as Chinese artifacts, such as lacquerware, demonstrating that the Kushans were linked into international commerce that extended from Rome to China.

The Kushan Empire was strategically placed to amass wealth. Many new cities sprang up along the trade routes, and as testimony to the wealth gathered there, palaces and private residences built from fired bricks were constructed. Kushan kings actively supported irrigated agriculture surrounding and supplying the cities. Of one such system at Khorezm, archeologists estimate that it took 15,000 laborers two months to dig the main canal and up to 7,000 workers a year to maintain it.

The Kushan kings claimed a heavenly mandate that legitimized their authority. They ruled through a governmental system they adopted from the Persian Achaemenids where governors maintained social order and collected taxes and tribute. Otherwise, however, the kings left the local administrative institutions to operate as they always had. Although the Kushans left no written documentation about their rule, several kings did stamp coins based on Roman weights and measures, suggesting at least a partially monetized economy existed.

The Kushans heavily patronized Buddhism. By encouraging its spread into China (first evidence in 65 CE), they facilitated not only the spread of one of the world's great religions but also the international commerce that was already growing across the Silk Road. Buddhist monasteries became commercial way stations, offering lodging to travelers and banking operations to merchants. Monasteries were revered for their sanctity, and as sacred places offering trust among strangers, they became prominent sites for economic transactions. Not accidentally, we find monasteries dotting the trade routes between east and west.

Moreover, Mahayana Buddhism, a popular variant of the religion, encouraged the donation of pious material gifts to monasteries and promised donors salvation in the afterlife and happiness in this one. "Seven treasures" were designated as the best gifts, and the gold, silver, lapis lazuli, crystal, coral, agate, and pearls were commodities, along with silk, that were in high demand in international trade. Mahayana Buddhism thus blended the value system of commercial exchange into its basic religious doctrine, and as wealth flowed across the Silk Road, many monasteries were enriched.

Kanishka I was an emperor of the Kushan dynasty in the second century (ca. 127–150 CE). He is known for his expansion of the Kushan Empire and for the spread of Buddhism within it. He ruled an empire that, at its greatest extent, stretched from Turfan in the Tarim Basin to the Gangetic Plain. His conquests and patronage of Buddhism played an important role in the development of the Silk Road. Controlling both the land and sea trade routes between South Asia and Rome seems to have been one of Kanishka's chief imperial goals.

Coins and royal seals issued by Kanishka provide excellent evidence about his reign. Coins, of course, suggest that the economy in which they circulated was at least partially monetized. A number of coins dating to the reign of Kanishka I have been discovered and provide sound evidence for an economy that thrived as the empire straddled important routes of trans-Asian commerce. We may presume that Kanishka struck coins at least in part to facilitate this commerce.

But coins, like royal seals, are also symbols of power. The imagery stamped on a coin or a seal usually portrays the monarch and the attributes of his authority. Frequently, these are religious, as kings associate their power with divinities. Kanishka's coins and seals are no different in this regard, but curiously, they portray images of divinities from three different cultural traditions—Greek, Persian, and Buddhist. This suggests that Kanishka's religious beliefs were either syncretic, an amalgam of various traditions Kanishka was enlisting to sanctify his authority, or that his beliefs shifted over the course of his lifetime.

FIGURE 9.1 A Gold Coin of Kanishka I. This gold coin shows Kanishka on one side (left), crowned and clad in the archetypical Kushan attire of a long, heavy coat and high boots. The inscription reads "King of Kings, Kanishka the Kushan." On the other side of the coin is a standing Buddha, inscribed with "Buddha" on the left and Kanishka's dynastic mark on the right.

The Parthian and Sassanian Empires (224–651 CE)

In southwestern Asia, two great empires arose in succession, first the Parthian and then the Sassanian. They shared several similarities. Both began as confederations of loosely affiliated territories, and both were ruled by kings who adopted the Persian Achaemenid notion that they were divine "kings of kings." Like the Kushans, the Parthians and Sassanians collected tolls and custom duties on the trade routes that crossed their realm, both overland toward the Silk Road and maritime routes through the Persian Gulf (the empire encompassed its northern and eastern coastline).

In 238 BCE, the Parthian Empire was established and lasted for over 400 years. When incessant wars with Rome led to loss of territories and weakened the Parthian kings, however, they were vulnerable to rebellion among their own wealthy subjects. In 224 CE, a Persian aristocrat named Ardašir revolted against his Parthian overlord. Victorious in battle against him, while still on the battlefield, Ardašir declared himself King of Kings and established the Sassanian dynasty. Two years later, he took the Parthian capital Ctesiphon.

Initially, however, Ardašir had to confront others like himself—aristocrats with the military means to exercise considerable power. To secure his own position, he had to win their loyalty. Initially, he won over former Parthian vassals by granting them relative local autonomy and giving them new lands when they fell vacant.

At first, then, the Sassanian kingdom appeared like the Parthian, a confederation of separate kingdoms and smaller lordships in varying degrees of dependency on the central authority. However, Ardašir realized that his power could best be secured and enhanced by increasing governmental centralization in both the administration and the military. Aggression against the Romans followed, and Ardašir used warfare as a means to command the loyalty of his subjects. His successors, such as Shapur I, continued this practice. By the end of the third century and for centuries to come, the Sassanian Empire would be a highly centralized, bureaucratic state.

The Sassanian monarchs became more self-consciously Persian in their style of kingship, as the deification of the Sassanian king far exceeded that of Parthian practice. Ardašir and Shapur invoked the **Zoroastrian religion** to legitimize their power, and this religion was increasingly harnessed to the state. The Sassanian King of Kings was openly styled after the Zoroastrian deity Ahura Mazda. As this creator deity had battled chaos in the cosmos, so the Sassanian king, who claimed divine descent, brought order to his earthly realm. This political theology promoted the notion that the well-being of the people was secured by the king and his priesthood.

Administratively, the Sassanians also departed from Parthian practice, for royal power was enhanced by the formation of a central imperial bureaucracy that carried out much of the affairs of government through councils, ministries, and officials. Indeed, an increase in hierarchy in government was matched by a pronounced drift toward inequality in society.

By the fifth century, the Sassanian Empire had developed into a legally enforced and universally recognized system of four main social ranks or estates arrayed in descending order beneath the absolute authority of the Shahanshah, or King of Kings. The highest rank was held by priests of the Zoroastrian religion called magi, followed by the military, the scribes (including various administrators, as well as physicians, poets, and astronomers), and, at the bottom, an undifferentiated class of cultivators, craftsmen, and merchants, all lumped together as people who worked to earn their livings. The many slaves in Sassanian society, mostly captives from war, had no formal estate and so existed outside and below the official hierarchy.

In practice, advancing administrative centralization, coupled with state sanction of Zoroastrian orthodoxy and the concentration of military and political matters in the landed nobility, created an enormous and impassable gulf between the aristocracy and higher ecclesiastics on one side and peasants, artisans, and traders on the other.

This concentration of wealth and power among the aristocracy was supported by Sassanian law that protected the inheritance of property, including offices of state, in this way securing the unequal distribution of wealth down through generations. Landowning and officeholding remained the foundation of wealth and power.

Amid this drift to unequal hierarchy, Persian literary sources attest and archeology confirms pronounced population growth, urbanization, and sustained agricultural production that was essential to feed the growing cities. Various Sassanian rulers encouraged this urbanization. Ardašir and Shapur were both renowned for encouraging the development of cities, often populating them with Roman captives and, in some cases, such as Jundishapur, naming them after themselves. Urbanization is a result of the investment of a significant portion of a society's surplus in a built environment that establishes and reinforces political, economic, and ideological power. The Sassanian cities, like the imperial capital Ctesiphon, seem no exception. These cities magnified power, and the rulers built roads and dams (for irrigated agriculture) to support them.

Occasionally, the rulers imported skilled workers to populate and, in some cases, to help build new or to reestablish cities. Often, these workers were Roman captive soldiers and engineers. Shapur I, for example, not only defeated and captured the Roman emperor Valerian in battle at Edessa in 260, but he also transported thousands of Roman captive workers and engineers to his eastern cities.

Persian urban industry seems to have thrived, perhaps as a result of the acquisition of technological knowledge from beyond the empire, especially concerning the production of silk textiles and metals. Persian silks came to rival the Chinese in western markets. Sassanian Persia also earned the reputation as the "armory of Asia" for the metal weaponry it produced. The cities were thus manufacturing sites and commercial centers, located on roads and rivers where economic activity was most intense. The Sassanian government left the actual commerce to private traders but secured the commercial facilities and, of course, taxed the trade.

A later Muslim historian praised the Sassanian kings for their well-ordered state and the prosperity of it. His blanket praise could apply to several Sassanian rulers, but it fits best the most renowned of them, Khosrow I (r. 531–579). The trend toward governmental centralization, ambitious urban planning, agricultural development, and technological improvement reached its apogee during his reign.

Khosrow expanded upon and rationalized a system of taxation begun by his father. Based upon a survey of landed possessions, taxes were levied on the amount of land possessed and the value of its produce. In this way the great landholders, who were not tax exempt, were further brought under the yoke of the king while the royal coffers swelled with revenue.

Khosrow was active in generating royal revenue in other ways as well. Archeologists note great activity during his reign in the dredging of canals and the building of ports, caravanserais (inns and warehouses along trade routes), and bridges. As with Roman emperors, such actions were likely guided more by a desire to promote the grandeur of the ruler and fund his wars than any preconceived notion of economic growth resulting from planned investment in infrastructure, but the result seems to have been an expansion in trade and further urbanization.

Connections and Transfers Across Asia

Empires and trade across the vast landmass of Asia are closely connected. Rulers of these various states all seemed to recognize that maintenance and extension of their authority rested upon commanding the wealth that transit trade through their territories could bring. Long-distance trade through Asia confronted enormous challenges, and only rare and high-value goods made the journey, but beginning in the second century BCE, connections between east and west were made by the Silk Road, linkages that will last for millennia.

Trade in the Ancient World

How was surplus mobilized, moved, and consumed? This is a timeless and fundamental question. When we consider the movement of goods over long distances, central Asia during antiquity surges in importance because it was there and then that, for the first time, the sedentary peoples of East and West Eurasia were first connected. Clearly, as we have seen, empire building and conquest contributed mightily to this linkage, but so did trade. However, trade is not simply a process by which resources are most efficiently allocated by supply and demand through the market. Noneconomic factors, such as environment, social relations, and politics, affect trade as much as market mechanisms.

Demand reflects desire for someone else's products, but its historical dimension must take into account environmental, social, and political factors that affected distribution and consumption. Ecology, for instance, creates conditions where some form of exchange is desirable, as different ecosystems produce unique resources absent from others. Social status and political power channel traded products within and between polities. Indeed, the unequal distribution of wealth in ancient societies determined the commodities of long-distance trade.

"Luxury" does not connote an intrinsic quality of a good but rather reflects a capacity to consume, an indicator of the possession of wealth. Luxury consumption, in turn, becomes a means of social differentiation. "Fashionable" women, to take an example, wore lavish clothing and used expensive cosmetics and perfumes, often imported from far away, to mark themselves as separate from social inferiors.

The institutions of the various states play central roles in distribution and consumption too. Both infrastructure and war, as we have frequently seen, greased the wheels of trade. When considering trade in the ancient world, then, it is helpful to think of that world as made up of overlapping spheres of exchange, where the boundaries between different ecosystems came to be overlaid with political boundaries that shaped the patterns of distribution.

The essential movers of goods were, of course, the merchants, and these individuals were forever in pursuit of profit. And profit has always been weighed against potential for loss. Managing risk and reducing cost were central to the merchant's calculus and so, therefore, was infrastructure. Harbors for protection from storms, market buildings or caravanserais for securing goods in transit or concentrating buyers and sellers, laws to regulate and enforce business agreements, standardized weights and measures, coinage—all of these and more can be found in varying times and places to have been provided by governments and were good for trade.

Ancient governments no doubt had their own purposes for creating such infrastructure—to tax and thereby generate revenue to support an army and expand the power of the ruler was invariably crucial—but the wide economic ramifications are undeniable. Indeed, the nature and effectiveness of governing institutions and infrastructure, whatever their intent, are keys to understanding the divergent paths of historical change and to explaining economic growth, stagnation, or contraction.

Nomads, Chinese, and Sogdians

Sources that survive from antiquity do not allow an accurate measurement of the total volume of long-distance trade, but the historical importance of that trade rests on the role it played in connecting East and West Eurasia for the first time. Transport across the Silk Road may have been slow and expensive, and trade most certainly immensely risky to person and property, but a line of communication, even if it resembled a line of ants linking distant anthills in China, Persia, India, and Rome, nonetheless came into being, and goods moved along it.

This link (see Chapter 7 and Chapter 8) has been called the Silk Road, and though many more products than the luminous textile were hauled along it, the route is nonetheless aptly named because of the volume and importance of silk. As we have seen, the relations between the Chinese and the nomads of the steppe were instrumental in the development of the silk trade. Even with the collapse of the Chinese central government of the Han dynasty in 220 CE and the dissolution of the Xiongnu Empire, trade did not disappear. Sogdian merchants and Buddhist monasteries sustained the trading routes.

In the oasis towns along the northern routes of the Tarim Basin at the base of the mountainous Tian Shan, we find many Sogdians who had migrated there from their home in western central Asia and controlled the transit trade. The oases along the southern route at the foot of the Kunlun Shan were sustained by Buddhist establishments visited by Kushan-Yuezhi traders. Western demand in the Roman and Sassanian Empires for Chinese products still made profits possible for the intrepid merchant who dared continue in the trade, and many did.

Later, under the Türks and Uighurs, the Sogdians played an even more prominent role as key middlemen in the international commerce. By the sixth century, Sogdian had become the main language of commerce along the Silk Road, and a century later, the Uighur khaghan converted to their religion. Sogdians were numerous in central Asian cities, such as Samarkand, Bukhara, and Ordu Baliq, and many settled in cities within China, especially the capital Chang'an. The Türks and Uighurs, as we have seen, sent thousands of horses to China annually in exchange for silk, and the Sogdian merchants not only handled the horse trade but also moved the silk toward western Eurasian markets.

Kushans, Parthians, and Sassanians

The Yuezhi had been Chinese trading partners before they were driven west by the Xiongnu, and so they took their knowledge and familiarity of the Chinese with them. When Zhang Qian was sent west by the Han emperor in 138 BCE, he encountered the Yuezhi and reported that they were uninterested in forming a military alliance against the Xiongnu, but they were eager to resume trading relations with the Chinese. Thus, when Chinese silks emerged at the western end of the Tarim Basin, some of it was channeled southward into the Yuezhi-Kushan Empire. Because the Kushans controlled the Indian ports on the Arabian seacoast (notably Barbaricon and Barygaza), they delivered silks to the Roman Empire and moved Roman goods, especially glass, red coral, gold, and silver, east (see Map 7.4).

Goods from the East moved through the Parthian Empire as well as the Kushan. Despite Parthian military confrontations with the Romans, trade between the empires was only intermittently affected. Goods from the Silk Road came to Parthia by way of Samarkand, Amul, and Merv, while India supplied Parthia with precious stones, perfumes, opium, slaves, and spices (above all, pepper).

During the Parthian period, Dura-Europos and Palmyra emerged as principal points of transit trade between east and west. The diversity of the population of these cities revealed its commercial nature, as Syrians, Jews, Macedonians, Greeks, Arabs, and Persians thronged there to conduct business. In Dura-Europos, they concentrated their activities in a large agora recently excavated by archeologists. By the second century CE, the chief trading city in Mesopotamia was Palmyra, which moved goods up and down the Euphrates and to and from the Persian Gulf harbor of Charax where ships from India docked.

Another important route ran from Zeugma to Edessa, Nisibis, and Seleucia near Ctesiphon. As evidence to the vitality of this trade, a huge annual fair was held at Zeugma, well stocked with Indian and Chinese products. Parthian armies secured the safety of the caravan trade, building fortresses along the way and by their actions directed and controlled the traffic. Fixed uniform tariffs were assessed and collected by Parthian officials, and the cities that were the pivots of this international trade shared with the Parthian rulers the substantial revenues that the commerce brought with it.

The Sassanians, like their predecessors the Parthians, showed a strong interest in close economic relations with east and west. The Sassanian rulers no doubt recognized that custom duties from the transit trade of goods bound to and from Rome generated essential revenues for the royal treasury. The border between the empires was by no means impermeable, nor was it heavily fortified. Many daily contacts occurred—joint markets, sharing agricultural products, even intermarriage—often mediated by the numerous Christians and Jews living there who easily served as conduits of trade.

Early in the Sassanian dynasty, the Persians sought to control Mesopotamia (and thereby tap the trade wealth of the Persian Gulf and India). They marched their armies into southern Mesopotamia and the western coastal regions of the Persian Gulf and eastern Arabia and threatened the Roman colony of Palmyra over the lucrative luxury trade with India.

Both Romans and Sassanians contended as well for control of the well-fortified caravan city of Hatra in northern Mesopotamia, a key junction for caravan routes from Nisibis to Ctesiphon. Hostilities between Romans and Sassanians were resolved by a treaty in 298 in which trade with the East was clearly important to both powers. As a result, the city of Nisibis in Mesopotamia surged in importance because the treaty granted it a monopoly of all exchanges between the two empires. It became the seat of the Roman governor of Mesopotamia and emerged as a huge transshipment center. At Nisibis, all goods were taxed by both Sassanians and Romans.

Control of the Persian Gulf remained crucial to the Sassanian economy. Persian merchants were the ubiquitous middlemen in the trade between India and the Mediterranean, and much of it flowed through the Persian Gulf. According to the sixth-century Greek writer Procopius, the Persians "locate themselves at the very harbors where the Indian ships first put in … and are accustomed to buy the whole cargoes."[2]

By the sixth century, the rulers had built ports in Oman. One of the main exports of the Sassanians was silk, for they developed their own state-run workshops and, using imported raw silk from China, the finished products rivaled that of the Chinese. They also exported Arabian horses, woolen textiles, carpets, leather, and pearls.

Sassanians turned their attention eastward as well. Like the Parthians, the Sassanians maintained active foreign relations with China. Chinese documents report on 13 Sassanian embassies to China. Commercially, land and, apparently, sea trade with China was increasingly important to both the Sassanians and the Chinese. Large numbers of Sassanian coins have been found off the coast of China dating from the fifth and sixth centuries, confirming maritime trade, while ample evidence on taxes and customs testifies to considerable overland trade as well. Indeed, the sixth century marks a new stage in the development of overland trade, as Türkic armies pacified it and Persian, Chinese, and above all Sogdian merchants increasingly integrated it.

Review Questions

1. How did the environment determine or condition human activity in central and southwestern Asia?

---

[2] Touraj Daryaee, *Sassanian Persia: The Rise and Fall of an Empire* (London: I.B. Taurus, 2009), 138.

2. What did the Xiongnu, Türks, and Uighurs have in common?
3. How were the Kushan, Parthian, and Sassanian kingdoms similar and different?
4. How and why did political rulers play a role in the patterns and development of trade across Eurasia?

Further Readings

Barfield, Thomas J. *The Perilous Frontier: Nomadic Empires and China, 221 BC to AD 1757*. Cambridge, MA: Blackwell, 1989.

Beckwith, Christopher. *Empires of the Silk Road: A History of Central Eurasia from the Bronze Age to the Present*. Princeton: Princeton University Press, 2009.

Christian, David. *A History of Russia, Central Asia, and Mongolia*. Vol. 1, *Inner Eurasia from Prehistory to the Mongol Age*. Oxford: Blackwell, 1998.

Curtis, Vesta Sarkhosh, and Sarah Stewart, eds. *The Age of the Parthians*. London: I.B. Tauris, 2007.

Daryaee, Touraj. *Sassanian Persia: The Rise and Fall of an Empire*. London: I.B. Tauris, 2009.

De La Vaissière, Etienne. *Sogdian Traders: A History*. Translated by James Ward. Leiden: Brill, 2005.

Dignas, Beate, and Engelbert Winter. *Rome and Persia in Late Antiquity*. Cambridge: Cambridge University Press, 2007.

Grousset, René. *The Empire of the Steppe: A History of Central Asia*. Translated by Naomi Wahlford. New Brunswick: Rutgers University Press, 1997.

Liu, Xinru, and Lynda Norene Shaffer. *Connections Across Eurasia: Transportation, Communication, and Cultural Exchange on the Silk Roads*. New York: McGraw-Hill, 2007.

Wiesehofer, J. *Ancient Persia from 550 BC to 650 AD*. Translated by Azizeh Azodi. London: I.B. Tauris, 2001.

Figure Credits

Map 9.1: Copyright © by Koba-chan (CC BY-SA 3.0) at https://commons.wikimedia.org/wiki/File:Eurasia.jpg.

Fig. 9.1: Copyright © by Classical Numismatic Group, Inc. (CC BY-SA 3.0) at https://commons.wikimedia.org/wiki/File:Coin_of_Kanishka_I.jpg.

CHAPTER 10

Imperial China Under the Tang Dynasty, 618–907

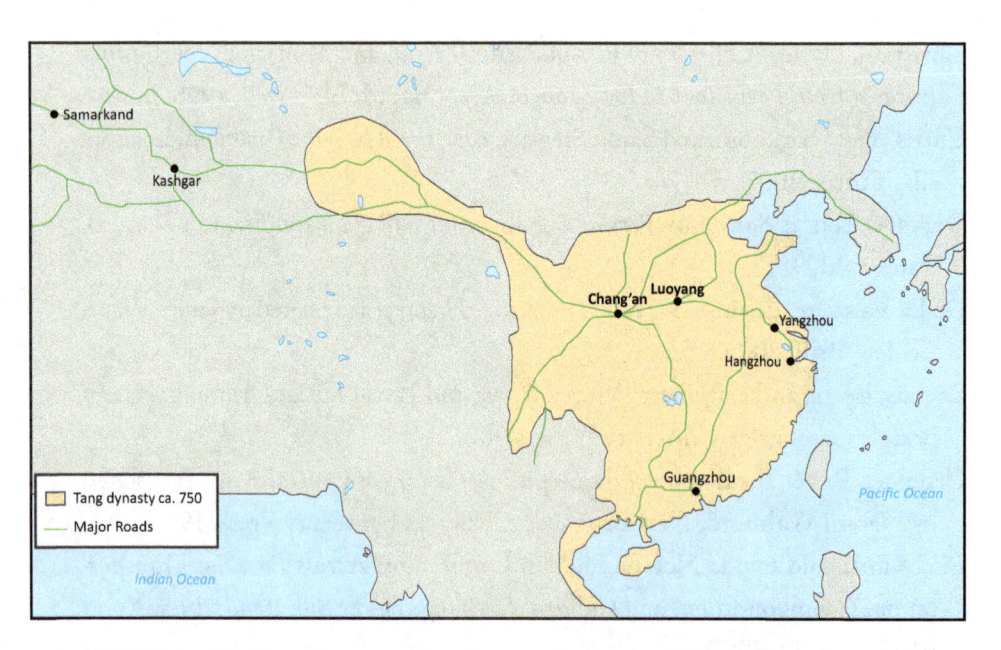

MAP 10.1   The Tang Dynasty at Its Greatest Extent, ca. 750.

Unification, Expansion, and Governance

The Tang emperor Taizong effectively consolidated his authority while expanding the empire to the greatest geographical extent of a Chinese empire before the 17th century. While his armies defended the far-off frontiers, in his capital, Chang'an, the emperor legitimized and secured his authority and kept his warlords in check by claiming the Mandate of Heaven, enacting a law code, expanding a bureaucratic cadre of educated officials, and efficiently taxing his subjects to fund these initiatives.

The Emergence and Consolidation of the Tang Dynasty

The Li was an aristocratic family in northwest China under the short-lived Sui dynasty (581–618). Recently sinicized (embracing the traditional characteristics of Chinese culture), the Li nonetheless retained the martial and horse-riding prowess of the steppe nomads from whom part of their family descended. When a rebellion erupted against the increasingly unpopular Sui emperor in 613 due to his ineffective war against the Korean state of Koguryo, Li Yuan, a former garrison commander in the North and part of the aristocracy that formed the core of the Sui political elite, seized the opportunity to expand his power.

With the help of the Eastern Türks and the quiet complicity of many other members of his class, Li Yuan marched on the Sui capital of Chang'an in 617. He forced the emperor's abdication and in 618 founded the Tang dynasty. Local elites quickly rallied to his cause in exchange for titles and offices, for these aristocrats were more interested in preserving their own power than supporting the defeated Sui regime. Li Yuan's younger son, Li Shimin, killed his brothers and imprisoned his father in a coup in 626 and became Emperor Taizong (r. 626–649).

Taizong consolidated his rule internally with the help of the Eastern Türks, subordinating the various local warlords that his father had briefly empowered. The Türks, for their part, hoped that the new Tang emperor would reestablish the tributary system under which the Türks and other nomads, such as the Xiongnu, had previously thrived. They were to be sorely disappointed. In 630, Taizong turned on them, defeating them in battle and capturing their khaghan. Taizong then launched expansionary military conquests. After each campaign, however, Taizong was careful to demobilize his army and return its generals to the imperial court where he could keep an eye on them and better ensure their loyalty.

By 642, Taizong accepted the formal submission of the khaghan of the Western Türks, reinforced by his successor in another military victory in 657. The Tang now were masters of central Asia, even occupying oases along the rims of the Takla Makan Desert. Tang armies also marched into northern Vietnam in the south, and in the northeast, they established colonies in southern Manchuria and Korea. By 750, a Chinese empire had reached its greatest extent prior to the Qing dynasty in the 17th century.

Tang Governance

Within this sprawling empire, the challenge for the Tang emperors was not simply to conquer but to govern. This meant providing military security on the frontiers, restoring the traditional bureaucratic governmental system of previous dynasties, stabilizing tax revenue collection, and checking the power of the warlords, those great militarized landowners.

To pacify the frontiers, Taizong created relatively autonomous districts in which tribal peoples were administered by their own chieftains. These chieftains, however, were provided with imperial military forces loyal to the Tang emperor and had their authority legitimized by the emperor who bestowed upon them their titles and seals of office. To keep these frontier peoples pacified, the emperor did not subject them to the taxes that were exacted from the interior Chinese population.

Emperors of new dynasties always sought to legitimize their authority, and Taizong was no exception. Upon accession, he claimed the Mandate of Heaven by which, according to Chinese tradition, heaven vested authority in this founding ruler and his descendants. He reinforced this claim by strict adherence to the correct forms of traditional state ritual. According to Confucian thought and practice, harmony between heaven and earth would be preserved by scrupulous attention to ceremonies of state. Rituals of offerings and sacrifice, if properly performed, were taken to be manifestations of heaven's grace upon the ruler.

To further legitimize his rule, in 637 Taizong promulgated a new law code. Laws were considered the written expression of the will of the emperor empowered by Heaven's Mandate. Like all Chinese law since the Qin code in the third century BCE, the Tang Code embodied Confucian principles that supported the notion of an unchanging hierarchy of legally distinct social status groups with government officials at the top and merchants at the bottom.

The Tang emperors also inherited a tradition of governance whereby Confucian intellectuals, many of whom were selected through competitive civil service examinations, staffed an extensive bureaucratic system. The Sui dynasty, which immediately preceded the Tang, had restored these exams that had been abandoned since the fall of the Han dynasty. The Tang emperors continued and expanded this practice.

The early Tang emperors were keenly aware that a cadre of career officials with shared Confucian values about social order and statecraft that connected them to the imperial court further legitimized the emperor's authority. They also knew that, by having no territorial power base, these officials formed an important check against powerful aristocratic families and warlords in the provinces. Early Tang emperors avoided bestowing semi-independent kingdoms upon imperial princes or aristocrats as the Han had done. Instead, they quickly erected a bureaucratic system with an elaborate central, regional, and local administration.

Following Confucian teaching, this system established the supremacy of civil administration over military, but the needs of security on the frontiers required some sort of a military command structure. The emperor stood at the pinnacle of this system, but the loyalty of his military governors was a constant concern. To help control them, the emperors felt that the efficient and rapid movement of imperial officials and documents between the court and the frontiers of the empire was essential. So the state built and maintained a vast network of roads that radiated from the capital of Chang'an. Every 10 miles, a relay station was erected, and there were 1,300 of them dotting the empire.

Taxes

Next to restraining the autonomous impulses of the rich and powerful, the most pressing issue for the early Tang emperors was to replenish a treasury emptied by war. The state collected taxes on salt, tea, liquor, ores, and metals as well as a miscellaneous array of commercial taxes on markets and merchants. However, for the early Tang emperors, the most important source of tax revenue was by far the land.

To ensure a steady flow of tax income, Taizong and his immediate successors reinstituted the **equal-field system** that had been in use during the Northern Wei dynasty (386–534). As China expanded territorially under the Tang, the emperors claimed large tracts of formerly unoccupied land (all land, in theory, belonged to the emperor). Peasants were moved onto these state-owned lands and granted equal plots to farm them. The emperor then collected taxes (in grain and silk) and labor service from them. The state kept meticulous records based on empire-wide household registration, to be revised every three years. Indeed, in the 720s, 800,000 new households were registered, increasing the flow of land taxes to the imperial treasury.

Technically, these lands were reserved for the peasantry and, as the emperor's property, could not be sold. For a time, this seems to have been the case, and the equal-field system provided the state with ample tax revenues. Gradually, however, wealthy landowners, tax-exempt Buddhist monasteries, imperial officials, and commanders in the army found ways to acquire many of these lands and to pass them down to their heirs.

In the late 600s, Empress Wu Zetian (who usurped the throne from her son and declared herself Huangdi, or emperor, in 690) continued to support the equal-field system, but how effective she was in forestalling the acquisition of peasant lands by wealthy landlords is debated. Certainly, over the long term, such acquisition usually resulted from foreclosure, for often, wealthy landlords loaned funds to peasants and then foreclosed on the land if the debt went unpaid. Some dispossessed peasants remained as tenant farmers of the rich, some drifted into the army, while others made their way to cities or migrated south to farm new land there. By the mid-eighth century, the equal-field system had fallen into disuse.

Militarism and Civilian Governance

Tang emperors, like their predecessors in previous dynasties, had to confront the perpetual problem of keeping the warlord in check. Problems arose when the state was threatened by enemies at its frontiers and was forced to enlist these warlords in its army. Emperors tried to adhere to the Confucian principle that civilian governance must supersede the military, but if army leaders decided to turn against the emperor, as the Tang general An Lushan did in 755, the survival of the dynasty was at risk. The dynasty survived An Lushan's rebellion, but never again during the Tang dynasty was centralized civilian authority effective in curtailing the power of the provincial warlords. During the final century of the dynasty, the empire fractured into nearly autonomous regions, and when an agrarian crisis struck in the late ninth century, rebellions swept the land and eventually ended the dynasty in 907.

Tang Armies

From its beginning, the Tang dynasty confronted powerful warlords within China and nomadic tribes that threatened the frontiers. As we have seen, there was a recurrent tension in Chinese history between the central authority of the imperial court and the forces of regional autonomy. As conquerors, the Tang commanded an enormous military force and incorporated great warlords within it. Mindful of the necessity of the supremacy of the imperial court, however, the early emperors kept the military structure independent of the civil bureaucracy and, in keeping with Confucian principle, subordinate to it. They periodically demobilized expeditionary armies as a means to this end.

However, as frontier defense against the nomads to the north and the Tibetans to the west became a constant demand, such demobilization proved impractical. The expeditionary armies, and the militia system in general, gradually gave way to permanently garrisoned professional armies comprised of a mixture of some steppe nomads and displaced peasants from the interior and under the command of powerful military governors. Predictably, the costs of military expenditure for the imperial treasury increased so dramatically that by 750 its cost was the single highest item in the imperial budget. Effective defense came at a price, however, for it encouraged that antithesis of centralized, bureaucratic governance—autonomous warlordism.

The An Lushan Rebellion

The seeds of imperial weakness lay within its strength, for if these powerful military governors acted independently of the court, they could destroy the dynasty. This is precisely what happened during the An Lushan Rebellion that broke out in 755.

An Lushan, born of a Türkish mother and a **Sogdian** father, was a Tang commander of over 150,000 troops in the north. He rose in rebellion against an unpopular emperor, Xuanzong, and his court ministers. The emperor had been blamed by the populace for a series of natural disasters, palpable evidence that he had lost the Mandate of Heaven and thus the right to rule. An Lushan's army swept toward the capital and, after the emperor fled, routed the imperial palace guard and entered Chang'an. Although An Lushan proclaimed himself emperor and established a new dynasty, internal dissension weakened his claim. After he was assassinated by one of his sons, a Tang army allied with Uighurs counterattacked, recaptured the capital, and drove the rebel forces in retreat to the north.

Imperial Weakness and Collapse

The Tang dynasty survived the An Lushan Rebellion. It even regained internal stability in the first half of the ninth century. Its central bureaucracy, however, was never again able to assert the supremacy of civilian governance over the military. Some emperors, such as Xianzong (r. 805–820), were aggressive in reasserting imperial authority, but their efforts were short-lived. Increasingly, virtually autonomous provinces in the North and West under military governors took control of what was becoming a decentralized fiscal system there and carved out large chunks of tax and grain revenues for their own armies. This sharply reduced the imperial take.

The civilian bureaucracy in these areas, formerly dominated by an aristocracy whose social prestige was linked to state service, gave way to local administrations controlled by the military. The Tang dynasty thus lost control of many of the northern and western parts of its empire. It survived, however, largely because it could depend on a relatively unmilitarized South whose civilian bureaucracy could still effectively channel enough tax revenues and grain to the court. The South more and more became the economic basis of whatever imperial power remained.

By the second half of the ninth century, famine and drought pushed increasing numbers of desperate peasants off their land, providing ample recruits for local and regional armies and even gangs of bandits that roved across the empire unchecked. All grappled among one another for local control. As the imperial court lost any real ability to assert its authority beyond the capital, these armies fought one another over establishing the next dynasty. It was in this context that another rebellion arose, led by Huang Chao, beginning in the mid-870s and lasting until Huang's death in 884.

Huang Chao capitalized on imperial weakness and adverse economic conditions and, with a following of several thousand impoverished farmers and fellow salt smugglers (Huang had made a career of salt smuggling), he joined the numerous rebellions that were erupting in the area. Huang's army swelled with masses of desperate farmers and outlaws and met with initial success against startled and disorganized Tang military forces.

Venting hatred for the government and the wealthy, the rebels attacked and looted cities, such as Guangzhou in 879, and reportedly massacred thousands of Tang officials and rich inhabitants, many of them foreign Arabs, Persians, Jews, and Christians. In late 880, the rebel army swung north and captured Luoyang before moving against the capital Chang'an. In early 881, the emperor Xixong fled to Sichuan province, and Huang's troops entered the capital. Once again, a few days after occupying the city, Huang's rebel troops looted the homes of wealthy residents and government officials and slaughtered many of them. In the poem "Lament of the Lady of Qin," Wei Zhuang recorded in verse the suffering of one of the victims:

> In house after house blood flows like boiling fountains;
> In place after place victims scream; their screams shake the earth ...
> My neighbor in the west had a daughter, lovely as a goddess ...
> So young she didn't know what happened outside her doors.
> Some thug leaps up her golden staircase,
> Rips the dress to bare half her shoulder, about to shame her,
> But dragged by the clothes she refuses to go through the vermillion gate,
> So with rouge powder and perfumed cream on her face
> She's stabbed down till she's dead.[1]

---

1   Mark Edward Lewis, *China's Cosmopolitan Empire: The Tang Dynasty* (Cambridge, MA: Harvard University Press, 2009), 272–73.

Huang then proclaimed himself the first emperor of the Da Qi dynasty. He was unable to secure a sufficient food supply for his newly conquered city, however, and he had no agenda to govern effectively or to consolidate his authority. In 883, he was forced to abandon Chang'an by a counterattacking Tang army that was supported by the cavalry of some Türkish tribes. Huang Chao fled eastward with the remnants of his army and held out until 884. His army was finally crushed in battle by a Tang general.

Huang's rebel troops scattered, but Tang governmental control over the country was never reestablished. The dynasty quickly collapsed, the death knell delivered by Zhu Wen in 907 when he drove the last Tang emperor from the throne. Zhu was one of Huang Chao's former generals, and though he tried to establish a dynasty himself, several decades of civil war, called the Five Dynasties and Ten Kingdoms period, followed until the Song dynasty was created in 960.

Producing Wealth: Agriculture and Manufacturing

Despite the varied political fortunes of the Tang rulers and the occasional droughts, floods, and famines, the economy during the dynasty showed significant overall growth. Population increased dramatically and shifted southward as large numbers of Chinese colonists migrated toward the Yangtze River valley and beyond. The vast majority of Chinese farmers were peasants who worked small plots of land, either as owners or tenants, but the greatest beneficiaries of the growing economy were the wealthy landlords.

An unmistakable development that contributed greatly to the growth, even as it fostered an unequal distribution of wealth, was the increase in the number of large agricultural estates. These operations produced much of the surplus food, notably rice from the South that was essential to the growth of cities, which also mushroomed in size. Technological innovation also enhanced productivity, and these innovations, because of their expense, were chiefly used on the large estates. Manufacturing grew as well, especially in the production of porcelain and silk.

The Conditions for Economic Growth

Regardless of its fluctuating political and military fortunes between roughly 500 and 1000, China's economy grew enormously. Its population surged by 50 percent over this half millennium, from about 50 million to 75 million people. The conditions for growth varied. Climate played its part, as China became wetter and cooler, especially beneficial for agriculture in the relatively arid regions north of the Yangtze on the North China plain where the bulk of the population lived. **Epidemiology** also played its part in population growth. China escaped any major visitation of epidemic diseases, such as plague, during these centuries and, with the advent of widespread tea drinking that entailed boiling and thus sterilizing water, avoided many water-borne diseases.

Importantly, over these centuries a marked shift in the economic center of gravity of China occurred. As population grew, many Chinese of the northern floodplain between the Yellow and Yangtze Rivers found good land harder to come by. Moreover, restive nomadic tribes at the frontiers and warlords jostling for regional domination made many a farmer's life precarious. Therefore, many migrated southward to the Yangtze River basin.

Before the arrival of this migratory wave, the southern lands had been sparsely populated by non-Chinese indigenous peoples. The steady migration of northern Chinese marked a colonization process of massive proportions. This migration and colonization was a powerful motor for economic growth. Whereas around 500 CE 75 percent of the population still resided in the Yellow River basin, by 1000, about equal numbers lived south of it, and more and more south of the Yangtze. The Yangtze River basin was increasingly drained and opened up to agriculture. It had a longer growing season, allowing multiple cropping (e.g., wheat, millet, barley, legumes, and beans) on land that produced higher yields than that of the North.

The Great Estates

The land and its produce was the fundamental source of wealth in Tang China, and three important and interrelated developments increased its productivity. First, land was increasingly concentrated into great estates dominated by wealthy landlords and Buddhist monks. Second, a steady stream of peasants and landlords migrated south and opened up new lands, producing an increasingly diverse yield of grains. And third, there is widespread evidence for innovations in agricultural technology.

As part of a long tradition, imperial China prized the idea of the small, independent family farm, an idea that, at least in part, informed the restoration of the equal-field system by the emperor Taizong. As we have seen, wealthy families and Buddhist monasteries gradually found ways to acquire these lands and amass great estates. In theory, it was forbidden to sell these fields, but exceptions were granted by rulers, such as the empress Wu Zetian, to powerful regional families in exchange for their loyalty or simply out of an increasing inability to enforce the law. People began to buy and sell land openly and relied upon private contracts, not formally recognized in Chinese law, to record these changes in ownership. Land increasingly became a commodity, and the market in it contributed to economic growth and to the increasing polarization of wealth in China.

Buddhism, which entered China significantly in the fifth century CE and reached its high-water mark in the seventh and eighth centuries, played a prominent role in the concentration of wealth in land. Monasteries received gifts from donors hopeful that sins committed in this life could be redeemed by the prayers of Buddhist monks. Monasteries often invested their wealth in land acquisition. Monks also operated as creditors for impoverished peasants, charging 50 percent interest payable from the next harvest. In the case of default, the monastery acquired the peasant's land through foreclosure. As a result, the amount of state-owned land decreased over time as great private estates owned by wealthy lay families and monasteries and farmed by wage laborers or peasant tenants (who paid half the crop in rent to the landlord) emerged.

Whatever the impact on state tax revenues or an independent peasantry, in purely economic terms, agriculture became increasingly productive, first in the northeastern part of the empire where military landlords were among the first to form large estates. Their agricultural efforts were aided by the fact that the Tang capital, Chang'an, was located in the North. To supply the city with tax grains and textiles, the state maintained an elaborate canal system of waterways connected to the Grand Canal that had been greatly restored by the Sui dynasty. This network stretched from Hangzhou all the way to the capital, Chang'an. It thus linked the Yellow and Yangtze River basins and regions further south. When landlords tapped into the canal system, they not only had access to water to irrigate their fields (and grow more crops) but also had access to commercial routes across which they could move their surplus produce to cities and markets.

Rice and Tea

Chinese migrants pushed down the river valleys south from the Yangtze. This brought them increasingly into a wet and swampy terrain. The most pressing challenge to these farmers was drainage, irrigation, and flood control, and only wealthy landowners had access to the necessary capital to accomplish this. As they opened new land, their estates grew in size and productivity, especially in rice, which is more dependent on water than soil for its nutrients—and thus the supreme importance of water control. Rice became a central food crop of the empire. It contributed to the increasing concentration of wealth in the great landlords, as it provided the sustenance for a significant expansion of the Chinese population.

Rice emerged as a primary food for China during the Tang period, but a nongrain crop also extended its reach across the empire: tea. Evidence of tea production and drinking can be found in Sichuan Province during the Warring States period (481–221 BCE), and during the later Han dynasty, it had spread into the Yangtze River basin.

During the Tang dynasty, tea cultivation and consumption penetrated the North first because of its widespread use in Buddhist monasteries. Tea's caffeine aided sustained periods of meditation by the monks, and it became an expression of hospitality to travelers staying in monasteries along pilgrimage and trade routes. Quickly, however, tea drinking spread across society, in the process becoming a cultural marker of being Chinese.

Tea plants, whose taste and character varied by region, were grown on hillsides throughout the empire and rapidly became an important cash crop for its growers and processors. Tea leaves were usually steamed, pounded, and pressed into a cake in an iron mold, then dried and shipped to market. Consumers roasted the cake, scraped off a powder, placed it in a sieve, and poured hot water over it.

Technology

The great landlords were well-positioned to develop another significant means to improve productivity and further increase their wealth: technology. A more effective plough was sporadically introduced in the eighth century. The new implement had a curved shaft (that transferred more animal power to the plough share) and a harness with a shorter beam suitable to the yoking of oxen. Moreover, the depth of the furrow could be adjusted by the farmer to work a variety of soils. And the new harness permitted a shorter turning radius, which meant that the plough could be used on new, more irregularly shaped, or sloping fields so common in the hilly terrain of southern China.

Use of draft animals in the fields provided the added benefit of fertilizer, and farmers were clearly aware that manuring fields increased productivity. Indeed, human excrement also was employed for this purpose to such an extent that procuring "night soil," as it was called, became a commercialized business as quantities of it were collected in cities and sold in the countryside.

All of these technological innovations were mentioned in printed manuals that found wider and wider circulation among literate landowners due to the development of **woodblock printing**. The great landowners were the primary beneficiaries of these developments in agriculture—the expansion of landed estates, the migration southward, and technological innovation.

Manufacturing

Tang China was a manufacturing powerhouse of small handicraft shops and state-run industries. The dynasty witnessed widespread and increasing production of metal tools and objects, boats and ships, leather goods, lacquerware, herbal medicines, wine and spirits, paper, ink, and a host of other commodities. Most important of all, however, were silk, porcelain, and salt.

The concentration of land into great estates drove many peasants from the land, and some of this surplus labor spurred manufacturing. Urbanization and commercialization, as we will see, also greatly stimulated the development of handicraft industry during the Tang dynasty. Chinese peasants had long been involved in textile, above all silk, production (recall that silk was collected along with grain in taxation), and during the Tang period, it became increasingly refined and delicate. Its splendor became both a sign of elevated social status domestically and a commodity of enormous demand in an expanding international economy.

The porcelain ceramic industry also entered a new phase during the Tang dynasty, driven by escalating demand both within China's growing wealthy social ranks and beyond the empire's borders. The invention of furnaces capable of reaching unprecedentedly high temperatures made this production possible. Marked innovations in glazing occurred, and the finest and most desired wares were the green celadon porcelain potteries from the Yue kilns in the South and the white porcelains from the Xing kilns in the North.

An early and continuing success story for the state was the production and distribution of salt. The state maintained a tightly controlled monopoly over salt, and for good reason. Salt was an essential commodity for food preservation everywhere before the advent of refrigeration in the 20th century. In China the monopoly was administered by special government agents working throughout the empire. After the An Lushan Rebellion in 763, the state salt monopoly became the single most important source of state revenue, accounting for more than 50 percent of income by 780. The most important sources were two salt lakes at Xie and Anyi where it was produced by state workers and then sold to merchants at an enormously inflated price. Staff working for the Salt Commission had many opportunities for personal enrichment, as did the merchants who distributed and sold the essential commodity throughout the realm and smugglers, like Huang Chao, who trafficked illegally in the trade.

Moving Wealth: The State, Cities, and Commerce

The Tang rulers inherited from previous dynasties the Confucian suspicion of commercial activity, assuming that it destabilized the ideal hierarchy of social relations. Consequently, the state, at least before 750, attempted to regulate it. Yet the state also used tax revenues to invest heavily in infrastructure—building and maintaining roads, canals, bridges, and so forth—which, contrary to government intentions, contributed to the ease of movement of goods and people and so to trade and economic growth. Cities also grew. As a commercialized system steadily emerged, it eventually overwhelmed the state's ability to regulate the economy. After 750, the state largely abandoned the attempt. Despite the weakening of the central government in the later Tang period, domestic commerce in China as well as long-distance overland and maritime trade beyond its borders became more extensive than ever before. China assumed a preeminent place in the Old World economy.

State Regulation and Commercial Growth

As with so much of the history of Tang China, the mid-eighth century was a watershed. This is true for the subsequent dramatic expansion in urbanization and commercialization. During the early Tang period, there was a fairly dense pattern of village settlement, especially in North China, but comparatively few small towns beyond the administrative county seats. During the later Tang period, however, many small- and medium-sized towns came into existence, clustered around great landed estates, civil and military posts, and large market centers on China's waterways.

Early Tang emperors perceived commerce as a threat to the prescribed, stable order of society laid down in the traditional Confucian texts and its timeless theory of the four hierarchical classes that placed merchants at the bottom. Official policy intended to ensure a rigidly regimented society obedient to the all-powerful state. Merchants were tolerated as a necessary evil, useful for the movement of goods, but they were considered parasitic, producing nothing, and reviled for their materialistic, profit-oriented mentality that ran counter to Confucian moral values.

As a reflection of this regulatory vision, early emperors legislated that all cities be constructed with spatially distinct political, residential, and commercial quarters. Government officials were expected to regulate and control commercial transactions. Chang'an, for a time, illustrated this vision. Similar to Han Chang'an, the Tang capital was divided into wards, with commerce restricted to the specified eastern and western markets. The markets, about a square kilometer each, were enclosed by earthen embankments.

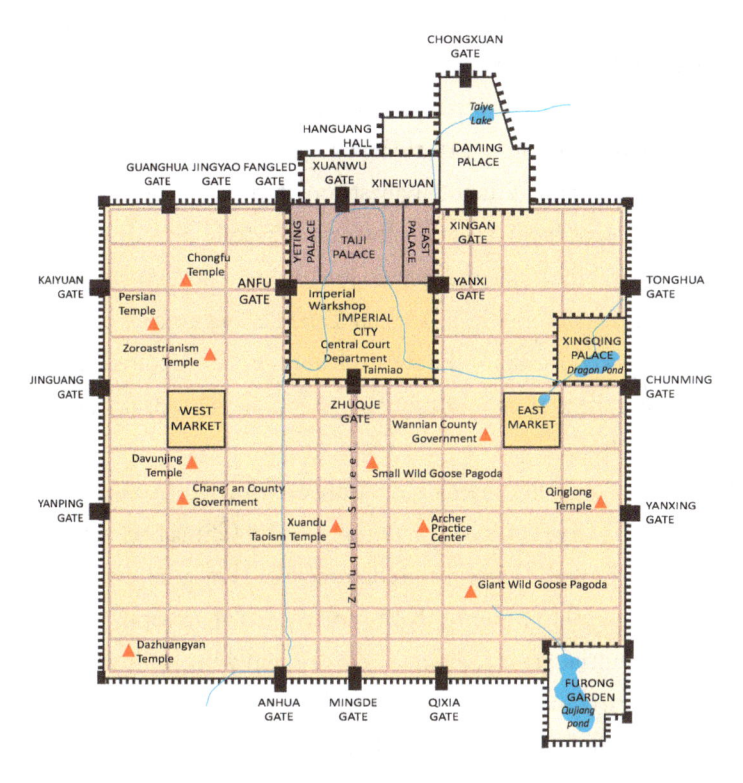

MAP 10.2 Chang'an During the Tang Dynasty

Within these walls were several thousand vending stalls, and each category of manufacturing and commerce was grouped in its own sector and alleyway. Also like the Han markets, imperial officials surveyed activities from a central tower. From here they sent out inspectors to assure that the goods being sold met prescribed quality standards and conformed to legal weights, measures, and currency. Indeed, sales in certain commodities, like slaves and livestock, were permitted only after an official had granted a certificate for the transaction.

Despite the state's longing for a stable and controlled economy, its own commitment to constructing an infrastructure for the efficient movement of tax goods and official state correspondence contributed greatly to subsequent commercial growth. This growth, in turn, undermined the very stability the state so much desired.

Tax revenues and provisions for the court and armies, collected in grain and textiles, were huge. In the 730s, for example, every year 2 million metric tons of grain and 13 million lengths of silk and hempen cloth poured into Chang'an, all moved by countless merchants. Observing the Grand Canal in the seventh century, an official wrote that "great ships in thousands and tens of thousands carry goods back and forth. If they lay unused for a single moment, 10 thousand merchants would be bankrupted."[2] The extensive and interconnected road and, above all, river and canal systems certainly helped the state collect its revenues, but they were also a boon to private trade.

The Tang government unwittingly stimulated economic growth in other ways too. For example, to facilitate tax collection, Taizong introduced a standardized copper coin that joined silk and hemp cloth as currency. By the 780s, taxation in cash exceeded taxation in kind. By then Tang copper coins were cast annually in nearly 100 imperial mints. Whatever advantages these coins might have served the state in tax collection, unquestionably they contributed, as money always does, to an increased liquidity in the commercial economy.

Despite the emperors' fears of instability arising from commerce, the capital and the emerging large cities in different regions of China became important trade centers during the early Tang period before 750. They grew even more during the later Tang from 750 to the early 10th century. The partitions in these cities that separated residential areas from markets gradually broke down.

In large cities, commerce spilled beyond the designated marketplaces into inns, hostels, and lodgings that often doubled as warehouses. Wineshops, restaurants, and street food vendors were everywhere. Thriving night markets appeared, eloquently testified by a Tang poet who rhapsodized, "From night markets, lamps by thousands lit the azure clouds."[3] Indeed, Tang China may have become the world's earliest nation of shopkeepers.

One of the most striking features of China after 750 is the sharp expansion of trade and the amassing of vast fortunes by merchants and government officials who invested deeply in it. As central authority deteriorated in the later eighth century and cities and commerce continued to grow, the state was forced to abandon regulation of the commercial economy.

---

2 Lewis, *China's Cosmopolitan Empire*, 24.

3 Heng Chye Kiang, *Cities of Aristocrats and Bureaucrats: The Development of Medieval Chinese Cityscapes* (Honolulu: University of Hawai'i Press, 1999), 82.

Credit and Domestic Trade

To grease the wheels of commerce with credit, moneylending and pawnbroking became important financial activities. These businesses were dominated by Sogdians before the An Lushan Rebellion but with significant participation of Buddhist monks. Indeed, in nearly every urban market, especially in Chang'an, moneylending Buddhist monks worked their loan stalls.

Foreign merchants were everywhere too. Many sold luxury items, such as jade and pearls, brought to China from central Asia along the Silk Road. Even though many of these commercial activities were technically illegal, they were still taxed, notably through a levy on the increasingly recognized private contracts in widespread use. The revenue they generated impelled imperial officials to tolerate or, in the case of many regional administrators, to encourage such commerce.

The growth and consolidation of large agricultural estates were clearly linked to the growth in trade, both local and long distance. Unregulated rural markets and periodic fairs sprouted up, usually at road junctions, fords, and bridges or near Buddhist monasteries, temples, or shrines. Here, local producers, large and small, sold whatever surpluses they had and purchased goods (sometimes via brokers) from travelling merchants.

More and more, a commercialized system of agriculture was taking hold across China. The increasingly autonomous provincial governors saw it in their interest to abandon the Tang policies of regulation. Thriving market towns in their jurisdiction, they saw, increased their tax revenues. Merchants (above all those trading in salt and tea), military officers, and men serving in the administrative staffs of the provincial governors were the big winners. These men, in turn, invested their new wealth in land.

A network of local market towns stocked with local goods (and dominated by the surpluses pouring from the great estates) connected with the network of waterways and supplied the larger cities. More and more Chinese people became dependent upon the market for their daily necessities, and farmers great and small increasingly produced goods for those markets with an eye toward profit. Entire regions began specializing in particular products destined for near and distant markets, a development that will increase dramatically during the subsequent Song dynasty (960–1279). Cities along the Grand Canal burgeoned, thriving on a pronounced growth in bulk trade in such goods as timber, rice, wheat, and millet. Many a commercial transaction was handled by a swelling population of brokers who arranged shipping for traders and coordinated relationships between travelling wholesale merchants and local retailers.

Many urban centers were created by trade. Consider booming Yangzhou, located on the Grand Canal just north of the Yangtze River. As its population soared from under 100,000 in 627 to nearly a half million a century later, it became China's premier emporium. Goods from the increasingly productive south poured through here. It became the main transshipment center for such commodities as salt, tea, wood, precious gemstones, copper wares, medicinal herbs, silks, and brocades.

Yangzhou was also important for its well-developed shipping and financial services, the latter increasingly employing silver. Although not yet minted into coin, silver became the normal medium of exchange for large transactions. Many silversmiths in large cities acted as bankers and as sources of credit.

Long-Distance Trade

During the Tang dynasty, long-distance trade enriched many cities and some of their inhabitants. The Tang upper class exerted a strong demand for luxurious foreign goods that reached China from both the West and the Southeast. Trade with and tribute to the nomads to the north and west remained important in the exchange of goods. The defeat of Tang armies by Muslim troops in 751 at the Battle of Talas ended the Chinese march westward, but the Chinese still controlled the Silk Road far into central Asia.

Sogdian merchants furnished the very substantial market of the imperial court and its attendant aristocracy with the exotic and luxury goods they increasingly demanded—saffron, medicinal herbs, carpets, jewels, brass, furs. Indeed, the Western Türks sent 38,000 marten fur pelts to the Chinese court in one year, 642, all transported by Sogdian merchants.

FIGURE 10.1 Foreign Ambassadors at the Tang Court. This image is from a mural in a royal tomb in Qian County, Shaanxi Province, about 50 miles from the Tang capital of Chang'an (today Xi'an). The two men depicted on the right are ambassadors from Korea, and the bald man in the center with the long nose is a European ambassador from the West.

Just as importantly, Sogdians were the key middlemen in the supply of horses by the Türks for the Tang cavalry, by the mid-seventh century reaching 700,000 a year. The Sogdians and a host of other foreign merchants then channeled silk in the other direction, paid by Tang rulers as tribute to nomadic tribes in the Northwest as the price of their pacification on the frontier. The capital Chang'an, a city of two million inhabitants in the eighth century and a terminus point of the Silk Road, counted among its residents merchant colonies of Türks, Uighurs, Arabs, Indians, and, of course, Sogdians, all involved in the overland long-distance trade to the West.

Increasingly, commerce during the Tang dynasty moved onto the waters off the eastern and southeastern coasts. The migrations of people southward and the new agricultural cultivation there facilitated this shift. Coastal provinces, like Guangdong, Fujian, and Zhejiang, were well-placed to take advantage not only of the increasingly integrated commercial system within China but also of the newly opened sea routes on the South China Sea. Large-scale, water-based commercial shipping would transform these provinces and their burgeoning cities of Quanzhou, Guangzhou, and Hangzhou, as the demand from long-distance trade rippled powerfully through the entire Tang economy. A contemporary described how at Hangzhou, an enormous harbor city in Zhejiang Province that sits at the eastern end of the Grand Canal and the Yangtze River delta, the masts of more than 30,000 ships stretched along the canals for almost nine miles.

Quanzhou in Fujian Province reflects the surging importance of seaborne trade. Until the eighth century, Quanzhou comprised a few scattered settlements along the banks of the Jin River, populated by colonizing Chinese migrating from the North. During the ninth century, it became a bustling transshipment center. By then it even exceeded Guangzhou, formerly the greatest Chinese port, in trade volume.

When the cargoes hailing from across the seas reached these coastal cities of China, they were carried by Muslim traders (overwhelmingly Persians) who had dropped anchor there. These Persian traders off-loaded such goods as cloves from Indonesia, pepper from Burma and India, coral and pearls from Sri Lanka, and aromatics from Arabia. In exchange they took on Chinese cargoes of silk and porcelain (the latter serving double duty as valuable commodity and ballast in the ships' bottoms). These cherished products were destined for Southeast Asia, India, the Red Sea, and the Persian Gulf.

As testimony to Muslim dominance in this overseas commerce, Persian became the common language among maritime traders engaged in it. As yet, no Chinese merchants ventured onto the high seas, but for the first time, this sea-based trade in bulk commodities linked China to an emerging economic system centered on the Indian Ocean and established China as the single greatest participant.

Review Questions

1. How did Tang emperors consolidate their authority?
2. What recurrent tension in Tang governance threatened the stability of the Chinese state and eventually led to its collapse?
3. Why did the Chinese agricultural and manufacturing economy grow during the Tang dynasty, and what were its main effects?
4. What role did the state and cities play in the economic history of Tang China?

Further Readings

Adshead, S. A. M. *T'ang China: The Rise of the East in World History*. London: Palgrave MacMillan, 2004.

Benn, Charles. *China's Golden Age: Everyday Life in the T'ang Dynasty*. Oxford: Oxford University Press, 2002.

Clark, Hugh R. *Community, Trade, and Networks: Southern Fujian Province from the Third to the Thirteenth Century*. Cambridge: Cambridge University Press, 1991.

De La Vaissière, Etienne. *Sogdian Traders: A History*. Translated by James Ward. Leiden: Brill, 2005.

Gernet, Jacques. *Buddhism in Chinese Society: An Economic History from the Fifth to the Tenth Centuries*. Translated by Franciscus Verellen. New York: Columbia University Press, 1995.

Graff, David A. *Medieval Chinese Warfare, 300–900*. London: Routledge, 2002.

Hansen, Valerie. *Negotiating Daily Life in Traditional China: How Ordinary People Used Contracts*. New Haven: Yale University Press, 1995.

Kiang, Heng Chye. *Cities of Aristocrats and Bureaucrats: The Development of Medieval Chinese Cityscapes*. Honolulu: University of Hawai'i Press, 1999.

Lewis, Mark Edward. *China's Cosmopolitan Empire: The T'ang Dynasty*. Cambridge, MA: Harvard Belknap, 2009.

Perry, John Curtis, and Bardwell L. Smith, eds. *Essays on T'ang Society: The Interplay of Social, Political and Economic Forces*. Leiden: E. J. Brill, 1976.

Twitchett, Denis. "Merchant, Trade and Government in Late T'ang." *Asia Major* News Stories 14, no. 1 (1968): 63–95.

Twitchett, Denis. "The T'ang Market System." *Asia Major* News Stories 12, no. 2 (1966): 202–248.

Wechsler, Howard J. *Offerings of Jade and Silk: Ritual and Symbol in the Legitimation of the T'ang Dynasty.* New Haven: Yale University Press, 1985.
Wright, Arthur F., and Denis Twitchett, eds. *Perspectives on the T'ang.* New Haven: Yale University Press, 1973.
Xiong, Victor Cunrui. *Sui-T'ang Chang'an: A Study in the Urban History of Medieval China.* Ann Arbor: Center for Chinese Studies, 2000.

Figure Credits

Map 10.1: Copyright © by Nicolas Eynaud (CC BY-SA 3.0) at https://commons.wikimedia.org/wiki/File:Emp%C3%A8ri_Tang.png.

Map 10.2: Copyright © by SY (CC BY-SA 4.0) at https://commons.wikimedia.org/wiki/File:Chang%27an_of_Tang.jpg.

Fig. 10.1: Source: https://commons.wikimedia.org/wiki/File:Li_Xian%27s_tomb,_ambassadors.jpg.

CHAPTER 11

The Fragmentation of Europe, ca. 400–ca. 750

After the Roman Empire in the West

In 400, the Roman world was a relatively stable one and in no sense would have seemed to its inhabitants to be doomed to an inevitable dissolution. And yet, even though the political, military, and economic complex of institutions and practices that characterized the Roman Empire did not abruptly end, there is no masking the reality of the breakdown of state structures, the shrinkage and sometimes disappearance of cities, the increasing localization of the exchange economy, and the militarization of the landed aristocracy that began during the fifth century.

Barbarians and the Disappearance of the Imperial State in the West

The Roman Empire, administratively, had been a union of hundreds of cities with jurisdiction over their surrounding territories, and as the residences of civilian officeholders, cities gave government its coherence. Roman law, uniform across the empire, was also a unifying force, as was the Roman aristocracy. Though aristocrats drew their wealth from vast and dispersed landholdings, they were vested in this unified empire, all sharing a common literary education and commitment to civilian governance.

Of course, the army was huge—in 400, half a million soldiers filled its ranks—but it was mostly concentrated on the Rhine, Danube, and Persian frontiers. It was enormously expensive to supply, but the imperial tax system, based on an accurate and systematic collection of land tax, generated sufficient revenue to accomplish that. A well-developed distribution system moved huge quantities of grain (mostly from Egypt, Sicily, and, above all, North Africa), wine, and oil to the troops, a logistical system that was the lifeblood of the empire. And Roman agriculture was up to the task, for there is no evidence that it was in decline as the fifth century dawned.

Before 400, the main "barbarian" groups (as the Romans called them, considering them inferior peoples compared to the "civilized" Romans) that lived beyond the borders of the empire were the Franks across the lower Rhine River, the Alemmans beyond the middle and upper Rhine, and the Goths north of the lower Danube. These barbarians were not nomads, but farmers. Nor were they united ethnic groups, but rather loose confederations of tribes with elected kings.

Barbarians had been entering the empire for decades before 400, usually to be absorbed into the Roman army, but late in the fourth century and into the fifth, unprecedented numbers of them poured into the empire. The first were the Goths. Pushed against Rome's European frontiers along the Danube by the advancing Huns from further east, the Goths asked for refuge inside the empire. The Romans let them in but remained wary of them. When the Romans cut off supplies to them, the Goths rose in rebellion. Shockingly, the Romans suffered a devastating defeat by the Goths at the Battle of Adrianople in 378. The emperor Valens was killed, and the best army of the Roman Empire was routed.

By the early fifth century, tens of thousands of barbarian warriors were on the move, slamming across the Rhine frontier and sweeping into Gaul and, later, Spain. The Goths, under their king Alaric, swung west and entered Italy in the early fifth century and in 410 even sacked Rome (see Map 7.2).

The critical blow to the Roman state came at the hands of the Vandals, a migrating tribe of barbarians that ravaged Gaul and Spain before sweeping across North Africa. In 439, the Vandal army reached Carthage, a primary outlet for grain exports that were essential for feeding the empire's cities and army. When they captured Carthage, they not only controlled one of Rome's most important grain-producing provinces but, by cutting off exports, they also severed the jugular vein of the western empire. With one blow, they interrupted the food distribution network that had held the empire together. Consider that it took 7,500 kilos (nearly 16,000 pounds) of grain and 450 kilos (nearly 1,000 pounds) of fodder per day to feed an imperial legion of 5,000 men, and the necessity of maintaining a supply system stands in bold relief.

In the 440s, we have evidence that existing taxation was insufficient to pay imperial troops. For the same reason, the city of Rome, though no longer the empire's administrative capital in the fifth century, saw its population plummet with its food supply. In 400, Rome counted half a million inhabitants; a century later, scarcely 70,000.

Despite this interruption of the food supply, however, the bureaucratic and military institutions of the imperial state did not suddenly collapse. In fact, contemporaries well into the fifth century saw no imminent danger of that. Choked from the loss of almost all its revenues from taxes and grain shipments, however, it is nonetheless clear that the political and economic system was fragmenting and, in large parts of the empire, withering away. Though emperors continued to claim the throne until 476, by then effective governance and military defense had largely disappeared. What would replace it?

By 500, the western empire had broken into half a dozen main barbarian kingdoms—Vandal Africa, Visigothic Spain and Southwest Gaul, Burgundian Southeast Gaul, Frankish northern Gaul, and Ostrogothic Italy. Post-Roman kingdoms shifted away from Roman government structures only gradually. Visigothic and Burgundian kings legislated, taxed, moved grain around to feed their armies, often under Roman generals, and employed Roman officials. But there no longer was an emperor or an imperial center to look to, the local aristocracies were much more militarized than the Romans had been, and the fiscal structures and exchange networks of these kingdoms were less integrated and much more localized. This end of political unity, gradual as it may have been, was not a trivial shift.

Barbarian Kingdoms

The barbarians came into the Roman Empire to settle, not simply to plunder, and their leaders, like the rich Roman aristocrats, wanted to be a ruling class. To do this, they needed landed estates, and as conquerors they were in a position to get them. Likely, this transfer of lands resulted from a settlement in which portions of the property of Roman landowners were ceded to the barbarians. Some land, no doubt, was taken by force. Kings acquired more of this land than any aristocrat, and in the new barbarian states, they sat at the top of the political and economic hierarchy. By 500, kings and aristocrats were paying their armies by way of rents from private landowning. Public taxation no longer was the basis of the state as it had been under the empire, land was.

This new system of governance required the complicity of landed aristocrats, both barbarian and the surviving Roman landowners. With no central structure of the empire to rely on, all aristocrats turned to the new rulers of the successor kingdoms to protect them and advance their interests. The new rulers, for their

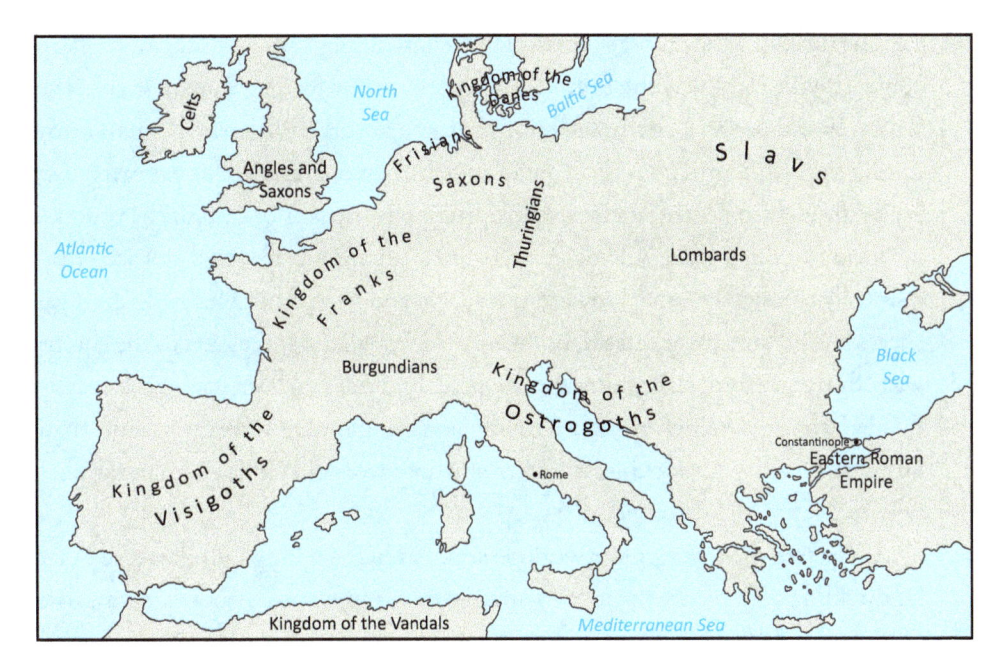

MAP 11.1   Barbarian Kingdoms, Sixth Century

part, needed the allegiance of the aristocracy and, in exchange for military service from them, doled out land and luxurious gifts. Frankish Merovingian kings more than any other rulers possessed immense landed resources, and this wealth was the basis of royal authority. Royal courts bustled with aristocrats jockeying for favors, and though individual kings might frequently be toppled in palace coups, all aristocrats were overwhelmingly committed to this personal rather than institutional system of governance that was based in reciprocity.

All the barbarian kingdoms shared these basic notions of governance, but different regions experienced very different conditions. Italy, the heart of the Roman Empire in the West, is an extreme example of the fragmentation that resulted from the collapse of the imperial state. In the fifth century, it saw its tax revenues and grain shipments dry up as a result of the Vandal conquest of North Africa. In the next century, it suffered nearly constant warfare. The Byzantine emperor Justinian I (r. 527–565), as we will see, launched an invasion of reconquest in 535 against the Ostrogothic kingdom in Italy, known as the Goth Wars. Soon after these wars ended in 554 and the Byzantine armies had withdrawn to the Adriatic Coast and to southern Italy, the Lombard invasion began from the North. So widespread and thorough was the destruction that Italy's political system splintered into many local polities, and its economy was severely dislocated.

THE FRAGMENTATION OF EUROPE, CA. 400–CA. 750

The successor state most successful in reconstructing public authority, in sharp contrast with Italy, was the Frankish kingdom in the former Roman Gaul. The Salian Franks were a Germanic tribe that was absorbed into the Roman army during the fifth century. As the Roman state withered, Frankish kings emerged as regional rulers in northern Gaul, appropriating vast tracts of land in the process.

One Frankish king, Clovis (r. 481–511), expanded the royal domain dramatically through conquest toward the south, and he and his Merovingian royal successors became the greatest landowners. Although the succession to the throne was often contested, civil war not infrequent, and the kingdom itself periodically divided, the possessions of the Merovingian royal families were far greater than any of their aristocratic subjects, many of whom were old Gallo-Roman families who had inhabited the region for years.

Whatever the strengths or weaknesses of individual kings, all possessed vast landholdings. To secure the loyalty and military support of their aristocrats, the kings granted them land. What evolved was a relationship between king and noble that was mutually beneficial. The Frankish aristocracy built local power bases in land, but the royal court became the place where aristocrats clustered, everyone jostling for royal favor that was the source of wealth and power.

Merovingian kings sought to legitimize their rule by aligning themselves with their imperial predecessors. One way they did this was to embrace the Catholic Church of Rome. Catholic Christianity, based upon the acceptance of the idea of the Trinity, had become the official religion of the Roman imperial state in the fourth century, and the structure of this church survived the collapse of the imperial system. Frankish kings, beginning with Clovis, became Catholic Christian and granted bishops (all of whom were aristocrats) and monasteries land in exchange for religious sanction for their rule.

From a platform of legitimacy, both political and religious, Merovingian kings embraced another imperial legacy, and one that again reveals the importance of land to the entire system. Beginning with Clovis, they decreed a system of law, called the Salic Law. Initially an oral code, during the early sixth century it was written down in Latin, the language of the Roman Empire. These laws focused mostly on inheritance and crime and show a pronounced awareness of the importance of property. To keep landholdings consolidated within a patrimony, women were excluded by law from inheriting property (or the crown). Concerning crimes, their severity was measured in property values. Punishment was meted out in the **wergild**. The focus on property value in this system is a further reflection of the importance of land in the new politics of post-imperial western Europe. The king was its defender, and the landowning aristocracy a major beneficiary of it.

Rich and Poor

An enormously rich senatorial, aristocratic elite had sat atop the social hierarchy of the Roman imperial state. This elite gathered its wealth from civilian officeholding in the imperial bureaucracy and, especially, from its vast, dispersed landholdings that spanned the empire. These aristocrats profitably moved their products into the state-run food distribution system as well as into the general commercial market. The fact that individual senators held land in various parts of the empire meant they were dependent upon the system of imperial unity to prosper.

When the imperial state broke up and the distribution system collapsed in the fifth century, this elite lost its coherence and had to adapt to a new, fragmented world. The aristocracies across the former empire became localized, much less wealthy than their Roman forbears, and, after 500 in the West and 650 in the East, increasingly militarized as their links with the various rulers tightened. By 700 in the West, the ability to read was unimportant and unnecessary to the military aristocrat, and so a literate civilian culture became largely restricted to the clergy of the Christian Church.

The channeling of wealth upward to aristocrat or king requires a system of economic extraction and labor control in which the landowner organizes production to allow his taking a share of the surplus. However, given the localization of landowning and the reduction in the scale of production during the fifth through seventh centuries, especially pronounced in Italy and Spain, there is little evidence outside of Merovingian Francia that most aristocratic landlords were much concerned with land management (recordkeeping fell out of practice). As long as the lord got enough surplus from the peasants farming his lands to support his military needs, he left his peasantry more or less alone.

Peasant society was far from egalitarian, and the key dividing line in status was between free and unfree. The latter were not slaves (the lord did not own their bodies and could not buy or sell them), but they were legally bound to the land and had no legal rights or involvement in village decision making. The free peasants (i.e, those who were not bound to the land and could move freely if they wished) either owned their own land or rented from a lord. The proportion of independent, free peasants, in fact, increased in the sixth and seventh centuries, probably partly as a result of plague that left large swaths of uncultivated land available, some of which whose owners had simply perished.

Cities radically contracted in size, and many simply disappeared. Under the empire, the urban poor and slaves were important social groups that numbered in the millions and had to be sustained by state charity to forestall urban unrest. As cities shrank, however, so too did this mass of humanity that henceforth fades from the historical record.

This state of affairs lasted until the 700s in the West. At that time, as we will see, there was an upturn in trade. The prospect of commercial profit then triggered a return to an intensification of agricultural production in which the landlord intervened more directly. This is evidenced by a surge in recordkeeping, as some lords more and more wanted to keep track of what and how much their lands were producing.

Peasants suffered from this aristocratic resurgence. They lost pastoral rights, saw their rents increase, and sometimes were displaced from the land altogether. Whatever resistance they mounted was largely futile, as the rulers and the aristocrats joined forces to maintain what we recognize now, and will explore in a later chapter, as the beginnings of the **manorial system**.

The Roman Empire in the East

The Roman imperial state survived in the East until 1453. The Byzantine Empire, or Byzantium, as the Roman Empire in the East became known, remained stable and prosperous during the fifth and sixth centuries when it was a prominent power in the eastern Mediterranean. Its fortunes would change dramatically in the seventh century. Military defeats from the Sassanians and then the Arabs sheared off much of the territory it had held. It survived, if barely, but its geographical extent was dramatically smaller in 650 than it had been in 400.

The Byzantine State

In 286, the emperor Diocletian divided the Roman Empire into two administrative parts, eastern and western. The emperor Constantine moved the capital of the entire empire to Constantinople in 324, a small city at the time but one strategically located on the Bosporus Strait between the Mediterranean Sea, the Sea of Marmara and the Black Sea. By 457, its population had grown to about 200,000 people.

Supreme authority rested with the emperor who supervised a bureaucracy of civic officials whose most important duty was the collection of imperial taxes. Byzantium in the fifth century was an ethnic melting pot, and the two great cultural unifiers were the imperial government topped by the emperor and Christianity. In fact, following the example of Constantine at the **Council of Nicaea** in 325 when the belief in the Trinity became official Christian doctrine, subsequent emperors continued to play important roles in defining the faith's accepted theology at any given time and so further secured a cultural coherence to the empire.

So, while imperial unity was disappearing in the West, the eastern part remained unified. Powerful rulers, like Justinian I (r. 527–565), embraced the Roman legacy of the emperor's legitimacy as head of state sanctioned by the Christian God. Legitimacy was reinforced scarcely two years into his reign by the codification of Roman law, the *Corpus Juris Civilis*, in which Justinian sought to reconstruct the basic civil and criminal laws of Rome and to reconcile contradictions within them. He further enhanced his legitimacy by sponsoring the construction of public buildings, palaces, roads, and, importantly, Christian churches, above all the spectacular church in Constantinople, **Hagia Sophia**, built in 532.

Justinian expanded the empire territorially as well. He launched his armies westward in 533 in an attempt to reconquer the parts of the Roman Empire that had fallen to the various tribes of invaders in the fifth century. His highly competent general Flavius Belisarius led an army to victory against the Vandals in North Africa, bringing the territory back under Roman rule and for a time channeling the grain that was the main source of Vandal wealth back into the Roman Empire. Belisarius then turned to Italy in what are known as the Goth Wars where he defeated the Ostrogoths and captured their capital of Ravenna in 540. But when the Sassanians invaded in the East, Justinian recalled Belisarius to fight them. It took another 20 years to completely vanquish the Ostrogoths in Italy,

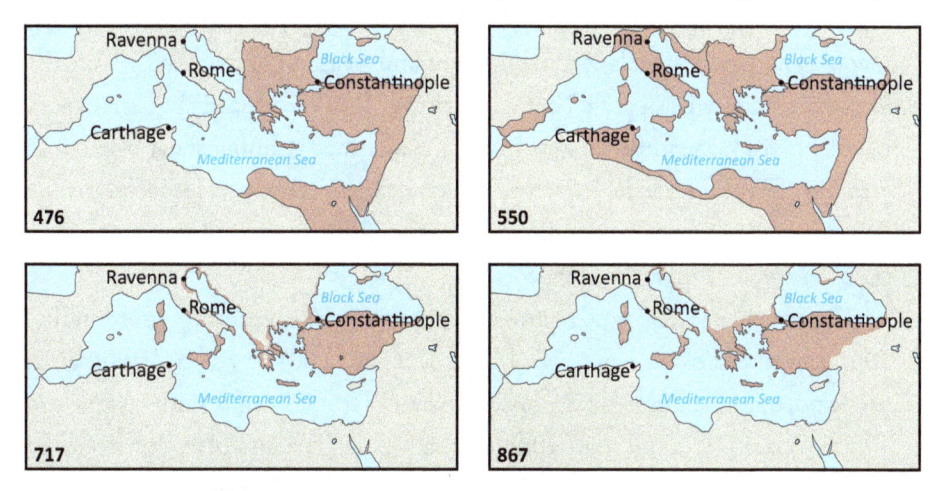

MAP 11.2 The Byzantine Empire, 476–867

but Roman forces were so weakened in the victory that when the Lombards invaded from the north in 568, the Byzantines were nearly driven from Italy. Byzantine armies were simply stretched too far and too thin, for they had too much territory to defend on too many fronts with too few troops.

Justinian's immediate successors lost much of the territory he had conquered. In 610, Heraclius (r. 610–641), a Byzantine commander in North Africa, became emperor. His armies were soon dealt devastating blows from the Sassanians and lost to them important cities in Syria and then all of Egypt in 620. Half of Justinian's empire was now gone and the all-important grain supply from Egypt cut off. The empire seemed doomed when the Sassanians attacked Constantinople in 626. They were driven back, however, and Heraclius launched a counterattack. He not only routed the Persian army but he even seized their capital, Ctesiphon. In the subsequent peace treaty, the Sassanians returned Syria and Egypt to the Byzantines.

Heraclius's success, however, was short-lived. Far more threatening to the empire in the East than the Sassanians were the Arab armies of the new faith of Islam. In 634, the Arabs conquered the Sassanian Empire, and by 642, North Africa, Syria, Palestine, and, most devastatingly, Egypt were lost permanently by the Byzantines. With them went imperial taxes and grain. Indeed, by these Arab conquests, the Byzantine Empire lost two thirds of its land area and three fourths of its wealth.

The threat to the very existence of the Byzantine state by the Arab conquests cannot be overstated. Now, the first priority for the emperor became the army. He needed one large enough to defend against the Arabs, but he had to fund it from an empire that had lost its richest provinces. The result was a fundamental military reorganization. Constans II (r. 641–668) created five military districts, called Themes, each with its own largely defensive army. The Themes drew their income and paid for their own equipment and weaponry from land grants from imperial estates within each Themes territory. This lessened the burden of salary payments from the imperial government, which was running short of cash. The creation of Themes cut the emperor's military expenses but gave local commanders dangerous amounts of power. Between 695 and 717, various Themes rose seven times in revolt against the emperor.

Crises of the seventh and eighth centuries changed Byzantium profoundly. In 780, it controlled barely one-third of the land it had in 602. It was far less urbanized as the population of its cities dropped 50 percent from the mid-sixth century, only 10 cities counting more than 10,000 inhabitants. The loss of Egypt decimated grain imports. Money in circulation decreased, although it did not disappear.

Nevertheless, a truncated Byzantium survived because the imperial government in Constantinople survived. The emperor and a civilian bureaucracy in the capital city continued to control the mechanisms of taxation and provincial administration, which held the state together. Unlike in the West, taxes, however reduced in volume, continued to be collected in coin. The state's bureaucracy administered a comprehensive system of land taxation where land was graded and assessed according to quality and use.

Moreover, the imperial court and the emperor remained the focus of the political community and remained closely tied to the Christian Church. Constantinople was filled with churches, relics, and hundreds of clergy. It was revered as a holy city at the heart of a sacred history that assumed Christian Romans were God's chosen people.

Social Stratification

The imperial state could not have survived without the complicity of the aristocracy, as both state and lord were dependent upon control of the extraction of surplus from agricultural production. Such a system of channeling wealth upward to nonproducers, as always, required force and legitimacy, and so, as in the West, the links between ruler and aristocrat tightened.

Also as in the West, the dominant elite in the East became sharply more military, above all in the provinces where military-governing hierarchies replaced city-based civilian ones after 600. The important exception—and this distinguishes the East from the West—was Constantinople where a civilian bureaucracy continued to wield statewide authority. Indeed, the central civil and imperial authority and provincial military powers worked together to control the land which, as in the West, more and more became the coin of politics.

The provincial aristocracy was enriched and empowered by land grants from the emperor that required peasants to pay rent and provide labor services to the aristocrats and to pay taxes to the state. In return, the emperor demanded loyalty and military service from the aristocracy, the latter more pressing than ever to meet the military threats from the Arabs after 642. A powerful, provincial, militarized officer class emerged, its wealth rooted in the control of land and its authority delegated and legitimized by the emperor.

Of course, it had not always been so. In the mid-fifth century, the apex of the social structure in the East was occupied by a small senatorial class of about 2,000 families clustered in Constantinople. In the provinces at the top of the social pyramid were members of the city councils of about 1,000 cities. Called decurions, they numbered about 50,000 and were the richest men in each city, although they possessed much less wealth than the senators.

Numerically, the social structure of the eastern empire was dominated by the peasantry. There were 14 million of them in the mid-fifth century, about 90 percent of the total population, dispersed across countless small villages of a few dozen people. Many were tenant farmers on estates owned by the emperor that comprised one-fifth of the land, about the same as the private estates. Thus, about 60 percent of land was owned by an independent peasantry farming small plots of land. Taxation was regular and heavy, and because it was collected in coin, it pushed peasants to produce a surplus that could be sold for cash in markets in the nearest city.

Women, especially peasants, were mostly confined to the household, preparing food, birthing and attending to children, repairing clothing, and tending small farm animals and small gardens. In cities, their activities ranged more broadly, although most working women were poor. Some operated boutiques and shops, prepared and served meals in small tavernas, and sold produce in open-air markets. Actresses, entertainers, and prostitutes could also be found in cities and invariably clustered at the bottom of the social scale.

Slaves, sometimes hundreds of them, were kept by the wealthy landowners, but Byzantine slavery, while it lasted, was mostly an urban phenomenon. They toiled in private households or workshops, preparing food, weaving baskets, making bricks, and so on, but their numbers declined steadily after the fifth century.

Byzantine cities swarmed with poor people who relied on the charity of the state and the Christian Church to survive. In the fifth century, the state still supervised the distribution of free bread, but gradually, charity became dominated by the church. The daily life of the poor was a monotonous routine of days spent scrounging for food, looking for odd jobs, or hawking found or stolen items in the street.

Mortality rates for everyone, rich and poor, were high. One-third of all babies did not live to see their first birthday, and for those who were fortunate enough to survive childhood, most would not see the age of 40. Of course, the life expectancy of the poor and destitute was even grimmer than these average figures might suggest.

The Economy in the West

The economy in the western part of the Roman Empire fragmented and contracted sharply when imperial unity disappeared. Population shrank in size, especially in cities, a trend accelerated by the outbreak of plague in 541 that swept widely across the former Roman Empire. Contraction in agriculture, manufacturing, and trade followed. During the seventh and eighth centuries, however, innovations in agricultural technology occurred, probably spurring enough production of surplus to feed increasing numbers of workers in manufacturing, notably in ceramics and metalwork. Trade shows a similar trajectory, from sharp contraction and localization in the fifth and sixth centuries to some growth and expansion in the seventh, especially in northern Europe as trading **emporia** came to dot the coastlines of the North and Baltic Seas.

Production: Plague, Population, and Technology

Bubonic plague, previously unknown in Mediterranean lands, broke out in the Egyptian coastal city of Pelusium in 541. It quickly spread, infecting thousands in Syria, Persia, Anatolia, and Constantinople before moving west to Greece, North Africa, Italy, Spain, and Francia. It followed river valleys and overland routes into the hinterlands and even leaped the English Channel and reached the British Isles. Although the disease never remained in one place very long, for two centuries it exacted its deadly toll. One-third to one-half of the population died from it in the first few years after it struck for the first time—perhaps 230,000 in Constantinople alone at a rate of 10,000 a day while it raged. The contagion infected rich and poor alike—even the emperor Justinian contracted it, although he was one of the fortunate ones to survive it. Zachariah of Mytilene, a Syrian historian, voices what millions must have thought of the disease: "It was a scourge from Satan, who was ordered by God to destroy men."[1]

Plague had significant economic effects. By quickly reducing population, its short-term effect was to disrupt farming and trade and to drive up the value of labor. It probably reinforced the growth in peasant autonomy already discussed, for lands lay vacant and lords were in no position to exploit a peasantry whose services increased in value.

What long-term demographic effects plague may have had is debated, for populations have a remarkable ability to rebound after catastrophic mortalities. There is little doubt, however, that the population of the former Roman Empire, in both East and West, contracted. Land everywhere went out of cultivation as the

---

1   Zachariah of Mytilene, *The Syrian Chronicle*, X 9, trans. F. J. Hamilton and E. W. Brooks (London: Metheun, 1899).

climate cooled, and overall agricultural production plummeted. This agricultural pattern is mirrored in metal and ceramic production.

Still, despite this contraction, archeologists find evidence of important changes in technological innovation during this period. We find scattered evidence of a new kind of plough being used around 600 in the lands north of the Alps in the West (although not in the East where the soil was not conducive to it). With a longer blade than the shallow scratch plough used previously, the new plough cut a deeper furrow, making accessible rich and fertile loams that characterized the heavy soil of these parts of Europe. Its curved moldboard, also a new addition clearly in evidence by the eighth century, turned it over. The new plough therefore increased productivity by moving previously untapped nutrients from the deeper soils to the surface.

The new plough was heavy and expensive. It took several oxen (and, later, horses fitted with a new type of harness that maximized the superior strength and speed of the horse) to pull, a cost few peasants could afford and certainly a factor that limited its use. In any case, where it was used, it covered more land in a given unit of time and so decreased the amount of labor involved. Fewer people, then, could produce larger harvests. In a time of population decline or stagnation, this was an important consideration. This may have released people to work in other specialized activities, such as manufacturing, construction, and trade.

Archeology also points to a gradual growth in ceramic production in certain locations in the early 700s, notably along the Rhine River. Here we find increasing evidence of standardized types of pottery being produced in concentrated workshops. Because these workers likely did not grow their own food, such specialization of labor points to at least some increased surplus food production and, importantly, to quickening systems of exchange through which these ceramics must have been sold.

One must be cautious about overstating the overall impact of innovative technology during these centuries, for its appearance was sporadic and far from general, but the growth in farming and in population that is evident in the eighth and ninth centuries, as we will see in a later chapter, owes something to changes slowly occurring during preceding centuries.

Trade in the West

What happened to commerce with the collapse of imperial unity in the fifth century? Certainly, the networks of the previous centuries were disrupted and fragmented, and in the West, the scale and volume of trade most certainly contracted.

Local economies appear to have become simpler. Artisan production was on a much smaller scale and, judging from archaeological evidence, involved less skill. The distribution range of most products was undoubtedly much reduced. The economy reached a low point in the West in the seventh century. Many fewer aristocrats were managing their lands with an eye toward trade across the Mediterranean Basin, as had been common among their Roman predecessors.

Still, trade never disappeared, and this suggests that in some places, in some commodities, surpluses were still being produced and exchanged. This in turn points to degrees of specialization of production because people swap what they make or grow for what they do not. Moreover, concentration on producing what can be traded suggests that the producer is, to some degree, paying attention to markets.

Clearly, the western half of the former Roman Empire was hit the hardest by the disappearance of imperial unity. As the trans-Mediterranean economic system collapsed, there was a distinct contraction in the scale of trade in the West and in the diversity of products exchanged. Cities shrank in size and in prosperity and in some places disappeared altogether. Likewise, there was a steady decline in the number of ships plying western waterways and a shrinking of the major ports. Many western harbors just faded away from disuse. By the 600s, almost all the ships involved in oceangoing trade on the Mediterranean Sea, even in the West, sailed from the East, but even their numbers had declined by two-thirds since 400.

During the Roman Empire, the Rhine, Rhône, and Danube Rivers were major water routes linking Rome's northern territories to its Mediterranean heartland. Between the sixth and eighth centuries, as the Mediterranean system withered and the Danube River fell under the control of hostile peoples from the East, the pattern shifted away from water toward land routes. Smaller Mediterranean markets no longer sustained a demand for bulk goods like wine that had arrived via the Rhône River in Gaul. What goods continued to trickle southward, such as metalware and weaponry, now hailed from Switzerland and the Rhine Valley and came to Italy and the Mediterranean world over the mountain passes of the Alps.

Contraction was especially pronounced in places like Spain and Italy that were tied irrevocably to withering Mediterranean shipping networks and markets. To the north, however, there were unmistakable signs of growth astir, even as early as the seventh century. In Merovingian Francia, as we have seen, the lay and clerical aristocracy remained rich and powerful, and these aristocrats were the source of demand that vitalized both regional and long-distance trade. A more complex and active exchange network existed there than anywhere else in the West. Pottery, metalwork, bonework, and glassware circulated across the Seine-Rhine region.

Although in total volume long-distance trade paled in comparison to regional and local, and all were far smaller in volume than during the days of the empire, it was far from inconsequential in its importance. Rich aristocrats prized luxury goods like silk (and the church desired it for its vestments and décor), which could only be acquired through long-distance trade. Periodic fairs and markets stocked these items, brought to market across tenuous but far-flung trade networks.

Coin finds from royal mints suggest that this exchange economy was at least partially monetized and that the Merovingian kings had an interest in its operation. Indeed, recent substantial coin and crafted metalware discoveries even beyond Francia in England and Denmark point to a hitherto unsuspected network of inland markets there.

Beginning in the seventh century and accelerating in the eighth, most of the spending of aristocratic and royal wealth was not directed southward toward the Mediterranean Sea but rather to the north. Archeological finds have uncovered a surprising amount of trade on the North and Baltic Seas at this time, with trade routes reaching into northeastern Europe, as well as to Byzantium. The Sutton Hoo ship, unearthed by archeologists in East Anglia, England, dates from the early seventh century. The site was discovered to be a burial, where an individual was buried within an entire ship and with exquisitely crafted items. The identity of the individual is unknown, but given the demands of labor and resources it must have taken to bury the ship and the value of the precious objects that were laid next to the body, he must have been a rich and powerful man, perhaps even an Anglo-Saxon king. An elaborate gold shoulder clasp, a gold-wrought buckle, precious gems, and 10 silver bowls are evidence of the man's wealth, and a ceremonial helmet, shield, and sword indicate that he was a warrior. Burying an entire ship illustrates not only the importance of the man but also the importance of seafaring and the connection of long-distance seaborne trade to great wealth. Not only were the silver spoons found among the many objects buried here likely from Byzantium but so, too, were the silver bowls, made in the eastern Roman Empire in the sixth century. The ship itself displays the shallow draft of seagoing ships typical of the period.

The hubs of this commercial system were new non-Roman urban settlements that dotted the banks of some rivers and the coastlines of the North and Baltic Seas. These new emporia, like Haithabu on the Baltic coast of Denmark, Birka in Sweden, Ladoga on the Volkhov River in northwestern Russia, and, above all, Dorestad at the confluence of the Lek and Rhine Rivers, were commercial and artisanal settlements, not centers of political or ecclesiastical power, nor were they residences of aristocrats. They certainly were protected by kings, however, suggesting that monarchs valued their function. They were gateway communities, ports of interregional and long-distance trade that imported and exported goods, responding to the demand of kings and aristocrats and exporting an array of commodities. An indication of the far-reaching trading networks that coursed through the Baltic and reach distant markets is a small bronze figurine of Buddha found at the island port of Helgo, Sweden. The statue was made in India, thousands of miles from Sweden.

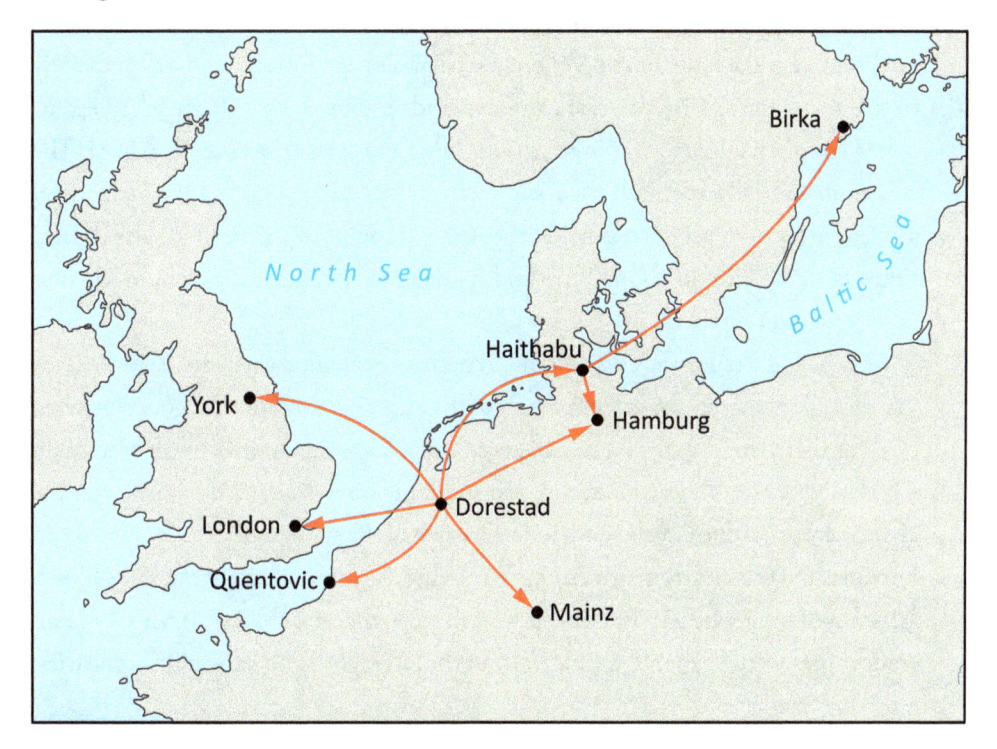

MAP 11.3 Trade Routes and Trading Centers in Northern Europe

Driven by demand from local elites and kings, the trade routes that crisscrossed the North and Baltic Seas were much more active during the seventh and eighth centuries than we once thought. The most prominent traders working these routes, at least until the ninth century, were the Frisians. They were present in most emporia. They likely sailed ships similar to the one excavated in East Anglia in England in the mid-20th century. The Sutton Hoo ship was a seaworthy craft that easily could have been used to transport goods across the North Sea, the Baltic Sea, the English Channel, and the Irish Sea.

Europe's rulers and aristocrats were seeking luxury goods through long-distance trade and exported amber ornaments, finely crafted metal tools and weapons, ceramics, and wine (great quantities of which were produced by **monasteries** in northern Francia). In the 700s, another commodity was added to the lists and in fact became the single most valuable export Europe had to offer—slaves. Most of them were destined for the Muslim world. Escalating demand for slaves in Islamic lands is plainly evident at this time. Muslim raiders descended on southern Italy, Sardinia, and Sicily several times between 700 and 710, returning to Sicily in force between 727 and 735, each time seeking and carrying off large numbers of captives. Most of them were young males, prized commodities in the slave markets across the Muslim Mediterranean.

It did not take long for the Venetians to spy a profit and respond commercially to this demand. The Mediterranean slave trade boomed. By 750, they had established commercial slave-trading relations with Muslims from North Africa. The Venetians initially acquired their supply from increasingly specialized squads of slave hunters who prowled outside the walls of towns or ranged into the coastal hinterlands to kidnap young boys and herd them to the beaches where Muslim slavers would buy them.

As the market for slaves grew, the Venetians expanded their operations. They increasingly acquired slaves from north of the Alps, trading Muslim goods or silver coin for them. In 748, the Venetians even ran a large slave market in Rome itself. The fact that the Venetians explode so suddenly on the commercial scene in the eighth century is due largely to their domination of the slave trade. This commerce in human cargo was clearly instrumental in reviving the sea routes between Italy, North Africa, and soon southern France. As we will see in the next chapter, Arab-Christian trade routes would expand dramatically in the late eighth and early ninth centuries.

The Economy in Byzantium

Despite the fact that plague swept the Mediterranean Basin beginning in 541, including Byzantium, it did not seem to drive the Byzantine economy into irreversible decline. Even though the Byzantine economy mirrors that of the West in a long-term trend toward contraction, it was still prosperous and well-integrated until 600. Population shrank, to be sure, but cities continued to exist, if on a smaller scale, and served as centers of manufacturing as well as markets for regional goods. Ships, although smaller than the classical galleys, carrying grain from Egypt continued to dock in Constantinople, which remained the dominant trading city in the East. Only with the loss of vast stretches of the empire, above all Egypt, to conquering Arab armies in 642 does the economy nearly collapse. Constantinople survived and so too, however truncated, did the Byzantine Empire and its economy.

Production: Agriculture and Manufacturing

Agriculture had always been the fundamental basis of Roman power, and that continued under Byzantium. The main grain production areas were Egypt (until it was lost to the Arabs in 642), Thrace, and the coastal regions of Anatolia. Indeed, Egypt's agricultural prosperity was fundamental to the health of the Byzantine economy. Egyptians had long ago learned how to turn the Nile floods toward robust agricultural productivity. It had been a primary breadbasket of the Roman Empire, and the remarkable fertility of the lands guaranteed substantial surpluses. Ships sailing upon the Nile had fashioned a complex and integrated economy that now was centuries old. This economy continued to sustain a dense urban population and, consequently, a diverse manufacturing base, including large-scale ceramic production. Indeed, Egyptian amphora production was enormous.

The entire Nile region remained linked and integrated, and the Byzantine state maintained the channels and dikes to control flooding. State officials also continued to administer an elaborate fiscal system with exact assessment and accounting. And the land tax continued to be collected.

Most of the soil in the Byzantine Empire beyond Egypt and Syria, however, was thin and rocky, meaning that the traditional scratch plough remained appropriate. This plough cut a furrow a couple inches deep, and such shallow ploughing conserved ground moisture. Indeed, unlike in the West, there was little change in agricultural technology in Byzantium before the 10th century. Most farming implements had iron blades mounted on wooden shafts. Olives and grain continued to be crushed and ground in water-driven mills as they had been in antiquity.

Though much smaller than in antiquity and contracting after the fifth century as the overall population shrank, cities still existed in Byzantium. They remained centers of local power; seats of administration, justice, and religion; and sites of artisan workshops and markets. In fact, although the evidence is scanty, the state apparently supervised commerce and manufacturing. In Constantinople, the prefect, called an Eparch, was an official appointed by the emperor charged with regulating a complex system of guilds of craftsmen and merchants. When these guilds and the Eparch came into being is unknown, but the prefect in medieval Byzantium enforced the use of standard weights, measures, and currency, and to protect guildsmen from harmful or unfair competition, he regulated the quality and quantity of production, the location of shops, and the prices retailers were allowed to charge for their goods.

There is no doubt that the state was especially keen to regulate silk-related occupations—spinning, weaving, dyeing, distributing and retailing, and importing—from abroad. For centuries, raw and woven silk from China passed through Sassanian Persia, but the Byzantines were at the mercy of high tariffs or choked supply. So Byzantium began producing silk on its own. Procopius tells the story of two Nestorian monks smuggling silkworm eggs into Byzantium in 553 and presenting them to the emperor Justinian. Whether true or not, in the mid-sixth century, the Byzantines did begin to breed silkworms and establish their own silk production under a jealously guarded imperial monopoly. The state also strictly controlled the production of a rare purple dye, already produced by Phoenicians centuries before, extracted from an eastern Mediterranean mollusk called a murex. The state-run Byzantine workshops gained renown for producing exquisite purple silks.

This luxury product was destined for the imperial court and for the churches in the East, but also for the export market west. Christian churches in Europe were a major consumer of Byzantine silks. Merchants in the fifth and sixth centuries who were associated with provisioning the churches grew fabulously wealthy, further testimony that the demand for luxury goods exerted by clerical aristocrats had commercial ramifications.

Trade in the East

The key date for Byzantine trade was 642. With the Arab conquests of North Africa, Syria, Palestine, and, above all, Egypt in the mid-seventh century, the Byzantine economy, like the state itself, was transformed. Eighty percent of the empire's cities contracted or were abandoned altogether, as building nearly ceased. The ones that remained were centers of military districts, buoyed only by enough demand to support small regional markets. Amphorae, once the standard shipping container across the empire, now were produced in local pockets. This clearly points to a breakdown in demand.

Constantinople was the only Byzantine city that continued to engage in sizable overseas trade. The demand for grain for its inhabitants (though many fewer than before the conquests, as the city's population plunged from 500,000 to under 70,000) kept ships at sea in the Aegean and, to a lesser extent, on the Black Sea. To pay for these imports, ceramic tableware was produced in state-run workshops in the capital for export.

Before 600, the economy of the Byzantine Empire, in contrast with that of the West, continued to prosper, if on a smaller scale than during the heyday of the Roman Empire. The Roman Empire in the East was largely a maritime state, with sea routes connecting its provinces. With the collapse of the state in the

West, trade across the Mediterranean between the East and West nearly dried up. However, in the East, regional trade continued to thrive. Cities like Constantinople and Alexandria in Egypt were bustling ports.

The Byzantine Empire and its neighboring regions were characterized by regional specialized products, all coursing across trade routes that converged in urban markets, above all Constantinople. Southern Greece and the Aegean Islands were known for olives and wine, inland Asia Minor for wool, meat, hides, leather, and parchment. From the upper Balkans came furs and metals, and from the western reaches of central Asia north of Byzantium came amber, furs, and slaves, and from further east came gems and jewels. Arabs brought fine ceramics, glass, and aromatics. From India, merchants hauled cargoes of ivory and spices, and from China, porcelain and silk.

Land travel was slow and expensive, the roads often plagued by bandits. Donkeys could carry a payload of 200–225 pounds, camels as much as 450 pounds, so the latter were preferred for longer hauls. Whenever possible, however, sea travel was used. It was cheaper, faster, and safer, and most of the population lived near coasts or navigable rivers.

Clearly, trade continued to be more vibrant in the East than the West until the mid-seventh century and coin, like the gold nomisma, more widely circulated there, but shrinkage in scale can nonetheless be seen everywhere by 650. From the fifth to the mid-seventh century, Mediterranean shipping both shifted eastward and contracted. By 650, the numbers of ships sailing this sea had dropped by two-thirds since 400, largely because of the end of the imperial transregional distribution system that had provisioned the empire's large cities and army. However, ships still sailed in and out of Constantinople, plying the waters of the Aegean and parts of the Black Sea. With the return of better fortunes for the empire in the ninth century, so, too, will trade in and out of Byzantium begin to grow again.

Review Questions

1. What were the results of the breakdown of imperial Roman governance in the West?
2. How and why did the Byzantine state change between 400 and 750?
3. In what ways did the economy in the West change between the fifth and the eighth centuries?
4. What effect did Arab conquests have on the Byzantine Empire?

Further Readings

Cunliffe, Barry. *Europe Between the Oceans: Themes and Variations 9000 BC–AD 1000*. New Haven: Yale University Press, 2008. (See, especially, Chapter 12)

Davies, Wendy, and Paul Fouracre, eds. *Property and Power in the Early Middle Ages*. Cambridge: Cambridge University Press, 1995.

Heather, Peter. *The Fall of the Roman Empire: A New History of Rome and the Barbarians*. Oxford: Oxford University Press, 2006.

Hodges, Richard. *Dark Age Economics: The Origins of Towns and Trade, A. D. 600–1000*. 2nd ed. London: Duckworth, 1989.

Hodges, Richard, and William Bowden, eds. *The Sixth Century: Production, Distribution and Demand*. Leiden: Brill, 1998.

Little, Lester K., ed. *Plague and the End of Antiquity: The Pandemic of 541–750*. Cambridge: Cambridge University Press, 2008.

McCormick, Michael. *The Origins of the European Economy: Communications and Commerce, A. D. 300–900*. Cambridge: Cambridge University Press, 2001.

Pestel, Tim, and Katharina Ulmschneider, eds., *Markets in Early Medieval Europe: Trading and Productive Sites, 650–850*. Bollington: Windgather Press, 2003.

Pohl, Walter, ed. *Kingdoms of the Empire: The Integration of Barbarians in Late Antiquity*. Leiden: Brill, 1997.

Smith, Julia. *Europe After Rome*. Oxford: Oxford University Press, 2005.

Wells, Peter S. *Barbarians to Angels: The Dark Ages Reconsidered*. New York: W. W. Norton, 2008.

Wickham, Chris. *Framing the Early Middle Ages: Europe and the Mediterranean, 400–800*. Oxford: Oxford University Press, 2005.

Wickham, Chris. *The Inheritance of Rome: Illuminating the Dark Ages, 400–1000*. New York: Penguin, 2009.

Wolfram, Herwig. *The Roman Empire and Its Germanic Peoples*. Translated by Thomas Dunlap. Berkeley: University of California Press, 1997.

Figure Credits

Map 11.1: Source: https://commons.wikimedia.org/wiki/File:Europe_at_the_close_of_the_6th_century,_showing_the_Gothic_monarchies_(14780052291).jpg.

Map 11.2: Copyright © by Roke~commonswiki (CC BY-SA 3.0) at https://commons.wikimedia.org/wiki/File:Byzantine_Empire_animated.gif.

Map 11.3: Source: https://commons.wikimedia.org/wiki/File:Dorestad_and_trade_routes.jpg.

CHAPTER 12

Conversion, Conquest, and Commerce in the Islamic World, 610–ca. 1000

The Prophet Muhammad and Early Islam

In 610, a Meccan merchant in Arabia began receiving what he believed were revelations from the God of the Judeo-Christian tradition. Believing himself to be the last prophet in that tradition, this communication from God to man would be, according to this prophet named Muhammad, the final one. The revelations came to Muhammad in Arabic in sporadic fashion over two decades. Muhammad frequently recited these revelations to his followers, some of whom must have written them down. The accumulated fragmented text of revelations became the Quran (alternatively, Qur'an or Koran), the holy book of the new religion of Islam. The political implications of the Quran are indirect. It implies a great deal about power and legitimacy, although it does not contain directives for the creation of an organized state, nor does it say anything about a succession of leadership of the Muslim community.

The Man and the Revelation

Muhammad was born around 570, lived in Mecca, worked as a caravaner, and married his employer, a rich widow named Khadija. Arabia was dotted with fairs and crisscrossed by caravan routes, and Mecca emerged as the most important commercial site during the sixth century when overland routes of the spice trade were diverted there due to political instabilities elsewhere. By Muhammad's day, Mecca had become an important caravan city. As such, Mecca attracted Christian, Persian, and Jewish traders as well as Arabs, and this extremely heterogeneous city was rife with religious diversity and economic competition. It was also increasingly socially stratified based on wealth.

The revelations that Muhammad heard reflect an uncompromising commitment to monotheism. Muhammad placed the revelations in the Judeo-Christian prophetic tradition that began with Abraham and included Jesus Christ. He considered Judaism and Christianity to be sibling religions to what would become Islam, but he parted company with Christianity because he did not believe that Jesus was the Son of God, and he thought that the doctrine of the Trinity split God in three and thus repudiated monotheism. Muhammad professed that he, like Jesus and all the other prophets before him, was a mortal man with no divinity and was simply God's chosen messenger.

The Mission

The revelations are directives given to the Muslim community. At first, that community was very small. The earliest converts—among them Abu Bakr, his cousin Ali, and his wife Khadija—accepted his ideas and gathered around him to hear him repeat his revelations. In 613, Muhammad began his mission, reciting the Quran in public places in Mecca. His new converts were rootless migrants, poor men, and members of weak clans who felt excluded from the power structure of Mecca that was dominated by wealthy mercantile tribes. The Prophet's message emphasized the importance of charity, compassion for the weak, and a merciful God and seemed to offer hope to marginalized people.

It also seemed to be an attack on the authority of the dominant tribes. As Muhammad became increasingly popular, the leading merchants of Mecca belittled and ridiculed his revelations, denouncing him as a phony soothsayer and a disreputable magician. They showered him with insults and harassed him and his followers.

Muhammad's message emphasized the creation of a community of believers who would be held together by fair and just treatment of one another, a message that caught the attention of bickering tribes in the nearby city of Yathrib whose leaders, in 622, invited Muhammad to arbitrate their disputes. Arab tribes were typically tight-knit kinship groups comprised of patriarchal families led by a chief, or shaykh. These clans and tribes were staunchly egalitarian and had no central commanding and enduring hierarchical institutions. Such was the situation in Yathrib.

The challenge for Muhammad, then, was to broker an intertribal harmony. He offered them equal membership in an overarching community of Muslims called the **umma**. This community was held together by common religious practices and a social vision it believed was revealed by God to Muhammad and was expressed in the Quran. Muhammad wrote the Charter, or *Constitution of Medina* (Yathrib was renamed Medina), which explicitly articulates the nature of this agreement.

The Meccan tribes quickly saw Medina as a rival. They began abusing Muslims who remained in Mecca and even confiscated their property. Muhammad received a revelation at this time, and, like many of them, this one was tied to a specific circumstance and gave specific directives to the community about how to respond to these circumstances. Muhammad harbored deep hostility toward these Meccan tribes and their treatment of Muslims, and this is the original context for the well-known verses in the Quran on holy "war" or "struggle," **jihad**. This quote is from the Quran itself:

> "Fight in pursuit of the way of God those who fight against you but do not provoke hostility. God has no love for those who embark on aggression. Slay them where ever you encounter them and drive them out of places whence they have driven you. Subversion is a worse thing than slaughter. Do not do battle with them, however, in the vicinity of the sacred mosque unless they are warring with you there. If they fight you, slay them; such are the desserts of those who deny the faith. But if they desist God is certainly forgiving and merciful."[1]

Islam is no more inherently violent than other religions. This call for jihad, in fact, stands in stark relief against most of the Quran, which emphasizes peace, harmony, justice, and compassion. This message, however, will be appropriated by some later Muslims to wage different wars in the name of God.

This revelation encouraged his followers to raid Meccan trade caravans. The conflict escalated to the Battle of Badr during which Muhammad's Muslims defeated a larger Meccan force. The victory was interpreted by many Arabs as a sign of divine favor and brought more converts to Islam from across Arabia. The city of Mecca sued for peace and surrendered to Muhammad who made his triumphal reentry into Mecca in 630. He magnanimously granted amnesty to all, destroyed the polytheistic idols of the Ka'ba shrine, and declared it the holiest shrine of Islam.

The Quran and the State

Muhammad's victory and message proved attractive throughout Arabia, and he became the most powerful leader on the peninsula. At the time of his death in 632, Islam was the dominant religion there. Two years after Muhammad's death,

---

1 Marvin Gettleman and Stuart Schaar, eds., *The Middle East and Islamic World Reader* (New York: Grove Press, 2003), 15.

the new leader of the community of Muslims created by Muhammad, Abu Bakr, ordered the manuscript of the Quran to be compiled into one copy. The third leader, 'Uthmān (d. 656), ordered copies to be made of this master copy and that all others be destroyed. This version remains the standard copy of the Quran to this day.

The Quran does not contain directives for the creation of an organized state, nor does it say anything about a succession of leadership of the Muslim community. Nonetheless, the Islamic state, as it evolved after Muhammad, monopolized coercive power within the community of Muslims and was charged with exercising it against evil-doers, those who, by their actions or words, had rejected God's law as the Quran defines it. The state and its leader, called the **caliph**, though initially not sacred in any way, were responsible for leading the community down the correct path to salvation as Muslims understood it.

Conquest and Expansion

The territorial expansion of Islam accelerated after the death of Muhammad. Unlike its generally peaceful spread through Arabia, the next waves of expansion were carried out by wars of conquest. The objective was religious in motivation, to fulfill God's will by extending Islam to the entire world. Muslim leaders believed that Islam was divinely ordained to bring to humanity peace and relief from oppression, to bring the protection of Islam to all peoples. Those who refused to accept it would be forced to submit, by military action if necessary.

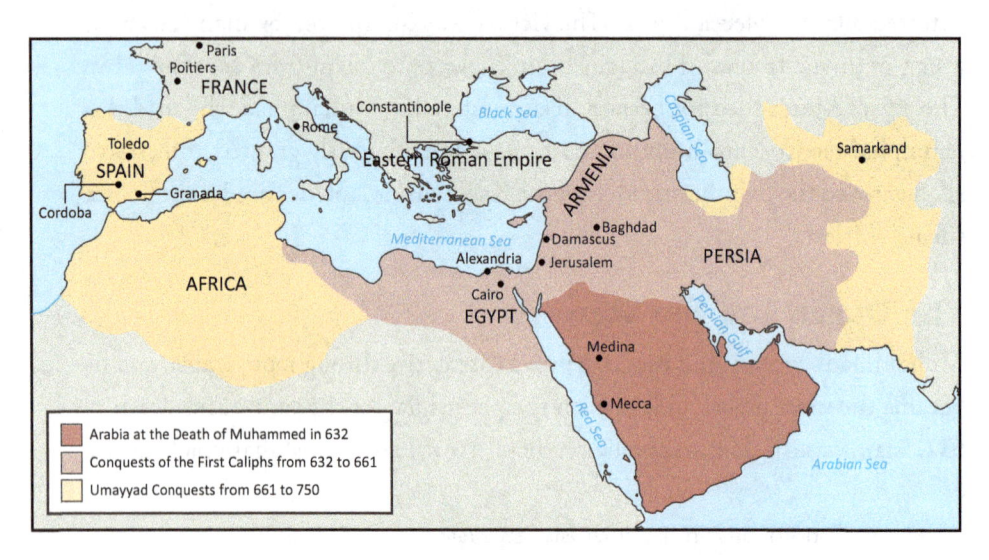

MAP 12.1   The Expansion of Islam

Difficulties arose when conquest turned to governance. How was such a sprawling and diverse empire to be effectively governed? Once Islam moved beyond the Arabian Peninsula, it ceased to be comprised of a community of Arab tribes. The world of Islam retained a religious unity, but politically, it became decentralized and fragmented.

Arab Armies and Non-Arab Lands

For over 100 years, the Arab armies were astonishingly successful. Between 639 and 642, the Muslim Arabs conquered two-thirds of the Byzantine Empire (notably Egypt and Syria) and all of the Sassanian. Regardless that these venerable empires had been weakened by years of fighting among themselves prior to the Arab invasions, the swiftness of the Arab conquest was nonetheless astounding.

Arab armies then marched east, north, and west. By 713, they had reached the lower valley and delta of the Indus River in India. Two years later, the ancient trading cities of central Asia, Bukhara and Samarkand, had fallen to the Muslim conquerors. The Muslim armies pushed further northwestward, capturing Tashkent in 751 and defeating the Chinese Tang army at the Battle of Talas in the same year. To the west, by 711, Arab conquerors had subdued all of North Africa and had entered the Iberian Peninsula. By 732, the Visigothic kingdom of Spain had capitulated, and Arab armies had crossed the Pyrenees into Francia. Their expansion was only halted in that year by the Christian victory in the Battle of Poitiers.

How was such rapid conquest possible? No Muslim written records from the time of the conquests survive to document them, so explanations are dependent upon non-Islamic evidence or Islamic texts written later. Indeed, except for the Quran, the history of Islam's first century from the Muslim perspective is dependent on sources written a century after the death of Muhammad. Understandably, this literature reflects the needs and perspectives of the later generations.

Concerning the conquests, these later Islamic accounts project a view of planned, operationally centralized, and ideologically motivated conquest. Early on, this may have been the case. Most of the commanders of the early Islamic armies were from Medina or Mecca, and though not necessarily from the same tribes, all knew each other personally and had helped Muhammad establish the nascent Islamic state in Medina.

Given such cohesion, strict control from the caliph may not have been necessary. Once this generation passed, however, the notion of an organized, planned conquest is more open to doubt. Non-Islamic evidence suggests it may have been more haphazard and, in some cases, even accidental. Arab armies were still likely stirred by Islamic ideological zeal, but whether the caliphs had any control over their conquering armies is questionable. Uncontrolled tribal raiding parties under autonomous war leaders acting on their own initiative may have accounted for some, perhaps most, of the conquests. Moreover, the Arab armies erupted across the region at a fortuitous time for them, for many of the states they conquered were suffering already from internal weakness.

The Arab armies could not have numbered more than 500,000 soldiers, yet within a century, they had conquered 20–30 million people. Often, the conquered peoples were willing to accept these new overlords and, in some cases, even to welcome them. When Muslim armies approached a new community and offered the protection of Islam, there were three options: first, to convert to Islam; second, to arrange treaties that acknowledged the sovereignty of Islam and paid tribute and special taxes to the new overlords in return for retaining religious and internal autonomy; and third, to refuse to submit, which was followed by Muslim armies attempting to force submission.

Usually, Arab rule was less oppressive than the Byzantine or Sassanian. Arab taxes were lower, and the new Arab rulers wanted as little as possible to disturb the agricultural productivity of the conquered lands. Initially, the Arab objective was to segregate Arabs from non-Arabs, the former serving as the military elite and the latter as producers and taxpayers. The armies were therefore settled in garrisons in cities. As a result, before 700, the new Muslim overlords did not live on the land, nor were they landlords or even farmers.

Political Decentralization and the Emergence of Inequality

The immediate result of the conquests was a scattered army of occupancy. Two problems promptly arose, however. First, how was the new empire to be held together? And second, what to do about the increasing numbers of non-Arabs who converted to Islam (often to avoid the tax imposed on non-Muslims)?

The Muslim community was headed by a political leader, the caliph, and theoretically, he had unquestioned command of the armies. In practice, however, he increasingly had little effective control of the conquered provinces that stretched from the Atlantic Ocean to the Indus River. Governors and generals were appointed by, and in theory responsible to, the caliph, but as we will see, actual caliphal control (and the access by the caliph to resources in the various provinces) deteriorated as time wore on.

Conversion by conquered peoples was increasingly problematic and in time would change the face of the world of Islam as much as its political decentralization. On the one hand, conversion to the true faith was theoretically encouraged, but in practice, Arab conquerors showed little interest in, and sometimes open hostility to, creating non-Arab Muslims. To the Arabs, society was defined by membership in tribes, and within these, a rough equality prevailed. There were no closed aristocracies or castes, and what hierarchy existed was fluid and open to advancement. The Muslim Arabs saw themselves as free, autonomous tribesmen chosen by God to be His carriers of His last revelation—spoken in Arabic, after all—and to be rulers of the world. Everyone else was misguided and, if necessary, worthy of conquest.

In such a vision, there was little room for the non-Arab Muslim. And yet, with the vast conquests, conversions mounted. Initially, the Arabs looked down upon the non-Arabs as inferior, but by the mid-ninth century, Arab Muslims were outnumbered by non-Arab Muslims, and Islam lost its specific ties to Arab culture and evolved into a religion that happened to have roots in Arabia.

By the 10th century, the Muslim world, now reaching far beyond Arabia, had become socioeconomically complex, rendering tribal organization obsolete. Even in the armies, Arabs became a minority. Society became increasingly defined by social and occupational strata, and the notion of egalitarianism that had marked tribal society was eroded. By the 10th century, Islamic social theorists can be found praising hierarchy in all its forms, arguing now that it pervaded the universe as God's natural order and therefore should be exemplified in human society as a reflection of His will.

The Caliphates: Governance and Legitimacy

Even as conquest carried Islam over vast reaches of territory, within the community of Muslims, dissension was its nearly constant companion. Muhammad said nothing about succession to the leadership of the community, and so it was frequently contested. The first four leaders, called caliphs, knew Muhammad personally, but after the death of the last one, the world of Islam was governed by two succeeding dynastic families called the Umayyads and the Abbasids. Both confronted the problem of governing a sprawling empire and both were torn by forces of decentralization led by powerful provincial generals and governors they could not control. They seized upon symbols of legitimacy to try to hold their empires together, but eventually, the countervailing winds of fragmentation effectively ended any real powers of governance from the center.

The Rightly Guided Caliphs, 632–661

Muhammad was the first unquestioned leader of the Islamic community, but he made no specific arrangements for his succession. Nor had Muhammad specified political systems or any particular political order that should continue after his death. Many of his followers in Arabia felt that their allegiance was to Muhammad himself and that upon his death their affiliation with the Muslim community ended.

Abu Bakr, Muhammad's father-in-law through the Prophet's marriage to Aisha and among his earliest converts, was joined by other close companions to Muhammad who were steadfast in believing that a single Muslim community must endure both in its adherence to the Quran and as a political entity. Abu Bakr was acclaimed by these companions as the true leader of the community, referring to him as Muhammad's representative, or caliph. He then made a momentous decision to bring the wavering tribes back into the Muslim community, by force if necessary. This set a precedent that would seem to justify the vast political expansion that soon followed and led to a shifting in the interpretation of the meaning of jihad to be broadened to include all enemies of Islam.

By 634 when Abu Bakr died, all the tribes of Arabia had been brought back into the Islamic political orbit. Abu Bakr named Umar, another early follower of Muhammad, to succeed him as caliph and instructed him to lead the Islamic army into Syria and Iraq and rid them of their Byzantine and Sassanian overlords. The task was made easier by the inhabitants often resenting Byzantine and Sassanian rule. Taxes were heavier and, in the case of the Byzantines, religious persecution against nonorthodox Christians was common. By the time Umar died in 644, assassinated by a Persian slave, the Byzantine Empire had been shorn of two-thirds of its territory, and the Sassanian Empire ceased to exist altogether.

The third "Rightly Guided Caliph," 'Uthmān, was also an early follower and son-in-law of Muhammad. His accession to the caliphate, however, was contested by some Muslims. They believed that Muhammad's cousin and another son-in-law, Ali (who was married to Fatima, one of Muhammad's daughters), was the rightful caliph and that Abu Bakr, Umar, and 'Uthmān were, therefore, usurpers. When 'Uthmān reasserted a tribal tendency and staffed his administration with members of his own clan, the opposition to him increased. He continued the territorial expansion of Islam, but enemies within the community assassinated him in 656.

After 'Uthmān's death, once again the succession was contested. Ali became caliph—but not without enemies of his own. Chief among them was Aisha, the daughter of Abu Bakr and one of Muhammad's wives (polygamy was permitted within Islam, and Muhammad himself had several wives). Aisha blamed Ali for not avenging the death of 'Uthmān by prosecuting his killers. She quickly rallied many tribesmen in Mecca to her standard and led an army against Ali who was on campaign in Syria. They met in battle outside of Basra in 656, with Aisha leading her troops into battle riding a camel. Ali prevailed at this Battle of the Camel, as it became known, and though Aisha survived and was treated with respect by the victors, Ali remained caliph.

Dissension, however, still tore at the fabric of Islam. Five years later, another civil war ended Ali's caliphate and his life. That the lives of three of the first four caliphs ended violently reflects the turmoil that beset the early Muslim community. This largely stemmed from disputes about succession to the caliphate that Muhammad had left unresolved at his death.

It is from this point, the death of Ali, that the first fissure in Islam occurred, one that continues to this day. Followers of Ali, called **Shi'a** (alternately Shi'ite) Muslims, believed that the true caliph and ruler of the Muslim community descended from Ali. In time they came to believe that this leader, called **imam**, inherited a secret knowledge and possessed exclusive authority to interpret the Quran (and eventually the practical statements and practices attributed to Muhammad, called **Hadith**) and to elaborate Islamic law, the **Shari'a**. The Shi'a never became a majority within Islam. Most Muslims, eventually called **Sunnis**, held to the notion that the caliph was the political leader only and that interpreting the Quran, Hadith, and the law was the preserve of learned jurists and scholars.

Despite the conflict over succession and leadership, Muslim conquests advanced and quickly brought enormous tracts of land into the Arabs' possession. Much of this land was left to the original owners and cultivators, and the Arabs adopted the system of taxation already in use, usually a land tax, and added a tax on non-Muslims. In parts of the former Byzantine and Sassanian empires, however, many elite landowners fled the invading armies and abandoned their land. The Islamic state, and thus the caliph, assumed ownership of these lands and was faced with formulating policies that could generate much-needed revenues. Most of this land was broken up into smaller farms. 'Uthmān introduced a system whereby state land was rented to individuals, leading to a substantial increase in state revenues. In Iraq, he also attempted to stimulate agricultural production by draining swamps, irrigating new fields, and importing slaves from eastern Africa to work the new lands. The demand for revenue was pressing because the Arab army, salaried and garrisoned, was paid from taxes and provisioned in their barracks by the state.

The Umayyad Caliphs, 661–750

In 661, civil war extinguished the last "Rightly Guided" caliphate as well as the life of the last caliph who knew Muhammad personally, Ali. A family related to 'Uthmān led by a general from Syria, the Umayyads, assumed the caliphate. They legitimized their claim as avengers of the murder of 'Uthmān and as members of his tribe, thus claiming blood relation with Muhammad.

However, the Umayyad caliphate was soon challenged by Husayn, the son of Ali and grandson of Muhammad (and a prominent figure in the emerging Shi'a sect of Islam). Husayn met the Umayyad army in the Battle of Karbala in 680 and was killed. His small army was massacred, securing the Umayyad hold on power and furthering the split within Islam between Sunni and Shi'a.

The Umayyads came to power when the Muslim community was still nearly entirely Arab, and the new rulers tried to retain Arab identity and power over a state that was rapidly coming to be extraordinarily diverse in peoples and traditions as the vanquished more and more outnumbered their conquerors. By 680, moreover, the emigration of armies from Arabia was slowing to a trickle, yet Muslim conquests of non-Arabic lands continued on a massive scale. The Muslim armies, therefore, comprised more and more non-Arabs, increasingly dominated by Syrians and then by slaves of Türkish and eastern European origin. Furthering the de-Arabization of the Islamic world, the Umayyads moved the capital from Medina in Arabia to Damascus in Syria.

By 700, the original segregation of Arabs from non-Arabs had broken down, as Arabs began assimilating into the local populations in the city and countryside. New cities emerged, and existing ones grew. Expanded economic opportunities beckoned. Departing from the practices of the first Arab conquerors, after 700, more and more Arabs became landowners and even peasant farmers. Tribal society rooted in lineage gave way to a society that was increasingly ethnically diverse and stratified on the basis of wealth and status. The Umayyads had tried to continue to privilege Arabs politically by placing them in the upper reaches of government and the military, and fiscally through favorable tax policy. By 720, however, they abandoned these practices, bringing Greeks and especially Persians into their administration and issuing legislation that granted all Muslims fiscal equality, whether Arab or not.

Many of the conquered regions remained economically vibrant—as we will see when we discuss the agricultural revolution occurring at this time—producing substantial surpluses, which in turn were tapped through taxes, which continued to be assessed and collected. Little of this revenue, however, found its way to the caliph's coffers in Damascus. In the case of Egypt, around 700, tax revenues sent to the caliph may have been as low as 5 percent, all of the rest kept in the province by its governor to support his own power base and, above all, the soldiers garrisoned in the cities.

This was probably the case in nearly every province across the vast Islamic world (with the exceptions of Syria and Palestine, which remained under the direct control of the caliph), from Iberia to India and central Asia. The Umayyad realm, then, became a loose federation of semiautonomous provinces controlled by independent-minded provincial governors and generals, local notables, tribal chiefs, and scholars of greater or lesser renown who were increasingly claiming the authority to interpret the meaning of the Quran and Hadith.

How, then, did the Umayyads remain in power? First, all Muslims, at least for a time, recognized that a caliph, however powerless in practice, was required within Islam. No one questioned the caliph as the theoretical figure who was charged with leading the community of believers to salvation. His existence was necessary for the legitimacy of all Muslim provincial governors, who claimed their authority from the caliph.

The Umayyads recognized that their authority—political, military, or fiscal—could not span the entire realm, but they do seem to have created a regional power base of their own that channeled enough revenue to their coffers to sustain them. Many of the caliphs claimed large swaths of conquered lands for their own family rather than for the state and its treasury, effectively creating royal estates that generated revenue directly to the caliphs. Most of these estates were in Syria and Palestine and thus close enough to Damascus that they could be effectively administered from the capital. In the early 700s, the caliph Hisham (r. 724–743), for example, was renowned for the detailed care he took over the management of his estates.

The Umayyads also secured their claim to power by adopting hereditary succession and abandoning the traditional tribal Arab-Muslim practice of election and consensual governance, further evidence of the waning of tribal tradition in Islam. They were criticized for turning the caliphate into a kingship and for raising family interests above those of the Muslim community.

Despite the opposition, the Umayyads more and more promoted an ideology derived from the Byzantine and, especially, Sassanian empires where the state and its ruler were the foci of ideological loyalty. In 695, for the first time a caliph minted gold and silver coins as the official currency of the empire, replacing Byzantine and Sassanian currency and struck with Arabic script to symbolize the sovereignty and legitimacy of the Muslim state by invoking the language of God.

The Umayyads came to define the caliph as God's deputy on earth. Caliphs were not as yet endowed with any personal sanctity, but they did present themselves as the sanctioned guides of the community toward salvation and exemplars of God's law in their practices and their architecture.

Two outstanding examples of Umayyad caliphs using monumental building to signify their power and authority are The Dome of the Rock, completed in Jerusalem in 691 by the caliph Abd al-Malik (r. 685–705), and the Great Mosque of Damascus, completed in 715 by the caliph al-Walid (r. 705–715). These buildings proclaimed the caliphs' dedication to the faith and promoted their own exalted standing within the Muslim community.

The Dome of the Rock is where many Muslims believe that Muhammad temporarily ascended to heaven where he spoke to Allah, who gave Muhammad instructions to take back to the faithful regarding the details of prayer. The Dome is located in the Old City of Jerusalem on the site of earlier Jewish temples and where, according to Jewish teaching, Abraham was going to sacrifice his son Isaac. Given the connection to Abraham, the building is clearly intended by the Umayyad caliph to assert the connection of Islam—and the Umayyad caliphate—with the prophetic tradition that was culminated by Muhammad. The building also reveals Greek influence on the Umayyads, for its architectural design was patterned after Byzantine churches, including the octagonal floorplan and the wooden rotunda, which were foreign to Islamic architecture at the time.

The Great Mosque of Damascus was constructed for much the same reason as the Dome of the Rock: to directly associate the caliph with the wellsprings of Islam—Muhammad and the Quran—and to place such a holy structure in the capital of his caliphate. A mosque in Islam is the place where Muslims come together to perform salat, or prayer, one of the "Five Pillars of Islam," as articulated in the Quran.

The Abbasid Caliphs, 750–1258

Yet another civil war wracked Islam between 744 and 750, ending with the transferring of power from the Umayyads to another family, the Abbasids. The leader of the rebellion against the Umayyads, Abū al-'Abbās, was a commander of a Muslim army in Khurasān, and with military victory, he was raised to the caliphate. Al-'Abbās claimed descent from an uncle of Muhammad and thus claimed blood relationship with Muhammad. The Abbasids, however, were ethnically more Persian than Arab, and their supporters definitely were. Indeed, the Abbasid rebellion in part was driven by the feeling that the Umayyads were ignoring the interests of Shi'as and non-Arab Muslims.

The Abbasids continued the Umayyad conception of the caliph as the vice regent of God on earth, appointed by God to follow in the ways of the Prophet and to lead the Muslim community along the path of salvation. This meant that they took it as their task to bring Muslim religious practice under state supervision. The mosque was the holy structure where Muslims performed the prayers and rites essential to their faith, and the Abbasids, like the Umayyads before them, sought to associate their rule with the construction and support of these religious buildings. All were monumental in scale, and many were adapted from Sassanian architectural style. At one time the largest mosque in the world, the mosque at Samarra, in present-day Iraq, was built in the mid-ninth century by the Abbasid caliph al-Mutawakkil (r. 847–861).

As reflected in architectural style and grandeur, Persian traditions came to influence Abbasid political culture on a major scale. Evident already in the ninth century, Persian influence acquired dominance in the tenth. The Umayyads had imported Persian ideas about statism (see the Persian Sassanians, Chapter 9), and the Abbasids continued this. Unlike their Islamic predecessors but akin to the Sassanians, however, the Abbasids claimed that the caliph's person was sacred and increasingly enveloped his actions in ceremonies that emphasized his grandeur.

The Abbasids promoted the notion that the caliph possessed unique powers to bring the order of the cosmos to earth. A Persian importation (with strong parallels to the Chinese conception of the Mandate of Heaven), the Abbasids appropriated the belief that the cosmos influenced the regularities of nature and that the sacred ruler's responsibility was to enforce a moral order that was in harmony with the cosmic one. As a reflection of this, initially, Abbasid caliphs intervened in theological doctrinal disputes to support a particular orthodoxy.

The Abbasids moved the capital from Damascus to Baghdad, a new city built in a strategic location between the Tigris and Euphrates Rivers and not far from the old Sassanian capital of Ctesiphon. It thus straddled the main trade and communication routes between Iraq, Syria, and Iran and rested amidst one of the most fertile parts of Iraq with ready access to an extensive water system. Above all, Baghdad was built to be an administrative and cultural center, and it grew so rapidly that under the Abbasids it became the largest city in the world outside of China.

In Baghdad, the caliphs continued to incorporate the Persian and Byzantine bureaucratic administrative structures into their own. Alongside these bureaucratic staffs, they appointed judges called **qadis** to administer Islamic law as it applied to worldly affairs. Thus, they further infused their political authority by way of jurisprudence with Islamic precepts. In the new city of Baghdad, the Abbasids built vast palace complexes (again, of Persian architectural inspiration) and created a highly visible and magnetic center of power and culture.

The first several generations of Abbasid caliphs are often referred to as a golden age, but already, opposition to their rule was stirring. Dissension focused first on their increasing reach into religious authority. Already, during the late Umayyad and early Abbasid period, a Hadith party independent of the state's bureaucracy was emerging. These men were scholars who believed that Muhammad's practices during his lifetime, called the sunna, were inspired by God and could be recovered from Hadith.

Although the Hadith—short statements and sayings of Muhammad—were distinct from the revelations in the Quran, they were nonetheless taken to be inspired by God. Often of a highly practical nature, dealing with Muhammad's solutions to specific legal, economic, or doctrinal issues, the Hadith were gathered from oral reports after the death of Muhammad and were only written down nearly a century later. They continued to be gathered and recorded during the ninth century, eventually numbering in the thousands.

The Hadith Party sought to define and circumscribe religious authority clearly in strict accordance with the Prophet's revelations and inspired statements. They therefore challenged the caliph's claim to religious authority. The definition of religious doctrine and orthodoxy was at stake, and gradually, this power shifted away from the caliphs and toward religious scholars acting independently of the caliphate. The caliph eventually was reduced to a merely executive role; the scholars defined orthodoxy, and the caliphs enforced it.

The increasing religious weakness of the caliph was mirrored, and no doubt reinforced, by a growing political weakness. The period of vast conquest largely came to an end with the Umayyads, and the challenge to the Abbasids was to administer the realm, to maintain the internal order and political unity of the caliphate. Initially, the caliphs rotated provincial governors frequently, attempting to deprive them of opportunities to establish autonomous power bases in their provinces. The caliphs also sought the separation of civilian and military powers. To avoid dependence upon provincial strongmen, the Abbasids relied upon an army of mercenaries, slaves, and freedmen, many of Turkish origin. Many of the generals and governors who came to challenge the authority of the caliph, however, came from these ranks.

Until about 860, the Abbasid caliphs were effective in asserting direct rule in the central provinces of Syria, Mesopotamia, Egypt, Iran, and Iraq. Long before that, in the more distant reaches of the empire, however, central control ceased to exist. The reasons for the breakdown of the political system were the same everywhere, even if the timing was different: The caliphs were dependent on local strongmen to assist in the collection of taxes and tribute. These strongmen created systems of patronage and clientelism that reached into the bureaucratic administration, resulting in a diminishing of control from Baghdad. Political fragmentation beset the caliphate, and power shifted to local or regional strongmen who commanded military force and who increasingly styled themselves emirs, kings, or sultans.

Spain had already escaped the Abbasid caliphate in 756 under a Umayyad prince; Morocco and Algeria broke away in 777 and 789 under sectarian leaders; and the rest of North Africa was no longer under the control of the Abbasid caliph by 800. By the early 10th century, the Abbasid caliph's hold on the central provinces was slipping too. As we will see in Chapter 16, in 909, the Fatimids in Egypt seized control, while the Shi'a Buyids did so in Iraq shortly thereafter.

The Seljuk Turks arrived in Baghdad in 1055, and though they allowed the Abbasids to remain as caliphs, they were powerless puppets. The Turks deposed and sometimes even blinded them at will and kept them impoverished. Some of these regimes (like the Buyids and Seljuks) acknowledged the caliph as a religious symbol of the community of believers as a descendant of Muhammad, but only to legitimate their own regimes. The trend toward the secularization of politics accelerated as government ceased to be a part of religion in any meaningful way.

The Fruits of Conquest: Cultural Unity, Agricultural Revolution, and the Emergence of a Commercial System

Vast conquest may have carried the seeds of eventual political decentralization, but it also created an Islamic world that was nonetheless culturally unified under a common religion, a universal language (Arabic, which became the language of politics, theology, and commerce), and one law, the Shari'a. It facilitated an easy and accelerated movement of people, goods, technology, ideas, and information. Conquest also stimulated an agricultural revolution, as new crops were introduced into new areas and new farming and irrigation techniques followed. The production of vast agricultural surpluses fed an increasingly integrated commercial system, as well as a burgeoning population in the countryside and in cities.

An Agricultural Revolution

Conquering Arab armies swept into regions with very different agricultural systems. New crops, new farming techniques, and new irrigation technology were then diffused across an increasingly culturally unified world with revolutionary effects. Most of the new crops came from India. Rice, hard wheat, sugarcane, legumes, spinach, citrus fruits (e.g., sour oranges, limes, and lemons), bananas, and a host of others spread throughout the Islamic world. Many of these crops were summer crops, and the introduction of them into regions where farmers typically left their fields fallow in the summer introduced a longer growing season. New systems of crop rotation were used, harvesting crops from the same fields four times in a two-year cycle. Agricultural manuals recommended fertilization with manures, ashes, and even crushed bricks to replenish the soils. The new agriculture rendered land and labor much more productive.

The new plants required a great deal of water, a significant challenge in an arid climate that was typical of much of the conquered territories. Systems of artificial irrigation were needed. Such irrigation was known in antiquity, but everywhere, these systems had fallen into disrepair and neglect. In the early eighth century, a surge in repairing and extending these systems, and the building of new ones, became suddenly evident almost everywhere. New kinds of dams were built, as were underground canals and a wide variety of wheels for lifting water, often maintained by special teams of engineers. The Umayyads and their successors, in fact, established and maintained schools for the study of horticulture and methods of irrigation. By 1000, hardly a water source anywhere in the Islamic world—river, stream, spring, oasis—was untapped.

The new agriculture was expensive and drew investment from wealthy landowners, prosperous peasants, and even communities of farmers pooling their resources. And it was labor intensive. New, even marginal, lands came into cultivation, feeding the growing demand for a larger labor force. Much of this labor was provided by imported African slaves. So miserable was their condition (many worked to drain salt marshes) that many of them joined the Great Zanj Rebellion launched in 869 and lasting until 883. The rebellion was led by a Persian Ali ibn Muhammed who claimed descent from the Prophet's cousin Ali and rallied the slaves by promising them freedom and wealth. The rebel army, fortified by slave soldiers who defected from the caliph's army, seized control of southern Iraq and sacked the city of Basra in 871. In the early 880s, the caliph's armies regrouped and in 883 finally crushed the rebellion and killed Ali.

The agricultural growth that followed was largely the work of a prosperous free peasantry cultivating relatively small plots of land. This mattered to the state because it made it easier for the peasants to pay their taxes. Large estates existed, but even these were worked in sharecropping arrangements. During the Arab conquests, the large estates that dominated the agricultural systems of the lands they conquered were usually broken up into smaller farms.

The system thrived until the 11th century when a noticeable decline set in. Everywhere in the Islamic world was overrun by invaders—Seljuk Turks, Crusaders, Mongols, and a host of others. Irrigation works were destroyed, peasants fled, and land was turned over to grazing or, if cultivated, it drifted to the lower crop-yield fields of extensive agriculture where smaller amounts of labor and capital were employed in relation to the area of land being farmed and where cultivators relied upon the natural availability of water rather than irrigation.

Cultural Unity and Commercial Growth

The Arab conquest may have been motivated to spread the faith, but after it was consolidated, it also brought new crops and techniques. By the seventh century, the Mediterranean world was already a complex commercial entity, but the religious and cultural unity of Islam undoubtedly contributed to its fuller integration and expansion.

Commercial unity, despite the political decentralization, characterized the world of Islam. The first wave of conquests under the Rightly Guided Caliphs seems to have had no commercial motivation. With the Umayyads, however,

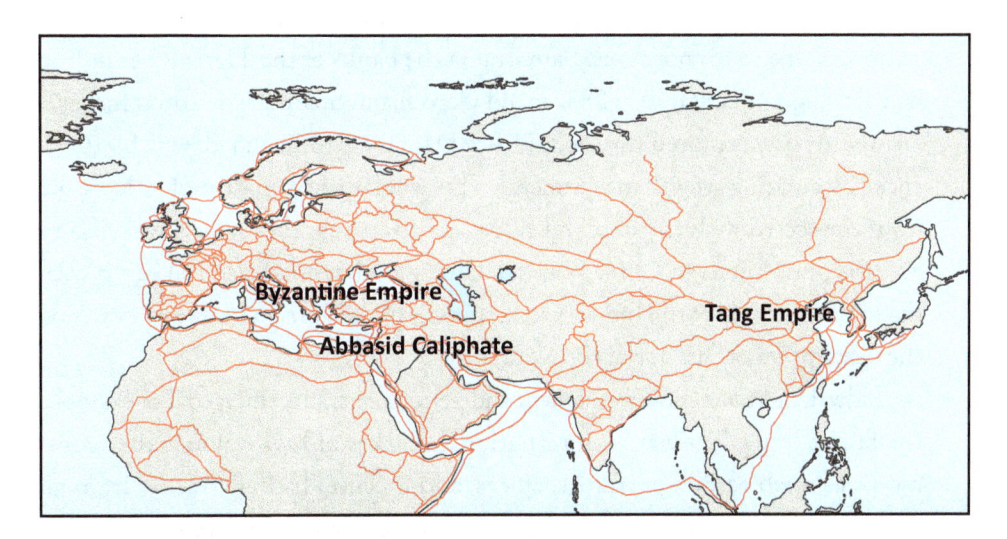

MAP 12.2 Major Trade Routes in 870

commercial aspirations played a role, as the conquerors spied a way to gain access to precious commodities and to control trade routes that would generate handsome custom revenues. North Africa, for example, provided access to the trans-Sahara gold trade, while the conquest of western India opened up the Indus delta for internal and overland trade on the Silk Road as well as linkages to the trade routes of the Indian Ocean. Conquest of Sogdiana and Ferghana in central Asia brought the fabled "heavenly" horses under Umayyad control, and with them came the endless demand for them from the Chinese.

Also beneficial to the mercantile economy was the stamping of new coins in 695, the gold dinar and the silver dirham, which corresponded to the actual value and denominations of earlier Sassanian and Byzantine coins and henceforth gained wide circulation within, and even far beyond, the Islamic world. Arabic coins have been found in the Volga River basin in Russia, in Scandinavia, and even in China. The increasing monetization of the commercial system enhanced liquidity, and money, as it always does, facilitated the speed and efficiency of business transactions.

Cities and Markets

Cities were integral to this booming commerce. Cities had never entirely disappeared in the eastern Mediterranean, but with the arrival of Islam and the agricultural revolution, they revived. The first several generations of Arab conquerors lived in cities, not the countryside, and they garrisoned their soldiers there as well. The extracted wealth from land and taxes, therefore, was channeled to cities, which then became vibrant administrative, transit, and consumption centers. Some were enormous. Samarra on the banks of the Tigris River in Iraq had a million inhabitants in 883, as did Cordoba in Spain in the 10th century.

The Abbasids moved the capital from Damascus to Baghdad, which experienced astounding growth in commerce. This was largely a product of its location, for it connected with the overland silk roads stretching through central Asia to its eastern terminus in China's capital, Chang'an. Baghdad also linked up with the maritime trade of the Indian Ocean by way of the Persian Gulf, aptly earning the description of "harbor of the world."

Indeed, more and more permanent and periodic markets emerged. For example, the fair at Jerusalem was an international market of high-value luxury commodities, such as silk, perfumes, spices, and incense. It drew traders from all over: Christian Europeans, Jews, Greeks, and, of course, Muslims. By the late 700s, all across the Mediterranean world—both Muslim and Christian—an expansion in exchanging goods is clearly evident. By 800, the economy appears highly monetized (liquidity being facilitated in part by collection of taxes in coin). Widespread evidence points to an astonishing diversity of agricultural and manufacturing products and the lively trading of them. Moneychangers and assayers were everywhere (often Christians or Jews). Some employed letters of credit and orders of payment for transfer of funds across regions.

New foods coming from new plants were clearly a response to wide demand in a complex commercial system. Beyond the agricultural products discussed earlier, urban markets were stocked with animals, timber, metals, textiles, fish, medicinal products, and spices. In the early ninth century in Basra, Iraq, as many as 360 different types of dates could be found in its market! Cairo, at the mouth of the Nile River and on the coast of the Mediterranean in Egypt, was another vast hub of commerce. Here, silk (in great demand in the Christian churches in Europe), porcelain, black pepper, and sandalwood were brought from the East, and aromatics, horses, ivory, cotton textiles, metal goods, and gold (to balance payments, as the eastern imports were of higher value than Mediterranean exports) were shipped east in return. Cairo was the most important transit point for goods from the Mediterranean and the Indian Ocean by way of the Red Sea. Muslims, Jews, Christians, and Hindus were all involved in this far-reaching trade.

Within Muslim commercial cities, the **funduq** emerged and developed. The funduq, eventually an institution found everywhere across Islam, was an essential component of the commercial system. It was a lodging house for traveling merchants that provided secure, locked warehouse space for storage of their cargo. These hostels evolved out of the earlier eastern Roman pandocheion, a waystation for travelers, but for Muslims, they became expressly economic. Attractive to merchants because of the security to person and property that they provided, funduqs catered to merchants of whatever ethnicity or religion (although they did segregate Muslims and non-Muslims). Public officials protected, inspected, and taxed these transit goods that are such a clear indication of regional and long-distance trade.

As we have seen in Chapter 11, in the mid-eighth century, Europeans, notably Venetians, dramatically increased the supply of slaves for sale in Italy and the Balkans. This was not the only source, however, for so great was the demand for the human commodity in the Mediterranean that vast numbers came from eastern Africa and central Asia too. The sellers were responding to surging demand for slaves by Muslims since it was about that time the vast Muslim conquests came to an end, and with them, the steady stream of prisoners of war used as slaves dried up.

In their place came slaves purchased from Europeans, from East African slavers plying a maritime trade in the western Indian Ocean, and from nomadic tribes to the north offering captured Turks for sale. Once purchased by Muslims (young males were in the highest demand), slaves were not only sent to work on agricultural plantations or in mines but also ended up as domestic servants or craftsmen, or as soldiers. Indeed, the Muslim armies became dominated by slave soldiers, and by the ninth century, these troops had become mounted slave warriors called Mamluks.

Islamic Economic Principles

Muslim merchants—retailers, wholesalers, travelers, brokers, auctioneers, and so on—not only shared a common language of business in Arabic but also shared assumptions about business practices that were rooted in the Quran, the Hadith, and the Shari'a. Unlike Christian ethics about trade that condemned the pursuit of commerce and profit, Islam explicitly endorsed it. This is not an ascetic, anti-materialistic religion. Muhammad, after all, was a merchant, and he voiced as part of God's revelation to him clear economic principles that subsequently found fuller articulation in the Hadith and Shari'a: deal justly, honor contracts and property rights, give true witness, and do not take usurious interest.

According to Islam, God owns all and grants trusteeship of resources to humankind as bounties from Him. "Wastage" (or using these resources inefficiently) is repeatedly denounced in the Quran. So is monopoly, while the principle of moderation is praised. The acquisition of great wealth is fully accepted. Sole proprietorship, partnership, and **commenda** (arrangements whereby an investor would entrust a merchant with capital and at the end of the venture share the profit in an agreed-upon division) were all explicitly approved by Muhammad, and profitable return on invested capital is encouraged. However, there is no encouragement of profit maximization (i.e., squeezing the greatest profit possible from each business transaction, which became a hallmark of modern capitalism) in Islamic economic ideology.

Because these economic principles are explicit in the Quran, it was the duty of political leaders to enforce them. Hence, the state provided the necessary security for business. It also assumed the role of protector of private property. Inheritance through generations is endorsed in the Quran and enforced by the state in Islamic law. This explicitly applies to women as well as men. It is true that the Quran assumes a patriarchal relationship between the genders, espousing that as men are responsible for the welfare of women, so women should be obedient to men.

However, the Quran explicitly dictates that women are to receive shares of the family patrimony through inheritance and that dowries brought to marriage are not to be given to the bride's father, as was traditional in tribal society, but to the bride herself. In a similar fashion, women are entitled to keep whatever wages they earn. This religion was not antithetical to economic growth and was no hindrance to the prospering commerce that is so evident in Islam before 1000.

Review Questions

1. During his lifetime, how did Muhammad's teachings change the Arab world?
2. What were the consequences of Islamic conquest?
3. How was governance legitimized among the caliphs of Islam from 632 to ca. 1000?
4. Why did the economy thrive in the Islamic world between 600 and 1100?

Further Readings

Bashear, Suliman. *Arabs and Others in Early Islam. Studies in Late Antiquity and Early Islam.* Princeton: The Darwin Press, 1998.

Crone, Patricia. *From Arabian Tribes to Islamic Empire* (Variorum Collected Studies). London: Routledge, 2008.

Crone, Patricia. *God's Rule: Government and Islam.* New York: Columbia University Press, 2004.

Egger, Vernon O. *A History of the Muslim World to 1405: The Making of a Civilization.* Upper Saddle River, NJ: Prentice Hall, 2003.

El-Ashker, Ahmed, and Rodney Wilson. *Islamic Economics. A Short History.* Leiden: E. J. Brill, 2006.

Goldsmith, Raymond W. *Premodern Financial Systems: A Historical Comparative Study.* Cambridge: Cambridge University Press, 1987.

Lapidus, Ira M. *A History of Islamic Societies.* 2nd ed. Cambridge: Cambridge University Press, 2002.

O'Shea, Stephen. *Sea of Faith: Islam and Christianity in the Medieval Mediterranean World.* New York: Bloomsbury, 2007.

Raaflaub, Kurt A., and Nathan Rosenstein, eds. *War and Society in the Ancient and Medieval Worlds: Asia, Mediterranean, Europe, and Mesoamerica.* Cambridge, MA: Center for Hellenic Studies, Harvard, 2001.

Watson, Andrew M. *Agricultural Innovation in the Early Islamic World: The Diffusion of Crops and Farming Techniques, 700–1100*. Cambridge Studies in Islamic Civilization. Cambridge: Cambridge University Press, 1983.

Wright, John. *The Trans-Saharan Slave Trade (History and Society in the Islamic World)*. London: Routledge, 2007.

Figure Credits

Map 12.1: Copyright © by Rowanwindwhistler (CC BY-SA 3.0) at https://commons.wikimedia.org/wiki/File:Conqu%C3%AAte_de_l%27Islam_%C3%A0_la_chute_des_Omeyyades-es.svg.

Map 12.2: Copyright © by Briangotts (CC BY-SA 3.0) at https://commons.wikimedia.org/wiki/File:Radhanites2.png.

CHAPTER 13

The Song Dynasty and Conquerors from the North: China from 900–1300

The Northern Song Dynasty (960–1127): Warlords and Bureaucratic Governance

The Tang dynasty eventually collapsed in 907 and was followed by civil war during which rival dynasties were established yet soon collapsed. Amid these chaotic conditions, a military man named Zhao Kuangyin succeeded in establishing a dynasty that would last. This was the Song dynasty, and it endured because its emperors were able to establish civilian, bureaucratic governance and tame the warlords.

The Collapse of the Tang Dynasty

The Chinese imperial dynasties of the Han and the Tang exhibited remarkable longevity and, at times, internal peace and stability. Still, a constant problem for Chinese emperors was to keep their wealthy and powerful aristocratic subjects in check. Restraining these warlords from pursuing independence and autonomy in their provinces was often the mark of successful emperors trying to govern a centralized and consolidated state. Ultimately, both the Han and Tang dynasties ended by their failure to do so.

During the late years of the Tang dynasty in the late 800s and early 900s and for a half century after its collapse in 907, China was engulfed by civil wars. The once-unified empire broke up into an array of local and regional polities as a series of warlords tried to establish dynasties of their own. None lasted very long. Warlords, often former military governors, and clans comprised of families who had entered the Tang officeholding bureaucracy seized control of whatever governing apparatus was at hand.

Moreover, already in the late 800s a market in vacant lands had sprung up in the wake of unrest and rebellion and the increasing breakdown of central authority. Many of the buyers of these vacant lands were imperial officials eager to establish themselves as rural landlords. As a result, large areas of China were taken over by powerful local men who put a floating, poverty-stricken population of people, uprooted by the chaos of war, to work on their estates as tenant farmers. With the essential support from the emperor gone, the traditional Tang hereditary aristocracy gradually disappeared, replaced by this new class of landholders intent on accumulating estates who had unprecedented opportunities to do so. A sharp polarization of wealth followed.

The First Song Emperor, Taizu

Amid this chaos, many a warlord dreamed of establishing a new dynasty. The gap between dreaming and accomplishing was wide, however, for the successful emperor had to bring his fellow warlords to heel. Proclaiming oneself huangdi, or emperor, was one thing, making the claim stick another. Zhao Kuangyin assumed the challenge. He was a military man from a northern Chinese family serving an emperor of the short-lived Later Zhou dynasty (951–960) as an adviser and inspection commander in the palace army. He had marched north with his troops to fight enemies along the border, but when that emperor unexpectedly died and left a six-year-old boy on the throne, Zhao seized his chance. His troops proclaimed him Son of Heaven, and his generals, following a ritualized practice, asked him to become emperor. He accepted, took the name of Taizu, and established the Northern Song dynasty.

Taizu knew that his success or failure rested upon two things. First, he had to break the hold that other warlords and the eminent clans had on local and regional power that they had seized after the collapse of the Tang and continued to hold under the weak Later Zhou dynasty. Second, he had to be strong enough militarily to keep enemies beyond China at bay. Success would prove to his subjects that Taizu had the Mandate of Heaven, that his dynasty was legitimate.

As part of Taizu's strategy to consolidate his rule, he seized upon a long-standing Confucian tradition that the imperial state was a civil government in which military men were expected to be obedient to the emperor and the imperial officials who carried out his dictates.

To disempower the regional warlords, Taizu moved quickly to pension them into a sumptuous retirement and replaced them with men loyal to him. This was part of an aggressive move to centralize governance under civilian control and fashion a military that was strong and loyal to Taizu. Later Song emperors never wavered from Taizu's precedent, a commitment to the Confucian principle of civilian governance. They devoted continual attention to creating, expanding, and supporting a class of imperial officials.

Civilian Governance of the Northern Song

The Song emperors after Taizu were committed to the Confucian principle of civilian governance administered by imperial officials, many drawn from those new families that had carved out landed estates in those tumultuous post-Tang years. The Song invention of movable type in printing in the 11th century had something to do with reinforcing civilian governance, for it enabled an explosion of printed works praising and popularizing the Confucian principle that statecraft should be in the hands of the emperor's civilian officials. As the Song emperors resumed, controlled, and expanded the venerable civil service examination system (established under the Han a millennium earlier), they were able to create a scholarly officialdom educated according to these values. These exams were the gateway to the prestigious jinshi degree and subsequent appointment to the imperial bureaucracy.

A meritocracy of sorts took hold. The scholar-official class comprised only a tiny minority of the population (it was dominated by a few thousand families in a population of at times 100 million), but it was nonetheless much larger than under the Tang. A clear bureaucratic hierarchy emerged. In exchange for their loyalty and obedience to the emperor, these officials were generously rewarded in cash and in material goods. They also received a partial tax exemption on their lands. This exemption was important because the ownership of land was the foundation of wealth for the official class.

This class created alliances through marriage that helped secure political influence, privileges, and economic prosperity. Daughters from affluent households brought property and dowries to their marriages. Some were daughters of wealthy merchants, and through marriages, these families could now enter the landed scholar-official class. Indeed, many of these wives managed the household finances for their scholar husbands who concentrated on self-cultivation and government affairs. These women bought and sold land, kept accounts of rents and taxes, and dealt with commercial activities that arose as the produce from the land entered a thriving commercial market system.

The scholar-official class became the backbone of Song imperial governance. Many of these well-educated bureaucrats developed and staffed the Song state's sophisticated economic management system. They centrally managed state granaries for famine relief. Perhaps even more important, they administered the state treasury, dispensing funds for such essential governmental tasks as public works projects, such as draining marshes, building and maintaining canals for secure transport and irrigation, and the timely and efficient payment of salaries. Crucially, they also managed the collection of taxes. Good accounting procedures and recordkeeping became pressing as the Song state shifted to collecting taxes in cash as the economy became increasingly monetized in silver and copper coins.

Indeed, the most important financial matter for the state was taxation. In 1069, Wang Anshi, an advisor with the full trust of the emperor at the time, instituted sweeping changes in state finance. His immediate objective was to find a way for the small-scale farmer to prosper so that he could more readily pay taxes to the state. Wang Anshi's reforms therefore offered these farmers state loans at low interest rates (much lower than private lenders were offering). These loans were considered an investment in agricultural productivity. From the growth, Wang believed, the loans could be repaid and regular tax payments collected.

The Land Survey and Equitable Tax System of 1072 was central to these reforms. It called for regular land surveys, which would be the basis of rural taxes assessed on cultivated acreage. The value of the land and the income from rents and nonagricultural endeavors were taken into consideration. Buddhist monasteries, Daoist temples, and even private land owned by scholar-official families lost previous exemptions. This created a firestorm of opposition to the reforms that ensured their doom, but the attempted reforms of Wang Anshi provide a clear example of the sophistication and organization of the Song financial system.

Conquerors from the North and the Southern Song Dynasty

A perennial recurrence in Chinese history has been border raids from the north by nomadic, militaristic peoples. These raiders, like the Xiongnu, Türks, and Uighurs centuries before the Song, had no interest in settling deep in China. They preferred instead to use the threat of invasion to extort wealth from the sedentary Chinese rulers. With the Khitan and Jurchen nomadic warriors, this changes because now conquest of Chinese territory became the objective.

The Khitan Liao Empire

Abaoji, a chieftain of the militaristic nomadic Khitan people who traditionally lived by herding, fishing, and hunting, was the first to break with the tradition of raiding and to concentrate on territorial conquest. Abaoji began his military campaigns in 901, and by 907, he had successfully established Khitan rule westward into the steppe, eastward into Manchuria, and southward into the North China plain. Abaoji proclaimed himself emperor, and in 916, he founded a dynasty, the Liao. He died in 926, but the Liao Empire would reach its greatest power in the early 11th century. It lasted until 1125.

MAP 13.1 The Northern Song and the Khitan Liao Empires in the 11th Century

The Khitan Liao state bordered the newly established Song Empire. In return for halting further invasion south, the Khitan demanded annual payments from

THE SONG DYNASTY AND CONQUERORS FROM THE NORTH   257

the Song emperor. By the Treaty of Shanyuan in 1005, the Song ruler agreed to send 200,000 rolls of silk cloth and 100,000 ounces of silver to the Khitan Liao. The tribute was increased in another treaty in 1042 to 300,000 and 200,000, respectively. These amounts represent a significant transfer of wealth, but as testimony to the vast resources of Song China, they represented less than 4 percent of the state's annual revenues. By keeping the peace, moreover, the Song and the Khitan Liao could engage in trade. So robust was the Song economy that the profits from the trade more than paid for the annual tribute because the silver sent in tribute tended to flow back into China in purchases by the Khitan for valued Chinese products.

The Khitan Liao state contained both nomadic tribal people in the steppe and sedentary Chinese people in northern China. Its rulers therefore crafted a dual administrative system that comprised a traditional tribal confederation among the nomadic Khitan clans and a bureaucratic system of salaried officials in the conquered areas in China. Both, however, were subordinate to a system that kept the state under military rule. Gradually, the Khitan Liao state became sinicized as it adopted elements of Chinese culture. Tea drinking, for example, universally practiced by the Chinese, was broadly adopted among the Khitan. Following Chinese practice, the Khitan people harvested tea leaves and pressed them into cakes, then sliced and steamed them in urns. The Khitan also placed a growing emphasis on literacy, and they employed the Chinese-style civil service examinations in the 930s. And, again following Chinese practice, they developed an efficient and rational fiscal system aimed especially at effective taxation.

Khitan women, like women generally in steppe tribes, possessed considerable freedom and authority, more than in the sedentary East Asian societies. They could possess wealth and property in their own names, could initiate divorce and remarry, and some elite women could even hold civil and military positions. Some Khitan Liao empresses could even be co-rulers with their husbands or sons.

The Jurchen Jin Empire

Another tribal, nomadic people, the Jurchen from forested Manchuria, posed a military threat to both the Khitan Liao state and the Song. Pursuing the traditional practice of extorting tribute to forestall invasion, in 1123 the Jurchen demanded, and received, from the Song a staggering tribute payment of 200,000 ounces of silver, 300,000 bolts of silk cloth, and 1 million strings of cash (the coin currency of Song commerce). The subsidy supported the Jurchen war machine and led to the sudden conquest of the Khitan Liao state. Part of the routed Khitan army joined the ranks of the Jurchen, while the rest fled westward. The Jurchen then leveled their sights on the Song Empire. They invaded in 1125 and swept across the North China plain. Within two years, they drove the militarily weak emperor Gaozong from the capital city of Kaifeng.

MAP 13.2 The Jurchen Jin and Southern Song Empires in 1127

Gaozong fled to Hangzhou south of the Yangtze River and established what came to be known as the Southern Song dynasty. The Jurchen remained in possession of North China and proclaimed the Jin dynasty. To secure the peace and halt further Jurchen invasion into the south, the Song emperor again agreed to an enormous one-time indemnity of 300,000 ounces of gold, 12 million ounces of silver, 10,000 cattle and horses, and 1 million rolls of silk fabric. As great as this tribute was, it paled in comparison to the booty the Jurchen Jin hauled back north in countless wagons and carts after sacking Kaifeng and other northern

Song cities. Treasures of jade, pearls, and precious stones joined the staggering loot seized from imperial warehouses that included 3 million gold ingots, 8 million silver ingots, 1,5 million rolls of patterned silk, and 54 million rolls of tabby silk. This treasure filled the Jurchen Jin war chest for years.

The Jurchen Jin now commanded an empire that encompassed a large sedentary Chinese population and a much smaller pastoral, nomadic one in the forests of Manchuria and the former Khitan-controlled steppe to their west. They replicated the Khitan Liao system of dual administration with parallel military and civilian hierarchies. The Jin were careful, however, to keep Jurchen in the dominant positions in both, and no Chinese were permitted in the high military command.

Beneath this Manchurian umbrella, however, sinicization occurred, much as it had with the Khitan Liao. Sedentary Chinese accounted for 90 percent of the Jin subjects, and to govern this part of the empire, the Jin adopted the existing bureaucratic system and the Chinese officials who staffed it. They adopted Chinese as their administrative language. They even incorporated the Tang Code of law into their own Taihe Code in 1201, allowing, however, certain minor modifications to favor Jurchen interests.

The conquest and turmoil in North China drove not only the Song emperor and his court to the south but it also proved a catalyst for a general migration of Chinese people in the same direction. Indeed, for 30 years after 1127, a colder climate and increased flooding followed by drought joined the disruption caused by conquest in the north to push peoples south on an unprecedented scale. The Southern Song dynasty (1127–1279) thrived as a result. The next century or so marked the highpoint of the scholar-official elite ideal. The dynasty's political philosophy was infused with a neo-Confucianism that embraced the ethical demand that government exists to benefit the people. As a result, there was great emphasis placed on practical effectiveness in statecraft.

The Song Economic Revolution: A Market Economy

With political stability within Song China came economic prosperity. Agricultural productivity, aided by technological innovations, generated vast surpluses of food to feed the inhabitants of burgeoning cities and sustained workers in manufacturing who turned out of their shops enormous quantities of goods, notably iron, porcelain, paper, and silk. So great were the surpluses that a commercial revolution occurred, built upon an increasingly integrated market economy where goods moved along roads, canals, and rivers. The state left the economy largely unregulated. The wealth that was produced was unequally distributed, a disproportionate amount ending up with lords on great estates and merchants engaged in commerce.

Agriculture and Urbanization

Before the invasions and conquests by the Khitan and Jurchen disrupted the lives of farmers in North China, the Northern Song Empire had witnessed a dramatic increase in agricultural productivity. This boom became the foundation for great cities, vast trade, and an expansive state structure that came to characterize Song China. The boom continued in the Southern Song Empire in the 12th and much of the 13th centuries.

Cities grew enormously. The urban population of China came to equal or surpass that of cities in the rest of the world. Obviously, Chinese farmers were producing a surplus to feed it. Migration southward had already begun during the late Tang years, bringing more rice, the primary crop in the much wetter south, into the Chinese diet. In the early 11th century, a Northern Song emperor imported from Vietnam 30,000 bushels of rice seeds of an early-ripening and drought-resistant type of rice called champa. Its cultivation spread rapidly in the South. It rendered two rice crops per year and, in some places, three. Moreover, more land was coming under the plough in the South. The Song government encouraged this expansion of arable land by providing low-interest loans and tax rebates to wealthy families who reclaimed land from marsh or river bottom.

The pressure to open new lands to support a booming population was keen. The population of all of China doubled in the 11th century. In some places, like the Fujian Province in the Southeast, it surged even more, quadrupling over the course of the three centuries of the Song dynasty. The great landlords benefitted the most from the resultant surging demand. They employed refugee peasants from the North to clear and reclaim land from river bottoms, swamps, coastal flats, and marshes and then to work as tenant farmers on their land. As a result, great landed estates were created and most densely concentrated in southern and southeastern China.

All across China, the use of manure and lime for fertilizer increased, including harvesting the vast quantities of human waste generated by the ever-growing cities. Innovation in agricultural techniques, however, was the preserve of the great landlords, and again was most prominent in the South. These lords had the wealth to invest in technology. Given the necessity for water control in wet-rice cultivation, ditches and canals had to be dug, and devices to lift water into and out of the paddies had to be designed, built, and maintained. Complex and expensive water-powered machinery, pumping water to irrigate or drain fields, appeared across many a great estate in the South. Machinery also was used to thresh and mill grain.

FIGURE 13.1 Hydraulic Watermill for Grinding Grain. Song engineers were extraordinarily sophisticated. Notice the water pouring onto the blades of the horizontal wheel below, providing the power to turn the grain-grinding round millstones on the second floor. This water-powered mill is depicted in an early Song painting on silk by an anonymous artist.

The Song government once again showed an interest in facilitating economic development. For example, it published practical manuals on farming and water control. Indeed, the government encouraged scholars to invent new technologies in agriculture, as well as in textile, ceramic, and iron production.

The state was interested in economic productivity because it stood to benefit in increased tax receipts from such growth. The Song emperors, like those before them, based their taxation system on household registration. Great estates had their importance, but the countless small, independent farms were no less essential to the economy. The anonymous and voiceless mass of small-scale farmers comprised about two-thirds of all farming households in China and paid the bulk of the taxes. Like the great estates, these farms produced surpluses and moved them to market along an increasingly well-developed and maintained transportation system of road and water. Tenant farmers comprised the remaining third of rural households, and though their landlords paid the taxes on the land, these farmers were less well off than their independent brethren. Taxes were paid in cash, kind, and labor service, although there was a clear trend toward cash under the Song. Whereas in 997 40 percent of taxes were paid in cash, by 1085 the percentage had jumped to 70.

Manufacturing

Like agriculture, iron production thrived during the Song dynasty. Mines were mostly under government control, and those in private hands had to sell their ore to the state, which monopolized iron manufacture. Although iron smelting in China traces back at least to the Zhou dynasty in the fifth century BCE, iron founders during the Song period developed the first blast furnaces in history. These furnaces, superheated by air forced into them, were hot enough to melt the iron that would then be poured into molds. Countless pots, ploughshares, chisels, nails, locks, hatchets, hoes, and even iron chains to support suspension bridges over canals were produced in these ironworks. So intensive was this iron production and so hungry were the foundries for fuel that deforestation spread during the 11th century, as trees were felled for the wood for fuel. With dwindling supplies of charcoal from wood available, ironmakers turned increasingly to coal, and even invented coke (ordinary coal baked to remove carbon impurities that made iron more brittle). Coke would not be used in iron manufacture in the West until the Industrial Revolution some 800 years later.

A great deal of iron was used to equip an enormous army. Despite the Song emperor's weakness in the face of the Jurchen invaders in the early 12th century, he still commanded over a million soldiers then, all of them users of iron products. The armament industry correspondingly yielded 16 million metal arrowheads and 32,000 suits of armor per year at the time, as well as innumerable horseshoes. In 1078 alone, the blast furnaces of Hebei-Henan Province, the geographic heart of the iron industry, produced 125,000 tons of iron. When the Jurchen seized control of this province in 1126, they continued the production (with Chinese workers). What iron they did not use themselves they traded to another emergent nomadic, militaristic people from the steppe, the Mongols.

Other industries boomed too. Porcelain ceramics had reached unchallenged standards of artistic achievement under the Tang. This continued under the Song but on an even greater scale as more ordinary porcelain ware was mass produced and marketed in a growing consumer economy.

Paper production surged as well. Made from bamboo, its production expanded enormously during the Song period, stimulated partly by the demand from an officialdom increasingly intent on recordkeeping. As literacy spread, printing did too, further stimulated by the elite scholar class that was consuming more and more printed books for both knowledge and prestige. Indeed, the surging population spiked demand for paper even among ordinary people, and paper products of every kind appeared on the market, including toilet paper.

All across the manufacturing landscape in Song China, remarkable development can be seen. This was especially true in textiles, notably in hemp cloth and silk fabric. Hemp cloth was inexpensive and thus the dominant textile for ordinary people. Although the evidence slightly postdates the Song dynasty, a spinning machine for hemp with 32 spindles powered by a waterwheel was in use by the early 1300s. An agronomist at the time who described the machine in a treatise on agriculture commented that the machine was more productive and cheaper than the labor of several women. Silk was purchased within China by the upper classes in the population. It was also prized on the international market. Hundreds of thousands of bolts of silk cloth left China, some as tribute into the hands of the Khitan and Jurchen, and was sent westward across the venerable Silk Roads. Silk was also loaded on ships embarking on the South China Sea with cargoes destined for the markets of the Indian Ocean and beyond.

The late Tang and the Song dynasties saw impressive advances in the silk industry. Certain geographical areas increasingly specialized in producing silkworms and the mulberry leaves the worms consumed. Specialized markets cropped up for these items. Silkworm fairs periodically appeared in the most important silk-producing areas where buyers could find not only worms and leaves but also silk-reeling machines, caldrons for boiling the cocoons, vast varieties of tools, and even live mulberry trees.

Silk production was decentralized, all of those countless bolts produced in innumerable peasant households. Silk reeling, for example, a technique for producing a continuous thread of silk several hundred meters long from an unwinding cocoon, had been practiced for two millennia by the time of the Song, the reeling frames operated by women since time immemorial.

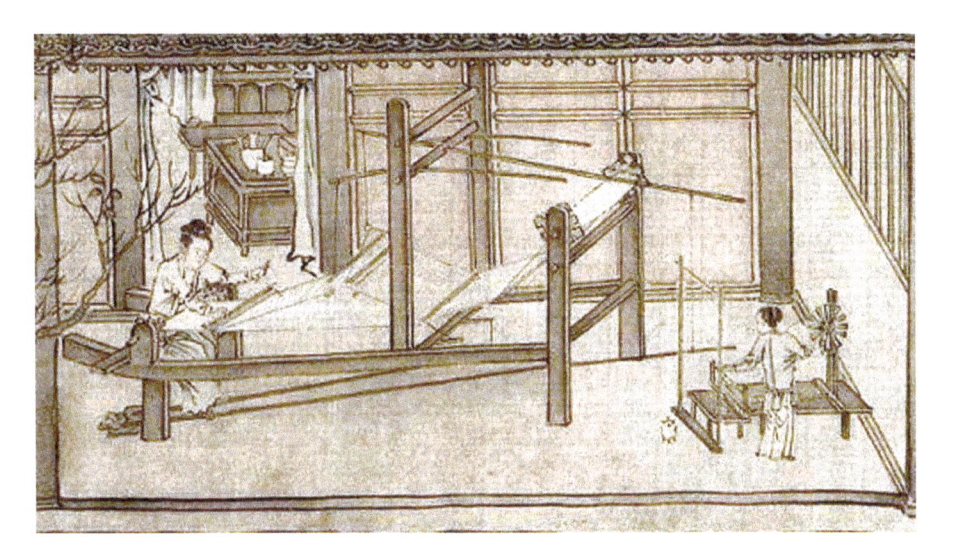

FIGURE 13.2 Silk Production in the Early 13th Century. Producing silk fabric required several steps and involved both men and women. First, women placed silkworms on trays with mulberry leaves. Men then placed the fattened silkworms on heavy frames where they would spin their cocoons. The cocoons were then sorted, weighed, and soaked by women. The fibers within the cocoons were then reeled, spun, and woven into fabric (pictured), tasks often performed by women.

A Commercial Revolution

> Sometimes ... the head of the family ... will buy gold and silver and hoard them away. This is an act of great folly. Assuming that one has 100,000 pieces of gold and silver, and that these are used to buy income-yielding property, the yearly takings are bound to be 10,000 pieces. After 10 years or so one will have recovered what may be regarded as the 100,000 and the rest will be profit. What is more, this 100,000 may be made in its turn to yield profits. If it is used for a pawnbroking business, a profit of a hundred percent will be realized within three years. ... It can, moreover, be doubled again in the next three years. ...What reason can there be for storing it in strong-boxes rather than taking advantage of it as a source of profit and benefitting everyone?[1]

As these observations made by Yuan Ts'ai in the 12th century illustrate, a commercial, profit-oriented mentality had taken hold in China. During the late Tang

---

1 Shiba Yoshinobu, *Commerce and Society in Sung China*, trans. Mark Elvin (Ann Arbor: University of Michigan Press, 1970, 1992), 195.

period and throughout the Song dynasty, a national market economy emerged and regional specializations developed. Obviously, these developments were made possible by the production of vast surpluses of foodstuffs and manufactured items. These goods made their way to various markets for distribution and consumption. As markets grew and diversified, more and more producers geared their production for the needs and demands of the market.

Many a peasant hauled his own products to market on foot, carrying bags of rice, grain, or raw silk on his back. Likewise, the granaries of landlords periodically released rice, millet, or wheat into the markets. Grain would often be sold to brokers who would then channel it to the public. In the case of the booming rice trade, brokers sold the grain to retail rice shops or to warehousemen, who would store it for later sale. Silk moved along similar circuits. Brokers bought raw silk from rural producers, then sold it both to rural and urban households with looms for weaving it into cloth. The brokers would then pay the weavers, take the cloth, and sell it to merchants, who in turn sold it to retail shops or to international brokers for marketing abroad.

More and more marketplaces offering a wide range of consumables popped up in cities, most highly specialized. There were 68 markets in Kaifeng to hire maidservants, for example. In its heyday, the capital had 72 high-quality wine restaurants, all with sumptuous entrances several stories high. Suburbs and villages saw markets pop up in their midst. Some, like fairs, were scheduled to coincide with religious celebrations, while other markets were more permanent and larger. Clustered by these marketplaces were shops selling garments and shoes, wineshops, snack booths, restaurants, guesthouses, and even beauty parlors, many run by women.

The roads of North China were jammed with carts and people on foot, heading toward cities like the capital Kaifeng. Some carts were so large that they required 20 mules to pull them. Fed overland from the north, Kaifeng was situated on the Yellow River, part of an extensive waterway system connecting the capital with the South (see Map 13.1).

In central and southern China, goods moved primarily on water, up and down the many rivers and canals. Indeed, China's extensive canal system was inherited from Tang times and was extended and improved under the Song. It connected the growing rice supply from the South as well as centers of silk and tea production in the Southeast to the densely populated North (at least before the Jurchen conquest in 1127). Tens of thousands of boats and barges, ranging from 18 tons displacement to 600 tons, plied these waterways. By way of comparison of scale, consider that the largest English ship in 1588 displaced 400 tons, while Christopher Columbus's *Nina* a mere 110 in 1492.

With the Jurchen Jin invasion in 1127 and the fall of Kaifeng, the thriving Song market economy shifted even more to the south and southeast. Hangzhou became the capital of the Southern Song dynasty, and by the mid-12th century, it could count over a million inhabitants. This city was at the terminus of the Grand Canal. It boasted gigantic warehouses along its banks stocked with everything from timber, coal, textiles, and iron to rice, pork, seafood, tea, and alcoholic beverages. Further to the southeast was Fujian Province, laced with rivers and a coast with excellent harbors. Its most important city, Quanzhou, evolved from being a transshipment center to the hub of an integrated regional economy that connected to international commerce as well as interior markets of China. By 1120, its population had reached 500,000.

The Role of the State

Tang emperors attempted to regulate the commercial economy. By a law decreed in 707, markets were only permitted in prefectural and county capitals and only in specified areas within these cities. Public officials were charged with registering all transactions as well as guaranteeing reputable weights and measures, and they were forbidden from engaging in commerce themselves. This regulatory system collapsed in the chaos of the late Tang period. When the Song dynasty rose from the ashes, the emperors did not try to structure and regulate markets.

The Tang principle that trading and commercial activities had to take place in prescribed areas broke down. It was swamped by a dizzying diversification of commercial transactions, in both city and countryside. For example, as small businesses flourished and farms geared production for market, a new valuation of property took hold. Now property value was simply determined by its commercial usefulness to buyers, for shops or rental properties in cities, for productivity in the countryside. Moreover, new laws permitted government officials to invest in commercial and real estate markets. The increasingly wealthy scholar-official elite, therefore, proved to be an important motor powering this market economy. Indeed, alongside the imperial court itself, scholar-officials were the biggest landlords in Kaifeng, a city in 1100 with well over one million inhabitants.

Merchants, too, amassed fortunes from the Song economy. Although officially lacking in prestige, merchants often invested their wealth in property and in the placement of their sons in officialdom through education and marriage. They had been prohibited by law from doing this before the ninth century. All that changed under the Song, reflecting the increasing importance of the market economy and the merchant's role within it.

As we have seen, agriculture and manufacturing were increasingly geared toward the market. This transformation had much to do with surging demand (especially in cities), but the state's shift toward requiring payment of taxes in cash rather than in kind during the 11th century played a prominent role as well. The small-scale, independent farmer, therefore, needed to convert his produce into cash, which could only be done through market transactions.

Of course, this put pressure on the state to mint coinage, which it did. Coins were cast from copper, iron, silver, and gold at an increasing rate. Whereas in 752 only about 6 coins per capita were in circulation, by 995 it was up to 17, and in 1080, it had reached 212. Never again in the history of imperial China would the supply of coins reach such a scale. The infusion of cash into the economy may have facilitated tax collection, but it also increased liquidity and so fueled further economic growth. In the 1120s, to relieve the shortage of cash caused by a war with the Jurchen, the Song state issued paper money with full convertibility into hard currency, providing yet another stimulus to the economy.

The Song state collected the lion's share of its revenue from land taxes and silk requisitions, but commercial taxes assumed a greater importance as the market economy spread. By the 1070s, they represented between 5 and 10 percent of state income, a doubling since the late 10th century. The state levied a charge on brokerage transactions and assessed a 2 percent toll on merchants moving their goods along canals, rivers, and roads. The state made the roads secure from banditry by erecting a watchtower every two and a half kilometers.

Foreign Trade

By the time of the Song dynasty, the Silk Road as an avenue of trade between East and West had existed for over a millennium. Under the Song it continued, but in terms of volume, it was eclipsed by maritime commerce. Still, it was a well-trod and profitable route, an important conduit that brought horses, amber, fine carpets, steel swords, and silver to the Chinese and moved west raw and woven silk, silk brocades, tea, and paper. The tribute treaties with the Khitan Liao and the Jurchen Jin actually stimulated this trade, bringing currency back into China as the dynasties to the north became dependent on this trade with China.

Seaborne commerce, nonetheless, was destined to become the most important medium for foreign trade under the Song. Regular trade between China and ports in the Indian Ocean had begun in Tang times, but the Chinese merchants at that time had never ventured onto the high seas. Instead, Southeast Asian, Persian, and Arab ships had come to Chinese ports. Many a foreign merchant could be found in the great fairs where goods from the West were sold.

Under the Song, this model of maritime commerce changes. Now Chinese merchants and sailors handle much of the shipping in the South China Sea and the Indian Ocean as far as Malabar and perhaps as far as the Persian Gulf and the eastern coast of Africa. By the 1070s and 1080s, Chinese merchants from Quanzhou were ranging throughout the Southeast Asian archipelago and up to Manchuria, Korea, and Japan. They operated through partnerships, rudimentary joint stock companies where even small, relatively poor investors could invest. They also engaged in commenda arrangements whereby an investor would entrust a merchant with capital and at the end of the venture share the profit in an agreed-upon division.

The fall of North China to the Jurchen Jin in 1127 and the dramatic increase in productivity and commerce in the South and Southeast further stimulated overseas commerce. Fujian Province became important under the Song in large part due to overseas commerce. Its greatest port, Quanzhou, replaced Guangzhou as the largest port in the empire. The Fujian merchant class was known far and wide for its wealth. It seemed to contemporaries that everyone in the province made their living in oceangoing trade.

During this time, the Chinese made great advances in shipbuilding. The large and fast seagoing junks made their appearance. Now the transport of bulk items like silk, tea, lacquerware, and paper with ballasts of porcelain and rice could be shipped westward in large quantities. The Chinese were hungry for imports from the West too, notably pepper from India. The number of pigs and chickens raised on scarce pasture land increased, and pepper was needed for preservation and flavoring the expanded meat and protein diet. The Chinese also craved incense from Arabia, ivory from Africa and India, fine cotton cloth from India, and above all silver from wherever they could get it.

Commodities flowed in both directions, but technology largely moved from east to west. From China came the sternpost rudder (a device that enabled more precise steering of ships in crowded harbors, river channels, and upon the open sea), the magnetic compass (first used in 1119), and ships with multiple masts and sails. Likewise, the West learned from the Chinese about the blast furnace for the melting and casting of iron, gunpowder, and the escapement device in clocks (a mechanism in a mechanical clock that allows for regular timekeeping).

The Mongols

In the early 13th century, the steppe to the north of China was once again astir. Another militaristic, horse-riding, bow-and-arrow-wielding, and nomadic tribal peoples, the Mongols, set their sights on the riches of China and embarked on massive raiding along its frontiers. Raids led to conquests, as the Mongols destroyed the Tangut Xi Xia dynasty in 1227 and the Jurchen Jin in 1234. By 1279, even the Southern Song Empire, weakened at the center by a succession of child emperors, fell to the Mongols. Kublai Khan, the grandson of Genghis Khan and conqueror of Southern Song China, declared himself the first emperor of a new dynasty, the Yuan.

Genghis Khan and Mongol Conquests

The rise of the Mongols as an unrivalled military power began with Chinggis, popularly known as Genghis (born Temujin in 1167). The Mongols on the northern steppe were a fragmented, leaderless, and relatively obscure nomadic group at the time, but that would change under Genghis. Unlike the Xiongnu, Türks, or Uighurs who rose to power by uniting imperial confederations around the leader's tribe, Genghis ruthlessly eliminated any challengers to his rule. He used treachery, terror, and unquestioned demand for personal loyalty to him to triumph in a civil war that ended when he was proclaimed Great Khan by the intimidated leaders of all the Mongol lineages in 1206.

Genghis had no notion of statecraft other than personal loyalty to him, and he built his army and government upon it. The highest positions went to the most loyal men, and he methodically murdered any challengers to his autocratic rule. He eliminated at least a dozen of his own kinsmen, including his half-brother. He paid scant attention to governance, but he did reorganize the army following Xiongnu practice. He divided his force of 100,000 mounted soldiers from various tribes into cohorts of 10,000 commanded by his most trusted and best generals (all Mongols). These cohorts were then subdivided into units of 1,000, 100, and 10.

This military machine was not only well-organized and disciplined but it was also noted for its ruthlessness and destruction. Like steppe tribes before them, the Mongols' initial objective was to raid and loot their enemies to the south like the Jurchen Jin, not to conquer them. Strike, plunder, retreat, and then extort payment to forestall future attacks was their strategy. In 1211, they attacked the Jurchen Jin Empire for the first time. They returned annually for three more years, each time looting and withdrawing back to the steppe. However, they were unable to extort tribute payments from the Jurchen Jin, who instead chose to resist the invaders militarily. The Jurchen Jin, after all, had a formidable army. It was no match for the Mongols, however, and the Jurchen Jin steadily retreated to the South, leaving North China to the Mongols.

The Mongols under Genghis had no interest in governing. Instead, they simply plundered the populous and wealthy North China plain and hauled the booty back to their capital in the steppe, Karakorum. The Jurchen Jin Empire finally collapsed in 1234 as one of Genghis's sons, Ogödei, captured Kaifeng. The immense scale of killing and destruction by the Mongol armies devastated North China. The invaders showed total disdain for Chinese farmers and no concern for resuming productivity, or even of taking over the Jurchen Jin system of taxation. The population of North China collapsed as a result, from 50 million in 1196 to under 9 million by 1235.

With the rout and retreat of the Jurchen Jin in North China, Genghis took much of his army west. In 1220, the great cities of Bukhara and Samarkand in Transoxiana fell to the Mongols with great loss of life. The next year, the Mongols overran Khorasan and by 1222 had reached the banks of the Indus River in India. Meanwhile, another branch of the army had gone north and rounded the Caspian Sea in 1223. This was the first time a major nomadic power from Northeast Asia had invaded and conquered sedentary states to their west. As in North China, however, Genghis's objective was conquest and plunder, not occupation and governing. The Mongol conquerors would only become rulers after Genghis's death, which occurred in 1227.

Death, Succession, and the Four Khanates

At the time of Genghis's death, his empire was vast, double the size of the Roman Empire or the Islamic Caliphate at their zenith. One of his sons, Ogödei, became the Great Khan after his father's death. In 1241, he launched an invasion of eastern Europe, laying waste to parts of Hungary and Poland following the defeat of the flower of Czech, German, and Hungarian knighthood at the Battles of Legnica and Mohi. The Mongols did not follow military victory with occupation or further invasion west, however. Instead, they rapidly withdrew following the unexpected death of Ogödei. Mongol tradition called together the leaders of the great clans to elect the next Great Khan, and Ogödei's death demanded such a gathering.

Mongol conquests were far from over, however, for the new Great Khan Möngke, a grandson of Genghis, sent his brother Hülegü at the head of an army against Persia. This army swept all the way to Baghdad where the last Abbasid caliph was executed in 1258. Möngke died in 1259, and four years of civil war followed. Möngke's brothers Kublai and Ariqboke struggled for the succession. Although Kublai won, his claim to Great Khan of the entire Mongol Empire was disputed, and the empire broke into four khanates. Hülegü remained in Baghdad and founded the Khanate of the Il-Khans. The Jochids (descended from one of Genghis's sons) remained on the Russian steppe and became known as the Khanate of the Golden Horde. The Chagatai (from another son of Genghis) remained in central Asia as the Chagatai Khanate, while Genghis's grandson Kublai retained the title of Great Khan and established the Yuan dynasty in China.

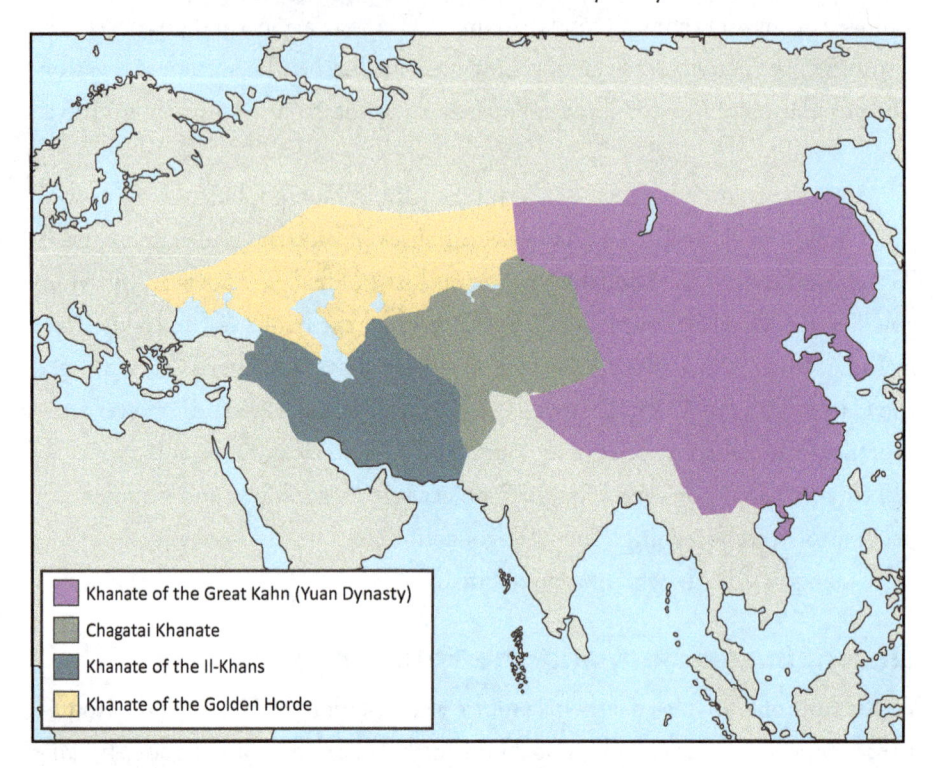

MAP 13.3   The Mongol Empire at Its Greatest Extent: The Four Mongol Khanates in 1294

Kublai Khan and the Yuan Dynasty in China

The Mongol invasion devastated North China, but unlike his forebears, Kublai remained in China and sought to return stable government to it. He moved his capital from Karakorum to Khan Baliq (present-day Beijing), and in 1271, he proclaimed himself emperor of a new dynasty, the Yuan, and claimed the Mandate of Heaven. Kublai then turned the Mongol armies southward, but he conquered with a difference. He sought to topple the Southern Song government, but to avoid destruction of its productive base, he prohibited reckless pillaging by his soldiers. He penetrated the South through its extensive rivers and canals. He ferried his cavalry on boats and barges and went ashore to fight only when necessary. With little damage done to the economy, the Southern Song dynasty fell with the conquest of Hangzhou and the dethroning of a four-year-old emperor in 1279.

Two problems immediately confronted Kublai: how to keep his powerful Mongol military men in check, and how to resume the flow of tax revenue to the imperial treasury that the Mongol conquests had disrupted. Traditionally, conquering khans had granted land and booty to their great warlords, with the assumption that such gifts would be used for military purposes in support of the khan when needed. With sedentary rule established in China, Kublai faced the prospect of these warlords forming autonomous local power bases beyond his control.

To disempower the warlords without destroying his own military strength, Kublai organized a state-supported army that bypassed these warlords. With their military function ended, many of these warlords sold their estates and were integrated in subservient roles within the new army.

This solution to the military problem, of course, depended upon the collection of imperial taxes to pay for it. In 1271, Kublai ordered an empire-wide household registration with the purpose of assessing taxes. He used Chinese officials to adapt the prior Chinese tax system, levying a cash tax on each household, an agricultural tax in kind based on production, and a duty on trade and commerce.

The Yuan state under Kublai appropriated a governing hierarchy that was essentially Chinese. Mongols, however, always were placed at its top, and the system was designed to preclude the formation of local power bases that could challenge the emperor. The victorious Mongols were vastly outnumbered by their new Chinese subjects, and Kublai and his favorite wife and trusted advisor Empress Chabi recognized that winning the goodwill of the conquered people would go a long way toward precluding rebellion and securing political stability. To this end, Chabi steeped herself in Chinese history, expressing interest in previous rulers of China. She and Kublai were especially intrigued by the renowned Tang emperor Taizong (624–649), and Chabi urged her husband to emulate him. She invited officials and scholars at court to compare the illustrious Tang emperor with her husband. Identifying the Mongol Khan with a hallowed figure in Chinese tradition was intended to ease the governance of China, and Chabi seems to have seen herself as part of the process.

A deeply centralized and vertical system linking all governance and revenue to the imperial court and the emperor himself could remain stable with a conscientious and capable emperor like Kublai. After his death in 1294, however, the system broke down. Weak emperors, corruption, palace coups, murders, and purges marked subsequent Yuan reigns, and by the 1330s, China was swept by widespread rebellions. One such uprising, the Red Turban Rebellion, toppled the Yuan dynasty in 1368 and ushered in another, the Ming.

Commerce Under the Mongols

The Mongols may have paid scant attention to agricultural and manufacturing productivity (content, apparently, simply to tax it), but they were active in nurturing and supporting the mercantile economy. Such favor of merchants began under Genghis, who protected and engaged foreign merchants even before his vast conquests. They provided him with information about neighboring tribes and states and served as his diplomats and official traders. All four great Mongol khanates that spanned Asia from China to Russia and Persia—the Yuan, the Chaghatid, the Golden Horde, and the Il-Khan—valued merchants and the commerce they brought to their territories. Merchants were the cherished purveyors of goods that the Mongol ruling class coveted, especially the luxury items destined for the courts of the ruling khans. All merchants traveling through the Mongol realms with proper documentation and authorization were protected. This reduced the risk of loss for merchants, and the security proved a great boon to overland trade.

The Mongol rulers recognized that a monetary policy would facilitate commerce by increasing liquidity as well as tax collection. Already, Genghis authorized the use of paper money shortly before his death in 1227, backing it with gold, silver, and silk. Under Ogödei, the Mongol government again issued paper currency backed by silk reserves. In 1253, Möngke established a department of monetary affairs to control the issuance of paper money to avoid inflation, this time linking the volume of notes with silver-ingot reserves. In China, Kublai also issued paper money backed by silver. Marco Polo, the famed Venetian merchant traveler who spent many years in Kublai Khan's empire, wrote at length about the khan's paper money, impressed by its economic importance and impact on trade. Coinage, of course, did not disappear. The various khanates mined gold, silver, and copper and minted the metals into coins that soon penetrated the vast reaches of Asia, from China to southern Russia, the Caucasus, and Iran.

This coinage flowed with an increasing volume of goods. The Golden Horde Mongols secured the relative safety for commerce across the northern land route of the Silk Road. Camel caravans linked central and East Asia with the Black Sea ports recently colonized by Italians. This, in turn, linked up with traffic flowing from northern Europe across the "northern arc" through eastern Russia. The Chaghatids of central Asia and the Il-Khans of Persia likewise secured the safety of the central and southern routes of the Silk Road. Travelling European merchants like Marco Polo and his uncles were dazzled by the splendid and thriving cities of Bukhara and Samarkand, Marco acclaiming the former as "the finest city in all of Persia."[2]

The Polos were not alone. Between 1250 and 1350, hundreds, perhaps thousands, of merchants from the West (some of them even Europeans) made their way across the resurgent land route connecting Europe to China. They trod relatively well-maintained roads. Marco Polo, who reached China across the central Asian land route and returned by way of the southern sea route, describes in his famous *Travels*, perhaps without realizing it, a vast and thriving system of international exchange. Foreign merchants, mostly Muslims, conducted business in great numbers in Asia, no doubt drawn to China by its fabulous wealth and unrivalled economic vitality. Polo himself was stunned by the incredible numbers of boats, barges, and ships that plied the elaborate canals and waterways linking the stupendous cities of China, all laden with every kind of good that could be imagined.

The *pax mongolica* (Mongolian peace) was not to last. The collapse of the Yuan dynasty in the 14th century disrupted international trade at its crucial eastern terminus in China. The overland route, the venerable Silk Road, ceased to be secure as hostile Turkic tribes seized its western end, and the Il-Khan Empire fell to the Safavids in Persia after years of chaos. Mongol unity likewise broke apart in central Asia as decentralized and warring Chaghatid princedoms were carved out of a once-unified khanate.

Review Questions

1. How did the Song emperors consolidate and legitimize their authority? Why is the scholar-official class important in understanding Song governance?
2. How did the Khitan and Jurchen nomadic invaders depart from the practices of previous nomads, such as the Xiongnu, Türks, and Uighurs, in how they governed their states?

---

2   Marco Polo, *The Travels of Marco Polo*, trans. Ronald Latham (London: Penguin, 1958), 35.

3. What were the elements, causes, and effects of the Song economic revolution?
4. How was the Mongol Empire established? What role did China play in it?

Further Reading

Abu-Lughod, Janet L. *Before European Hegemony: The World System A.D. 1250–1350*. Oxford: Oxford University Press, 1989.

Adshead, S. A. M. *China in World History*. New York: St. Martin's, 2000.

Barfield, Thomas J. *The Perilous Frontier: Nomadic Empires and China, 221 BC to AD 1757*. Cambridge, MA: Blackwell, 1989.

Birge, Bettine. *Women, Property, and Confucian Reaction in Sung and Yüan China (960–1368)*. Cambridge: Cambridge University Press, 2010.

Ebrey, Patricia B. *The Cambridge Illustrated History of China*. Cambridge: Cambridge University Press, 2010.

Headrick, Daniel. *Technology in World History*. Oxford: Oxford University Press, 2009.

Jackson, Peter. *The Mongols and the West*. London: Pearson Longman, 2005.

Kuhn, Dieter. *The Age of Confucian Rule: The Song Transformation of China*. Cambridge, MA: Harvard University Press, 2009.

Liu, William Guanglin. *The Chinese Market Economy, 1000–1500*. Stony Brook: The State University of New York Press, 2015.

Morgan, David. *The Mongols*. Hoboken: Wiley-Blackwell, 2007.

Mote, F. W. *Imperial China, 900–1800*. Cambridge, MA: Harvard University Press, 1999.

Rossabi, Morris, ed. *The Mongols and Global History*. New York: W. W. Norton, 2010.

Rossabi, Morris. *Khubilai Khan: His Life and Times*. Berkeley: University of California Press, 2009.

So, Billy K. L. *Prosperity, Region and Institutions in Maritime China*. Cambridge, MA: Harvard University Press, 2001.

Tao, Jinsheng. *The Jurchen in Twelfth Century China: A Study of Sinicization*. Seattle: University of Washington Press, 1977.

Twitchett, Denis. *Land Tenure and the Social Order in T'ang and Sung China*. Oxford: Oxford University Press, 1962.

Wittfogel, Karl, and Chia-sheng Feng, *History of Chinese Society: Liao (907–1125)*. Whitefish, MT: Literary Licensing, 2012.

Yoshinobu, Shiba. "Sung Foreign Trade: Its Scope and Organization." In *China Among Equals: The Middle Kingdom and its Neighbors, 10th–14th Centuries*, edited by Morris Rossabi, 89–115. Berkeley: University of California Press, 1983.

Yoshinobu, Shiba. *Commerce and Society in Sung China*. Translated by Mark Elvin. Ann Arbor: University of Michigan Press, 1992.

Figure Credits

Map 13.1: Copyright © by LiDaobing Yu Ninjie (CC BY-SA 3.0) at https://commons.wikimedia.org/wiki/File:China_11a.jpg.

Map 13.2: Copyright © by Augusta 89 (CC BY-SA 3.0) at https://commons.wikimedia.org/wiki/File:China_-_Southern_Song_Dynasty-fr.svg.

Fig. 13.1: Source: https://commons.wikimedia.org/wiki/File:Song_Dynasty_Hydraulic_Mill_for_Grain.JPG.

Fig. 13.2: Source: https://commons.wikimedia.org/wiki/File:Weaving_the_silk_(Sericulture_by_Liang_Kai,_1200s).jpg.

Map 13.3: Copyright © by Sting (CC BY-SA 2.5) at https://commons.wikimedia.org/wiki/File:Mongol_Empire_map_1297.png.

CHAPTER 14

Territorial Expansion and Economic Growth in Europe, 750-1300

The Carolingians

With the establishment of the Carolingian dynasty in 751 and the reign of its greatest ruler, Charlemagne (r. 768–814), a new Roman Empire straddled much of western Europe. In Charlemagne's hands, wars of conquest brought territorial expansion of the Frankish kingdom, which he renamed the Empire of the Romans, for he considered his state the reestablishment of the Roman Empire of antiquity. Able governance by Charlemagne brought political consolidation. Wealth was rooted in the land, and power accompanied its ownership. The royal family and the landed aristocracy, therefore, benefited most from the economic growth and quickening of trade that resumed in the middle of the eighth century and lasted well into the ninth, fueled by an expanding population.

Wars of Conquest

Under the later Merovingian kings, the mayors of the palace, managers of the king's household, gradually grew in power to become the most influential figures at the Frankish court. The first mayor of significance was Charles Martel, a warrior who led a Christian army that defeated a Muslim raiding party near Poitiers in 732.

This victory enhanced the stature of Martel and his family. His son Pepin succeeded him as mayor of the palace in 741. Pepin's ambitions reached higher, however, for he sent a letter to the pope, the head of the Christian Church in the West, asking for his support in deposing the Merovingian king, Childeric III (r. 744–751). The pope granted his approval and with it God's blessing, and Pepin was crowned king of the Franks in 751.

One of Pepin's sons Charles inherited the realm upon the death of his father in 768 and ruled jointly with his brother Carloman until Carloman died in 771. As sole ruler of the Franks, Charles immediately engaged in wars of conquest. Charlemagne (or Charles the Great), as he became known in history, invaded Saxony multiple times (in 772, 775, 782, and 785), but his armies also waged war in Lombardy, Spain, and Bavaria.

Over 20 years of campaigning, Charlemagne brought much of Europe under Frankish rule. His empire stretched from the Elbe River in the east to the Atlantic Ocean in the west, and from the North and Baltic Seas in the north to the Italian Lombard plain in the south. The wars gave Charlemagne immense prestige among his warrior aristocracy. With conquest came land, captives (who were sold into slavery), tribute money, and plunder for him and his warriors.

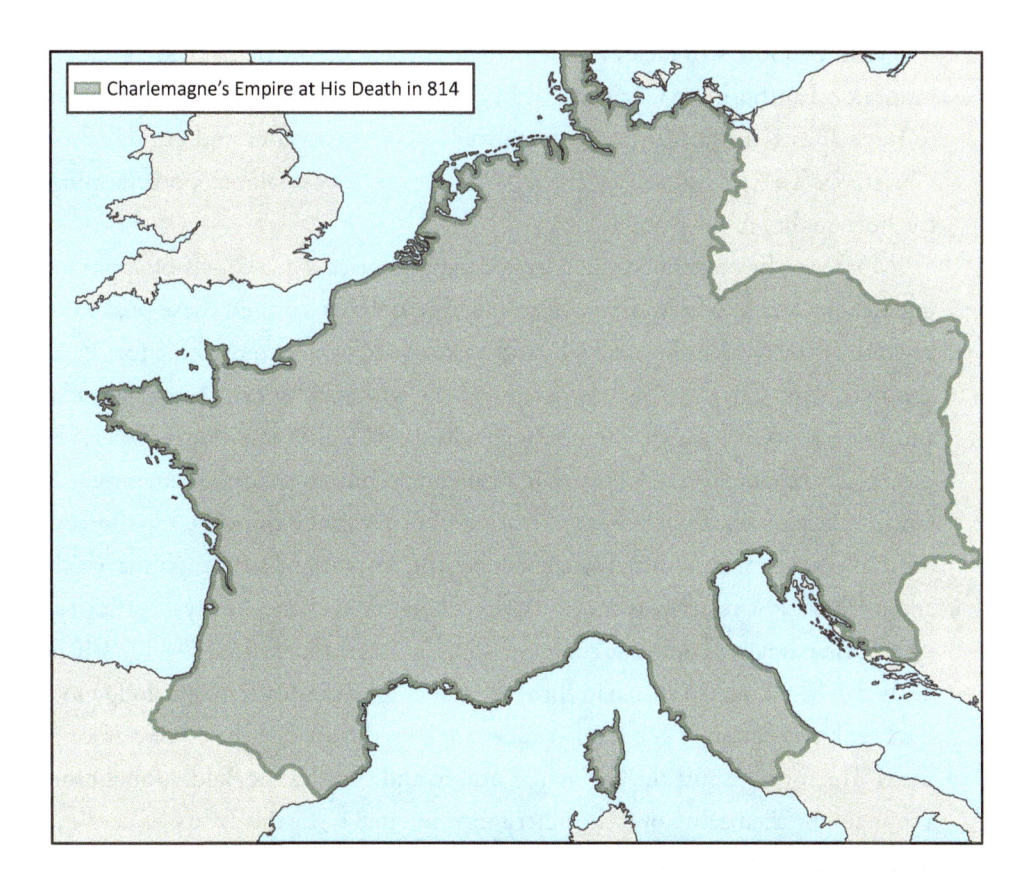

MAP 14.1   Charlemagne's Empire at His Death in 814

Warfare and conquest may have brought the Frankish king and his aristocrats wealth, but they also forced the king to govern. It became pressing to raise revenues to support the army once plunder dwindled after initial conquests. Within the Frankish realm, Charlemagne appointed his most trusted nobles to rule particular regions in his name.

Charlemagne began issuing laws, called capitularies, that treated a wide variety of topics. An ad hoc and brief pronouncement of the royal will rather than part of a systematic legal code, a royal capitulary nonetheless always superseded the local law. Many of the capitularies concerned the specific business of the king, such as terms of military service of his warriors or the administration of his royal estates. The **missi dominici**, direct agents of the king, carried the capitularies into the kingdom and extended the king's authority into provincial administration.

Charlemagne was crowned emperor of the Romans by Pope Leo III on Christmas Day in Rome in 800. Charlemagne did not, however, regard his authority as coming from the pope, but as a capitulary described the coronation, he was "crowned by God."[1] In fact, even before the coronation, he had already wedded his political authority to Christianity. In 796, in an official document, he referred to himself as King and Priest (*rex et sacerdos*) as the Leader and Guide of all Christians. To style himself as "priest," Charlemagne was pointedly proclaiming the holy quality of his person.

Moreover, he continued the Merovingian practice since Clovis of appointing bishops and abbots to their positions. The nobility coveted these positions because of the wealth they brought and so curried favor with the king for these appointments. Charlemagne also assumed the authority to call church **synods** and to back up ecclesiastical injunctions with royal legislation. For instance, he issued laws supporting the Church's position on prohibiting marriage among close family relations under pain of confiscation of property by the king. He thereby tried to prevent the nobility from consolidating patrimonies through marriage among their close relatives from which they then might challenge royal authority.

Charlemagne had only one surviving son, Louis the Pious, (r. 814–840), when he died in 814. Louis in turn had three sons, and upon his death in 840, following the Frankish custom of equal inheritance for sons, he divided the empire among them. The sons—Louis the German, Lothair, and Charles the Bald—fought for a time among themselves over the inheritance, but in 843, by the Treaty of Verdun, they agreed to the partition.

---

1 From the *Annales regni francorum* 801, in Richard E. Sullivan, *The Coronation of Charlemagne* (Boston: D.C. Heath, 1959), 2.

No new Charlemagne emerged to reunite the empire, which, as succeeding rulers divided the kingdoms among their heirs, steadily splintered into dozens of polities. Indeed, even effective defense of its fragmented parts became impossible. For 100 years from the middle of the ninth century, the Franks were thrown on the defensive as Vikings invaded from the north, Muslims from the south, and Slavic Magyars from the east.

Feudalism, a political system in which the nobility held lands called fiefs granted by kings in exchange for military service, arose in the ninth century in the absence of centralized state government, or even any notion of public authority. Amidst these unsettled conditions for holding and defending property, lords waged constant if small-scale warfare against one another, seeking advantage over weaker neighbors. Lords needed loyal warriors for this fighting and embraced the idea of contract to secure their services. Military service was usually paid for with land, which remained the foundation of wealth and power.

The Carolingian Economy

As we saw in Chapter 11, the population of Francia had contracted for several centuries beginning in 500. By the late 700s, however, it appears to have begun to grow again, an expansion that continued into the early 900s. Population growth was joined by economic growth, stimulated in part by technological developments in agriculture. Although far from ubiquitous, the use of the heavy-wheeled mouldboard plough gradually spread, especially on the great estates of the king and the lay and clerical aristocracy. The Merovingian development of these great landed estates, in fact, accelerated under the Carolingians, as the descendants of Charlemagne are known. Surplus production increased and was concentrated more and more in the hands of the aristocrats, the king, and the church. Indeed, the monasteries and **bishoprics** of the church tripled their property holdings from 750 to 825 through pious bequests, grants of land to the church by lords in exchange for promises of salvation for their souls from the clergy. Monasteries, like the Abbey of Cluny, continued to receive these bequests for centuries, as the church became the greatest landowner in Europe.

Land was typically organized by manor. Manorialism, as this system of organization has been called, was dominant in France, England, and much of central and southern Germany and in the ninth and tenth centuries spread to northern Germany, Poland, the Balkans, and Ukraine.

Manors were typically farms between 750 and 1,500 acres with 15–30 peasant families working on it. Part of the land, called the demesne, was owned by the lord for his own use but was worked by serfs and free peasants. Serfs were not slaves, because the lord did not own their bodies, but without the lord's consent, they were unable to move or to marry off their daughters. Free peasants, like serfs, owed the lord service obligations, but they also had legal rights to own land in their own name. However, even free peasants paid the lord certain fees and dues, such as to use the lord's mills and ovens and for hearing legal cases in the lord's court.

Some especially large manors, like those between the Loire and the Rhine Rivers in Francia, were the primary motor driving the Carolingian economy. There is clear evidence for an increase in the production of wine and grain far beyond the needs of local consumers. Some of these manors were dispersed over large areas, especially those owned by the church, because pious bequests in land could come from a variety of benefactors spread across broad areas. When confronted with dispersed estates and to improve managerial efficiency, some ecclesiastical lords, such as the abbots of Cluny, employed *firmarii*, laymen who kept their positions as long as they kept the revenues flowing to the lord.

Evidently, many lords were becoming more profit-oriented during the ninth century. We find legal documents in much greater quantity than previously, asserting rights to land just when the great estates began keeping managerial documents called polyptiques, inventories that list the inhabitants and the physical resources of the various estates. Further evidence of this profit-oriented mindset is the investment by lords in watermills. These machines were expensive and complex. A lord would only make an investment in them if the return covered it. Evidently, it did, for during the ninth century, watermills cropped up everywhere that flowing water permitted.

The royal house was the greatest landowner of all, but beyond royal estates, lay the kingdom. In 793, Charlemagne tried to link the Danube and Rhine Rivers by digging a canal. Even though it was never completed, it showed royal interest in facilitating trade. Merchants (including Jews) operating in the Carolingian economy, often as agents of great estates, were protected and privileged by the king. The Carolingians also were aware of the importance of readily available coinage to the economy and surpassed the volume of their predecessors in minting it or melting down Arab or Byzantine coins and restamping them with the image of the emperor, as Charlemagne did. The royal treasury stood to benefit from these varied activities. Again, it is no accident that imperial toll stations stood at the entry and exit points of the key trade routes linking the empire to the rest of the world.

The Carolingian great estates were growing more agricultural products than could be consumed on the estate itself. Some agricultural products, notably wine, were transported over surprisingly long distances. The wine surplus from the monastery of St. Germain des Près near Paris, for example, was enormous. The monks shipped it down the Seine River to the periodic fairs at Saint Denis, which became the greatest wine market in western Europe. In the late 700s, these fairs lasted only a few days, but a century later, business had increased so much that they were held for a month at a time. International merchants were attracted to them. They brought with them luxury goods, like exotic furs, silk, and spices, that Frankish rulers, lords, and their wives coveted and carried away the prized wine destined for distant markets.

Indeed, export was an important aspect of the Carolingian economy. Goods travelled out of the empire along two fundamental routes. One reached to the north toward the Baltic and North Sea basins. The other ran to the southeast over the Alps and toward the Mediterranean Sea.

The Rhine River was the main highway for goods going north. Oak-casked wine, grain, metalwork, jewelry, weaponry, glassware, clay pottery, and lava grinding stones called querns all flowed down the Rhine toward Dorestad. Dorestad, as we saw in Chapter 11, was a thriving emporium at the junction of trade routes from the north and northwest. There, Frankish goods met products imported from the north—furs, hides, wax, amber, and slaves.

This Rhenish trade boomed from the 780s, propelled by demand across the north. A newcomer to this trade and a product of this demand was clay pottery. Manufacturing sites upriver on the Rhine near the city of Cologne appeared in the late eighth century, all responding to a market-driven demand. Plentiful clay, sand, water, and wood provided the raw materials and energy to sustain a centralized industry here where workers with specialized skills toiled in interconnected workshops.

Other important emporia, all with toll stations set up by various rulers, linked Baltic and North Sea commerce. Quentovic on the English Channel in northern Francia; Birka and Helgo in central Sweden; and Hedeby (Haithabu) in Denmark at the head of the River Schlei, which opens into the Baltic Sea, were all important ports and trading centers. They were loosely linked by maritime trade routes dominated by Frisian merchants (from modern-day Netherlands and western Germany) until well into the ninth century. As testimony to the increased volume of trade, there was a gradual evolution in ship design toward vessels with deeper draughts, which enabled the stowing of larger cargoes.

Frankish goods destined for foreign markets also exited the kingdom to the southeast, through mountain passes in the Alps and toward the Italian city of Venice. From here, the path opened onto the Mediterranean Sea. Venice at the northern end of the Adriatic Sea was the main point of entry of goods from the East (the coveted silks and spices) and of export of Frankish goods, notably slaves. The 700s witnessed a quickening of commerce on the Mediterranean Sea.

The Venetians entered Mediterranean commerce suddenly in the mid-700s, as we have seen in Chapter 11. Their ships were destined for Byzantine and, perhaps surprisingly, Muslim ports on the eastern and southern rim of the Mediterranean basin. A sudden influx of Arab coins into Charlemagne's kingdom in the late 700s points to intensifying linkages with the Arab world. Venetians hauled a variety of European products, but above all, their cargo was a commodity in keen demand, especially among Arab buyers—slaves. The demand for slaves seemed limitless. And Venetians were at the epicenter of the thriving slave trade and made their fortunes from it.

Venetians also acquired slaves from the Carolingians to the north. Many a prisoner captured during the Carolingian wars of conquest was enslaved and sold to Venetian traders. The slaves formed human caravans, and as they marched over the Alps, they nullified the cost of transport because they transported themselves through their own labor. Indeed, their value was enhanced by the fact that they could be forced to haul on their backs, at no added cost, additional wares (notably weaponry) destined for distant markets.

The Venetians were not the only intermediaries in trade between East and West. By the ninth century, Jews were everywhere—at the Frankish court, in the Muslim Levant, in Byzantine Constantinople, even in India and China. Important intermediaries between the various cultures in Eurasian trade, they greased the wheels of commerce. They were multilingual, speaking Arabic, Persian, Greek, Frankish, and Slavic, and they traded in everything—slaves, textiles, furs, swords—whatever was in demand.

Raiders, Traders, and Settlers

For centuries, Scandinavian people had largely remained isolated from the rest of Europe, alternately trading and raiding among themselves. Suddenly, in the late eighth century, they burst upon Europe, raiding and sacking one monastery and city after another. These Vikings, or Norsemen, as they later became known, for a time disrupted the economy of Europe, but as they settled themselves in new locales, the raiding ceased and trading became their primary activity. They played an important role in a trading system that connected the commerce of northern Europe with the well-established Asian and Mediterranean markets.

Raiders from the North

For centuries in Scandinavia, people had farmed, herded animals, fished, and traded and raided among themselves. These Vikings formed loose political organizations based on kinship. The men met in councils called Things, engaged in collective decision making, and appointed chieftains from among themselves who usually claimed some sort of divine ancestry and promised, with the favor of the gods, to secure the well-being of the community. Often, this well-being involved successful raiding of other communities. While the men were away on these frequent expeditions, women assumed the defense and management of the farm and household, raising the family, making and mending clothing, tending livestock, and supervising servants and slaves.

Suddenly, beginning in the 790s and continuing for the next century, the Vikings burst upon Europe in repeated and devastating raids. The most likely explanation for this dramatic intrusion upon foreign lands is overpopulation in the Vikings' homelands where agricultural productivity could not sustain a growing population.

The Vikings also knew that raiding overseas was both prosperous and, given their ship technology and sailing skills, attainable. The North Sea is one of the coldest and most treacherous bodies of water in the world, but the Vikings were able to navigate it in their heavy-beamed langskips (longships). These vessels were upwards of 100 feet long, and with a shallow draft and large capacity, they were ideal for carrying warriors and loot.

The Vikings struck the British Isles, the Carolingian Empire, and Ireland at a time when internal divisions weakened these targets and made them easy prey. Encountering no effective naval opposition on the seas or by the coasts, the Vikings from Norway and Denmark were able to travel freely, raiding with impunity. They first targeted the isolated and ill-defended monasteries, like Lindisfarne in northern Britain, sacked in 793. Gold and silver jewel-encrusted crosses and chalices made for easy pickings. They soon set their sights on the north and west coasts of Francia. Ermentarius, a monk at a monastery in the 860s, vividly described the Viking raids: "The number of ships increases, the endless flood of Vikings never ceases to grow bigger. Everywhere Christ's people are the victims of massacres, burning and plunder. The Vikings over-run all that lies before them, and none can withstand them."[2]

---

2   Gwyn Jones, *A History of the Vikings*, 2nd ed. (Oxford: Oxford University Press, 1984), 215.

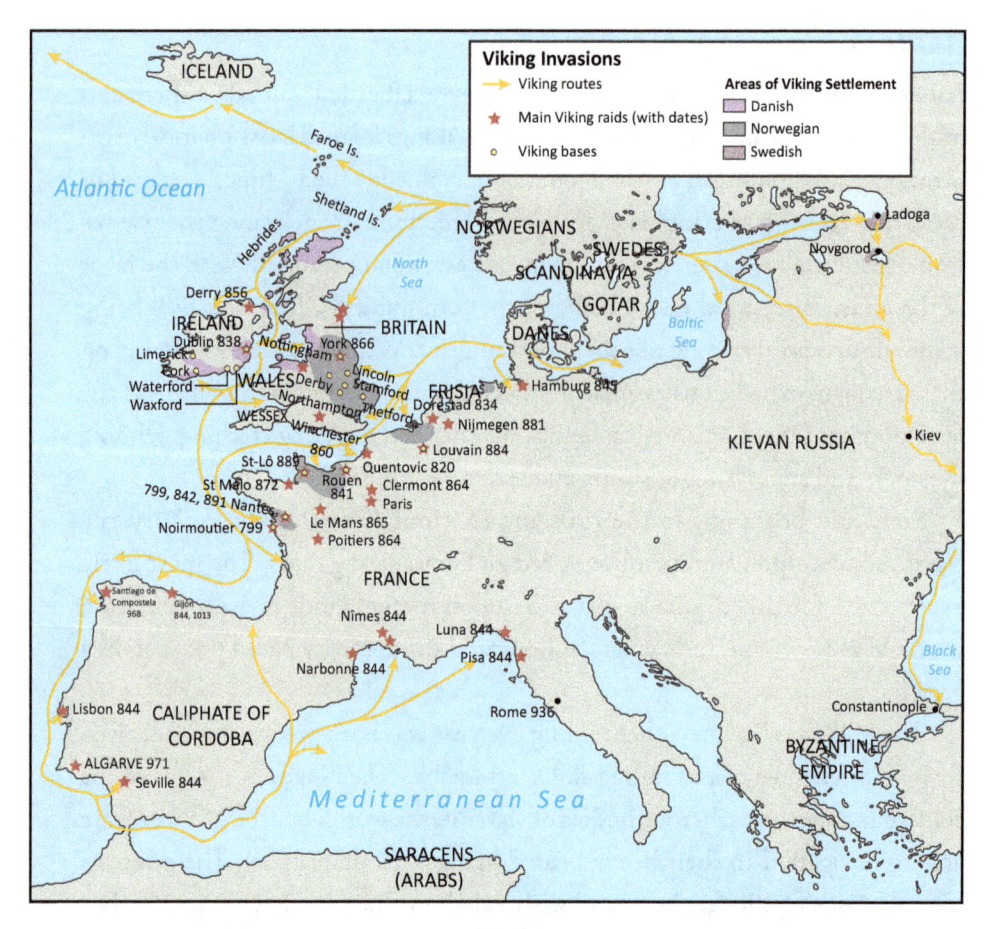

MAP 14.2 Viking Invasions in the Ninth Century

The raids continued throughout the ninth century as Viking ships cruised the coast and sailed up rivers to strike and loot wealthy emporia and cities. The Viking Halfdan even led an expedition of 62 ships through the Strait of Gibraltar and into the Mediterranean Sea. In the 860s, his warriors plundered cities in southern Spain, southern France, and western Italy. After his men sacked Pisa, they set their sights on Rome. They attacked and looted Luna, mistakenly thinking it was Rome. When Halfdan discovered his error, he furiously ordered the slaughter of all the men in the city and sold all the women and children into slavery. He never found Rome.

By the middle of the ninth century, the Vikings were now settling in the conquered areas. In 865, the Danish Vikings invaded the interior of England and remained there. Their advance was halted by the Anglo-Saxon king of Wessex, Alfred the Great (r. 871–899), but the Danes remained in England for centuries to come. Similarly, in Francia, the Vikings invaded and then settled in Normandy, which even became a principality of the Frankish kingdom in 911.

The Viking diaspora reached to the west as well. The Norwegians first settled the bleak Shetland, Hebrides, and Faroe Islands in the North Atlantic. They then pushed on to Iceland in 870, a century later to Greenland, and by the year 1000, to the shores of North America. They brought cattle and sheep and built homes and churches. The settlement in Iceland was permanent, unlike that of Vinland in North America and Greenland. Distance from the homeland and hostile native peoples quickly drove the Vikings from America, and a cooling climate gradually after several hundred years made Greenland inhospitable.

From Raiders to Traders and Settlers

Vikings from eastern Scandinavia (present-day Sweden) also joined the diaspora. Like their Norwegian and Danish brethren, the Swedes began with raiding, but within a generation or two, had become mostly traders and settlers. Their ships sailed to the south and east of Sweden, reaching the eastern shores of the Baltic Sea.

Like Vikings in the west, they sailed up rivers. They penetrated Russia via the Don, Dnepr, and Volga Rivers. Eventually, by way of the Black Sea, they connected to trade routes toward Byzantium. By way of the Caspian Sea, they linked up with the trade routes of the Abbasid caliphate and the caravan trains from central Asia bearing goods to and from China.

This trading system, centered in the Baltic and North Seas and which by the 10th century the Vikings controlled, is known as the Northern Arc. It connected the commerce of northern Europe with the well-established Asian and Mediterranean markets. The Vikings brought slaves, furs, timber, amber, honey, and walrus ivory and traded for silks, spices, glass pottery, and silver. So many Vikings settled in Russia that they created the Rus state. The trading center Novgorod was its first capital, then Kiev, likewise a trading center on the important waterway, the Dnepr River. The transit trade of the Northern Arc also created a thriving commercial center on the island of Gotland in Sweden. Nearly 100,000 Byzantine, Arabic, German, and Anglo-Saxon coins and vast caches of silver objects and jewelry have been excavated in Gotland.

The Byzantines

The Byzantine state had nearly disappeared by 650 (see Chapter 11), a victim of conquests from hostile neighbors on all sides. It survived because of its impregnable capital city, Constantinople, and after 780 began to expand its territory again. Over the next 250 years, a series of conquering emperors brought the empire to its greatest extent since the reign of Justinian in the sixth century. Favorable conditions for agricultural growth and trade buoyed the economy, filled the imperial treasury through increased taxes, and enriched a provincial, landed warrior class.

The Resurgent State

Unlike in the West, the state administrative apparatus of the Roman Empire continued in the East. Byzantium, as this state came to be known, was centered upon a great and impregnable capital city, Constantinople. Governance was highly centralized under the emperor and his imperial bureaucracy, and the economy was heavily regulated by the state. As the greatest landowner and the beneficiary of a comprehensive system of taxation, the state was the driving force in the expropriation of surplus wealth from the peasant producers.

This strong center provided a solid base from which to renew conquest and territorial expansion, which marked the years between 780 and 1025. A series of emperors reacquired western and northern Greece, most of Armenia, northern Syria, all of Bulgaria, and southern Italy. By the end of the reign of Emperor Basil II (r. 976–1025), Byzantium had doubled in size since 780.

Success did not come easy to Basil. Early in his reign, Basil had to contend with rebellious aristocratic families in Anatolia who had grown wealthy from their great estates and powerful from their command of large armies. They posed a formidable challenge to his rule. Shortly after Basil became emperor, his realm was plunged into civil war. With the aid of Vladimir of Kiev, he was able to quash his aristocratic rebels. With his restive nobility pacified, Basil was able to turn his attention to foreign conquests, and it was during Basil's reign that the Byzantine Empire grew to its greatest extent since Justinian. Perhaps his greatest victory came against Bulgaria, the empire's greatest foe on its northwestern frontier. Basil's conquest was as decisive as it was brutal. After one battle, he captured 15,000 Bulgars. He blinded most of them but allowed 1 in every 100 to retain sight in one eye to lead the miserable horde back to their king as a reminder of the power and might of the Byzantine emperor. Basil was subsequently nicknamed the Bulgar Slayer.

Unlike Justinian, these conquering emperors did not leave the state impoverished. Quite the contrary, in fact, for explosive growth in government revenues allowed Basil to leave a huge surplus in the treasury at his death. The state remained the largest landowner. Newly conquered land mostly became imperial holdings, and rents and taxes from these became a major source of revenue for the state.

The Aristocracy and the Peasantry

As in the West, the ninth century in Byzantium saw more favorable conditions for agriculture. The heavy plough was never introduced here, as it was ill-suited to the thin and rocky soil. Still, some large landowners clearly had an eye toward surplus and profit, evidenced by investments in extensive irrigation systems and by the planting of vines and olives for the market.

The growth of agricultural production continued in the tenth and 11th centuries and altered the relationship between the state, the landowning aristocracy, and the peasantry. A new rural, landed, and military aristocracy had emerged in the seventh century (see Chapter 11) and taken its place at the top of the provincial hierarchy. The state became increasingly dependent upon this new aristocracy for local administration and, importantly, for military defense against perennially hostile neighbors. Such dependency came at a cost, and emperors faced the constant problem of an overly independent and powerful aristocracy.

To retain the loyalty and military service of the aristocrats, emperors not only had to grant them vast tracts of land but they also had to award them greater legal rights over the peasantry who worked for them. As a result, peasants increasingly saw larger portions of the produce from their farms taken by their lords in higher rents and imperially sanctioned labor services, whereby peasants were forced to work more on their lords' lands.

Moreover, the state increasingly demanded cash payment for taxes. This fell on lord and peasant alike, but the lords met their obligation by requiring rent payments in cash from their peasants. To satisfy the requisitions of lord and state, peasants were forced to sell on the local market whatever surplus they might squeeze from their land, only to turn the cash over to the landlord and the state. Thus, the gains derived from agricultural growth were divided between the state and the aristocracy but were denied to the peasant producer. In the 11th century, such fiscal demands seemed so excessive to the peasants that they rose in sporadic yet unsuccessful revolts. In 1065, for example, peasants in Thessaly in northern Greece rebelled, fruitlessly as it turned out, against a spike in imperial taxation.

Political Recovery and Economic Growth

With the fragmentation and breakup of the Carolingian Empire and the invasions across its borders in the ninth century came economic dislocation and contraction. For a time, production diminished and trade routes were disrupted. However, especially in the West and beginning in the late 10th century, new states emerged, population grew and migrated into new lands, and trade expanded in volume and became more diversified. The economy in Byzantium was not as robust as in the West, but there, too, we find quickening economic activity during these centuries, as foreign trade continued to be channeled through its key cities and across its major trade routes.

New States in the West

As the Carolingian Empire broke up, authority was exercised by rulers of territories that varied greatly in size. Some of these were so small that they barely encompassed what the lord could see from his manor. Other territories were larger, and the most stable and enduring of these were in northwestern Europe—the core of Francia. These enduring estates typically sat on fertile and productive lowland that provided the agricultural base essential to political survival because of the surplus it could produce. Wealth and power were never far apart.

Gradually, the rulers of these stable and productive territories fashioned governing administrations to extend and consolidate their authority. Francia provides the best illustration of the growth of monarchical power and the territorial extension of the kingdom. A new royal family, the Capetians, initially owed their crown to their weakness. Frankish nobles elected Hugh Capet king in 987 because he was weak and they feared no threat from him, yet they were desirous of a king who could theoretically legitimize their own authority as derived from the king's and, through him, from God's. Hugh may have been powerless, but his descendants, notably Philip II Augustus (r. 1180–1223), expanded the realm. Philip fashioned a relatively efficient administration through royal officials called bailli who were appointed by him, answered only to him, and could be removed by him.

This extension of royal authority did not go unchallenged, nor did it triumph everywhere. In fact, in many parts of Europe, landowning aristocrats found ways to consolidate their own authority in their territories and keep royal power at bay. In many places, they secured their property for their lineage by favoring the eldest son in inheritance. This practice of **primogeniture** (which was especially prominent in northwest France) kept the landed estate intact and permitted the transmission of resources from one generation to the next, thereby facilitating the consolidation of aristocratic "houses."

These aristocratic families, moreover, deepened and extended alliances among themselves through marriage, women being centrally important figures in these arrangements. They thereby formed increasingly tangled webs of powerful kin groups that served as counterweights to the exercise of royal power in their territories. In some places, like Poland, Hungary, and above all 13th-century Germany, the great lords dominated the political world. Indeed, between 1254 and 1273, there were no kings of Germany at all.

Somewhat earlier, England also experienced an aristocratic challenge to royal authority. The consolidation of royal authority had advanced during the 12th century but was abruptly contested in the early 13th during the reign of King John (r. 1199–1216). Shortly after the French king Philip II Augustus defeated John's armies at the Battle of Bouvines in 1214, which dispossessed John of the Angevin kingdom in France that the royal English family had held for generations, he faced a rebellion among his own nobles at home. John was forced by his barons to sign the Magna Carta, whose clauses explicitly limited regal authority and affirmed baronial privileges, above all the control of property and its passing down to heirs without royal interference.

John's successor, Henry III (r. 1216–1272), was equally in thrall to the power of his barons. In 1258, he was forced to appeal to them for funds (he was nearly bankrupt), and to get them, he was forced to sign the Provisions of Oxford. This agreement between king and lord reconfirmed the provisions of the Magna Carta that protected baronial property. Furthermore, it created a permanent council of barons that the king had to consult prior to any royal fiscal exactions in the realm beyond the king's own lands. The council came to be called a parliament, and the precedent was set that the king had to appeal to his barons for money.

Kings were not only challenged by their own lords in their own realms but were also challenged by the papacy. The Church of Rome had unrivalled access to resources because it was the most extensive landowner in Europe and levied a tax on its own clergy. After the year 1000, it expanded its authority and wealth, reaching a high-water mark in the 13th century. Pope Innocent III (1198–1216) convened the Fourth Lateran Council in 1215, and it was here that the church decreed its universality. Church administration and doctrine were both clarified and standardized. By the end of the century, a pope, Boniface VIII (1294–1303), could realistically assert that the pope held both the secular and spiritual swords, theoretically proclaiming the subservience of even kings to the papacy in all matters.

This resurgent Church of Rome was also fundamentally instrumental in the Crusades, an enormous military venture initially launched to recapture the Holy Land from the Muslims. In 1071, the Byzantine army was routed by the Seljuk Turks at the Battle of Manzikert. When word of the defeat reached the West, a rumor spread that the Byzantine emperor had issued a plea for military help to counter the rising power of the Turks.

Whether the emperor had made such a plea is unknown, but in Pope Urban II's famous speech in 1095 in which he called for a crusade, he acknowledged the emperor's plea. He pledged that anyone who took up the cross and returned the Holy Land to Christendom would earn salvation. He also saw a crusade as a way to alleviate the rampant strife among Europe's warrior class. The practice of primogeniture increasingly denied younger sons of knights access to the patrimony, leaving them with little to do but wage small-scale wars against other nobles. A crusade, for all of its religious motivations, would also draw off this restive group of warriors, reducing wars at home and promising land from conquest abroad. Following the pope's summons in 1095, thousands of knights and common folk trekked 2,000 miles across unknown lands to storm Jerusalem and return it to Christian hands.

No kings participated in the First Crusade (although they were prominent in later ones), nor was it guided or planned by the papacy, but scores of lesser Frankish nobles set off for the Holy Land. Eastern Mediterranean cities fell to the Frankish sword, culminating in the conquest of Jerusalem in 1099. The crusade was ostensibly a war waged against the Muslim infidel, but in fact, Jews and Christians (including women and children) were also slaughtered in appalling numbers as the European warriors slashed their way to conquest. Several Latin crusader states were created by the Europeans, mirroring the consolidation of monarchical states occurring back in Europe. Some of these states survived into the 13th century. The Crusades can be counted an early expression of European geographic expansion, a prelude to a vast movement exploding upon the world several centuries in the future.

TABLE 14.1 The Five Major Crusades and Their Outcomes

Crusades	Dates	Outcome
First Crusade	1096–1099	Conquered Jerusalem. Established crusader states of the Kingdom of Jerusalem (1099–1291), the County of Edessa (1098–1146), the Principality of Antioch (1098–1268), and the County of Tripoli (1109–1289), which was established after, but as a result of, the first crusade
Second Crusade	1147–1149	Failed to recapture the County of Edessa and the city of Jerusalem, both of which had been conquered by Muslim armies

Crusades	Dates	Outcome
Third Crusade	1189–1192	Failed again to recapture Jerusalem, which had been taken by the Muslim general Saladin in 1187
Fourth Crusade	1202–1204	Objective to retake Jerusalem, but when that failed, crusaders led by the Venetians captured the Christian city of Constantinople and temporarily created the Latin Empire of Constantinople (1204–1261)
Fifth Crusade	1213–1221	Failed again to recapture Jerusalem from the Ayyubid Sultanate (1171–1260)

Population Growth and Migration in the West

European territorial expansion occurred closer to home as well. The population of Europe tripled between 1000 and 1300, most likely the result of climate change marked by warmer conditions that extended the growing season that proved favorable to increased agricultural production. The explosion of cereal production was joined by the absence of endemic diseases, the end of foreign invasions, and a reduction in warfare among the aristocrats closer to home (aristocratic warriors were busy doing much of their fighting beyond Europe's borders). These conditions favorable to economic growth, moreover, had the greatest impact in northwestern Europe, above all in Francia, what is today France and western Germany.

By the 13th century, farmers, merchants, miners, and, importantly, knights from the old core of Francia had colonized vast reaches of the European continent. Indeed, land was the greatest prize. Much like the Crusades, the expansion of Europe was speared by an aristocratic diaspora, especially of Frankish knights caught in a frenzied scramble for new lands. Frankish knights intruded everywhere, pushing into Muslim Sicily and Iberia and above all into eastern Europe. Armored knights on horseback flanked by crossbowmen overwhelmed the technologically inferior existing aristocracies wherever they went. Once established by conquest, they often secured their hold on their new lands by marrying native women and building castles: first motte and bailey—fortifications where a wooden citadel sat atop raised earthworks and was surrounded by a courtyard and moat—but soon replaced by stone castles.

These conquering lords confronted an immediate and pressing need: labor to clear, drain, and farm their new lands. To obtain labor, they employed middlemen who recruited colonists and helped them settle on the new lands, marking out houses and fields. The lords further appealed to migrants by proclaiming favorable economic and legal conditions. The lords continued to own the land, but for fixed rents and certain dues, they permitted peasants to pass the land down through their own generations.

Economic growth benefited lord and peasant, although disproportionately favoring the former. Many lords paid increasing attention to land management. Recordkeeping increased on aristocratic, clerical, and royal estates. The *Domesday Book*, completed in 1086, is a startling example of this new mentality. William the Conqueror (r. 1066–1087) ordered a survey of his new English kingdom seized in 1066, with an express purpose to determine if more could be extracted from the land than was currently obtained.

By the 12th century, kings of England had instituted annual audits of income and expenditures from royal estates whose results were stored in central archives, a practice that monarchs on the continent increasingly employed as well. By the late 13th century, a technical literature on estate management had appeared.

With new settlers in eastern Europe came technological changes, noticeably the heavy plough and new mills that intensified and spread cereal cultivation. Wind power was increasingly harnessed by windmills, a medieval invention, for grinding grain, for pumping water from wetlands, and to power machines using camshafts and triphammers for fulling wool as the cloth was pounded to cleanse it of dirt and oils. Watermills with the more efficient, if more expensive, overshot wheel also made their appearance.

The growing surplus of foodstuffs triggered the emergence of new towns and markets, many clustered near castles, bridges, and harbors, as well as the growth of existing cities. Indeed, a market-driven demand for cereals altered the ecology, as many woodlands and marshes were cleared and drained.

Quickening Economic Activity in the East

By 1000, the Byzantine Empire encompassed Anatolia, Greece, and the Balkans and reached into southern Italy. As economic activity quickened in the 11th and 12th centuries, so too did the circulation of coinage in the empire: gold for taxes, copper for ordinary transactions.

The extent to which a commercial market penetrated the rural Byzantine economy, however, should not be exaggerated. Outside of the great port cities and above all Constantinople, demand was still meager. Indeed, demand in the Byzantine economy was dominated by purchases by the state, powerful landowners and their wives, and monasteries. In fact, much of state demand was for military needs, and much of this was requisitioned directly from state-controlled workshops or farms. Only a limited amount, in other words, was obtained through commercial transactions.

Constantinople and a handful of large trading cities, however, stood apart, and they played a major role in long-distance trade. The considerable length of its coastlines was a commercial advantage for the Byzantine Empire, making it conducive to maritime trade. Trebizond on the Black Sea, for example, was a major commercial center on the trade routes between Constantinople and Syria, the Caucasus, and central Asia.

The state monopolized silk production and trade. It exported the expensive and exquisitely purple-dyed fabric to the East through Trebizond as well as to the West where it was used in Church decoration and vestments. Private Byzantine traders, though heavily regulated by the state, imported luxury goods, like perfumes and spices, from the East and slaves and furs from the West and the North.

Byzantium, then, played an important role in recreating a Mediterranean-wide trading network for the first time since the collapse of old Roman Empire in the sixth century, even if the commercial activity was concentrated in a few cities and dominated by the state.

Trade

The generation of surplus from the growth of population and the expansion of agriculture in turn increased the volume of trade and the density of its networks. Kings were hungry for the luxury objects of distant origin that would be the outward symbols of their power and royalty, but there is clear evidence of an expansion of volume of trade and variety of goods of a more mundane nature.

Local and regional markets and fairs cropped up, as did new towns. Each served as nodes of increasingly integrated regional economies. Indeed, towns grew everywhere in Europe. This was especially the case during the 12th century and markedly in the newly colonized regions to the east populated by migrants from the central core of Europe. Increasingly populous and complex centers of manufacturing and consumption, towns also became important transshipment centers. There was also an unmistakable growth and increasing specialization of urban craftsmen.

One of the byproducts of the Crusades was the formation of the crusading religious order of the Knights Templar. Their military role in the Crusades was important, but their role in the expanding European economy was even more significant. Initially, they served to safeguard travelers to the Holy Land. Soon, however, they established banks at strategic points along the way so that a traveler, for a fee, could deposit money before leaving, receive a certificate of deposit, and withdraw funds as needed at distant Templar banks. The Templars rapidly grew into a large, rich, and powerful financial institution, eventually maintaining a private navy and engaging in merchant shipping operations.

The Templars, along with scores of merchants and moneychangers from across Europe, found the fairs of Champagne especially profitable. The fairs were ideally situated at the commercial axis where textiles from the Low Countries (present-day Belgium and Netherlands) met luxury goods from Italy. Provided political protection and legal guarantees to secure person and property by the Counts of Champagne, the fairs (which met at regular intervals) became a key locus of exchange for long-distance trade. They reached their zenith in the 12th and early 13th centuries.

The 12th and 13th centuries witnessed other signs of economic growth. Notably, the Hanseatic League was founded. Centered in the town of Lübeck on the Baltic Sea, the League began as a loose confederation of trading cities. By the 13th century, however, it had surged to monopolistic control of commerce on the Baltic Sea and was extending its reach into the North Sea. Forest products, furs, amber, resins, wax, grain, and fish were all channeled through League-controlled ports. By 1368, the volume grew to such an extent that 700 ships a year sailed into and out of Lübeck's harbor.

Member League cities entered formal agreements removing restrictions on trade among themselves. Scores of cities maintained lighthouses, provided harbor pilots, and offered inns and warehouses for League merchants. By the mid-14th century, the League had created a representative governing body, called a *Diet*.

Italy was also experiencing economic growth between 1000 and 1300. Cities had never disappeared from the Italian Peninsula, but after the year 1000, they grew noticeably. During the 11th century, the trading cities of Amalfi and Venice were joined in competition by Pisa and Genoa, all eager to tap the riches of the East. By the early 1300s, the Venetians and Genoese had forged to the front of the Italian pack of merchants. They could be found in every part of the western Eurasian trade network. The Latin crusader states offered new opportunities for these overseas traders, for the crusader states had no fleets of their own. The states were surrounded by Muslim states and thus heavily dependent on maritime supply, and so the Italians became the crusader states' lifeline.

The Venetians and Genoese also hammered out agreements with Byzantine and even Muslim rulers, and through these Italian intermediaries, trade between East and West grew. Italians were granted territorial enclaves in port cities in exchange for payment of fees and custom duties on the cargo they carried. More than anything, however, the Italians were eager to acquire spices—nutmeg, mace, cloves, cinnamon, pepper. Many cargoes of spices from the East channeled up the Red Sea and down the Nile River to Alexandria in Egypt, and Italian merchants flocked there. So many Christian traders came to Alexandria that the Muslim ruler built a special harbor for them, separate from the one used by Muslim merchants.

The spice trade was hugely profitable for the Italians. In 1300, for example, 100 pounds of nutmeg purchased in Alexandria would cost 10 Venetian ducats but would sell back in Venice for up to 50. Many Italian merchants became enormously wealthy and parlayed their wealth into political dominance in their home cities. Ostensibly **republics**, Genoa and Venice witnessed sharp polarization of wealth and power skewed toward the upper class of rich merchants.

Italian traders were keenly aware of the routes by which the luxuries of the East reached the West, and so both Venetians and Genoese also pushed into the Black Sea to tap them. The Genoese, for instance, founded trading ports and colonies on the Black Sea's northern shores, linking with trade routes to and from China. The most important colony was Caffa on the Crimean Peninsula, purchased by the Genoese from the Mongol Golden Horde in 1266. It became an **entrepôt** teeming with silk, spices, and slaves.

How were the Italians to pay for these products? They carried few commodities from Europe that the East valued, except for slaves, gold, and silver, and a steady stream of all three flowed eastward. The Venetian gold ducat became an international standard of value, but until Europe could produce items in demand in the East, a steady drain of coins from west to east will present a chronic goods-to-money imbalance for Europeans well into the 16th century.

The resulting shortage of gold and silver in Europe pushed Italians to innovate in business organization and mechanisms of credit. Borrowing heavily from Muslim practices, Italian merchant families pooled capital in partnerships and commenda, whereby one partner entrusts goods to another for delivery to market and shares in the profits.

The Italians also established permanent agents in far-flung cities in northern Europe, western Asia, and points in between. Through careful accounting, they expanded the use of credit and the mobility of capital. They apparently borrowed to great effect the Muslim practice of double-entry bookkeeping where revenues and expenses are kept in separate columns, and so profit and loss can be observed clearly. They also adopted the Muslim device of bills of exchange (much like a modern check, a contract governing later payment somewhere else). Moreover, both Genoa and Venice created systems of public debt to fund investment in infrastructure and defense. Wealthy citizens loaned capital to the state in return for redeemable shares of stock. This was an early instance of the state becoming a vehicle of credit and an outlet for profitable capital investment.

Review Questions

1. Why were the great royal, lay, and clerical landed estates important politically and economically?
2. What was the Viking diaspora, and what were its consequences?
3. How did the relationship between the state, the aristocracy, and the peasantry in the Byzantine Empire change between 750 and 1100?
4. What were the causes and consequences of European economic growth from 1000–1300?

Further Reading

Barraclough, Geoffrey. *The Crucible of Europe: The Ninth and Tenth Centuries*. Berkeley: The University of California Press, 1976.

Bartlett, Robert. *The Making of Europe: Conquest, Colonization and Cultural Change, 950–1350*. Princeton: Princeton University Press, 1993.

Crosby, Alfred W. *Ecological Imperialism: The Biological Expansion of Europe, 900–1900*. Cambridge: Cambridge University Press, 1986.

Cunliffe, Barry. *Europe between the Oceans*. New Haven: Yale University Press, 2008.

Duby, George. *Rural Economy and Country Life in the Medieval West*. Translated by Cynthia Postan. Philadelphia: University of Pennsylvania Press, 1999.

Duby, George. *Women in the Twelfth Century*. Translated by Jean Birrell. Chicago: University of Chicago Press, 1997.

Harvey, Alan. *Economic Expansion in the Byzantine Empire, 900–1200*. Cambridge: Cambridge University Press, 1989.

Hodges, Richard. *Dark Age Economics: The Origins of Towns and Trade, AD 600–1000*. London: Duckworth, 2001.

McCormick, Michael. *The Origins of the European Economy: Communications and Commerce, AD 300–900*. Cambridge: Cambridge University Press, 2001.

Nicholas, David. *The Growth of the Medieval City: From Late Antiquity to the Early Fourteenth Century*. London and New York: Longman, 1997.

Phillips, J. R. S. *The Medieval Expansion of Europe*. Oxford: Clarendon Press, 1998.

Pounds, N. J. G. *An Economic History of Medieval Europe*. New York: Longman, 1976.

Riché, Pierre. *The Carolingians: A Family Who Forged Europe*. Philadelphia: University of Pennsylvania Press, 1993.

Verhulst, Adriaan. *The Carolingian Economy*. Cambridge: Cambridge University Press, 2002.

Figure Credits

Map 14.1: Source: https://commons.wikimedia.org/wiki/File:Droysens-21a.jpg.

Map 14.2: Adapted from: https://commons.wikimedia.org/wiki/File:Princeton_Viking,_Magyar_and_Saracen_Invasions_in_9th_and_10th_Century_Europe.jpg.

CHAPTER 15

Trade and States in Sub-Saharan Africa, 8000 BCE–1500 CE

Geography, Ecology, and Human Settlement

By 400 CE, the shift from foraging to agriculture in Africa was largely complete, with only pockets of foragers still inhabiting areas in the center and south of the continent. Villages ruled by local chiefs became the norm, and in some places, cities appeared and chiefdoms gave way to larger kingdoms. Soil suitable for cultivation and a forbidding environment rife with infectious diseases in large parts of equatorial Africa directed the patterns of settlement. The densest village networks were initially in the **savannas** of the inland delta of the Niger and Middle Senegal Rivers, but as populations grew, Bantu speakers migrated eastward into the Great Lakes region and then southward. By 200 CE, they inhabited coastal cities on the Indian Ocean and by 400 had reached the southern tip of Africa.

Pastoralism and Agriculture

Africa is a vast continent. All of the continental United States and the continent of Australia would fit within it with room to spare. It has a half dozen distinct ecological zones. Along the northern shores is a strip of Mediterranean climate, which starkly gives way southward to the largest desert in the world, the Sahara. The **sahel**, or grassy **steppe**, borders the southern edge of the Sahara, and beyond it further to the south is a swath of savanna, marked by scrubland, scattered trees, and tall grasses, that stretches west to east nearly across the continent. South of the savanna are woodlands with a continuous tree canopy and then further south the dense jungles of the equatorial rainforest. The pattern is more or less repeated in the southern half of the continent.

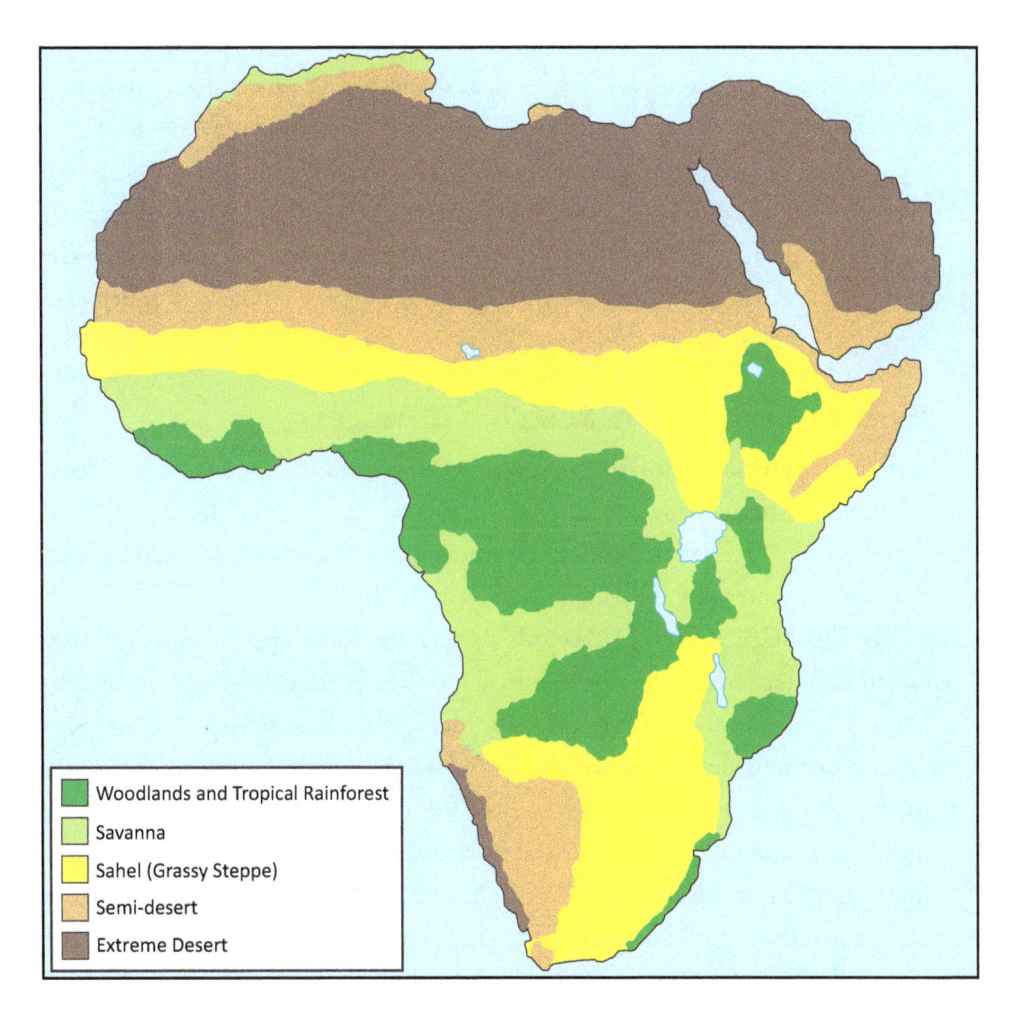

MAP 15.1 Ecological Zones of Contemporary Africa

Within this diverse ecology, much of Africa's soils are too poor for agriculture. In sub-Saharan Africa, disease also helped direct habitation patterns. The mosquito-borne diseases Malaria and Yellow Fever plagued humans in tropical and humid forested regions, and the tsetse fly carried Typanosomiasis, or sleeping sickness. This afflicted humans, while its close relative rinderpest was a killer of livestock. Thus, the areas where cultivation and herding could occur and diseases were kept at bay became relatively densely populated and, therefore, the sites of societal complexity and city and state formation.

As we read in Chapter 2, by 5000 BCE, **pastoralism** had spread into the central Sahara where during the next 1,000 years herding became the primary means of subsistence. Pastoralism had also expanded southward into the upper Nile valley by 4000 BCE. Climate change beginning around 3500 BCE gradually dried the Sahara and pushed some pastoralists southward along major rivers into the savanna in West Africa. They brought domesticated cattle, sheep, and goats into the grasslands above the bend of the Niger River and below the shores of Lake Chad. Crop domestication can be traced to the northern sahel and grassland savanna between 8000 and 7000 BCE, where cereals were grown, and to the woodland savanna by 5500 BCE, where yams and oil palms were harvested. The latter was the ancestral home of Bantu-speaking peoples, on the border between present-day Cameroon and Nigeria.

Expansion of Bantu-Speaker Culture

Agriculture provided the Bantu speakers with the means for gradual population growth, and they expanded eastward, seeking new farmlands. The agricultural crops and practices of the Bantu speakers, as well as their language, had reached the western shores of Lake Tanganyika by 1000 BCE.

By 500 BCE, Africans across this swath had developed iron metallurgy (whether independent of outside diffusion or as a product of it remains inconclusive). The natural-draft technique utilizing chimneys for heating furnaces (as opposed to bellows) was widely although not universally practiced. Copper smelting was also practiced at the time, but the hardness of iron made it preferable for weapons and for tools to clear and work fields, thus contributing to a further intensification of cultivation. As a result of the expansion of ironworking and cultivation, the population grew and many people migrated further to the east and south. This brought farming and iron to new areas. By 200 CE, Bantu-speaking migrants had settled on the east coast of Africa and by 400 had reached its southern tip. Iron ore is plentiful and widespread in the soil of Africa, so there were few geological impediments to the spread of this revolutionary technology.

It appears that with these developments, gender roles became clearly associated with particular tasks. Iron technology and land clearance became male activities, while women took up the tasks of farming and domestic cooking. Indeed, it appears that men jealously guarded their monopoly over iron production. They kept women from its secrets and invested the processes of smelting and ironworking with rituals that proscribed women from participation. The ability to produce iron was a powerful tool for these communities, and it was regarded as a male monopoly.

The spread of agriculture and ironworking coincided with an expansion of commercial relations both within and outside of Africa. An early trading emporium, Rhapta, appeared on the east African coast in present-day Tanzania early in the first millennium CE and thrived for several hundred years before disappearing with the temporary contraction in trade on the Indian Ocean in the fifth century CE. Here, African ivory, rhinoceros horn, and tortoiseshell were exported in exchange for south Arabian and Mediterranean products like glass beads and, most likely, fine textiles.

The Indonesian settling of Madagascar in the first century CE introduced East Asian crops to Africa, notably Asian yams, sugarcane, and, above all, new types of bananas. The Indonesians also brought pigs and chickens. Banana trees are highly adaptable to different soils, are 10 times more prolific in fruit per plant than the African yam, and the fruit is just as nutritious. These crops and animals spread widely inland and transformed village agriculture and diet.

The Nile Valley and the Ethiopian Highlands

For several thousand years BCE, state-building and trade were well-established across North Africa, as Egypt and Carthage attest. The Nile River was the lifeline

MAP 15.2 The States of Africa, First Century BCE–1500 CE

TRADE AND STATES IN SUB-SAHARAN AFRICA, 8000 BCE–1500 CE   303 of ancient Egypt, and it reached southward deep into Africa's interior all the way to its source in the Great Lakes region. It traversed Nubia to the south of Egypt, a region known by the Egyptian pharaohs as a source of gold. With the decline of Egyptian influence in the Nile valley, independent kingdoms and cities emerged first in Nubia and then in the Ethiopian Highlands.

The Kingdom of Kush

As discussed in Chapter 4, the state in tropical Africa emerged in Nubia after Egypt's New Kingdom fragmented in 1069 BCE and the Egyptians lost control of the middle Nile River valley. The Nubian state, commonly called the Kingdom of Kush, established its capital at Napata just downstream from the fourth cataract. The Nile has six **cataracts** (rocky, swift rapids that sharply impede, or even prevent, navigation across them and thereby provide a natural barrier against aggression). In 728 BCE, the Kushites invaded Egypt and ruled the country for about 50 years. But following the Assyrian conquest of Egypt, the Kushites moved further southward to the confluence of the Nile and Atbarah Rivers. On the east bank of the Nile, just downstream from the sixth cataract and between the White and Blue Niles, the Kushites established the city of Meroë. For nearly 800 years, from around 400 BCE until about 350 CE, the city of Meroë was the capital of an important kingdom that drew vast wealth from a rich agricultural hinterland, the extraction and manufacturing of iron, and trade.

Unlike the situation further to the north in Egypt where agriculture was dependent on the regular flooding of the Nile or the irrigation of fields close to the river, the area surrounding Meroë had a climate that produced enough rainfall to support the growth of cotton, sorghum, millet, and other cereals as well as an extensive grassland used for raising livestock. Cattle herding was enormously important, as men, even priests and kings, measured and displayed their wealth in the size of their cattle herds. This mixed-farming economy supported a large, diversified, and stratified urban population that, at its peak around 100 CE, numbered as many as 25,000 people. Within this population, most likely a gendered division of labor held sway. There were many ironworkers as well as other skilled craftsmen, most likely men specializing in a wide range of products, including finely wrought jewelry. Men also manufactured wheel-thrown pottery that was destined for the export market, while women molded pots from slabs of clay for household use.

The land around Meroë was rich in iron ore and timber (necessary for the voracious consumption of charcoal in iron smelting). The city emerged as one of

Africa's major centers of iron manufacture, here using bellows instead of draft through chimneys to heat the furnaces. Indeed, the Kushites may have chosen to establish their capital at Meroë precisely because of its ironmaking potential. The fact that iron was used in the city to manufacture many weapons as well as tools suggests that the Kushite kings were intent not only on protecting their territory from foreign invasion but also on hunting exotic animals that could be exported to distant markets for high prices.

The location of Meroë was not only favorable to farming and ironmaking but was also favorable to commerce. The city sat astride a major artery of trade linking Ptolemaic Egypt with inner Africa mainly through the Nile River connections. With the conquest of Egypt by the Romans in the first century BCE, Meroë entered the Roman economy via the Nile. Of course, waterborne traffic was the most efficient mode of transport, but goods also moved overland in caravans on the many roads that fanned out from Meroë.

Some of these roads were shortcuts bypassing several of the cataracts on the Nile, while others led southeast to ports on the Red Sea. Meroë, therefore, was also connected with trade routes into the Indian Ocean that channeled commodities to and from India. Meroë was, in short, an ideal transshipment center in the heart of a vast network of regional and long-distance trading links through which large quantities of gold, ivory, slaves, timber, food, and even elephants used for warfare and as beasts of burden were exported. Among the foreign imports to Meroë were luxury items from the Mediterranean, like fine glass and aromatics, and from India, such as fine cotton textiles.

The Kushite kings of Meroë initially patterned themselves after Egyptian pharaohs, appropriating the Egyptian god Amun as the divine source of royal authority. The Egyptian mother goddess Isis was also worshipped in Meroë, perhaps among ordinary women who called upon her as a healer. Gradually, the Kushites' own deities replaced the Egyptian ones, the most important being **Apedemek**, the lion-headed god. The rulers of Meroë kept a menagerie of live lions within their royal living area. Moreover, the royal compound was a large, stone-walled precinct in the heart of Meroë within which were built palaces, audience chambers, and quarters for palace officials. Throughout the city, the kings of Meroë also built lion temples with lion-figure reliefs to associate their sacral kingship with this god and to project themselves as divinely appointed.

Once the king was on the throne, his word may have been law, but he came to power only with the approval of military leaders, clan chiefs, high officials, and priests and most likely needed their favor to retain his supreme authority.

Indeed, Kushite kings were not as autocratic as Egyptian pharaohs and even on occasion were deposed by high priests. Queen mothers were significant political figures as well. They played an important part in the choice and coronation of the next ruler and sometimes may have wielded power in their own right. As we saw in Chapter 4, one such queen, Shanakdakhete, who lived in the middle of the second century BCE, may have been a builder of public monuments and temples and may have been buried under one of the stone pyramids for which Meroë is known. Nonetheless, the fact that the tombs of queens were smaller and less elaborately embellished that those of kings confirms that a gender hierarchy was in place that ranked men above women in the political and social structure.

Most of the subjects of the rulers were rural peasants and herders. They were left to the control of minor chiefs and heads of family clans so long as taxes were paid in the form of annual tribute to the king. The kings exerted more direct control over the city itself, however, for it was here that they commanded the chokepoint of trade, upon which they levied extensive import and export duties.

The collapse of Meroë came suddenly, in the early 300s CE. As occurred in so many other parts of the world, overexploitation of natural resources accelerated Meroë's decline. In this case, deforestation from the voracious demand for charcoal used in iron smelting and soil erosion caused by overgrazing and intensive farming contributed to Meroë's demise. The crowning blow was the decline of external trade. The Roman economy contracted during the crisis of the third century (see Chapter 7), and Meroë was cut off from the Indian Ocean economy by the rising kingdom of Aksum directly to the southeast. In fact, in 350 Meroë was conquered by the rulers of Aksum, and the city was abandoned.

The Kingdom of Aksum

The state of Aksum emerged during the first century CE in the Ethiopian Highlands, a mountainous region offering a range of relatively favorable environments for mixed farming. Varying in elevation from around 3,000 to over 12,000 feet above sea level, the highlands possess three different climatic zones: temperate, subtropical, and tropical. A combination of fertile soil and seasonal rainfall in many places allowed for the cultivation of a large number of different crops, such as wheat, barley, millet, chickpeas, lentils, and beans. By raising cattle, sheep, and goats in addition to growing a wide range of grains and vegetables, farmers in the highlands produced enough food to support the urban centers that arose in the Aksum kingdom.

Like Meroë in the Nile valley, the Kingdom of Aksum in the Ethiopian Highlands joined the long-distance commercial networks of the Roman provinces of the eastern Mediterranean, Egypt, South Arabia, India, and Sri Lanka. Although its political capital was inland, the key to the kingdom's rise and importance until the seventh century was its port city of Adulis and the trade that flowed in and out of it from the Red Sea. Foreign merchants docked at Adulis to acquire the prized commodities of ivory, slaves, frankincense, myrrh, emeralds, brass, copper, and exotic animal skins and, as at Rhapta and Meroë, brought with them an array of goods from distant shores—notably ceramics, glass, fabrics, clothing, oil, and wine. In the sixth century, the Aksum kings gained access to gold in the interior, which became another key export.

The Aksumite kings confined all trade to the port of Adulis. The duties on commerce that they efficiently levied through their retinue of royal officials supported military campaigns and the consolidation of kingly power. These kings, beginning with King Ezana (320s–ca. 360 CE), embraced Christianity in the fourth century, devoted considerable resources to church buildings, and appropriated the religion for ideological legitimation of their position. Vassal states paid regular tribute to the kings, further swelling the royal coffers.

Like that of Meroë, Aksum's society was stratified, with peasants and slaves providing food and material sustenance to urban centers whose functionally specialized populations included officials, temple priests, merchants, and skilled craftsmen. Archeological evidence suggests that Aksum society was highly stratified. Absolute monarchs, frequently depicted on Aksum coins wearing a crown, stood at the top of the social pyramid. A small number of elite individuals who lived in palaces and possessed luxury goods occupied a position in the social structure just below the king and his immediate family. Further down the social ladder was a group of skilled artisans who produced a variety of high quality goods made from iron, bronze, and ivory. Although nothing is known of the women in this society, a large number of peasants and slaves occupied the bottom position in this sharply hierarchical social order.

In its heyday, the thriving state of Aksum boasted impressive stone residences, palaces, and monuments; its own form of writing; and gold, silver, and bronze coinage. Indeed, it was the first state in sub-Saharan Africa to mint currency.

King Ezana is the best known ruler of Aksum, largely because of the artifacts that were created during his reign that proclaimed his power and accomplishments. A large stone tablet called the Ezana Stone bears inscriptions about a series of the king's military triumphs. The fifth and last known inscription praises the

Christian God for the first time before describing Ezana's conquest of the Kushite city of Meroë in 350 CE. The inscriptions are written in three different languages, Ge'ez (an Ethiopian language), Sabaean (a South Arabian language), and Greek, probably with the intent to communicate his religion and his power, which he took to be linked, as widely as possible. King Ezana declared Christianity the state religion and associated it with his authority and success as a ruler. After his death, the king was embraced as a saint by the Ethiopian Orthodox Church.

Aksum prospered as long as trade flowed on the Red Sea, one of the major sea routes of antiquity. With the spread of Islam in the seventh century and the relocation of the Umayyad caliphate to Damascus, however, trade was diverted to the Persian Gulf, and as trade on the Red Sea dried up, so declined the fortunes of the kingdom of Aksum.

Nubia

Around 350 CE, after the fall of Meroë, small Nubian states dotted the middle Nile valley. The introduction of the camel to trans-Saharan trade in the third century CE revolutionized transport and opened up new routes for commerce with sub-Saharan peoples. Among the beneficiaries of this new trade was a Nubian ruling class that, by the 400s, dominated three small kingdoms.

In the mid-500s, missionaries from Alexandria converted the Nubian kings and ruling class to Greek Orthodox Christianity. Under the sponsorship of these converts, pagan temples became churches and monasteries were built. Nubian kings wore Byzantine-styled crowns, cloaked themselves in Byzantine-styled robes, and, likely as part of the incentive to convert, appropriated the eastern Roman notion that kings had a divine sanction for their rule that came from the Christian God. Early in the 700s, a king united the smaller kingdoms, although the new rulers presided over a decentralized system where the kings retained the loyalty of their vassals, including churchmen, by granting them land.

The Nubian kings apparently did not tax their vassals or peasants, the primary source of royal income coming from taxes on merchant caravans engaged in long-distance trade. A treaty with Muslim Arabs in 652 is an indicator of the nature of this commerce, as it stipulated that Egyptian cloth, pottery, iron utensils, leather goods, and wine from the Arabs would be traded for ivory and slaves from the Nubians.

West Africa

The ecological conditions of West Africa were highly conducive to regional and, after camel transport opened the Sahara, long-distance trade with North Africa and the Mediterranean basin. Cities like Jenné-Jenno emerged as key transshipment centers, and great kingdoms like Ancient Ghana and Mali followed, their wealth based on access to raw materials, especially gold, and trade.

Trans-Saharan Trade

The Atlantic seacoast of West Africa has few natural harbors and no coral reefs, thus offering no protection to ships and sailors. Moreover, prevailing winds always blow from the north, so before the technological sailing innovations of the lateen sail and sternpost rudder that are necessary for tacking into the wind, sailing along the coast could only go in one direction with no chance of return, which is hardly suitable to trading. The Atlantic Ocean thus was a barrier, not a highway, and consequently, there was no oceanic trade to speak of before the arrival of the Europeans in the 15th century CE. From the perspective of a West African, the Atlantic Ocean was vast and empty, a kind of watery desert.

Within West Africa, however, the conditions for trade were very favorable. The close proximity of desert, sahel, grassland, and woodland savanna ecozones, each zone possessing resources that the others lacked, presented both the necessity and opportunity for their inhabitants to exchange raw materials and products across environmental borders. West Africa, that is, provided conditions conducive to the development of complex networks of regional trade, and we find evidence of it by 1000 BCE. Goods travelled along the Senegal and Niger Rivers but also were hauled overland on the backs of donkeys or the heads of humans.

To the north of the West African sahel and savanna is another sea, a sea of sand, the Sahara Desert. Like the Atlantic Ocean, it stood as a barrier as well, but not an impermeable one. Oases punctuated the desert, and desert dwellers inhabited them and used them as waystations, thus enabling some trade across the desert. Until about 300 CE, most trade involving the Sahara was a regional affair where rock salt moved south from the desert in exchange for varieties of food from the savanna. Middlemen in the sahel facilitated the trade. The Romans, inhabiting the Mediterranean shore of Africa, were aware of products from south of the Sahara. They were primarily interested in gold dust and red precious stones. Regular or direct trade across the desert, however, was a mere trickle, a highly risky venture that passed through the hands of several groups of desert dwellers before reaching its final destination.

By 300 CE, trade routes had been carved across the Sahara, but the volume of traffic would only increase significantly with the widespread use of the camel. Introduced by **Berber nomads** of the northern Sahara, camels revolutionized the scope and scale of trans-Saharan trade. The camel's ability to go days without water combined with its splayed, padded hooves made travel across long stretches of arid sand feasible.

Urban centers like Jenné-Jenno in the Niger River valley (in present-day Mali) thrived as a result of this trade. It became a major urban center around 300 CE and lasted until 900 (the current city was relocated). With a population of anywhere from 5,000–13,000 people, including nonagricultural craftsmen, it was a bustling hub of regional and long-distance trade in raw materials and luxury goods.

The spread of Islam in the seventh and eighth centuries was a further boon to this trans-Saharan trade, as Muslim merchants furthered the link of West Africa to the burgeoning markets of the Mediterranean (see Chapter 12). More and more caravans hauled increasingly large cargoes of **kola nuts**, ivory (from Hippopotamus tusks), ostrich feathers, slaves, and gold north across the desert, while textiles, sugar, tea, glass beads, and other manufactured goods moved south. The gold trade in particular expanded in the eighth and ninth centuries, as consolidated Islamic states to the north had a growing need for large quantities of gold to mint coins for their increasingly monetized economies (see Chapter 12). Further testimony to the demand for currency, caches of **cowrie shells** from this time have been discovered by archeologists along these trade routes. Cowries were a currency originating in the Maldive Islands southwest of India over a thousand miles away; their presence in the Sahara is vivid testimony to the extent of the commercial economy into which sub-Saharan West Africa was now increasingly integrated.

The Kingdom of Ancient Ghana

For the first time in the history of sub-Saharan Africa, in the 700s CE, a powerful consolidated state with a stratified and functionally specialized population in urban centers emerged in West Africa: the Kingdom of Ancient Ghana. As with the city Jenné-Jenno, this state emerged due to the increasing commercialization of the region, for its rulers were successful in controlling the transshipment points of the regional and, crucially, the trans-Saharan trade with the North African Islamic states on the Mediterranean coastline.

The origins of this state most likely lay in kin-based communal groups that collectively maintained control over land, as there was no sense of landed private property in most of sub-Saharan Africa. Most agricultural work in sub-Saharan Africa at this time was performed by women, although men controlled the land through marriages that granted men access to women's labor and reproductive capacities, and men typically had multiple wives. Moreover, men everywhere in Africa seem to have been the exclusive owners of cattle, a key source and indicator of wealth and power that was decidedly rooted in a gendered hierarchy.

Gradually, clans of the Soninke ethnic group in West Africa (in contemporary Senegal) banded together to form larger chiefdoms, which in turn joined together in a loose confederation sometime in the first century CE. If the Soninke were like most sub-Saharan ethnic groups, their society and political system were probably male dominated, although some women may have exercised power as queen mothers, royal wives, priestesses, and healers.

The impetus for this consolidation was likely that the Soninke, armed with iron weapons and cavalry, saw such cooperation as the best means to seize as much remaining arable land in West Africa (which was steadily desiccating with the spread of the Sahara) as they could; it also probably came at least partially in defensive response to increased raids by Berber nomads to the north during periods of drought.

The most important factor in Ghana's rise to power, however, was the advantageous geographical position of the Soninke, which positioned them to profit from the trans-Saharan trade. Their region was ideally located as a middle ground for exchanges of desert salt from the north and gold mined in the lands to the south. The volume of trade and accompanying prosperity for these middlemen surged in the fifth century, facilitated by the use of camels in trans-Saharan trade.

Ghana gradually became a consolidated state under a king who directly commanded a central region and indirectly commanded a periphery of tribute-paying vassal chiefdoms. At the apogee of their power between the ninth and 11th centuries, the kings of Ghana dominated the whole western sahel zone from the lower Senegal River in the West to the bend of the Niger River in the East. They therefore commanded the Middle Senegal Valley and the Inland Niger Delta. These were agricultural zones rich in foodstuffs to produce the necessary surplus for a ruling elite and several urban centers whose specialized craftsmen produced manufactured items of copper, iron, and gold.

Even more important to the growing power of the kings of Ghana, however, was their control of trading networks. Cotton cloth, dyes, iron goods, kola nuts, and wide varieties of foodstuffs flowed along the many regional trade routes between the sahel and the rainforests. The kings extracted levies and duties that made them rich and powerful. By the 11th century, an Arab observer reported that the Ghanaian king commanded an army of 200,000 soldiers.

But the influence of the kings of Ghana went well beyond regional commerce. They also controlled the supply for the trans-Saharan trade of two commodities—gold and slaves—in sharp demand across the Islamic world as Islamic states became more and more commercialized and monetized. Berber caravans from the north, financed by Arab merchants, brought vast quantities of rock salt, a necessary commodity lacking in West Africa, across the desert to trade in exchange for West African gold and slaves.

The kings of Ghana monopolized access to the West African goldfields of Bambuk of the upper Senegal River. As the gold passed through their kingdom, the kings shaved off a portion for their own coffers. Moreover, as we have seen in Chapter 12, the rise of the newly rich ruling classes of Islam in the eighth century brought a surging demand for slaves. Ghana's kings fed the demand with captives seized in raids on less powerful peoples to the south. Like the Venetians far to the north and at roughly the same time, the kings of Ghana made fortunes from commerce in human beings.

Just as the kings of Ghana rode control of trade networks to power, so their loss of that control spelled their demise. In the 11th century, the Almoravids, a group of North African Muslims dedicated to the strict adherence of Islamic law and jihad, or holy struggle against the infidel (Ghana's kings only later would convert to Islam), set their sights on the northern reaches of the kingdom of Ghana. Fired by religious zeal and the promise of plunder, in 1055, the Almoravids followed their conquest of the northern Saharan city of Sijilmasa (in present day Morocco) with the seizure of the Ghanaian city of Aoudaghost on the desert's southern edge. This gave the Almoravids control of the two termini of an important route of the trans-Saharan gold trade.

At the same time, slave-mined goldfields in Bure (southwest of the Bambuk fields, spanning the Niger River but beyond the borders of the Ghana Empire) opened up, the gold being traded along new trans-Saharan routes to the east beyond the control of Ghana. The Ghanaian rulers had no access to the wealth of this trade and suffered from its competition for their own gold fields at Bambuk. Compounding their dire situation, the agricultural and grazing lands of the kingdom became increasingly exhausted and could no longer support a dense population or a state that depended on it. By the early 13th century, the vassal chiefs were in rebellion, and one of these, Sundiata, would found another West African empire, the Kingdom of Mali.

The Kingdom of Mali

The new kings of Mali had resources similar to the Ghanaian kings and likewise built an empire from them. At the peak of their power, the kings commanded a large and economically diverse population from the Atlantic Ocean in the West to Timbuktu, Tadmeka, and Gao in the East, and from the dry steppe of the Sahara fringe in the North to the edge of the rainforest in the South. Beyond amply providing manpower for the king's armies, the people of these diverse ecozones also created a richly diversified economy. The Niger flood plain produced cereal crops, pastoralists provided animal and forest products, and people along the Atlantic coast and river banks netted vast quantities of fish. All contributed to an expanding commercial economy.

The kingdom sat astride bustling trade routes, and as the kings taxed the flow of goods coming and going, their state became one of the wealthiest in the world by the 14th century. The Mali kings recognized that it was in the royal interest to maintain security for merchants, an increasingly professional class of traders who were mostly Muslims, to travel freely across their dominions. They thus deployed some of their soldiers to patrol the trade routes.

Of utmost importance to these kings was the importance of gold and the gold trade. The Mali controlled the sources of gold at Bure in the savanna of the upper Niger River and later at Akan further to the east. Indeed, for a time they controlled all of the gold fields of West Africa and the trans-Saharan gold trade. Tellingly, the Mali kings built their capital at Niani near the Bure goldfields. The Akan goldfields further east especially benefited Timbuktu, which became an increasingly important exchange port linked to trans-Saharan trade routes. Through here, as with other ports on the sea of sand, caravans hauling sub-Saharan products (e.g., gold, ivory, kola nuts, and slaves) headed north, passing southbound camel trains carrying Mediterranean products and, importantly, salt.

Like their Ghanaian predecessors, the Mali kings ruled through vassal chiefs who paid tribute. The king's army also was deployed to secure this important flow of resources. These chiefs collected a portion of the surplus produced by an independent peasantry. They kept part of it for themselves and shipped the rest to the royal treasury. The Mali kings themselves owned vast state farms where slaves produced food for the army and the court.

The Mali kings embraced Islam; in fact, they claimed to be the descendants of an African from Ethiopia named Bilali Bunama, an early convert to Islam and a close companion of the prophet Muhammad. By claiming such descent, the kings linked themselves to early Islam and used it to legitimize their rule.

The most famous of the Mali kings is Mansa Musa (r. 1312–1337), known largely for his extravagant commitment to Islam. He endowed Timbuktu with three mosques, and in one of them, the Sankoré mosque, he founded a madrasa (a school) endowed with an extensive and important library. Timbuktu soon became a renowned center of Islamic learning.

Mansa Musa is also known to history because of the well-documented pilgrimage he made to Mecca in 1324. His journey was recorded by many contemporaries who were staggered by the gold he brought with him, a testimony to how much of the precious metal the Malian kings commanded. It was reported in contemporary sources that among the 60,000 men in his entourage were 12,000 slaves, each of whom carried a four-pound gold bar! Eyewitnesses reported that 80 camels each carried another 50–300 pounds of gold dust. To demonstrate his piety, he showered the poor with so much gold along the way that as it entered the monetary system it devalued the metal and inflated the prices of goods.

As so often is the case in these kinds of polities, the strength of the empire depended upon the strength of the ruler at the center, and every king was not like Mansa Musa. In the late 14th century, a series of weak kings with brief reigns invited dynastic succession struggles. Vassal chiefs in the outer provinces broke away and launched pillaging raids into the crumbling empire. In 1433, Timbuktu fell to Tuareg nomads, and so the Malian kings lost an important source of wealth. By 1500, the once-great Mali Empire had largely been supplanted by another, the Songhai, and although the Mali kingdom survived, it had contracted to a powerless and unimportant state.

FIGURE 15.1 Mansa Musa. This detail from the Catalan Atlas of 1375 depicts Mansa Musa, king of Mali, holding a scepter and a large piece of gold.

East Africa

Bantu speakers had reached and begun settling the East African coast early in the first millennium CE. Some of them recognized the advantages of trade within the Indian Ocean commercial network and established port cities there. Unlike the west coast of Africa, the east coast has an abundance of coral reefs, inlets, harbors, coves, and bays, all conducive to coastal trading. Gradually, the coast became dotted with cities stretching from Mogadishu in the North to Sofala in the South. These cities linked trade with the interior of Africa with the well-established Indian Ocean commercial network. From this trade, especially in gold, the inland kingdoms of Mapungubwe and Great Zimbabwe thrived.

Coastal Port Cities and Indian Ocean Trade

The coastal region of East Africa was called Azania by the author of the *Periplus of the Erythranean Sea* (that invaluable guidebook for Greek traders written around 50 CE). The city of Rhapta, which rose to trading prominence in the first century CE, was for a time the southernmost and apparently the most important of these coastal cities. It has since disappeared, so its exact location remains unknown (it seems likely that it sat at the mouth of the Ruffiji River), but as a trading city linked to Indian Ocean commerce, it was a harbinger of similar cities to come.

The arrival and spread of Islam during the eighth and ninth centuries revitalized Indian Ocean commerce. The coastal cities of the former Azania once again began to merge their regional economies into a transoceanic one. Arab, Persian, Indian, and Indonesian traders, all Muslims, arrived with the monsoon winds blowing towards East Africa between November and March. At the port cities, they traded with the resident Africans for African products drawn from the interior and caught the monsoon winds blowing out toward India from April to October. To facilitate their entry into this economy, many Muslim merchants settled in these port cities and married daughters from local aristocratic clans who were familiar with the trading networks of the region. By the ninth century, this ruling class had embraced Islam, although conversion of the lower classes in the cities and those who lived in the interior from the coast who practiced indigenous religions was only slowly accomplished. Not only did these independent port cities thrive from this renewed trade but also the interior Great Lakes and Eastern Rift regions were increasingly linked to the sea.

The Great Lakes and Eastern Rift regions (present-day Uganda, Kenya, and Tanzania and known to Arab traders as the Land of Zanj) spanned different ecological zones and thus rendered different products in adjacent lands. As in West Africa, this diversity encouraged trade. Market centers cropped up in environmental transition zones, notably along the southern slopes of Mount Kenya and Mount Kilimanjaro. Ironworking was well-established there by 700 CE, as was banana cultivation and cattle raising. Thus, by 1000, inland East Africa was experiencing population growth and an intensification of regional commerce through regular markets.

By the ninth century, there were a number of well-established market towns along the Swahili seacoast, as it was called because of the Bantu language that was spoken there, from Mogadishu in the North southward to Mombasa, the Lamu Islands, Zanzibar, Kilwa, and, at the southern end, Sofala. The merchants generally exported raw materials drawn from deep in the African interior, even as far as the Congo Basin. In exchange, they traded cloth manufactured in the coastal cities and salt in plentiful supply along the coast but lacking in the interior.

The most prized commodities from the interior were ivory, in high demand in China, and slaves. Slaves were tellingly referred to as Zanj by the Arabs, and they were destined for the insatiable Islamic markets of the Middle East. Many male slaves worked the large farms in Iraq or were incorporated into the caliphs' armies while many females became domestics and harem girls. Timber, plentiful in Africa but rare in Southwest Asia, also was exported in great quantities from these city-states.

After 1000, another commodity was added to the export list—gold. Goldfields in southcentral Africa were opened. Merchants of some of the coastal cities of East Africa, notably Kilwa, controlled the flow of the precious metal down the Zambesi and Limpopo Rivers to the coasts where it was traded to foreign merchants. These valuable exports made possible the importing of manufactured goods and luxuries, such as Chinese porcelain and silk clothes, Mediterranean glassware, and Indian fine cottons.

By 1000, these coastal city-states were well established (there were about 40 of them between Mogadishu and Sofala). They were ruled sometimes by Muslim sultans and sometimes by oligarchies. Like their merchant subjects, these rulers grew wealthy from oceanic trade, charging import and export duties of up to 50 percent.

The social structure of these cities was clan-based and stratified, with Muslim merchant patricians and rulers at the apex, far above the lower classes who for a long time did not convert to Islam and retained their indigenous practices and beliefs. The elites commanded the lion's share of the wealth generated by trade.

They wore fine robes of silk and cotton and bedecked themselves with gold and silver jewelry. They ate off exquisite Chinese porcelain. They lived in cities with palaces, public buildings, lavish private residences, and mosques built of cut coral and stone. All of this reflects not only a concentration of wealth in the hands of the ruling classes but also considerable craftsmanship and functional specialization in the urban population as a whole.

One of these city-states, Kilwa, has left an impressive archeological record that testifies to a prosperity that reached its high point between 1200 and 1500. Indeed, by then it was the wealthiest of all the Swahili city-states. At the most southerly point to which overseas merchants could sail in one season, Kilwa was ideally located to control the southern trade, above all in gold. Ibn Battuta, an intrepid Muslim traveler, marveled in 1331 that Kilwa "is one of the most beautiful and well-constructed towns in the world."[1] When the Portuguese arrived on the eastern coast of Africa in the late 15th century, they, too, were impressed by the city's splendor. One wrote that the city of 12,000 inhabitants was surrounded by "trees and gardens of all sorts of vegetables, citron, lemons, and the best sweet oranges that were ever seen ... and a great abundance of flocks, especially sheep." He also noted that "in the port there were many ships."[2] The Portuguese were also impressed with the intensity of the gold trade, and in the early 16th century, they seized control of Kilwa and Sofala and appointed a puppet sultan to rule on their behalf.

The Mapungubwe Kingdom and Great Zimbabwe

Between the 11th and 15th centuries, the southern Swahili cities of Sofala and especially Kilwa were trading with the interior of Africa and drawing ivory, slaves, and especially gold to the coast and into the commercial networks of the Indian Ocean. Inland on the Limpopo River, the Mapungubwe kingdom emerged around 1070, its lifeblood trade with the coastal Swahili cities. Already, in the early 900s, villagers in the area began to mine gold, and it remained a major export from the region for centuries. The Mapungubwe kingdom's capital city of the same name counted 5,000 inhabitants, among them skilled craftsmen turning out sophisticated ivory and gold figurines. Little is known of the ruling class or of the power structure other than Mapungubwe was ruled by kings who claimed spiritual

---

1   Erik Gilbert and Johnathan Reynolds, *Africa in World History*, 2nd ed. (Upper Saddle River, NJ: Pearson Education, 2008), 132.

2   Gilbert and Reynolds, *Africa in World History*, 132.

authority derived from local gods and oversaw a chief priest who performed rain-making ceremonies. The kingdom only lasted a little more than a century, most likely absorbed by the emerging powerful state to its north, Great Zimbabwe.

West Africa was not the only important source of gold flowing from Africa to the larger world. Gold deposits in the Zimbabwe Plateau facilitated the emergence of a powerful, formally organized state, Great Zimbabwe, which rose to prominence in the 13th century and reached its apogee a century later. Impressive stone ruins give silent witness to a once thriving capital city (with perhaps 18,000 inhabitants). Within the city, a precinct reserved for wealthy elites and rulers was surrounded by walls nine meters high, crowned by impressive turrets, suggesting the need for defense not just from outsiders but also perhaps from an underclass restive from such an unequal distribution of wealth. Elsewhere in what must have been a substantial city are ruins of a wall stretching 244 meters and reaching 10 meters in height and 5 meters in thickness. The powerful Zimbabwean elite and ruler commanded not only the city itself but also surrounding regional centers and smaller towns, each with their own elite group subservient to the rulers in the capital city.

The Zimbabwe Plateau was ideally suited for trade and habitation. It is bordered by the Zambezi River valley to the north and the valley of the Limpopo River to the south, giving it easy water access to the east coast as well as to areas in the interior of Africa. At 1,000 meters in elevation, it escapes the harmful insects, like the tsetse fly, that carried disease. The fertility of the plateau proved conducive, for a time, to mixed farming of agriculture (sorghum and millet) and animal husbandry (mostly cattle raising—cattle, as in most societies in Africa, being a means to amass wealth in a negotiable form).

The working people of Great Zimbabwe spun and wove cotton textiles, and slaves likely mined the region for iron ore, copper, tin, and gold. Iron metallurgy produced utilitarian tools like hoes, axes, and spear- and arrowheads, while gold, tin, and copper were worked into decorative objects displaying wealth, prestige, and status, much of it (as archaeological evidence from graves has shown) adorning the bodies of elite women. A range of specialized and sophisticated craftsmen must have inhabited the city to produce such varied-quality wares and to build such impressive stonework.

Evidence for trade with the coastal cities of East Africa is substantial. Archaeological evidence reveals that wealthy Zimbabweans imported an extraordinary assortment of exotic objects, among which were Persian glazed ceramics, Chinese celadon porcelain, and Mediterranean glass beads. Cowrie shells, a widespread currency in international trade at the time, also have been found in abundance in the ruins of Great Zimbabwe.

Above all, however, the prosperity and power of this state rested upon the gold trade, its crucial export. Gold was in sharp demand in the Indian Ocean commercial network until the mid-14th century, and Great Zimbabwe was poised to prosper as long as the supply and the demand continued. With the sag in demand for gold in the wake of the pandemic of bubonic plague, the **Black Death**, that dramatically contracted the population in the Mediterranean basin in the mid-14th century, however, Great Zimbabwe suffered. As its population grew to such a point that it depleted the soil necessary to sustain it, the kingdom fell into decline, and its capital city was eventually abandoned altogether.

Slavery in Africa Before 1500

Multiple forms of slavery and servitude have existed around the world throughout history. Africa is no exception. In some places in the world and in Africa, chattel slavery was the norm, where slaves were simply a thing to be owned by another human. Elsewhere and at different times, slavery may be a temporary status, and still at other times and places, slaves were recognized as human and with certain protections from their masters defined by law. Whatever their status, slavery and the slave trade were central to the history of the world and of Africa before 1500.

Slavery, the Slave Trade, and Islam

Slavery was an integral part of the economic and social structure of African societies, although it seems that after around 1000 the number of slaves increased there, perhaps driven by the expansion of the trade in slaves to destinations beyond Africa. West Africa had known slavery on a small scale before the coming of Islam in the eighth century, but Islamic monarchs, like the Mali kings, greatly increased slave owning and trading. These kings were powerful men with large armies, and waging war for captives to enslave was endemic during their rule. A Venetian traveler commented that the Mali had numerous slaves obtained by pillage, many who were put to work cultivating fields. Slaves were also put to work mining the goldfields and, of course, continued to be traded across the Sahara, destined for the Mediterranean market, or from ports of East Africa to the Middle East, India, and beyond.

The numbers of slaves exported from Africa before 1500 is difficult to estimate. We know from Roman sources that most African slaves of the ancient Roman

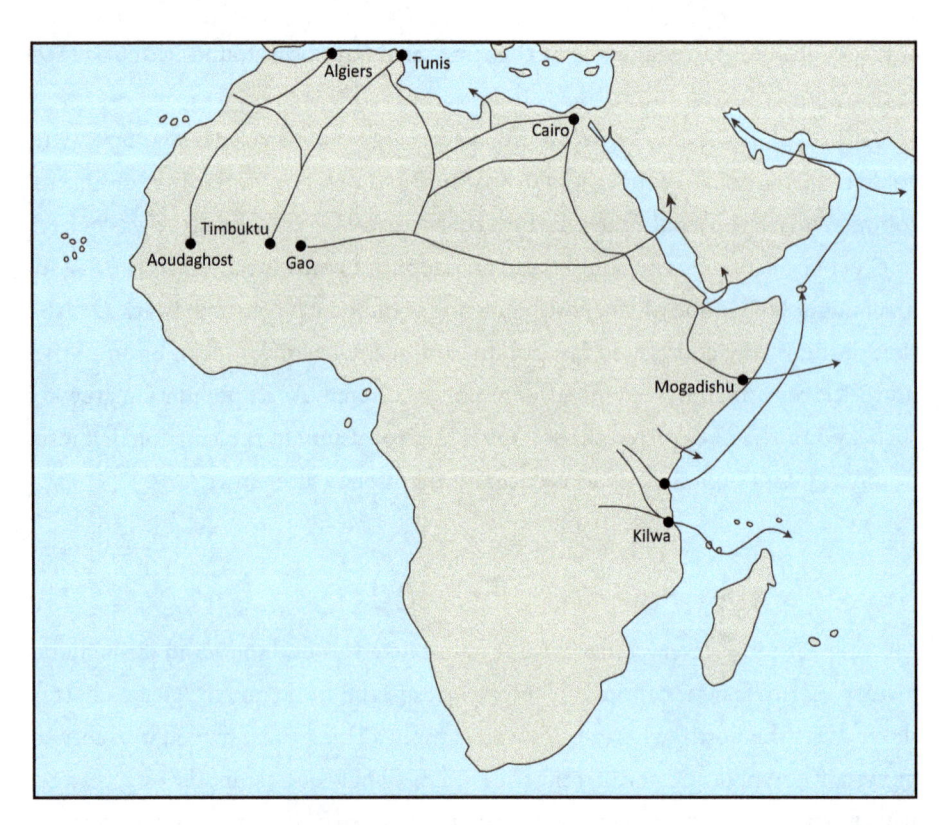

MAP 15.3   The Main Slave Trading Routes in Africa Before 1500

world came from Ethiopia through Egypt, but some came into the empire by way of a caravan route that was opened in the second century from Leptis Magna in Libya (present-day Tripoli) to sub-Saharan West Africa. Documentary evidence from the Nile valley records that slave trading was regulated there by treaty, even after the eclipse of the Roman Empire. For example, a treaty in 652 obliged the Nubians to deliver 360 slaves a year to Egypt.

Already, around 50 CE, we read in the *Periplus of the Erythranean Sea* of a maritime slave trade from the East African coast to Egypt. This seaborne trade continued and expanded throughout the first millennium, with slaves (reportedly including women and children) along with gold and ivory embarking from East African ports en route to Persia, India, Indonesia, and even China. From the eighth century, this Indian Ocean slave trade was controlled by Muslim merchants. It has been estimated that during the ninth and tenth centuries a few thousand enslaved people were taken each year from the East African coast, as slavers captured peoples from the interior and brought them to the littoral. This trade accelerated after 1000, as superior ships with greater cargo capacity led to more trade and increasingly helped to meet the demand for labor on plantations in the Abbasid caliphate.

The religion of Islam was introduced into sub-Saharan Africa in the ninth century, not by conquest as was typical elsewhere, but by Muslim merchants and missionaries who converted African elites with whom they traded. We know little about the conversion process of these elites and nothing about it among ordinary people. The process for the latter no doubt was slow, for we have evidence that Islamic rulers in East African port cities controlled populations who retained their indigenous religions.

In any case, Islamic law, the Shari'a, allowed slavery but prohibited the enslavement of Muslims. Thus, the main target of slave raids and even war were pagan people who lived in the frontier areas of Islamic states in Africa. Islam accepted slavery as an unquestionable part of human organization, though the law of Islam, unlike those of Rome, denied masters the power of life and death over the slave. Nonetheless, slaves were eagerly sought in the Islamic world. Ibn Battuta, who visited the ancient kingdom of Mali in the mid-14th century, recounts that the local inhabitants vied with each other in the number of slaves they had and was himself given a slave boy as a hospitality gift.

The Status of Slaves

It is impossible to generalize about the fate or status of the unfortunate people who were enslaved, although nowhere before the Atlantic slave trade of the 17th and 18th centuries (see Chapter 21) was the status of slaves associated with race. Many communities had hierarchies between different types of slaves, for example, differentiating between those who had been born into slavery and those who had been captured through war. Within certain societies, like the Soninke of the Ghana Empire, slaves were hierarchically arranged into three strata, with village slaves the most privileged. They lived in their own part of the village and took orders directly from the village chief. Domestic slaves, another category, lived with families and performed household tasks and could not be sold. The lowest level among slaves were those who were used in the slave trade and therefore could be bought and sold.

Some worked hard labor in the agricultural fields of the Middle East, conditions so miserable that they spawned an enormous slave uprising in Mesopotamia in the ninth century, The Great Zanj Rebellion (see Chapter 12). Others toiled in goldfields in West Africa or in salt mines in the Sahara Desert. The princes of Bahrain in the Persian Gulf in the 11th century were reported to own 30,000 Black slaves, mostly employed in gardening and agriculture. Throughout the region, girls and young men were especially sought as servants, concubines, and warriors. Slave girls of Aoudaghost, on the upper Niger, were prized as cooks, particularly skilled, writes an Arab traveler, at making pastries out of nuts and honey. The late-10th-century Umayyad caliph of Cordoba in al-Andalus, al-Hakam II, reportedly had a Black slave bodyguard. Indeed, some slaves joined the courts of Muslim rulers and held important administrative positions, some no doubt the children of caliphs and their slave concubines.

Review Questions

1. What were the consequences of the development of agriculture and iron-making in Africa?
2. Why did the states of Kush and Aksum thrive for a time, and why did they decline?
3. Why was trans-Saharan trade important for the cities and states of West Africa?
4. How did trade patterns affect the Swahili city-states and the kingdoms of Mapungubwe and Great Zimbabwe?

Further Reading

Chittick, Neville. *Kilwa: An Islamic Trading City on the East African Coast.* Nairobi, Kenya: British Institute in East Africa, 1974.

Connah, Graham. *African Civilizations: An Archeological Perspective.* 2nd ed. Cambridge: Cambridge University Press, 2001.

Curtin, Philip, Steven Feierman, Leonard Thompson, and Jan Vansina. *African History: From The Earliest Times To Independence.* 2nd ed. Upper Saddle River, NJ: Pearson, 1995.

Ehret, Christopher. *The Civilizations of Africa: A History to 1800.* Charlottesville: University of Virginia Press, 2002.

Falola, Toyin, ed. *Africa. Vol 1: African History Before 1885.* Durham, NC: Carolina Academic Press, 2000.

Gilbert, Erik, and Jonathan T. Reynolds. *Africa in World History: From Prehistory to the Present.* 2nd ed. Upper Saddle River, NJ: Pearson-Prentice Hall, 2008.

Kent, Susan, ed. *Gender in African Prehistory.* Walnut Creek, CA: Altamira Press, 2000.

Levitzion, Nehemia. *Ancient Ghana and Mali.* Teaneck, NJ: Holmes and Meier, 1980.

Maat-Ka Re Monges, Miriam. *Kush, The Jewel of Nubia*. Trenton, NJ: Africa World Press, 1997.

Munro-Hay, Stuart. *Aksum: An African Civilization of Late Antiquity*. Edinburgh: Edinburgh University Press, 1992.

Shaw, Thurstan, Paul Sinclair, Bassey Andah, and Alex Okpoko. *The Archaeology of Africa: Foods, Metals and Towns*. London: Routledge, 1993.

Shillington, Kevin. *History of Africa*. Oxford: Palgrave, 2005.

Timingham, J. Spencer. *The Influence of Islam upon Africa*. 2nd ed. London and New York: Longman, 1980.

Vansina, Jan. *Paths in the Rainforest: Toward a History of Political Tradition in Equatorial Africa*. Madison: University of Wisconsin Press, 1990.

Figure Credits

Map 15.1: Source: https://commons.wikimedia.org/wiki/File:Africa_Climate_Today.png.

Map 15.2: Source: https://commons.wikimedia.org/wiki/File:Africa_%28satellite_image%29.jpg.

Fig. 15.1: Source: https://commons.wikimedia.org/wiki/File:Catalan_Atlas_BNF_Sheet_6_Mansa_Musa.jpg.

Map 15.3: Copyright © by Runehelmet (CC BY-SA 3.0) at https://commons.wikimedia.org/wiki/File:African_slave_trade.png.

CHAPTER 16

Fragmented States and Commerce in the Islamic World, ca. 900–1500

MAP 16.1   Political Fragmentation in the Islamic World, 900–1500

The world of Islam covered vast stretches of territory, and as we have seen in an earlier chapter, the forces of political fragmentation set in almost as quickly as the territorial spread of Arab conquests. Such centrifugal forces continue to fragment the political world of Islam from 900 to 1500. Still, despite this political diversity, the Islamic world continued over these years to exhibit a notable commercial cohesion.

The Muslim Regimes in North Africa

Although the Abbasid caliphate lasted until 1258, already in the 10th century rival caliphates arose that sheared off large chunks of territory from it. The Fatimids from North Africa were the first to do so. The Fatimids were Shi'ite Muslims who rejected the legitimacy of the Abbasids and endowed their caliphs with a divine aura. Then, from Morocco came the Almoravids and later the Almohads, Berber tribes driven by a rigorous and uncompromising understanding of the Quran that justified conquests, which, for a time, brought the trans-Saharan trade routes, as well as much of North Africa and southern Spain, into their caliphates. The Fatimid caliphate ultimately met its demise when the Kurdish Ayyubids defeated them in Egypt in 1171 and established a new dynasty. Like so many Islamic regimes, however, the Ayyubid state was decentralized, and the lack of unity made conquest by the Mamluks that much easier. Although the Mamluk **Sultanate** would endure until 1517, it was plagued by frequent assassinations of the sultan.

The Fatimids

The first Muslims to rule Egypt who were not a part of the Abbasid caliphate in Baghdad were the Fatimids. Unlike the Abbasids who were Sunni Muslim, the Fatimids were Shi'ite. They derived their name and claimed descent from Muhammad's daughter Fatima who was the wife of the fourth caliph, Ali. Fatimid rule did not begin in Egypt, however, but further west in North Africa where a rival caliphate to the Abbasids was established in Tunisia in 909.

In the 960s, the Fatimids then launched an invasion of Abbasid Egypt, conquered it, and built a new capital, Cairo. Eventually, Fatimid warriors (comprised mostly of Berber tribal forces and Sudanese slave regiments) pushed their empire across the Sinai Peninsula into Palestine and Syria. Here, they abutted the frontiers of both the Abbasid and Byzantine Empires. At its territorial zenith, the Fatimid caliphate stretched from North Africa and Sicily in the west, eastward across Egypt and Syria, and southward to the Red Sea coast of Africa, Yemen, and the Hejaz.

When the Fatimids established a new caliphate in Tunisia in 909, they were the first Muslim regime to challenge the Abbasid caliph's claim that his authority was the universal expression of God's will. The Abbasid caliph's actual power was certainly limited by this time, but no Muslim questioned his theoretical supremacy until the Fatimids. Claiming to be the true imams as direct descendants of Fatima and Ali, the Fatimids further legitimized their rule by appropriating Neoplatonic philosophy—part of the classical revival then sweeping the intellectual centers of Islam. **Neoplatonism** held that God brought life and spiritual wisdom to the world through divine emanations that were received by true believers, and Fatimid caliph-imams claimed to be the privileged recipients of these emanations.

These caliphs expressed their exalted status in court ceremony, art, and architecture. The ruler sat on a gold throne, wore a special crown, carried a sword and scepter that were the signs of his sovereignty, and built sumptuous and grand royal palaces and mosques in the new capital of Cairo. The Fatimid caliphs believed themselves to be sent by God to rule and to dispense the justice of Islamic law, the Shari'a. The name of one of the caliphs, al-Hakim bi-Amr Allah (r. 986–1021), means "Ruler by God's Command." As Shi'ites, the Fatimids were both theologically and politically opposed to the Sunni rule of the Abbasids in Baghdad whom they took to be illegitimate usurpers.

The Fatimid single-minded ideological stance in Shi'a Islam aimed at delegitimizing the Abbasid caliphate. In their own realm, however, the Fatimids were pragmatic, tolerant of religious and ideological diversity when it suited their needs. Advancement in government positions was based more on merit than on heredity or even religious affiliation. Offices were open to Sunnis and even Christians and Jews, who occupied some of the highest positions in government. Indeed, the financial administration was filled with **Coptic Christians**. As with all Muslim dynasties, Fatimid power was founded upon a strong army. Military personnel were paid in cash and, increasingly, with landed estates, as the booty from pillaging dried up with the consolidation of Fatimid rule.

The Almoravids, Almohads, Ayyubids, and Mamluks

The Fatimids built their realm through conquest and lost it the same way. In the early 11th century, the Almoravids seized western North Africa from them. The Almoravids, a coalition of Berber peoples, were united by religious fervor and doctrine. Fired by the mission to fight holy war against the pagan sub-Saharan peoples, the Almoravids conquered Morocco in 1070, and their leader assumed the title of caliph. From their capital in Marrakesh, they commanded the vital and lucrative trade routes across the Sahara Desert. By 1090, their armies had swept eastward through much of present-day Algeria.

The Almoravids would also set their sights on Spain. As early as the eighth and ninth centuries, small Christian kingdoms at the southern base of the Pyrenees Mountains in Spain began to reconquer and recolonize areas that had fallen to the Umayyads. Called the **Reconquista** (reconquest), it began as a trickle but ended as a flood. Before the 11th century, Christian armies only incrementally moved southward, but the weakness of the Umayyad caliphate in Spain and its disintegration in that century opened the possibility for rapid expansion of various Christian kingdoms. In fact, when Christian armies retook Toledo in 1085, the threatened Muslim **emirs** asked the Almoravids in North Africa to come to their aid. They came, and stayed, defeating the Christian army but claiming the conquered area as a province to be ruled from Marrakesh.

The Almoravids were, in turn, conquered by the Almohads in the mid-12th century. The Almohads believed that the Almoravids had become too lax in their adherence to the dictates of the Quran and rose in rebellion against them. By 1172, they had subsumed the rest of Muslim Spain in their North African–based empire. The Christian Reconquista resumed in the 13th century, with Cordoba falling to Christian armies in 1236 and Seville in 1248. Only Granada remained in Muslim hands, surviving until 1492 when the last light of Islam was extinguished on the Iberian Peninsula.

The Almoravids and Almohads for a time, then, spelled trouble for Christians. They also threatened the Fatimids, but it wasn't just the Almoravids and Almohads that the Fatimids had to confront. After about 1070, the Fatimid hold on the Levantine coast and parts of Syria was challenged first by Seljuk Turk invaders and then by the European Christian crusaders. Fatimid territory shrank until it consisted only of Egypt, and in 1169, even that fell to Kurdish horse-mounted warriors under the leadership of the renowned Salah ad-Din, known in the West as Saladin. Saladin had served in the Fatimid army, but with his father, he rose in rebellion against it and brought it down.

Despite Saladin's well-known military successes against the crusaders, the Ayyubid dynasty he established suffered from the same centrifugal forces that beset most Islamic regimes. Within only two decades of its founding, Saladin was forced to divide his state into emirates, forming a decentralized federation. The Ayyubid rulers held their regime together by bestowing land upon loyal soldiers. The recipient was required to maintain the infrastructure (e.g., dykes, irrigation canals, bridges, etc.) and to see that the land was properly cultivated. He was also charged with collecting taxes and channeling a portion of them to the ruler, keeping the balance for himself.

The Ayyubids were politically decentralized, making common defense that much more difficult. Like most Muslim regimes, they also had grown dependent on slave soldiers, now mostly Turkish, in their armies for defense. One of these soldiers led his fellow slaves in a successful overthrow of the Ayyubid ruler in Egypt and established the Mamluk Sultanate in 1250. The Mamluks preserved and consolidated their rule in 1260 when they halted the Mongol advance into Southwest Asia with a victory at the Battle of Ain Jalut, earning legitimacy as the defenders of Islam.

Although the Mamluk regime would last until 1517, the security of any given sultan on the throne was precarious, for none could effectively control the turbulent soldiers in their ranks. Sultans were made and unmade by these soldiers, reigned on average for less than seven years, and usually did not die peacefully in their beds. In spite of the dangers the sultans faced at home, the dynasty survived largely because of its military strength and success abroad. Slave soldiers fiercely loyal to their commanders, if not always to their sultan, presented a formidable fighting force.

Mamluk sultans and their soldiers were preoccupied with military exploits and left domestic governance and land-tenure systems of Egypt and Syria largely unchanged from that of the Fatimids and Ayyubids. Much government administration remained in the hands of Coptic Christians and Jews. Lands continued to be allocated as **fiefs** to loyal soldiers, although the sultans abolished their heritability and would not permit contiguous holdings for fear of consolidating a landed aristocracy that could challenge their rule.

The Muslim Regimes in Southwest Asia

The Abbasid caliphate lingered in Southwest Asia until 1258, when it was brought to an end by the Mongol invasions. For 50 years, the Mongols simply ravaged the newly conquered territories, but in the early 14th century, the Ilkhans, as the Mongol rulers were known, tried to stabilize the regime by granting land to the warrior aristocracy in exchange for their compliance in raising revenue for the central treasury. By the middle of the 14th century, the Ilkhan Empire was little more than loosely allied provincial states and easy prey for the forces of yet another Mongol ruler from central Asia, Tamerlane. Tamerlane invaded and absorbed them into a vast empire that lasted as long as the leader was alive but dissolved rapidly upon Tamerlane's death in 1405. The disruption of Southwest Asia caused by the Mongol invasions opened opportunities for ambitious chieftains to carve out and expand their authority in the destabilized area. One such ambitious chieftain was Osman, the first Ottoman ruler, who launched a dynasty that would last for centuries and, under conquering sultans, whose empire would encompass vast territories in Southwest Asia, North Africa, and Southeast Europe.

The Mongol Ilkhans and Tamerlane

Shortly after the Mamluks seized control of Egypt and Syria, the Mongols swept into Persia and Iraq. Hülegü, a grandson of Genghis Khan, led an army of 70,000 mounted warriors into Baghdad in 1258, sacked the city, and executed the last Abbasid caliph. The swiftness and effectiveness of Mongol empire building largely rested upon a seemingly invincible cavalry. These mounted troops were equipped with curved bows, metal-tipped arrows, swords, and lances. These archers possessed the remarkable skill of firing arrows accurately up to 500 feet while at full gallop. The use of saddles with stirrups (an invention of the Chinese and adopted by nomadic peoples of central Asia, like the Mongols) allowed the horseman to pivot his upper body and to shoot in all directions, even facing backwards. Obviously, the horse was key to Mongol military power. Each soldier usually maintained three or four, always keeping one fresh so the army could move rapidly for days at a time, covering up to 100 miles a day. Such speed and distance often caught opponents off guard and unprepared for assault, for no one had ever imagined an army could cover such distance so quickly.

The new Mongol rulers who toppled the Abbasids, called the Ilkhans, spent the first 50 years of their occupation plundering and slaughtering countless inhabitants. Ruinous taxes followed, the Mongols only interested in extracting as much wealth from their new possessions as possible. The population plummeted, and the economy deteriorated. Peasants were reduced to serfdom, and vast tracts of land went uncultivated or were converted to pasture to graze the animals of the nomadic Mongols. What land was cultivated was sold or distributed by the rulers to loyal followers. Ilkhanid agriculture became marked by large landed estates owned by a small minority of extremely wealthy lords.

After a half century of catastrophic rule, the first Muslim Ilkhan, Ghazan (r. 1295–1304), attempted to change course toward economic recovery. He reformed taxes to assist the revival of town life, restored the currency with a firm rate for the silver coin, rebuilt dilapidated irrigation works, and encouraged agriculture and trade. The Ilkhan state was still a military one, however, with a warrior aristocracy allied to the ruling dynasty. Ilkhan rulers distributed land to military chiefs who in turn distributed it among their followers, but all were responsible for channeling a share of tax revenues toward the khan, or Mongol ruler.

In 1336, the Ilkhan regime faced a crisis of succession (typical of Mongol dynasties that had no clear policy on succession) and rapidly dissolved into competing provincial states. Later in the 14th century, Timur, known historically as Tamerlane (r. 1370–1405), descended from the Chagatai branch of the Mongols in central Asia, invaded and absorbed them into a new empire. Tamerlane was a military adventurer whose marauding army swept aside lesser chieftains and, with the promise of plunder, absorbed many of the defeated warriors into his army.

Like Mongol invasions nearly everywhere, Tamerlane's devastated the conquered areas and destroyed the economic base of the region. He did, however, spare the vital caravan city of Samarkand, which was the gateway to the Silk Road to China, and established it as his capital. By the time of his death in 1405, his empire engulfed Iran, northern India, Anatolia, and northern Syria.

As a Muslim, Tamerlane justified his conquests and rule as the spreading of Islam and the Shari'a, but in practice, he confronted much the same obstacles of most conquest regimes—the centrifugal forces of decentralization. He tried to centralize power in himself by ruling through loyal generals who, in turn, oversaw governors of provinces who were frequently rotated to preclude creation of independent local power bases. Still, local clan-based warriors, many of them Mongol and Turkish immigrants, remained in a semi-independent state. They constantly sought opportunities to press for more power by challenging the authority of their supposed military superiors.

The Ottomans

The Mongol invasions had a profound impact on Southwest Asia. Destruction was widespread, and empires were obliterated. One such empire was that of the Seljuk Turks. When the Mongols defeated the Seljuks and destroyed their empire in 1242–1243, small bands of warriors and nomads who had lived on the fringes of the Turkish Seljuk Empire found themselves pushed westward. A steady flow of displaced Turkish warriors from the east gathered around local chieftains in Anatolia. These chieftains led them in raids for booty into the neighboring borderlands of the Byzantine Empire, its military defenses long weakened by wars with the Mamluks to the south and the Seljuks to the east.

Osman, the first Ottoman ruler (r. 1299–1326), was one such Turkish chieftain, but in addition to raiding the Byzantines, he embarked on conquest. His descendants followed his lead for centuries. From the beginning, the Ottomans pursued a dynamic conquest policy, and military concerns always dominated imperial policy. In the 14th century, Ottoman armies conquered large portions of the Byzantine Empire in Southwest Asia and, in the 1360s, pressed into the Balkans. The regions they conquered were overwhelmingly Christian, but the Ottomans were often welcomed by the populace because the former Christian regimes usually levied onerous taxes and coerced labor demands. Under the Ottomans, non-Muslims could live and work in relative freedom, so long as they paid their taxes. Indeed, the new Muslim rulers often enlisted many Christian Greek advisors to help them administer the conquered lands, brought Christian warriors into their armies, and even arranged marriages between Ottoman princes and Christian princesses, thereby sealing alliances with local dynasties.

The 15th century witnessed the reversal of the long-standing trend toward political decentralization that Islamic regimes had experienced for centuries with the extension and consolidation of Ottoman rule in the Balkans, the conquest of the rest of Anatolia (the Byzantine capital and last holdout of the Roman Empire, Constantinople, fell in 1453), and the coastal lands on the north shore of the Black Sea.

With the defeat of the Mamluks in 1517, Egypt and Syria fell under Ottoman rule, and when the western coast of Arabia soon followed, the Ottoman Empire commanded large parts of three important bodies of water—the Red Sea, the Black Sea, and the eastern half of the Mediterranean Sea. By 1500, not surprisingly, the Ottomans had built a formidable navy.

The sultan ruled over the empire, and the Ottomans secured an uninterrupted succession by departing from the Turkish tradition of multiple heirs and a divided inheritance. Instead, one son was selected to succeed, and all other brothers were exterminated, known as the Ottoman Law of Fratricide. Sultans had multiple wives (many were slave concubines), guaranteeing the infusion of new blood into the dynasty and preventing inbreeding.

The authority of the sultan combined patrimonial, imperial, and Islamic dimensions. The territory of the empire was the sultan's personal property to disperse as he wished, the soldiers of his army his personal slaves. As the enforcer of the Shari'a, his rule, much like caliphs in other regimes, was legitimized by Islam. The Ottoman state centered on the sultan's palace, with a central administration run by a bureaucracy there and supported in the provinces by military and civil governors and local judges. The judges, known as qadis, all were trained in a state-supported educational system of **madrassas** where they learned Islamic and sultanic law, the latter a flexible code made up of ad hoc pronouncements by the sultan.

The backbone of the sultan's authority, however, was the army, and Ottoman sultans used it to counter powerful aristocrats who from time to time opposed the consolidation of the sultan's power. Murad I (r. 1360–1389) was the first Ottoman to use slave military units as his bulwark against aristocratic challenges (a strategy many other Muslim rulers would use). His successors built upon this foundation by levying a human tax upon conquered populations, taking young boys from their families and raising them as the slave soldiers known as janissaries.

Janissaries were infantry troops, and in the Ottoman army, they were complemented by a cavalry comprised of free Turks. To keep the latter loyal and in the sultan's military service, sultans granted them timars, akin to the fiefs used in other Muslim and even medieval Christian feudal regimes. Timars were assignments of land owned by the sultan but that generated rents and taxes that in part went to the timar holder. Continual conquests by the Ottomans brought much land into the timar system. Conquered lands became the property of the state—and the sultan—and were his to dispense as he saw fit. Unlike Christian feudal knights, timar recipients did not own the land and could not pass it down through generations. Indeed, a timar could be revoked by the sultan and, in cases of perceived disloyalty, sometimes was.

The dynamism of Ottoman conquest was driven by two imperatives: to bring revenue to the sultan's treasury and to acquire land for the timar system. To determine how much revenue could be extracted from a conquered region, immediately upon conquest and at regular intervals thereafter state-administered surveys were taken for tax purposes, listing villages, households, and adult males. The land was then organized into plots that were worked by a family that had sufficient labor and a team of oxen to plow the fields. Each unit was then taxed on its surplus. The overarching goal of the government, then, was to bring land under productive cultivation to generate tax revenue.

By far the largest part of state expenditures was for military purposes: cash for soldiers' salaries and to purchase food, clothing, and weapons. The perennial imperative for the sultan was to keep the imperial revenues adequate to meet expenses incurred by war. This fiscalism was the central concept of the Ottoman state: conquest was the motor that drove imperial expansion *and* the necessity to pay for it. The Ottoman state, then, was a thoroughly militarized one and, for centuries, a continually expansionist one.

The Commercial Economy of the Islamic World

Perhaps surprisingly, amid the political decentralization and warfare that characterized the various Islamic regimes from the tenth to the 14th centuries, the economy of the Islamic world thrived. For all of the militarism of the Islamic regimes, most of their leaders recognized the value of trade and pursued policies to facilitate it. This was especially the case for long-distance trade and the various trade routes to the riches of the East—overland through central Asia or by sea down the Persian Gulf or the Red Sea. More commodities moved along these routes than ever before. Populations grew everywhere during these centuries, and though the conditions of the producers—rural peasants and urban craftsmen—were often miserable, increasing volumes of a vast array of both luxury and bulk commodities were traded by affluent merchants from Spain in the western end of the Mediterranean basin to Southwest Asia and beyond.

The Growth of Trade

Despite political fragmentation, the Muslim Mediterranean, like its Christian counterpart, enjoyed pronounced trading prosperity from late in the 10th century with the establishment of the Fatimid dynasty in Egypt until the mid-14th century when the pandemic Black Death dealt a withering blow to all economic activity in the Mediterranean basin.

By the 10th century, there were several key trade routes that connected the Mediterranean world with Asia (see Map 12.2). There was the northern route from Constantinople to the northern shores of the Black Sea and across the land mass of central Asia north of the Caspian Sea to the important caravan cities of Bukhara, Samarkand, and Kashgar and thence on to China.

A middle route linked Constantinople to an artery that ran along the southern coast of the Black Sea, then overland to Tabriz. In Tabriz, it joined one of two important routes from the Levantine Mediterranean coast. One of these ran to Baghdad, then north to Tabriz and eastward south of the Caspian Sea, eventually reaching Merv and linking with the northern route in Bukhara or branching off to Balkh where it connected with several routes into Afghanistan and India.

A third route from the Levantine coast went southeastward to the Indian Ocean by way of Baghdad, Basra, and the Persian Gulf. Yet another route was further south, starting in Alexandria and Cairo (or, more accurately, the nearby port city of al-Fustāt) and running up the Nile River, then briefly overland to the Red Sea and Arabian Sea and into the Indian Ocean. At different times and for different reasons, the northern and middle routes thrived or contracted, but until the rise of the Ottomans, the Red Sea route was consistently the most important.

All of these routes had long carried luxury goods from the East—silks, fine cotton fabrics, and spices—but the 11th and 12th centuries saw an increase in the volume of these commodities now destined for expanded markets. On maritime routes, luxury products were joined in the 13th century by bulk commodities, such as timber, rice, sugar, wheat, barley, and salt. The arrival of bulk cargoes, in turn, signal a change in maritime technology, as new, more seaworthy ships with larger cargo capacity made their appearance. Mediterranean galleys, Indian Ocean dhows, and Chinese junks now plied the maritime trade routes, all increasingly guided by the new **magnetic compass** (a Chinese invention from the 11th century) that allowed open-water sailing far from the coast.

In the Muslim Mediterranean, world-trading cities found ways to lodge increasing numbers of merchants and to securely store growing volumes of goods in transit. To accomplish this, they expanded the traditional **funduqs,** which flourished nearly everywhere. Major trading cities might have 100 within their walls. Not only were these inns and warehouses but they also were sites where government officials could efficiently collect taxes and long-distance traders could gather to conduct commercial transactions. Because funduqs were lucrative sources of revenue, governments often protected them and in some cases, like the Ayyubids, constructed new ones. Muslims, Jews, and Christians all met within funduqs to trade (although they were segregated by religion for lodging). With the growth in the number of Christian traders that flocked to Muslim markets from the tenth through the mid-14th century, specific funduqs (called fondacos by the westerners) were designated for them. In Alexandria, for instance, each foreign "nation" (e.g., Genoa, Venice, Pisa, etc.) had its own funduq. Funduqs remained common into the Ottoman period.

Egypt and the Supremacy of the Red Sea Route

For several hundred years after the 10th century, the Red Sea route eclipsed the northern and middle routes in commercial importance for political reasons. Egypt was the heart of the Fatimid caliphate and the Mamluk Sultanate, and it flourished economically under them. The Fatimids encouraged the development of an extensive trade network in the Mediterranean and Red Seas that linked up with the Indian Ocean and extended all the way to Song China. Fatimid government officials rarely interfered with the economy, although they did maintain a monopoly on the trade in goods that were necessary for the military (above all iron for weapons) and for securing an adequate food supply to the cities. Their chief concern was collecting tax revenues from trade.

Fatimid troops also secured the caliphate's control of the trade routes across the Sahara Desert, thus assuring a steady supply of gold to Egypt and providing the regime with an exceptionally pure gold dinar. Stable currency was a strong stimulus for an expanding economy, especially in long-distance trade. Fatimid Egypt's India trade flourished, and the Red Sea route came to be the preferred highway linking the Mediterranean economy with that of the Indian Ocean. Al-Fustāt-Cairo and Alexandria thrived as transit points, and Italian traders were drawn to their harbors for the eastern goods they could acquire, carry back to Europe, and sell for enormous profits.

The Christian traders, however, were allowed no further than the port cities, and they were not permitted to compete with the Karimi merchants for the transit trade from the Indian Ocean. The Fatimids, as well as the Ayyubids and Mamluks, protected this group of wholesale merchants, granting them monopolies over crucial commodities; building funduqs exclusively for them in al-Fustāt, Alexandria, and Red Sea ports; and even providing military escorts to protect their annual seaborne caravan on the Red Sea from pirates. Of course, the government taxed the transit trade.

Fatimid domestic industries also thrived for a time, with some products, like textiles and sugar, finding export markets in Europe. This export trade may have benefited the mercantile classes, but not all subjects of Fatimid rule thrived. As with all premodern societies, wealth in Fatimid society was sharply polarized; peasants and urban workers saw their standard of living steadily erode. In the early years of the caliphate, the population grew, pushing prices up and wages down. As a result, by the second half of the 11th century, famine periodically occurred, and desperate peasants, impoverished townsmen, and disgruntled **Bedouins** sometimes rose in revolt. One such rebellion occurred in Tyre, Lebanon, in 996 when a sailor named 'Allaqa and his followers rose up against the Fatimids. It took two years for the caliph to retake the city, but when he did, his troops slaughtered the rebels, captured 'Allaqa, flayed him alive, and then crucified him. This and other rebellions had no impact on the condition of the peasantry or the poor urban classes, which continued to deteriorate.

The Mamluks succeeded the Fatimids in Egypt and further enhanced the Red Sea route to the East. Indeed, for a century after taking power in 1250, they maintained exclusive control over the sea gateway between the Mediterranean and the Indian Ocean. They intensively developed Red Sea ports and continued the Karimi merchant monopoly by granting the merchants trading privileges and military protection. During the first century of Mamluk rule, the state constructed a more integrated network of roads, especially from Nile ports to the Red Sea, and increased the security for travelling merchants upon them.

The Red Sea route benefited from the decline of the middle route to the Persian Gulf. The middle route through Iraq and Iran to the Persian Gulf had long stood as rival for the lucrative India trade with the southern route through the Red Sea. After 1250, however, the middle route collapsed as a result of the

Mongol conquest and the depredations of Persia and Iraq that sacked important cities and destroyed much of the economy there.

In the last decade of the 13th century, the Ilkhan ruler Ghazan, the first Mongol to convert to Islam, attempted to foster trade across the northern land routes toward China and met with some success. As Mongols did everywhere, he took steps to secure the safety of merchants upon these roads. Many great Mongol landowners lived in cities and invested heavily in trading ventures operated by long-distance-trading wholesale merchants who grew wealthy from this resurgent overland trade with China. Tabriz (in present-day northwestern Iran) was the capital city of the Ilkhan kingdom and became a great emporium of the international caravan trade. The intrepid Venetian adventurer Marco Polo testifies in his famous *Travels* to the vibrant trade that flowed across these trade routes.

The Persian Gulf route suffered not just from the Mongol Ilkhans, however. With the expulsion of Christians from the last Latin crusader state in 1291 by the Mamluks, Italian traders lost easy access to the Persian Gulf. The Mamluks gained control of Syria and Palestine and, to favor the Red Sea route, blocked access to the Gulf route. Italian traders thus focused not only on the southern route through Egypt but also on the northern route through the Black Sea (see Chapter 14).

The Genoese especially pushed into the Black Sea and established trading posts, such as Caffa, on its northern shores. Here they traded for slaves to supply the seemingly limitless demand of the Mamluks. The slave sultanate employed a system of manumission for soldiers after a period of time in service and so created a constant need to replenish the military ranks with slaves. By Islamic law, only non-Muslims could be enslaved; therefore, regions like Circassia north of the Black Sea were prime recruiting grounds.

Like the Fatimids and other, shorter lived Egyptian dynasties, such as the Ayyubids, the Mamluks allowed trade with Christians in the Mediterranean but permitted no European to transit their territory. This strong and militaristic government closely watched Christian merchants. When Italian ships entered the harbor at Alexandria or al-Fustāt, they could only unload after state customs officials had boarded their ships, registered their goods, and assessed a tax on the cargo. These same officials then oversaw the transport of goods to specified funduqs.

The Mamluk state actively encouraged the production of linen and cotton textiles for export. It owned the land that produced the flax and cotton crops and owned the workshops where the fabrics were manufactured. Indeed, its domestic economy was essentially state run and depended on coerced and intensive labor to produce surpluses. As under the Fatimids, gold imports from sub-Saharan Africa stabilized the monetary system.

As long as population levels remained buoyant, which they did until the mid-14th century, the Mamluk economy and the state could thrive, if not the peasantry and the manufacturing class. However, when the Black Death descended on the Mediterranean basin in 1347 and swept away one-third of its inhabitants in just a few years, Mamluk production sharply contracted. Domestic industries suffered from depopulation and increased competition from now superior-quality European wares, and these industries effectively collapsed. Only the naturally productive soil of Egypt kept the economy afloat, but now its products were not destined for domestic workshops but rather for export to Europe as raw cotton and flax.

From 1350 until the final defeat at the hands of the Ottomans in 1517, the Mamluk state was marked by an eroding economic base, military reversals, and a gradual loss of territory. In the late 15th century, the Mamluks faced increased military competition on their northern flank from the Ottomans, adding pressure to an already extended military budget, and suffered a crushing loss of Red Sea commerce when the Portuguese opened up trade routes around the southern tip of Africa and began carrying products from India directly to European ports. Their commercial base gutted, the Mamluks were no match for Ottoman armies, who toppled the regime in 1517.

The Ottoman Economy

The Ottoman state was a militarized one, and the overriding necessity of providing resources for the army stimulated trade and a rapid growth in the size and diversity of markets. Indeed, among the objectives of Ottoman conquests from the beginning were the control of trade routes and productive resources. The scale of Ottoman military campaigns was so grand that they demanded tens of thousands of camels (each carrying up to 500 pounds of cargo, or twice what a horse can carry) just to supply the army.

The demand for food to feed the army lured the Ottomans into the Balkans in an early wave of conquest. They allowed the port city of Dubrovnik to remain an independent republic in exchange for channeling products from the Balkan interior to Dubrovnik for export to Ottoman ports. For the same reason Ottoman armies pushed northward in the Balkans and into the lower Danube basin in the 15th century. From there, through trade relations, they reached further northward into unconquered regions of east-central Europe and southern Germany. The Danube River became an important artery channeling goods into the Ottoman

Empire, and the city of Brasov on the Wallachian-Transylvanian border emerged as a key transit center.

Ottoman armies marched southward and northeastward from Anatolia for the same reasons (to command resources) and with similar effects (stimulating the growth of trade). Conquests to the south in Arab Syria and Palestine and Mongol Iraq were followed by Persian Iran and, in 1517, Mamluk Egypt. These conquests revitalized the Persian Gulf route to the Indian Ocean and access to cherished eastern goods.

The northern route was similarly revitalized by Ottoman conquests. Tamerlane had deliberately destroyed the route that skirted north of the Black Sea by waging devastating war against the Golden Horde, seeking thereby to advantage the more southerly route to China that ran through the heart of his empire toward his prize city and capital, Samarkand. With the extension of Ottoman power into the area in the 15th century, the northernmost route returned to importance.

Here, control of the Black Sea trade was the Ottoman goal. Trade across this body of water included enormous quantities of grain, again necessary to feed the army, but the route also served as a highway for furs and captive humans. The Genoese had lodged themselves at Caffa and profited enormously by channeling furs and slaves southward from Circassia (along the northeast shore of the Black Sea), Muscovy, and Poland. The Ottomans were steady buyers. Ottoman slaves, like those of the Mamluks, were usually eventually manumitted, and the constant erosion of the slave population proved a strong stimulus for the slave trade. After 1475, the Ottomans succeeded in driving the Italians out of the Black Sea, removing the middleman in the lucrative trade there.

The revitalization of the northern route also stimulated trade with the East. By the mid-14th century, Bursa in northwest Anatolia (present-day Turkey) became a thriving market between east and west, Ottoman rulers building monumental **caravanserais** there to handle the trade. By the 15th century, Bursa was joined by Izmir south of Constantinople on the Aegean Sea as the most important commercial centers in Anatolia. Through these cities goods came from and went to the Black Sea, linking the Ottoman Empire with Ukraine, Poland, and Russia to the north and eastward across the Silk Road and to China.

The city of Aleppo in Syria thrived for reasons similar to Bursa and Izmir. It was a center of exchange between Asia Minor, the Balkans, and the Black Sea from one direction and from Syria, Egypt, Arabia, Iran, and India from the other. Indeed, all of these cities were crucial transit points for what was the most coveted commodity of international exchange until the 18th century: silk. The demand for Iranian and Chinese silk thread surged in the 15th century as the Italians abandoned the production of silk thread and devoted their energies to weaving silk cloth from imported thread from the East.

Ottoman sultans recognized that vibrant trade not only fed their armies but also brought revenues to the imperial coffers. The state, consequently, was actively involved in tapping the wealth generated by the economy. The empire was divided into customs zones to tax transit trade, and taxes were levied on goods brought to urban wholesale and retail markets. The state stimulated land traffic by building bridges and caravanserais and garrisoned soldiers at major road junctions for security. After the conquest of Christian Constantinople in 1453, the city (today Istanbul) experienced a feverish rebuilding. By 1481, 209 mosques, 24 schools, 32 public baths, and 12 bazaars had been constructed. The burgeoning city's markets grew proportionately, especially the food markets that provisioned the capital. The need for food in a large urban center in turn stimulated the growth of large agricultural estates in Anatolia.

The Ottoman state may have been active in the economy, but it left international trade largely in the hands of non-Muslims, above all Jews and Christian Armenians, Greeks, and Italians. The markets of the Ottoman Empire were extraordinarily heterogeneous, with Muslim and non-Muslim merchants mixing freely in the marketplaces. Jews were welcomed into Ottoman lands after their expulsion from Spain and other Christian states, and they built up a formidable trading diaspora.

Al-Andalus

Spain, or al-Andalus in Arabic, was an integral part of the Mediterranean economy until the mid-13th century. Commercially, it was the western terminus of a bustling east-west trade axis across the Mediterranean Sea and an important component of the resurgence in trade in the Mediterranean basin beginning in the 10th century. Through Egypt, eastern goods found buyers in Andalusian markets, as merchants from all over the Mediterranean world could be found in Spanish ports. Jewish traders were everywhere (at least until the religiously intolerant Almohads expelled them in 1150), often shipping their goods on Muslim vessels. Christians entered Andalusian trade in the 11th century as a result of the rise of the Italian maritime presence and were ubiquitous in Spanish markets.

Bustling Muslim Andalusian ports led by Almeria dotted the southern and eastern coast of Spain, emporia through which eastern goods, such as spices, paper, and fine cotton and linen textiles, and Adalusian products, such as silk fabric and

FIGURE 16.1 A Christian and a Muslim Playing Chess in al-Andalus. This image comes from *Book of Games, Dice and Tables*, a Christian text produced during the reign of Alfonso X of Castile (r. 1252–1284). It supports other evidence that Christians and Muslims (and Jews) intermingled in the market and port cities of al-Andalus. Here a Christian (left) is playing chess with a Muslim (right).

leather, found their way northward into Christian European markets. Northern European furs and slaves as well as bullion were in turn traded southward. Most merchants handled a broad range of commodities, including medicinals, aromatics, dyes (indigo was especially prized), and mordants like alum (for fixing dye in fabrics), all coveted commodities because their low weight, small volume, high demand, and limited geographical availability pushed up prices and profits. Bulkier items joined the trade too, however, as thousands of barrels of Spanish olive oil and bales of woven and raw silk, wool, flax, and cotton traversed Mediterranean shipping lanes annually.

Joining the key Andalusian exports of olive oil and high-quality silk fabrics (produced in a cottage industry of hundreds of workshops in which women spun and men wove), were leather hides and timber (for shipbuilding, especially in demand in the unforested Muslim eastern Mediterranean). In addition, slaves sold by Christian traders were joined by slaves brought from Africa by the Almoravids and Almohads and Christian slaves from northern Spain captured in warfare and border raids by Muslim emirs. Most of these captives headed eastward to the insatiable Muslim slave markets.

As in all Muslin ports, upon arrival in Andalusian ports, cargoes had to clear customs for tax collection and were then stored in prescribed funduqs. The various rulers all recognized the value of the commerce entering and leaving their ports, and they subjected the trade and the funduqs to close scrutiny and oversight. Muslim, Jewish, and, increasingly, Christian traders could be found in these ports. Genoese and Pisan traders increased their presence as a result of favorable treaties signed in the 12th century with the Almohads that gave them their own funduqs and reduced tariffs.

Indeed, Genoese mercantile activity in Andalusia often involved female investors. Surviving contracts show that Genoese women enjoyed considerable financial independence and often used their money for commercial investment in Iberian trade. Moreover, wives often acted as their husbands' agents, and widows were known to continue their deceased spouses' businesses.

Within Andalusia, merchant activity shifted increasingly into Christian hands after the mid-12th century. Before this time, Christian merchant ships (both Latin and Byzantine) had dominated the sea routes along the northern coast of the Mediterranean Sea, while Muslim vessels monopolized the southern one along the African coast. During the 11th and 12th centuries, however, the southern route deteriorated, and the northern Mediterranean sea lanes controlled by Christians, above all Italians, surged in importance.

Christian traders continued to enter Muslim ports in Spain, but Muslims were denied reciprocal access in Christian ones, which were growing in number as a result of Christian conquests during these centuries. By the early 13th century, power was permanently realigned in Iberia favoring the Christians, the Reconquista increasingly reorienting Spanish trade northward into the European Christian world and away from the Muslim Mediterranean world. By 1500, the Spanish economy had become largely dependent on northern European markets and was increasingly drawn into the overseas commerce emerging in the Atlantic basin.

Review Questions

1. What do the Fatimids, Almoravids, Almohads, Ayyubids, and Mamluks have in common?
2. How was the Ottoman system of rule and generation of revenue different from the Mongol regimes that preceded it?
3. Why did the four main trade routes linking the Islamic world with the East thrive or wither when they did?

Further Reading

Abu-Lughod, Janet. *Before European Hegemony: The World System A.D. 1250–1350.* New York: Oxford University Press, 1989.

Ashtor, E. *A Social and Economic History of the Near East in the Middle Ages.* Berkeley: University of California Press, 1976.

Barkey, Karen. *Empire of Difference: The Ottomans in Comparative Perspective.* Cambridge: Cambridge University Press, 2008.

Boyle, J. A. ed. *The Cambridge History of Iran, Vol 5: The Saljuq and Mongol Periods.* Cambridge: Cambridge University Press, 1968.

Constable, Olivia Remie. *Trade and Traders in Muslim Spain.* Cambridge: Cambridge University Press, 1994.

Constable, Olivia Remie. *Housing the Stranger in the Mediterranean World: Lodging, Trade and Travel in Late Antiquity and the Middle Ages.* Cambridge: Cambridge University Press, 2003.

Goffman, Daniel. *The Ottoman Empire and Early Modern Europe.* Cambridge: Cambridge University Press, 2002.

Greene, Molly. *A Shared World: Christians and Muslims in the Early Modern Mediterranean.* Princeton: Princeton University Press, 2000.

Inalcik, Halil. *An Economic and Social History of the Ottoman Empire. Vol. 1, 1300–1600.* Cambridge: Cambridge University Press, 1994.

Lapidus, Ira M. *A History of Islamic Societies.* Cambridge: Cambridge University Press, 2002.

Lev, Yaacov. *State and Society in Fatimid Egypt.* Leiden: E. J. Brill, 1991.

Petry, Carl F., ed. *The Cambridge History of Egypt. Vol. 1, 640–1517.* Cambridge: Cambridge University Press, 1998.

Valensi, Lucette, *The Birth of the Despot: Venice and the Sublime Porte.* Translated by Arthur Denner. Ithaca: Cornell University Press, 1993.

Figure Credits

Map 16.1: Copyright © by Koba-chan (CC BY-SA 3.0) at https://upload.wikimedia.org/wikipedia/commons/0/02/Eurasia.jpg.

Fig. 16.1: Source: https://commons.wikimedia.org/wiki/File:Alfonso_X_Libro_F64R.jpg.

CHAPTER 17

The Americas, ca. 1 CE–1533

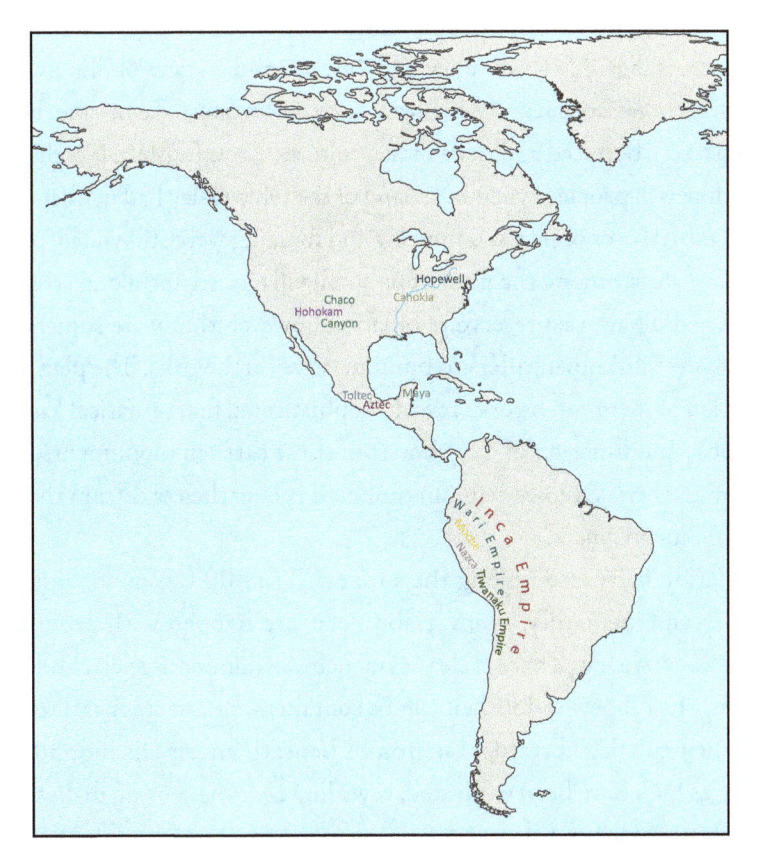

MAP 17.1 The Americas

The Indians of North America

Many important American Indian cultures of North America—the Woodland Hopewell, the Mississippian, the Hohokam, and the **Pueblo**—were mainly sedentary cultivators, and some became urbanized and formed into extensive states with a dominant political elite. Like all the Indians in the Americas, North American Indians were impressive builders, their work ranging from massive earthworks to sophisticated irrigation systems to enormous masonry dwellings. As their agriculture generated surpluses, they engaged in trade, at times far-reaching, and they lived in stratified societies in which a small social elite possessed the majority of the wealth.

The Woodland Hopewell

Between 1000 BCE and 900 CE, known as the Woodland period, Indians settled the floodplains of the many rivers east of the Mississippi River, learning to cultivate the thriving native seed-bearing plants there. As agriculture gradually took hold, a sedentary lifestyle emerged. Sometime in the first century CE, maize from Mexico joined the cultivated mix. A distinct culture, called Hopewell, appeared. By 400, it stretched across the Ohio River valley into the present-day states of Illinois, Indiana, Ohio, southern Wisconsin and Michigan, and southwestern Tennessee. Hopewell influence also can be traced in various Indian cultures in southeastern North America.

The Hopewell people in their heartland of the Ohio valley had neither cities nor fully agricultural economies, and hunting and foraging were still widely practiced. They lived instead among the numerous small villages strung along streams and rivers. They did have vast reservoirs of labor, however, that were somehow marshaled by as yet unknown rulers to build massive earthworks. The planning and construction of these earthworks reveal a sophisticated mathematical knowledge. The purpose and function of the greatest of these earthen monuments, Serpent Mound in southern Ohio, remain unknown. It is nonetheless certain that no one lived within its precincts.

Population increased among the Hopewell to 400 CE or so, and societal complexity and inequality, as invariably seems to happen with production of surpluses, grew with it. There is clear evidence of a dominant social and political elite among the Hopewell, for their tombs contain rare artifacts that dramatically marked their privileged status. Log tombs beneath enormous mounds two to three stories high have been excavated, revealing ceramic serving dishes, jewelry, and sometimes sacrificed slaves.

Some of these artifacts point to long-distance trade in materials like sheet mica from the southern Appalachian Mountains. Other unearthed items originated from as far away as the Rocky Mountains to the west, the Great Lakes to the north, and the Gulf of Mexico to the south. All of this suggests that the Hopewell had extensive trading links.

For unknown reasons, Hopewell culture declined in the fifth century CE and disappeared entirely by 500. Although no culture like Hopewell emerged from its ruins, over the next four centuries the cultivation of maize did spread across many eastern regions of North America with suitable soils. Most likely carried by migrating bow-and-arrow-wielding peoples, it provided for the sustenance of a gradually expanding population.

Mississippian Culture

For 300 years following the collapse of Hopewell culture around 500 CE, the cultivation of maize gradually spread across the Ohio and Mississippi River valleys. After 800, there is evidence of an intensification of land clearance in the region and thus the spread of agriculture. By 900, a diverse array of peoples lived along the Ohio, Illinois, and Mississippi Rivers and their tributaries. Gradually, communities were becoming more integrated as surplus food production took hold.

Suddenly, around 1000 CE, the region surrounding the confluences of the Illinois, Ohio, and Missouri Rivers with the Mississippi River, called the American Bottom, began drawing people to it from other areas. People were abandoning their villages and hamlets and migrating to the American Bottom. As the name suggests, the area topographically was fertile floodplain bottomland in the broad valleys of these major rivers whose frequent flooding enriched soils and maintained wetlands that teemed with wildlife. Because these prime conditions attracted migrants, population in the American Bottom surged, from perhaps 3,000 people in 1000 to 15,000 scarcely 50 years later.

A rural labor force that was largely gendered—hoe agriculture and spinning seem to have been performed by women; harvesting, hunting, and perhaps weaving by men—must have rendered a substantial surplus in the region, supporting the rapid development of the political and ceremonial center of Cahokia, the great Native American settlement in the American Bottom. Some of the surplus crops, meat, and fowl brought into Cahokia were kept in storage facilities for periodic distribution supervised by central administrators, notably to the workers engaged in the massive construction projects.

Exotic raw materials from far away were imported into Cahokia where they were fashioned by urban craftspeople into finished objects. Shells, mica, quartz crystal, and copper came from the Gulf of Mexico, the Appalachian Mountains, western Wisconsin, and the shores of Lake Superior. They were funneled through down-the-line trading partners to Cahokia along waterways that eventually led to the capital. Down-the-line trade describes relations where no single trader ranged far from home. Cahokia commanded the midcontinent's principal transportation corridor. It sat astride the confluence of the Missouri, Illinois, and Mississippi Rivers near present-day St. Louis and controlled traffic that moved along it.

At its zenith, Cahokia dominated the entire American Bottom and exerted indirect influence well beyond it. Largely due to Cahokia, Mississippian culture spread into the Southeast. Agricultural chiefdoms there came into contact with Cahokia and adopted its cultural forms of platform mounds and rectangular public plazas as well as its pantheon of deities. Monks Mound is the largest earthen platform-mound pyramid constructed at Cahokia and the largest north of Mexico. It stands 100 feet high, nearly 1,000 feet long, and over 800 feet wide. Between 1100 and 1200, several parts of the Southeast became integrated in a regional exchange network directly related to Cahokia.

The late 1100s, however, were a turning point for Cahokia. Now, the population contracted, and trading relations to the North ceased. After 1250, long-distance exchange dried up in every direction, and in the Southeast, warfare between chiefdoms increased noticeably.

Astonishingly, Cahokia was abandoned almost as rapidly as it grew. Indeed, the once-thriving American Bottom was effectively vacated by 1300. Climate change most likely had something to do with this. The 13th century did experience cooling, likely of planetary sweep, and drought usually came with it. In Cahokia, environmental deterioration may also have played a leading role. The Bottom was increasingly deforested. The removal of trees for fuel and farmland caused erosion that deprived farmland of its fertile topsoil.

Whatever the cause, most people had left the American Bottom by 1300, many migrating south and west. Cahokia was not succeeded by large polities anywhere, people instead gathering under village chiefdoms. Endemic warfare ensued well into the period of European contact after 1500. The peoples of these chiefdoms were only semisedentary. They often moved seasonally across networks of trails or along the extensive rivers and swamps in the Southeast. They travelled not only to hunt and wage war but also to trade. Coastal people, for example, traded salt, fish, and shells to the tribes in the interior for flint, pottery, and animal skins.

Although beyond the influence of Cahokia, eastern woodland peoples from the Ohio valley to the Atlantic Seaboard also were organized politically in chiefdoms that occasionally became federated nations. They, too, were traders, hunters, farmers, and warriors. They traded and travelled extensively, and the plentiful deer in the region provided meat as well as skins useful for trade. By the 10th century, maize cultivation was known here, followed soon by beans and squash.

The importance of these staple crops, in turn, increased the value of good farmland, which, because of the topography of the eastern woodlands, was concentrated and in limited supply. Villages were fortified to defend it, and the entire region was wracked by nearly constant wars of conquest for the prized farmlands and their crops. Indeed, the Susquehanna River in present-day Pennsylvania became a "war road" that Iroquois war bands from the eastern Great Lakes and Mohawk Valley traversed regularly.

The Indians of Southwest North America

Maize cultivation appeared in the Southwest of North America much earlier than it did east of the Mississippi River, perhaps as early as 1500 BCE. Maize was most likely an import from Mesoamerica. By 500 BCE, further Mexican influence can be seen in the style of pottery being made and in the similarity of religious beliefs and practices. Unfortunately, we know little about the nature and extent of these cultural contacts. Perhaps the North American Southwest was settled by migrants from Michoacán in west-central Mexico, for there are clear similarities in both places in rock art, textile designs, platform temple mounds, and ball courts.

At the beginning of the first century CE in southern Arizona, there is evidence of concentrated villages along the Gila and Salt Rivers. These settlements were supported by maize fields watered by irrigation ditches. Hohokam culture, as it became known, lasted in the area for over a thousand years. In some places, towns emerged, like Snaketown south of contemporary Phoenix. Here, irrigated maize, squash, and cotton fields sustained hundreds of town dwellers. Two ball courts have been found along with trash and ceremonial mounds. Residences surrounded a large central plaza, suggesting that several thousand people may have lived in Snaketown at its zenith in the mid-11th century CE.

By the seventh century CE, the Hohokam people were making a distinctive style of pottery. Their towns and villages were linked by trade and military alliances. They also had developed long-distance, most likely down-the-line, trade with Mexico. Copper bells and macaw birds were brought up from Mexico in exchange for the semiprecious stone turquoise, which was being commercially mined by the Hohokam people.

By the ninth century, Hohokam culture in the Gila-Salt River basin spanned a large area, perhaps 100,000 acres, and its population reached 25,000–50,000 people. The entire region was interlaced by elaborate and sophisticated canal systems. Some canals were as deep as 15 feet and as wide as 30; one even extended 20 miles, reflecting engineering knowledge about gradients.

Water in this arid climate, of course, was a precious resource. Control of it seemed to be the basis of political power. Society was organized in family groups, the heads of which would convene in councils to negotiate governance. The heads of these lineages were prosperous landowners, and the distribution of water was their fundamental concern. There were 16 canal systems in the Gila-Salt River basin, each with a gate on the rivers. The family that controlled the gate controlled the use of water in that canal system.

The 11th century marked the greatest development and extent of Hohokam culture. However, perhaps testimony to a growing reliance upon trade with Mexico, with the fall of the Mesoamerican Toltec Empire in 1168 (see below), the Hohokam lost a vital trading partner, and trade withered. After that, Hohokam culture shrank geographically to a Phoenix basin core. Drought in the 12th century, no doubt, also played a significant role in the contraction of this culture, just as it likely did in Cahokia. The end came in 1356 with a devastating flood that inundated the region, destroying irrigation ditches, fields, and homes.

The Southwest also witnessed the emergence of Pueblo culture. Around 750 CE, people on the Colorado Plateau began to build distinctive dwellings and workshops out of sandstone and mud, characterized by joined rows of rectangular rooms. By 1000, these pueblos, as these buildings are called, were made of solid masonry, and by the 13th century, large connected blocks of these buildings, often two or three stories high, had been constructed.

The best known of these settlements was in Chaco Canyon in northwestern present-day New Mexico. Between 800 and 1150, a town with eight large masonry pueblos housing perhaps 2,000 people came into existence. The largest pueblo, the Pueblo Bonito, was a bustling political and ceremonial complex with 700 rooms. One of a dozen such "great houses" in the canyon, a burial crypt with 14 skeletons of both men and women and over 11,000 turquoise pendants and beads (by far the most found in the entire Southwest) has been excavated in the Pueblo Bonito. Such wealth exhibits exalted, perhaps royal, status. Nine of these skeletons had maternal DNA, suggesting that their aristocratic or royal status was passed down from the mother, which in turn suggests that elite women in this society may have held religious, political, or even economic importance. The town of Chaco Canyon was at the center of a basin within which small dams, sluices, and channels were built to maximize the limited rainfall and to irrigate fields that fed the townspeople.

Chaco Canyon thrived because of turquoise. Powerful clans controlled the rich turquoise mines, extracting the valuable stone and exporting it southward to a hungry Mexican market. Chaco Canyon thrived into the mid-12th century but then collapsed suddenly. Perhaps like Hohokam culture, its demise was related to the fall of the Toltecs (and the collapse of the Mexican market) but also certainly from a prolonged drought that struck the region then.

The Indians of Mesoamerica

Mesoamerican Indian cultures, from the earliest Olmecs (see Chapter 4) in the second millennium BCE to the city-states in the Valley of Mexico and the Maya of the Yucatán Peninsula to the Toltecs and to the Aztecs in the 15th century CE, shared many common characteristics. Among these were the construction of huge pyramids and monuments, the organization of large markets and trade networks, the practice of human sacrifice, and the institution of a complex religion.

Everywhere, human muscle was overwhelmingly the source of energy. None of the Indian cultures had mills powered by water or wind, and none had knowledge of sailing techniques or iron metallurgy. They had no domesticated draft animals and thus no need for wheeled vehicles, confirmed by the absence of the wheel from the archeological and written record.

All of these Mesoamerican cultures based their diet on maize, squash, beans, and chili peppers. These cultures spanned diverse geographies and ecological zones, rendering an array of natural and cultivated products and dictating that no one region would be self-sufficient. Such ecological diversity in close proximity, as we saw in Africa in Chapter 15, bred interdependence and encouraged trade.

Teotihuacán

The heart of Mesoamerican culture was the fertile Valley of Mexico. It stood at an elevation of a mile and a half and covered 3,000 square miles. Olmec city-states like San Lorenzo and La Venta thrived for a time, as we saw in Chapter 4, but both collapsed suddenly in violent cataclysms, San Lorenzo in 900 BCE and La Venta around 400 BCE. River channels around San Lorenzo and La Venta most likely shifted, making the region unsuitable for intensive farming. Perhaps these environmental changes destroyed the confidence of the people that their ruler still commanded the supernatural favor of the gods and so led to insurrection. Or perhaps unknown invaders swept upon a weakened city and destroyed it. Whatever the cause of its demise, by 400 BCE La Venta was gone. Large areas once inhabited by Olmecs lay abandoned; the trade networks they had controlled withered. Mesoamerica then lapsed into several hundred years of chronic warfare between small, independent city-states.

One of these city-states was Teotihuacán. By the first century CE, it was growing larger than all the other warring city-states. Fully urbanized, its cityscape, at its peak in the early fourth century CE, covered eight square miles. The city was built in a grid plan that was divided into residential wards, some dotted with palaces of lords and many more with humble dwellings of small-time traders and artisans. Anywhere from 125,000 to perhaps 200,000 nonfood producers crowded into this city. This sizable urban aggregation is again testimony to a robust surrounding agricultural sector that fed the population and a power structure that controlled surplus and could channel it into the city.

As so often is the case in urbanized societies, social and economic inequality was extreme, and power and wealth were concentrated in a small elite topped by a ruler. When the lords of Teotihuacán died, immense pyramids entombed them. Although it is unknown if it served this purpose, the largest, the Pyramid of the Sun, peaked at over 200 feet high and is the largest monument in Teotihuacán and the third highest pyramid in the world. Of course, prodigious labor was demanded to erect these monuments, labor that was provided from the territory they ruled.

And the territory reached far, for Teotihuacán fashioned a trade and tribute empire that stretched north into the desert and south to Guatemala. Expansion and consolidation most likely were driven by the desire to control trade networks that could channel commerce and tribute (in both goods and labor) to the capital city and wealth to its elite classes. The empire's success was primarily due to fielding the most formidable military force in Mesoamerica armed with the new thrusting spears and protected by quilted-cotton armor.

Teotihuacán reached its apogee of influence and power between 375 and 500 CE, after which it declined. It collapsed in the early seventh century, again, like San Lorenzo and La Venta, the result of deliberate destruction. Archeological evidence shows that the city was burned in a conflagration aimed directly at the elite and its symbols of power. This destruction, in turn, points to an internal rebellion. The ruling class and the ruler were probably blamed for their failure to win the promised favor of agricultural bounty from the gods. In this case, it likely had something to do with deforestation coupled with an increasing drought that beset all of Mexico at this time. The result was agricultural collapse and destruction of a political order that could not bring on the rains.

Maya

The Maya people populated the Yucatán Peninsula in an environment ranging from highlands to tropical forest lowlands. Like other Mesoamerican Indians, they practiced human sacrifice and a **pantheistic religion** that centered on the idea of a cosmic mandate to semidivine rulers who were ritually responsible for maintaining the favor of the gods to provide for the prosperity of their people.

Around 2000 BCE, village farming began in parts of the Yucatán Peninsula, and by the beginning of the first century CE, cities had emerged. At that time in the lowlands at Tikal, large stone tombs and temples were erected, evidence of a social and political elite that was commanding vast resources of labor and agriculture. The demands for administrative recordkeeping for city-states like Tikal prompted the beginnings of **hieroglyphic writing**. In the Mayan system of writing, symbols called glyphs, which were only decoded beginning in the 1950s, are phonetic and can represent whole words or just syllables. There were 300 glyphs that were commonly used.

The Maya region was fragmented into numerous city-states that were never politically unified. Most of the Maya period was marked by frequent warfare among the city-states, competing with one another for tribute, labor, and warriors. The powerful city-states of Tikal and nearby Calakmul, for example, were deadly enemies.

Despite frequent warfare, Mayan culture thrived during the years from 250 to 800 CE and centered in the lowlands of the southern Yucatán, northern Guatemala, Belize, and parts of Honduras. A population of anywhere from eight to ten million people lived here by 750 (in a global population of about 210 million) amid a flourishing economy with extensive trade. Their agrarian economy was dominated by hereditary aristocrats who possessed vast private estates. These lands were worked by a combination of free laborers and slaves.

With no sailing vessels, the Maya carried goods for trade along waterways and the coastline in dugout canoes propelled by human muscle. Trade in heavy, bulk commodities, then, was not practical over long distances, but lighter weight luxury goods were exchanged widely. Certain regions specialized in certain products that were prized by Mayan elites, like fine pottery, cotton fabric, jade, **green obsidian** blades, exotic bird feathers, jaguar pelts, and **cacao** for the cherished chocolate drink. Large swaths of the Yucatán Peninsula, as a result, became highly commercialized and dotted with markets through which these goods passed. Indeed, luxury trade relations extended to Teotihuacán in the Valley of Mexico.

The influence of Teotihuacán was felt in other ways too. After 400 CE, its armies invaded and conquered parts of the northern Yucatán highlands, and though local elites remained in power as vassals of their new masters, the grip of Teotihuacán was tight.

After 800, the southern lowlands fell into decline, victim of some cataclysm that shook the area. Overpopulation, soil erosion and depletion, and, above all, drought were the likely culprits. Dense populations could no longer be sustained, and once again, rulers incapable of winning the favor of the gods by bringing rain fell from power. Warfare among city-states increased as they competed for diminishing agricultural resources. By 830, monumental building had ceased.

Sometime around 1000, Toltec influence among the Maya seems likely. The architecture and sculpture at Chichen Itza, for example, shows parallels with Toltec buildings in Tula in central Mexico. Chichen Itza became the new power center from which the rulers dominated the northern half of the peninsula for several centuries. How the Toltec influence got there remains a mystery.

This political order collapsed for unknown reasons in the 13th century. Once again, the area fragmented into rival city-states, each coveting the lands, labor, and resources of the other and waging constant warfare to get them. When the Spanish arrived in the northern Yucatán in the early 16th century, they encountered 16 independent Maya city-states, totaling between 600,000 and a million inhabitants, and still frequently at war with one another.

Toltecs

After the collapse of Teotihuacán in the early seventh century, central Mesoamerica was once again plunged into chronic warfare among small and aggressive states ruled by entrenched warrior castes. Meanwhile, great migrations of peoples from the Northwest of Mexico, notably the Chichimeca people, entered central Mexico. The Chichimeca, who in their northern habitat were desert-dwelling hunters, foragers, and subsistence farmers, joined other migrating tribes and settled in Tula.

The Toltecs, as these inhabitants of Tula became known, organized a large army equipped with a new weapon, the short sword. They thereby asserted their dominance over the region and by 900 had created the Toltec Empire. Tribute, as usual, was collected in agricultural produce and labor. Monumental construction soon followed and continued for two centuries. The capital at Tula was fashioned into a political and religious center of some 30,000–40,000 people. Here, the rulers, like all others in Mesoamerica, performed religious ceremonies, including human sacrifice, to curry favor with the gods and to legitimate their rule by mediating between the gods and the human community.

The empire's inhabitants produced goods for internal consumption but also, importantly, for export. In Tula itself, perhaps 40 percent of the inhabitants were carving obsidian for sale in distant markets, and the Toltecs controlled the great mines of green obsidian to furnish these workshops. Not surprisingly, Toltec trading networks were extensive. Other items besides obsidian were also exported, such as copper bells and macaw birds. Affluent Toltec families acquired the prized turquoise stone from Hohokam and Chaco Canyon in Southwest North America and fine pottery from the Pacific coastal plain near Guatemala.

Tula's immediate environment was only marginal for farming and required irrigation dams and canals to render it productive. Progressive drought struck the region in the mid-1100s (as it apparently did throughout the Americas) and destroyed the agricultural base. A Toltec diaspora followed, as did a cataclysmic end to the city of Tula itself in 1168. Archeological evidence confirms a furious destruction, but at whose hands remains unclear. Once again, a united empire was followed by political fragmentation as small city-states filled the vacuum.

Aztecs

For thousands of years before the arrival of the Spanish in the early 16th century CE, the Valley of Mexico, with its great fertile soils and its diversity of natural resources, had been a destination of migrating peoples. The Aztecs, a name anachronistically given to three allied peoples in the 15th century, were the last of these migrants before the European conquest.

The Mexica people, the progenitors of the Aztecs, migrated from the north into the Valley of Mexico at the beginning of the 14th century. They were proficient and ruthless warriors. They were useful at first as mercenaries for the city-states and small kingdoms already established in the valley, but they were also viewed with disgust by the sedentary peoples as uncultured, repulsive savages. They were thus repeatedly denied permanent residence. The Mexica eventually found refuge on some swampy, unoccupied islands near the western shore of the great lake Texcoco in the center of the Valley of Mexico. The island capital of Tenochtitlán was soon established. One group of Mexica soon broke away and settled on the northern shore of the lake, creating the city-state of Tlatelolco. Another city-state on the lake and bearing the lake's name, Texcoco, had been settled before the arrival of the Mexica, probably by Chichimeca migrants in the 13th century.

Along with the inhabitants of Texcoco, the Mexica of Tenochtitlán and Tlatelolco expanded their influence and power in the valley in the 15th century and so came up against the Tepanec kingdom, which had dominated the valley up to this time. In 1426, the city-states formed the Aztec Triple Alliance to challenge and destroy the Tepanecs.

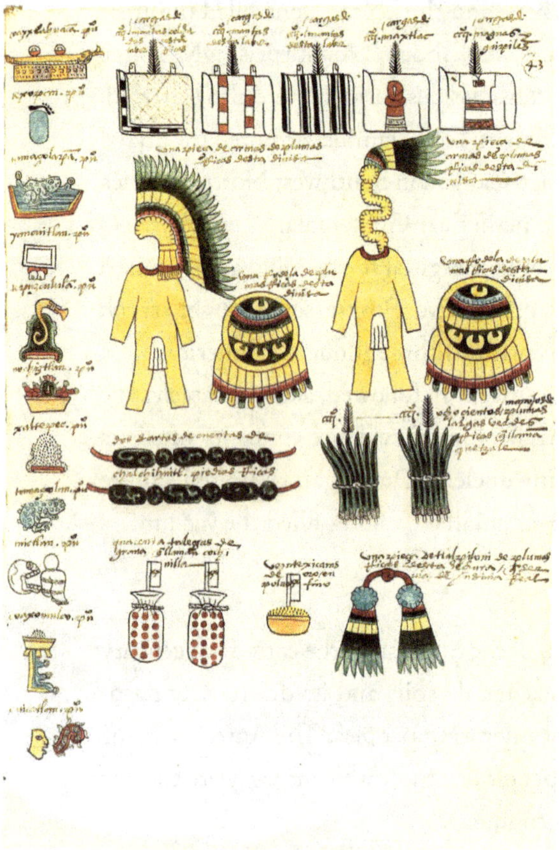

Led by the Mexica of Tenochtitlán, the Triple Alliance continued a program of conquest and brought most of central Mexico under their rule. In 1473, the Mexica of Tenochtitlán turned on their former ally Tlatelolco and conquered them, thereby further consolidating the Aztec state. When Hernán Cortés and the Spanish arrived in 1519, the Aztecs had already brought the city-states to the south to heel and were engaged in war with the states of Tlaxcala to the east and Tarascan to the west. Although they never conquered Tlaxcala or Tarascan (who joined the Spaniards to fight the Aztecs), by 1519 the Aztec Empire subsumed as many as 11 million subjects. It was administered from the capital city of Tenochtitlán, home itself to 200,000 inhabitants. Seville, the largest city in Castile, by contrast, had a population of 60,000 in 1520.

The Aztec state was organized for war. Imperial expansion was undertaken for tribute and for the capture of enemy troops for human sacrifice. So great was the flow of tribute to the ruling class that Aztec social

FIGURE 17.1 Aztec Tribute. Depicted here is a page from the Codex Mendoza, created by the Spaniards 14 years after they conquered the Aztecs. It reproduces Aztec pictograms with Spanish commentary. It contains a history of the Aztec rulers and their conquests, a list of the tribute paid by the conquered, and a description of daily Aztec life. There were many pages dedicated to listing items and quantities paid in tribute, but on this page, the tribute demanded included loads of fine cloth and blankets, two sets of richly plumed armor and feathered shields, and containers of grain. Because the Spaniards simply appropriated the Aztec tributary system upon conquest, this document gives an indication of the Aztec system itself.

structure was fundamentally altered. When the Mexica entered the Valley of Mexico, their society was an egalitarian system of kinship groups, but as nearby territories were conquered, a ruling warrior class was rewarded with land, and thus, social and political stratification began.

Great landowners emerged, providing farmland to commoners to work in return for rent in kind and labor services. The farmland surrounding Tenochtitlán was densely cultivated and irrigated by a sophisticated, interconnected water-control system of dams, sluice gates, and canals.

As territorial expansion continued further away, land no longer was the reward for the ruling elite. Instead, tribute was channeled to them. With the collection of tribute as their main objective, the Aztecs did not control their empire by a centralized administrative bureaucracy. Rather, they relied on compliant local leaders from whom the Aztecs secured loyalty through arranged marriages with Aztec princes and princesses. So long as these conquered regions paid tribute in the form of food, firewood, and labor (for the massive construction projects of temples and palaces in the capital), the Aztecs largely left them alone. Those who did not comply were ruthlessly punished.

The Aztecs had a king, but as the nobility's wealth grew and their power became more consolidated, kings were chosen from the royal lineage by a council of nobles, priests, and high-ranking military officers. Brothers of kings came to be elected more often than sons.

The ruling elite of the Aztec state in the 15th century had a cosmic vision of the Aztecs' central place in the universe. This belief demanded a specific history that portrayed the empire as the favorable outcome of a cosmological unfolding. The Aztecs saw themselves as a chosen people and self-consciously promoted themselves as the true heirs of Toltec culture and tradition. The Aztecs believed that they had a divine mission and one that required human sacrifice to the gods to retain their favor and to ritually proclaim the exalted status of their ruler. Indeed, human sacrifice was the highest level of an entire range of offerings that included birds, animals, food, and even insects. Through these sacrifices, the Aztecs sought to repay their debt to the gods, who, according to a widespread Mesoamerican belief, had long ago sacrificed themselves so the earth would produce bounty to support all forms of life.

Tenochtitlán was the center of the Aztec Empire and, according to the Aztec vision, at the center of the universe. The city's sacred precinct, with its great temples stained with the blood of sacrificial victims, was its spiritual heart. The city was also the empire's economic heart, a thriving residential, manufacturing, and commercial entity. Tenochtitlán became an enormous manufacturing center, with whole neighborhoods specializing in certain products, from weapons, quilted armor, gold and silver jewelry, copper bells and ornaments, to obsidian objects, combs, and needles. The workshops of the city pumped out goods that reached across the empire.

In a fundamental sense, the Aztec Empire was an economic empire, based in part on the provision of tribute. It also had a highly commercialized market system (where cacao beans were widely used as money) through which moved the varied products of a diverse ecosystem that the Aztecs ruled. Market centers dotted the empire, but none was as great as the Great Market of Tlatelolco across the lake from Tenochtitlán. Perhaps 25,000 people thronged it daily, surging to 40,000–50,000 on special days. This market was abuzz with the buying and selling of clothing, foods, pottery, tools, slaves, and even cigars. The Spaniard Bernal Díaz del Castillo wrote, "When we arrived at the great marketplace, called Tlatelolco, we were astounded at the number of people and the quantity of merchandise that it contained, and at the good order and control that was maintained."[1]

The Aztecs were keen on increasing the quantity and reliability of trade across their empire. They therefore guaranteed the safety of merchants who travelled along the routes that linked the realm's many city-states and their flourishing local markets. Merchants who engaged in long-distance trade were called pochteca, and became a powerful, well-respected hereditary group in Aztec society. They procured luxury goods, such as feathers from tropical birds, precious gems, and finely crafted pottery and jewelry, for the nobility and the royal palace.

The pochteca travelled hundreds of miles from the capital to acquire these rare goods, often ranging far beyond the limits of the empire itself. They could be found as far south as the southern Gulf of Mexico and as far northwest as Zacatecas and Durango where they connected with a down-the-line system of trade that brought turquoise from New Mexico and Arizona. This was the empire that the Spaniards encountered and conquered in the early 16th century, an empire with a restive population eager for the overthrow of their Aztec overlords.

The Andean Indians of South America

The Andean Indian cultures of South America—Nazca, Moche, Tiwanaku, Wari, and Inca—were like their Mesoamerican and North American counterparts

---

1 Richard F. Townsend, *The Aztecs* (London: Thames and Hudson, 2009), 180.

in many ways. Cultivation of maize was essential, they constructed impressive monuments central to a religious ceremonial system that included human sacrifice designed to curry favor with the gods, and they had stratified social structures with a warrior class at the top. Some of them were confronted with arid climates and so built complex irrigation systems, while others created vast empires that were held together by extensive highway networks and integrated systems of food distribution. And like the Indian cultures to the north, most were dependent upon favorable climate conditions, and when these turned unfavorable through prolonged droughts, their empires collapsed.

The Nazca and Moche Cultures

The Nazca culture, located in river valleys along the dry southern coast of present-day Peru, dates from about 1–750 CE. These peoples are known for an impressive irrigation system of underground aqueducts, the production of extremely complex textiles and elaborately decorated polychrome pottery, and, above all, their **geoglyphs**.

The fundamental Nazca crops, besides maize and squash, were sweet potato, manioc (an edible starchy root), and cotton. Given the arid climate, survival depended on adequate water. Sometime after 450, the Nazca people created an underground aqueduct system to tap streams to irrigate their crops. Dug into the mountainside, these channels directed water to fields as well as to reservoirs for later use.

The aridity of the climate also guided Nazca religious beliefs, which were based in a pantheon of powerful nature gods worshipped to bring rain and fertility to crops. Such worship, led by **shamans** who consumed parts of the hallucinogenic San Pedro cactus to induce religious visions, centered upon the ceremonial site of Cahuaci with its immense earthwork mounds and plazas. Nazca craftsmen produced elaborate pottery painted with as many as 15 distinct colors, often with images of nature gods in the form of mythical creatures with human and animal characteristics.

Nazca craftsmen (and perhaps women) also produced beautiful and technically complex cotton textiles. Excavations show that some women were clad in them, the quality of craftsmanship and the materials indicating high social status. Many of these women's garments were woven with images of various creatures that suggest religious purposes.

The Nazca people were not unified in a state or empire, political authority being located in local chiefs. They came together periodically at Cahuaci to worship the same gods, but warfare seems to have been endemic among them. Some pottery visually depicts decapitations by men dressed as warriors while archaeological excavations have uncovered large numbers of severed heads, increasing dramatically in number between 450 and 550. All of the skulls are drilled with a hole through the forehead, suggesting that the head was a trophy that could be displayed on a rope. Successful headhunting most likely enhanced the prestige of the leaders of Nazca society.

The Nazca people are best known for their mysterious geoglyphs, a series of large geometrical and animal figures (spider, monkey, birds) laid out in the dry highlands and on valley slopes. The makers of these geoglyphs, with astonishing precision, removed dark colored pebbles on the surface to reveal the light-colored soil underneath. The purpose of these figures is unknown. Perhaps they beseeched the gods above, perhaps they served as a calendar laid out in astronomical alignment, or perhaps they were pathways for ceremonial processions.

FIGURE 17.2 Nazca Hummingbird Geoglyph. The Hummingbird Geoglyph is one of a series depicting animals and birds.

After 500, there are signs of Nazca decline, and by 750, the culture had disappeared. Climate change likely had something to do with it, as widespread flooding interspersed with prolonged droughts became more frequent. When water no longer coursed through the Nazca irrigation system, society was doomed. Its people were likely absorbed by the rising Wari Empire.

During the same centuries as Nazca culture, the first to the eighth, Moche culture arose and thrived for a time along the arid northern coast of Peru. It shared many similarities with the Nazca. Like the Nazca, the Moche people built platform pyramids, made of dried mud bricks, as ceremonial centers to invoke the favor of the gods. Both cultures had stratified social structures with a warrior class at the top and fragmented political authority where different chiefs ruled over separate valleys. Like the Nazca, the Moche also constructed irrigation systems for their crops in the arid climate, also tapping streams running down the Andes Mountains and channeling the water into a system of canals. Similarly, both cultures produced sophisticated craft goods, including pottery painted with images that bear upon their religious beliefs. Both were warlike, the Moche sacrificing prisoners of war to their gods, followed by the ritualized drinking of their blood. And both probably collapsed for the same reason: climate change that brought catastrophic flooding and widespread drought.

FIGURE 17.3 Moche Warrior Tomb. Archaeologists recently excavated this tomb near the village of Sipán that contains the skeleton of a Moche warrior, perhaps a king. Buried with him were displays of his wealth and status: jewels, precious metals, fine craftwork, and a copper figure representing the dead man. His tomb is flanked by four others, perhaps sacrificial victims.

The Tiwanaku Empire

Around 1000 BCE, perhaps earlier, small farming villages were settled in the southern Andes Mountains near Lake Titicaca in what is Bolivia today. By 100 CE, the population of these people, the Tiwanaku, had grown to the extent that they began to erect large platform mounds and temples. This site became the capital of an empire that between 400 and 1000 CE dominated the southern Andes. Administrative centers and economic colonies sprawled across the high plateaus of Bolivia and Peru and spread along the seacoasts of southern Peru and northern Chile.

To populate these colonies, the Tiwanaku rulers forcefully relocated people to them. These colonists in turn provided the empire and the capital city with a diverse range of products drawn from the great variety of ecological zones they spanned. Vast caravans of llamas, the primary pack animal of Andean Indians, organized by the ruling class and supervised by state officials, moved these goods throughout the empire and especially to the capital city itself.

As is everywhere the case, the power of the rulers rested upon the wealth they could extract from the land and its people. The Lake Titicaca basin, which was a productive environment with abundant rainfall, was intensively farmed in raised and ridged fields interlaced with canals. The canals irrigated the crops, but they were also stocked with fish and were dredged periodically for a rich sludge that was used to fertilize the fields. Farmers paid tribute to their overlords in the city in produce and labor, the latter put to work in building the great ceremonial monuments that proclaimed and legitimized the authority of the ruler. The capital was thus a religious center, the site of human sacrifices carried out atop the platform temples. The empire disintegrated between 1000 and 1200 CE, likely a victim of a changing climate that brought great droughts after 1000.

The Wari Empire

About 1000 kilometers north of Tiwanaku in the south-central Andes of present-day Peru, another empire emerged at roughly the same time, that of the Wari. Its future capital, also known as Wari, was first settled around 200 BCE, and like Tiwanaku, it grew rapidly into an urban, ceremonial, residential, and administrative center with monumental temples and tombs as well as residences for the ruling elite.

The Wari expanded their empire through a series of military conquests, likely to acquire more farmland and to access the products of the many diverse ecological zones in the region. At its greatest extent, the empire encompassed most of highland and coastal Peru, subsuming both the Nazca and Moche cultures. It was tightly controlled from the center. Its economy was based on agriculture and herding of llamas and alpacas (similar to but smaller than llamas). Their terraced farms rendered not only maize, chili peppers, and squash but also potatoes, fruits, and peanuts. A large share of the produce was stored in state-sponsored facilities. This reserve would be distributed to the people in the event of a meager harvest or in times of need. To facilitate the collection of these products and to distribute them as needed, the empire was divided into administrative centers linked by a state-constructed highway network.

The extent of a trade network beyond the state-controlled storage and distribution system is unknown. There is evidence, however, that manufactured items of pottery and stonework from the capital city of Wari made their way to some of the empire's colonies. Like Tiwanaku and around the same time, the Wari Empire collapsed, probably for the same reason: climate change and ensuing drought.

The Inca Empire

The disappearance of the Tiwanaku and Wari Empires left small, warring states in the vacuum, as political fragmentation swept the region. It is from this world that the Inca Empire would emerge. The Inca people arrived in Cuzco around 1200 CE. Like their neighbors, the Inca engaged in localized military raids in the Cuzco Valley for several hundred years, gradually increasing their regional influence through strategic alliances and marriages. In the 15th century, however, they embarked on far-reaching military conquests that rapidly created a vast empire. By midcentury, they controlled the entire Cuzco Valley, and from there they steadily expanded.

Successful warfare concentrated power and wealth in the hands of a ruling elite and a ruler who drew much of his prestige from his prowess as a military leader. The ruling elite formed a small kin group, the Incas, this caste comprising anywhere from 15,000–40,000 people. From this group came the sacred emperor who, as the Son of the Sun, claimed a divine mandate to rule. His words and actions were believed to be inspired by the gods, and in his person was concentrated political, military, and sacred leadership.

The Inca believed that the world was shared with the dead and the gods and that human well-being depended on the deceased ancestors' and the deities' goodwill. To gain this goodwill, upon which the legitimacy and authority of the emperor rested, the emperor prayed and at times sacrificed human beings.

In practice, the emperor was advised by a council of close relatives, all Incas. Each province of his empire was headed by a governor, also always from the Inca caste. This council determined the imperial succession, for it was not necessarily passed from father to son. It remained within the male bloodline but was granted to the man the council believed was the most able. Not surprisingly, murderous palace intrigues and sometimes outright civil war were often a result. For example, when the emperor and his appointed heir died of smallpox in 1527 (which had been introduced by Europeans in Mexico preceding the Spanish conquest of South America), rival claimants created a political crisis, and civil war ensued.

The emperors ruled directly over the central part of the empire in the Cuzco Valley. It was from this region that they drew most of the wealth that sustained their power. All newly conquered land technically belonged to the emperor, the people only having use of it. In practice, however, some lands were owned as private estates by the ruler, some by Inca family members (both men and women who could pass it down to the next generation), and some by religious establishments to maintain shrines and sustain priests and priestesses.

For the rest of the empire, however, the most important objective of the emperor was the extraction of labor. The empire was organized into 80 provinces. Each provincial governor's most important tasks were the supervision of the census that recorded births, deaths, and marriages and the mobilization of labor for the emperor and ruling elite. Labor was conscripted to work the lands of the Inca rulers; to erect monumental public works to exalt them; to build and maintain canals, roads, and storage facilities; and to quarry stone and mine gold and silver.

Labor was also drafted for the imperial armies, as thousands of soldiers might be mobilized and remain in the field for months or years, engaged in conquest or, increasingly, employed to suppress internal insurrections. To preclude the latter, upon conquest of a particular area, the victorious Incas would relocate about a quarter of the populace to a distant province.

The military was organized through a system of garrisons, forts, and storehouses, all linked by a vast and efficient infrastructure of royal highways built and expanded upon the prior network of the Wari. The system stretched 40,000 kilometers. Two main trunk roads ran north and south, and they were connected laterally by shorter highways. A Spanish soldier 20 years after the conquest marveled that "in human memory, I believe that there is no account of a road as great as this, running through deep valleys, high mountains, banks of snow ... and wild rivers. ... In all places it was clean and swept free of refuse, with lodgings, storehouses, Sun temples, and posts along the route."[2]

The highway system also served administrative and economic purposes. Not only were soldiers supplied by the state-run storage depots (a practice the Incas adopted from the Wari) but so too was the entire populace. Remarkably, the Inca economy had no market system, no currency, and no merchant class. The production, distribution, and use of commodities were centrally controlled by the government, all without wheeled vehicles or draft or riding animals.

The state-controlled storage facilities contained dried maize, quinoa, potatoes, beans, seeds, clothing, metal tools, and weapons. Using an as-yet-undeciphered knotted cord system, official accountants carefully recorded and distributed necessities to each inhabitant. The operation of this system is all the more astonishing given that the Inca ruled over a diversity of environments, from the driest of deserts, to the world's second highest mountain range, to lush tropical lowlands of the Amazon Basin. The entire expanse contained a population of perhaps 10 million people.

To minimize the demands of long-distance transport, the Inca encouraged as much regional self-sufficiency as possible. Exchange networks did exist, however. Because some regions produced surpluses of unique products due to the ecozone they were located in, goods were exchanged between zones. Local lords acting for the state oversaw the exchange and redistribution of these goods, but again not through a market system, but rather following government orders.

The state also owned vast herds of llamas and alpacas and employed tribute labor to weave their wool into state-owned cloth. Similarly, thousands of skilled craftsmen, including metalworkers and potters, provided manufactured goods for what has been called a "supply and command" economy.

Unlike Aztec Mexico, the Inca Empire was not heavily urbanized. Most inhabitants lived in dispersed rural hamlets. The few cities of the empire were ceremonial centers and residences of the ruling elite. Cuzco was the most important of these, for it was the residence of the emperor and the sacred center of not only the empire but also of the cosmos. Its construction was deliberately designed with temples and plazas and reflected its ceremonial and sacred purpose. When the Spaniards captured the emperor and Cuzco, they struck a mortal blow to the empire's sanctity, and it fell quickly to Spanish occupation in 1533.

---

2 Terrance N. D'Altroy, *The Incas* (Oxford: Blackwell, 2002), 3.

Review Questions

1. In what ways were the Indian cultures of North America different from one another?
2. What do the structures built by the Mesoamerican Indians reveal about them?
3. How did the Wari, Tiwanaku, and Inca hold their empires together?

Further Reading

Blanton, Richard E., Gary M. Feinman, Stephen A. Kowaleski, and Peter N. Peregrine. "A Dual-Processual Theory for the Evolution of Mesoamerican Civilization." *Current Anthropology* 37, no. 1 (1996): 1–14.

Bragdon, Kathleen J. *The Columbia Guide to American Indians of the Northeast*. New York: Columbia University Press, 2001.

Coe, Michael D. *The Maya*. New York: Thames and Hudson, 2005.

Coe, Michael D., and Rex Koontz. *Mexico: From the Olmecs to the Aztecs*. London: Thames and Hudson, 2008.

D'Altroy, Terrance N. *The Incas*. Oxford: Blackwell, 2002.

Emerson, Thomas E. *Cahokia and the Archaeology of Power*. Tuscaloosa: University of Alabama Press, 1997.

Hassig, Ross. "The Aztec World." In *War and Society in the Ancient and Medieval Worlds: Asia, The Mediterranean, Europe, and Mesoamerica*, edited by Kurt Raaflaub and Nathan Rosenstein, 361–387. Washington, DC.: Harvard Center for Hellenci Studies, 1999.

Hudson, Charles. *The Southeastern Indians*. Knoxville: University of Tennessee Press, 1976.

Kehoe, Alice Beck. *America before the European Invasions*. London: Pearson Longman, 2002.

McEwan, Gordon F. *The Incas: New Perspectives*. New York: W. W. Norton, 2006.

Mann, Charles C. *1491: New Revelations of the Americas Before Columbus*. New York: Vintage, 2006.

Pauketat, Timothy R. *Ancient Cahokia and the Mississippians*. Cambridge: Cambridge University Press, 2004.

Pauketat, Timothy R., and Thomas E. Emerson, eds. *Cahokia: Domination and Ideology in the Mississippian World*. Lincoln: University of Nebraska Press, 1997.

Townsend, Richard F. *The Aztecs*. London: Thames and Hudson, 2009.

Webster, David. "Ancient Maya Warfare." In *War and Society in the Ancient and Medieval Worlds: Asia, The Mediterranean, Europe, and Mesoamerica*, edited by Kurt Raaflaub and Nathan Rosenstein, 333–360. Washington, DC: Harvard Center for Hellenic Studies, 1999.

Figure Credits

Map 17.1: Copyright © by Serg!o (CC BY-SA 3.0) at https://commons.wikimedia.org/wiki/File:Topographic_America.png.

Fig. 17.1: Source: https://commons.wikimedia.org/wiki/File:Codex_Mendoza_folio_43r.jpg.

Fig. 17.2: Copyright © by Diego Delso (CC BY-SA 4.0) at https://commons.wikimedia.org/wiki/File:L%C3%ADneas_de_Nazca,_Nazca,_Per%C3%BA,_2015-07-29,_DD_52.JPG.

Fig. 17.3: Copyright © 2018 Depositphotos/marktucan.

GLOSSARY: VOLUME 1 (CHAPTERS 1–17)

adaptive radiation	Emergence of new species as hominins moved into different environments.
agora	The market area in Greek towns for the exchange for local goods, such as shoes, pottery, and tools.
alluvial soil	Sedimentary matter, such as sand, mud, or silt deposited by flowing water.
Amphorae	Clay jars used as shipping containers in the ancient economy.
Apedemek	The lion-headed god worshipped by the Kushites.
barbarian	A term used originally by ancient Greeks to disparage all foreigners as inferior.
Bedouin	A nomadic Arab of the North African desert.
Berber nomads	Ethnic people native to North and West Africa with no permanent abode.
bipedal	Walking upright on two feet.
bishop	A high-ranking official of the Christian clergy in charge of an administrative unit called a diocese and empowered to confer holy orders upon priests.
bishopric	A district under a bishop's authority, usually a diocese.
Black Death	Plague that struck the Mediterranean world and Europe beginning in 1347.
Bosporus Strait	The strategic waterway connecting the Black Sea with the Sea of Marmara and then with the Aegean and Mediterranean seas.
Brahman	Ganges valley priests who performed ritual sacrifices in hopes of pleasing the gods and assuring the well-being of their entire clan.
bubonic plague	A deadly disease caused by bacteria transmitted to humans and rodents by insects, usually fleas.

Buddhism	A major religion founded around 563 BCE in the middle part of the Ganges valley by Siddhartha Gautama, who eventually came to be known as the Buddha (the Enlightened One).
cacao	Beans from a small tropical Mesoamerican evergreen tree from which chocolate is made.
caliph	Political leader of the Islamic community regarded as the successor of Muhammed.
capitulary	An ad hoc and brief pronouncement of the royal will rather than part of a systematic legal code; it always superseded the local law.
caravanserais	Inns or waystations along trade routes used by merchants for overnight stays and securely storing their goods.
carbon dioxide	An odorless, colorless, incombustible gas that can accumulate in the earth's atmosphere.
cast iron	At a temperature of 1130 degree Celsius, iron combines with carbon and turns into liquid that can be poured into molds.
caste system	A hierarchy of Indian social classes, fixed at birth according to the purity of their occupation.
cataract	Rocky, swift rapids that sharply impede, or even prevent, navigation across them.
Celtic	A term that pertains to an early Indo-European people who from the second millennium BCE to the first century BCE spread over much of Europe.
census	An official recording of all Roman citizens and their property conducted by the state at regular intervals for the purposes of taxation.
champa	A type of rice that is drought-resistant and matures quickly and therefore allows for two, sometimes three, harvests in a single season. It was introduced in China from Vietnam during the reign of Emperor Shenzong and dramatically increased food production.

civil service examination system	Created during the Han dynasty, a test that assessed the knowledge about Confucian principles that established the supremacy of a civilian bureaucracy. Individuals who passed the test usually entered the government's service.
codex	A manuscript whose pages are bound into a book.
coke	A solid residue from coal baked to remove carbon impurities. It was a fuel used for the first time by the Chinese that made iron less brittle in the smelting process.
commenda	Commercial arrangements whereby an investor would entrust a merchant with capital and at the end of the venture share the profit in an agreed-upon division.
Coptic Christians	Adherents to a branch of Christianity, the Coptic Orthodox Church, based in Alexandria, Egypt.
Corpus Juris Civilis	A legal code compiled at the command of the Emperor Justinian in the sixth century that comprised a collection of past laws and interpretations of learned jurists in Roman history, dating to the time of the Republic.
Council of Nicaea	A Christian church council convened in 325 CE that established the doctrine of the Trinity in the Christian faith.
cowrie shells	Shells of mollusks (sea snails) originating in the Maldive Islands southwest of India and used for currency.
cuneiform	A system of writing in which a stylus with a triangular end is pressed into clay to form wedge-shaped characters.
debased coinage	The reduction of the content of silver in coins and replacement of it with a cheap metal alloy, like bronze.
debt slavery	Peasants who could not pay their debts sometimes lost their land to aristocrats and ended up as bound servants working for aristocrats.
Delian League	An alliance of Greek city-states led by Athens and formed in 478 BCE in response to fears of attacks from Persian forces.

diaspora	Migration of any species to different parts of the world.
domestication	Human actions that change the genetic composition of wild plants or animals.
egalitarian societies	Communities without significant differences in access to wealth and power other than those based on age or gender.
emir	A Muslim military commander, local chief, or ruler.
emporia	Principal centers of commerce.
entrepôt	A commercial center where exports and imports were traded.
environmental degradation	Decreases in the quality of the land, water, or air in an area.
epidemiology	Scientific study of diseases in defined populations.
equal-field system	A system of land allocation first used during the Northern Wei dynasty (386–534) and reinstituted during the Tang dynasty when emperors claimed large tracts of formerly unoccupied land and, in exchange for redistributing the land to peasants in equal plots, the state registered households and collected taxes from them.
ethnographic studies	Scientific examinations of the beliefs and behavior of different societies.
evolution	Genetic changes in organisms as they adapt to their environment.
feudalism	A political system in which the nobility held lands, called fiefs, granted by kings in exchange for military service.
fief	Land granted by lords or kings to loyal soldiers in exchange for military service.
floodplain	A nearly flat area formed along the course of a river that periodically overflows its banks.
fossil	Any remains, impression, or trace of an animal or plant of an earlier geological age.
funduq	A lodginghouse for traveling merchants that provided secure, locked warehouse space for storage of their cargo.

geoglyph	A large design produced on the ground by arranging stones, rocks, or gravel to depict an image.
green obsidian	A naturally occurring hard volcanic glass.
greenhouse gases	Fluid substances, such as carbon dioxide, that can trap heat from the sun and thereby raise global temperatures.
Hadith	Record of the traditions or sayings of the prophet Muhammad, considered by Muslims as a source of religious law and moral guidance second only to the authority of the Quran.
Hagia Sophia	A spectacular church built by the Emperor Justinian in Constantinople in 532.
Harappan	The inhabitants and their urban society that emerged in the Indus valley around 3000 BCE.
Hellenistic	Pertaining to the Greek language and culture that flourished in the eastern Mediterranean and southwestern Asia between the death of Alexander the Great in 323 BCE and the Roman conquest of Egypt in 30 BCE.
Hellespont	The narrow waterway, now called the Dardanelles, connecting the Aegean Sea to the Sea of Marmara and through it and the Bosporus to the Black Sea.
Hexi Corridor	A narrow stretch of plain between the Mongolian plateau to the north and the Tibetan Plateau to the south that served as a fundamental trade route of the Silk Road.
hieroglyphic writing	Mayan system of writing in which symbols, called glyphs, are phonetic and can represent whole words or just syllables.
hieroglyphics	A unique form of writing employed by Egyptian scribes using sheets of paper-like material made from reeds growing along the banks of the Nile.
hominin	Bipedal creatures that did not develop brains that were much larger than African apes.
Homo	Lineage of hominins that gradually evolved into modern humans.

hoplite	Greek soldiers who fought on foots while carrying round shields made of bronze and wearing expensive cast bronze armor paid for by themselves.
Iberian Peninsula	A region, comprising Spain and Portugal, located in the extreme southwest corner of Europe.
Imam	A spiritual leader among Shi'a Muslims who was believed to possess knowledge to correctly interpret the Quran.
ingot	Metal cast into a size and shape, such as a bar, convenient to store or ship for further processing.
insulae	Multistory tenement buildings, usually crowded and in dilapidate state of repair, providing the housing for the urban poor.
Ionian cities	Greek settlements, located along the shore and on offshore islands, in the central region of the Aegean coast of Anatolia.
Jainism	A religion founded in India during the 6th century BCE by the Jina Vardhamana Mahavira who preached against the teachings of orthodox Brahmanism.
jihad	A holy war fought against the perceived enemies of Islam.
junks	Chinese sailing ships that became widely used during the Song dynasty in ocean-going, long-distance trade. Innovative hull and sail design increased cargo capacity, speed, and flexibility, as sails could be adjusted to permit sailing into the wind.
khaghan	Supreme chief of Turkic and Uighur nomadic tribes of central Asia.
kola nuts	The nut produced by a West African evergreen tree that contains caffeine and is chewed to extract flavor and stimulate mental concentration as well as for some medicinal purposes.
last glacial maximum	The most recent period when ice sheets reached their greatest extent.
Latin states	Independent city-states, located just to the south of Rome, whose inhabitants spoke Latin.

Levant	A geographical region along the eastern Mediterranean that includes areas of Lebanon, Syria, Jordan, and Palestine.
loess soil	Loosely compacted dirt deposited by the wind.
madrassa	Muslim school.
magnetic compass	A navigation instrument with a magnetic needle that aligns itself with earth's magnetic field and points due north.
Mandate of Heaven	A Chinese belief that emperors (Sons of Heaven) were granted the absolute right to rule by celestial authorities based on how well they provided for the well-being of their people. If the ruler failed in his obligations, he could be legitimately overthrown.
Manichaeism	A major religion founded in the third century CE by the prophet Mani in the Sasanian Empire, whose followers, like Zoroastrians, believed in a dualistic view of good and evil in the cosmos.
manorial system	The political and economic organization of rural communities in medieval Europe that vested legal and economic power in the lord of the manor, or farm.
missi dominici	Direct agents of the king who carried capitularies into the kingdom and extended the king's authority into provincial administration.
monasteries	Places occupied by communities of clergy, monks, or nuns following religious vows.
monotheism	Religious belief in one supreme deity.
monsoon	Prevailing winds that regularly change direction, blowing from east to west during warmer months and in the other direction during cooler months.
Muslim	An adherent of the faith of Islam.
neo-Confucianism	A moral and political philosophy that emphasized the acquisition of knowledge and moral awareness as a means to individual fulfillment and, through service to the state, as a means of creating a virtuous society and government.

Neoplatonism	A philosophy that held that God brought life and spiritual wisdom to the world through divine emanations that could be received by human beings as a form of enlightenment.
Old World	Eastern hemisphere.
oligarchy	A form of government in which a small number of people, such as wealthy landowners or powerful military figurers, have control over a country.
Olmec	A hierarchical society, ruled by powerful chiefs, that emerged in the gulf costal lowlands of Mesoamerica around 1200 BCE.
pantheistic religion	Based in the belief that divinity is immanent in all things.
partible inheritance	Inheritance whereby the father's patrimony was divided equally among surviving sons.
pastoralism	A form of animal husbandry where livestock are herded onto lands for grazing.
Peloponnese	A peninsula in southern Greece separated from the central part of the country by the Gulf of Corinth.
phalanx	Groups of soldiers, in close formation, carrying overlapping shields and long spears.
polytheistic	Religious belief in multiple gods.
primate	A related family of mammals that includes humans, apes, and monkeys.
primogeniture	The right of the first-born son to inherit the entirety of the father's estate.
Pueblo	Term that refers to (a) a distinctive type of dwelling of solid masonry made of sandstone and mud characterized by joined rows of rectangular rooms, sometimes multistories high; and (b) the Indians of the American Southwest who constructed these dwellings.
Punic	Inhabitants of ancient Carthage and their settlements around the Mediterranean.
qadis	Judges appointed to administer Islamic law.
Reconquista	The Christian conquest of Muslim-held territory in Spain.

Red Turban Rebellion	The final rebellion against the Mongol Yuan dynasty in China in 1368. It was led by Zhu Yuanzhang who founded a new dynasty, the Ming.
republic	A form of government in which power is held by the people or their representatives.
Roman Senate	A governing and advisory assembly of Roman aristocrats that was created in the eigth century BCE and endured through the dissolution of the Roman Empire in the fifth century CE.
Sahel	Topographical region of grassy steppe.
salinization	A process by which water-soluble salts accumulate in soil.
savanna	Topographical region of scattered trees and grassland.
sericulture	The raising of silkworms and the use of the filaments of their cocoons for the production of silk.
shaman	A spiritual person who is believed to interact with a spirit world through trances, sometimes induced by rhythmic drumming, chanting, or by consuming hallucinogenic substances, with the purpose of directing spiritual energies into the physical world, often for healing
Shanyu	Supreme chief among the Xiongnu peoples.
shari'a	Islamic law.
Shi'a	Branch of Islam whose adherents believe that the true caliph and ruler of the Muslim community descended from Ali, the fourth caliph and son-in-law and cousin of the prophet Muhammed (and thus reject the legitimacy of the first three caliphs).
silt	Fine particles of earth carried by a stream or river and deposited as sentiment.
Sogdian	An ancient Persian people from a region is central Asia known as Sogdia or Sogdiana.
species	Related organisms that resemble one another and can breed among themselves but not with members of other kinds of organisms.

stele	A stone or wooden slab erected in the ancient world as a monument.
steppe	A large topographical region of plains of grasslands without trees.
sultan	A Muslim ruler distinct from a caliph yet claiming sovereignty over a specified territory.
Sunni	Branch of Islam whose adherents accept the first three caliphs as legitimate leaders of the community of Muslims.
synod	An assembly of the clergy convened to decide an issue of doctrine or church administration.
Takla Makan Desert	A stretch of desert in central Asia flanked by the Tian Shan Mountains to the north and the Kunlun Mountains to the south. It is dotted with oases along the northern and southern rims.
tribute	A coerced or enforced payment or contribution.
Trinity	Christian doctrine established in 325 CE at the Council of Nicaea asserting that there is one God but that He is comprised of three eternal entities that are distinct but of one substance, the Father (God), the Son (Jesus Christ), and the Holy Spirit.
Umma	The community of Muslims.
untouchables	Despised outcasts who were viewed as belonging to the lowest and least pure group in the Indian status hierarchy.
vizier	Egyptian officials, serving as second-in-command to pharaohs, who headed a large civil service and oversaw all aspects of the government bureaucracy.
warlordism	A political and military order whereby a leader commands a territory of variable size within a larger political unit and retains military troops loyal to him.
Warring States period	A time of almost constant military conflict in China between 481 and 221 BCE.
wergild	A payment from a wrong-doer to the injured party or, in the case of his death, to his family.

woodblock printing A printing technique similar to modern woodcuts whereby images or symbols are carved in relief in a piece of wood that is then inked, covered by a piece of cloth or paper, and rolled.

ziggurat Massive stepped pyramids often serving as the foundation of temples.

Zoroastrian religion A major religion that appears in the fifth century BCE that is based on the teachings of the seventh century BCE Persian prophet Zoroaster that center on a dualistic cosmology of good and evil embodied in the supreme deity of good, Ahura Mazda.

BIBLIOGRAPHY

D'Altroy, Terrance N. *The Incas*. Oxford: Blackwell, 2002.

Daryaee, Touraj. *Sassanian Persia: The Rise and Fall of an Empire*. London: I. B. Taurus, 2009.

Gettleman, Marvin, and Stuart Schaar, eds. *The Middle East and Islamic World Reader*. New York: Grove Press, 2003.

Gilbert, Erik, and Johnathan Reynolds. *Africa in World History*. 2nd ed. Upper Saddle River, NJ: Pearson Education, 2008.

Groussett, René. *The Empire of the Steppes: A History of Central Asia*. Translated by Naomi Wahlford. New Brunswick: Rutgers University Press, 1997.

Jones, Gwyn. *A History of the Vikings*. 2nd ed. Oxford: Oxford University Press, 1984.

Juvenal. *The Satires*. Translated by Charles Badham. New York: Harper Brothers, 1855.

Kelly, Chrisopher. *The Roman Empire*. Oxford: Oxford University Press, 2006.

Kiang, Heng Chye. *Cities of Aristocrats and Bureaucrats: The Development of Medieval Chinese Cityscapes*. Honolulu: University of Hawai'i Press, 1999.

Lewis, Edward Mark. *The Early Chinese Empires: Qin and Han*. Cambridge, MA: Harvard University Press, 2007.

Lewis, Mark Edward. *China's Cosmopolitan Empire: The Tang Dynasty*. Cambridge, MA: Harvard University Press, 2009.

Lichtheim, Miriam, ed. and trans. *Ancient Egyptian Literature, Vol. III: The Late Period*. Berkeley: University of California Press, 1980.

Liu, Xinru. *Ancient India and Ancient China: Trade and Religious Exchanges, AD 1–600*. Delhi: Oxford University Press, 1988.

Meijer, Fik, and Onno van Nijf, eds. *Trade, Transport and Society in the Ancient World: A Sourcebook*. London: Routledge, 1992.

Morley, Neville. *Trade in Classical Antiquity*. Cambridge: Cambridge University Press, 2007.

Murray, Oswyn. *Early Greece*. Cambridge: Harvard University Press, 1993.

Parkinson, Richard B. *Voices from Ancient Egypt: An Anthology of Middle Kingdom Writings*. London: British Museum Press, 1991.

Polo, Marco. *The Travels of Marco Polo*. Translated by Ronald Latham. London: Penguin, 1958.

Pritchard, James B., ed. *The Ancient Near East: Supplementary Texts and Pictures Relating to the Old Testament*. Princeton: Princeton University Press, 1968.

Sullivan, Richard E., ed. *The Coronation of Charlemagne*. Boston: D.C. Heath, 1959.

Townsend, Richard F. *The Aztecs*. London: Thames and Hudson, 2009.

Yoshinobu, Shiba. *Commerce and Society in Sung China*. Translated by Mark Elvin. Ann Arbor: University of Michigan Press, 1992.

Zachariah of Mytilene. *The Syrian Chronicle*, X 9. Translated by F. J. Hamilton and E. W. Brooks. London: Metheun, 1899.

INDEX

A

Abbasid caliphs, 242–245
Abbasids, 248
Abū al-'Abbās, 242
Abu Hureyra, 26
accumulation of wealth, xx
Achaemenid clan, 108–110
Achaemenid kings, 111
Acheulean tools, 3
  hand axes, 3
acquisitive behavior, xx
adaptive radiations, 2
Africa
  Bantu-Speaker Culture, 302–303
  coastal port cities, 315–317
  crop domestication, 302
  east, 315–319
  emergence of humans in, 1–6
  farming in, 34–36
  pastoralism and agriculture, 300–302
  slavery in, 319–322
  urbanization and states formation in, 73–76
  west, 309–314
agora, 97
agricultural and industrial products, xx–xxi
agricultural communities, 20–22, 24
Agricultural Revolution, xxi, 20–21, 23, 161
agriculture, emergence and spread of, 20–21
  agricultural implements and lethal weapons, 63–64
  agricultural production in fertile valleys, 55
  farming, 22–23, 34–36
  in East Asia, 30–31
  in Europe and Central Asia, 24–25
  in North Africa, 34
  in North America, 37–38
  in Pacific Basin, 32–34
  in Southeast Asia, 31–32
  in Southwest Asia, 24–25
  in Sumer, 40–41
  irrigation systems, 23
  rice farming, 30
  social inequality and, 24
Ahura Mazda, god, 111
Ain Ghazal, 26
Aisha, 238
Akhenaten, 49
Akkadian Empire, 44
Aksum kingdom, 306–308
al-Andalus, 339–341
Alexander the Great, 115–116
Alexandria, 116, 118, 149–150, 229, 297
Ali, 238–239, 246
alluvial soil, 40
Almohads, 326–328
Almoravids, 312, 326–328
al-Mutawakkil, 243
Alps, 103
Amenhotep III, 49
amphorae, 145
Anatolia, 45, 86, 103, 108, 112, 116, 294, 331
Ancient Ghana, 310–313
Andean highlands, 37
Andean Indian cultures of South America, 356–363
An Lushan Rebellion, 201, 205
Antigonid kingdom, 117
Antioch, 152
Antony, Mark, 128
Aoudaghost, 312, 322
ape species, 1
Arab armies, conquest of, 235–236, 240
Arab Nabataean kingdom, 152
Arab tribes, 232
Aryan invasions, 55
Ashoka, King, 70–72
Ashur city, 45
Assyria, 45, 87
Assyrians, 92–93, 95
Athens, 85, 99–100, 108, 112–115, 136
Aurelian, Emperor, 137, 153
Award, 90
Ayyubids, 326–328
Aztec Mexico, 363
Aztecs, 353–356

B

Babylonia, 84, 87
Babylonians, 95–96
Baghdad, 248
Bakr, Abu, 232, 238
Balkan Peninsula, 27
Baltic communities, 17
Baltic Sea region, 17
Bantu-Speaker Culture, 302–303
barbarian invasion, 112
barbarian kingdoms, 212
  notions of governance, 213
barbarians, 211–215
Barbaricum, 150
Barygaza, 150
Basin of Mexico, 77, 81–82
Battle of Manzikert, 291
Battles of Legnica and Mohi, 271
Bay of Naples, 104
Bay of Salamis, 112
Bedouins, 335
Belisarius, 217
Belisarius, Flavius, 217
Berber nomads, 310
Beringia, 9–10
Bindusara, 69
bipedal species, 2
bishoprics, 281
bishops, 142
Black Sea colonies, 104–106, 297

Black Seas, 101
Black Sea trade, 275, 287, 295, 331, 333, 336–338
Blombos Cave, 5
Boniface VIII, 291
Bosporus Strait, 104, 216
Boxgrove, 4
Brahmanism, 68
Brahmans, 67
Bubonic plague, 221
Buddha, Lord, 68
Buddhism, 68, 71, 180, 199
Bulgaria, 29
Burgundian Southeast Gaul, 212
Burgundy, 104
burials, 36
   Celtic, 104
   of affluent foragers, 15–16
   of elite individuals in farming communities, 28–29
Byblos, 90
Byzantine armies, 213
Byzantine cities, 220
Byzantine Empire, 226–229, 235, 294–295
   agriculture and manufacturing, 227–228
   economy of, 228–229
   silk-related occupations, 227–228
   trade and trade routes, 228–229
Byzantine slavery, 220
Byzantine state, 287–288
   aristocracy and peasantry, 289
Byzantine State, 216–219
Byzantium, 104

C

Caesar, Julius, 127
Cahokia, 345–347
caliph, 234–236
Cambyses II, king, 109
caravanserais, 338
carbon dioxide, 26
cardamom, 149
Carolingian dynasty, 278
   consolidation of royal authority, 290–291
   economy, 281–284
   fragmentation and breakup of, 289
   political recovery and economic growth, 289–290
   trading and settlers, 284–287
   wars of conquest, 278–281
Carolingians, 282
Carpathian Mountains, 27
Carthage, 93–94, 96, 123–125, 211
caste system, 67
cast iron, 63
Catalhoyuk, agricultural settlement of, 26–27
cataracts, 46, 304
Catholic Christianity, 214
Cato the Elder, 147
Celtic peoples, 103
Celtic settlement, 104
census, 138
Central America, 37
Central Asia, 173–174
   trade in, 184–185
cereal production, 293
Chaco Canyon, 348–349
Chaghatids, 275
Chang'an, 167, 248
Changjiang, 58–59
Charlemagne, 278–281, 284
Childeric III, 278
chimpanzees, 1
China
   militant Chinese states, 61
   pastoral tribes, 63–64
   Qin empire, 64–65
   unification of, 61–66
   unified Chinese empire, 65–66
   urbanization and state formation in, 55–56
   warring states of, 62–64
Chinese metalworkers, 63
Chinese silks, 149
Christian Church, 142, 219–220
Christianity, 91
Christian traders, 335
cinnamon, 149
citizenship, 100
city-states, 42
classical China
   brewing industry, 166
   cities, 167
   coinages, 161
   economy of, 165–167
   exchange of silk for horses, 168–170
   iron smelting, 166
   land and taxes, 161–163
   landed estates, 163–164
   law of partible inheritance, 164
   merchants, 168
   papermaking, 165
   peasant unrest in, 164–165
   porcelain manufacturing, 166
   private enterprises and state-controlled manufactories, 166
   private land ownership, 163
   religion in, 158
   sericulture and textile manufacturing, 166
   silk industry, 166
   taxes and infrastructure, 159–161
   technology and production, 165–166
   unification of, 155–161
Cleopatra, 128
climate change and global warming, effects of, 10
Clovis, King, 214
Code of Hammurabi, 45
coinage system, 137, 143, 149, 161, 274
commenda, 250, 297
Confucianism, 157–159
Confucius, 62
Constans II, 218
Constantine, emperor, 216–217
Constantinople, 226–227, 294–295, 331, 333
Coptic Christians, 326
Corpus Juris Civilis, 217
Council of Nicaea, 217
cowrie shells, 310
cranium fossils, 5
Crete, 85–86
Cro-Magnons, 9
Crusades, 292
cuneiform, 43
Cuzco Valley, 361–362
Cyprus, 86, 116
Cypselsus of Corinth, 99
Cyrus, 109

D

Danube, 211
Danube River valley, 28
Daoist messianic religious sect, 164
Da Qi dynasty, 197
Darius, 109–112
De agricultura, 147
debased coinage, 137
debt slavery, 88
Delian League, 113
Diocletian, 138, 142
Dnieper River valley, 30
Dolni Vestonice, 8
Dome of the Rock, 242
Domesday Book, 294
domestication of plants and animals, 21–22

E

East Asia, cities and states in, 55–59
Eastern Han Empire, 171
Eastern Han Luoyang, 160
eastern Mediterranean exchange network, 84–89
   Israelites and, 91
   social and economic order in, 89
   social stratification, 88–89
   trade and diplomatic exchanges, 86–88
edicts, 72
egalitarian societies, 12
Egypt, 73, 84–85, 87, 116, 128, 218, 228–229, 297, 334–337
   agricultural prosperity, 227
   centralized authority and political fragmentation, 49–50
   maritime expeditions, 49
   military campaigns, 49
   urban development and state formation in, 46–50
Egyptian pharaohs, 46–49
Egyptian society, 46–47
   administrative purposes, 47
   commoners, 47, 49
   patriarchal society, 50
Eleutheros River valley, 87
emporia, 221
Enheduanna, 44

entrepôt, 297
environmental degradation, 21, 23
Eparch, 227
epidemiology, 198
equal-field system, 193–194
Erlitou, 56
Ethiopian Highlands, 303–304
ethnographic studies, 11, 14, 20
Etruscan aristocracy, 103
Etruscans, 103–104
Europe
   economic activity, 294–295
   new states in, 290–293
   population growth and migration, 293–294
   trade, 295–298
European mammoth, 8
European territorial expansion, 293–294

F

farming
   in Africa, 34–36
   in South Asia, 36
Fatimids, 325–326, 334–335
Ferghana, 248
Fertile Crescent, 25–26
Feudalism, 281
First Crusade, 292
Five Pillars of Islam, 242
floodplains, 31
food production, 37–38
foraging societies, 11–12
   European foragers, 12–13
fortified hilltop settlements, 104
fossil discoveries, 2
France, 221
Frankish aristocracy, 214
Frankish kingdom, 213–214
Frankish Merovingian kings, 213
Frankish northern Gaul, 212
Fu Hao, 58
Fujian, 207
Fujian Province, 261
funduq, 249
funduqs, 334

G

Gadir, 94–95
Ganges plain, 67

Ganges River valley, 36, 66–67
   chiefdoms and kingdoms, 68–69
   second urbanization, 67–68
Gaul, 132
Gautama, Siddhartha, 68
Gebel Barkal, 73
Genoese mercantile activity, 340–341
geoglyphs, 357
Ghaggar-Harkra River, 51, 55
Ghazan, king, 329
gold coinage, 149
Goths, 211
Gracchus, Gaius, 126
Gracchus, Tiberius, 126
great human diaspora, 7–8
Great Mosque of Damascus, 242
Great Wall of China, 66
Great Zanj Rebellion, 246
Great Zimbabwe, 317–319
Greek agrarian governments, 96–101
Greek city-states (polis), 101
   wars between, 98–99
Greek colonization, 101–102
   Black Sea colonies, 104–106
   in central Mediterranean, 102
   motives, 102
   urban centers and rural hinterlands, 102
Greek culture, 116
Greek Dark Age, 96–97
Greek farmers, 96–97, 99
Greek society, 96–97
   nature of, 100–101
Greek workshops, 98, 103–104
greenhouse gases, 26
Guangdong, 207
Guangzhou, 196, 207

H

Hadith Party, 244
Hadrian, 136
Hagia Sophia, 217
Hamadab, 76
Hammurabi's reign, 44–45
Han dynasties, 155–160
Hangzhou, 207
Hanseatic League, 296
Harappan cities, 54
Harappan society, 52, 54–55

383

decline of, 54–55
political organization of, 54
Harappan towns and cities, 52–54
Hatshepsut, 50
Hatti, 84, 87
Hattusa, 88
Hebrew Bible, 96
Hebrew scriptures, 91
Heidelberg man, 3–4
Hellenistic empires, 115–118
Hellespont, 113
Henry III, King, 291
Heraclius, 218
Hexi Corridor, 169, 174
hieroglyphics, 47
hieroglyphic writing, 351
Himalaya Mountains, 173
Hindu Kush Mountains, 179
History of the Han Dynasty, 170
History of the Jewish Wars, 135
Hittites, 87
Hobbes, Thomas, xx
Hohokam culture, 347–348
hominins, 1–4
Homo erectus, 3, 6
Homo ergaster, 3, 5
features, 3
migration, 3
tool manufacturing ability, 3
Homo heidelbergensis, 3
Homo neanderthalensis, 4, 6
Homo sapiens, 4–6, 8, 20
across Eurasian land mass, 6–7
Homo species, 2–3
Hopewell, 344–345
hoplites, 96, 98–99
horse-riding nomads, 175–176
Horus god, 48
Huang Chao, 196
Hülegü, 271
humans, evolution of, 1–6
ape species, 1
brain enlargement, 3–4
hominins, 1–3
language and social evolution, 5–6
modern humans, 4
origins of modern behavior, 5
hunter-gatherer populations, 11–12
technologies and trade, 12–13

Husayn, 240
Hyksos immigrants, 49

I

Iberian Peninsula, 124
Ice Age, 10, 12, 20
Ice Age burials, 14–16
Ice Age foragers, 11
Ice Age hunter-gatherers, 12–13
food resources, 13
semipermanent settlements, 13–14
Ice Age warfare, 13
Ilkhan regime, 328–330
imam, 239
Imperial University, 159
Inca Empire, 361–363
Indian cotton textiles, 149
Indian Ocean Trade, 315–317
Indian ports, 150
Indians of North America, 343–349
of Mesoamerica, 349–356
of Southwest North America, 347–349
Indus River valley, 23
cities in, 51
urban growth in, 51–52
industrial development, xxi
Industrial Revolution, 263
ingots, 86
Innocent III, Pope, 291
insulae, 133
intercity warfare, 42
Ionian cities, 108, 112
Ionian Greeks, 112
irrigation systems, 22–23
Islam, 91, 231, 233–234, 310, 322, 325
agricultural revolution, 246–247
cities and markets, 248–250
conflict over succession and leadership, 239
cultural unity and commercial growth, 247–248
economic principles, 250–251
governance and legitimacy of caliphates, 237–245
political decentralization, 236–237

territorial expansion of, 234–235
island of Salamis, 99–100
Israelites, 91, 95–96
Italy, 86, 102, 126, 132, 215, 217, 221, 296–297

J

Jade Gate, 174
Jainism, 68
jihad, 233
John, King, 291
Jomon culture, 17
Josephus, Flavius, 135
Jurchen Jin Empire, 258–260
Justinian I, emperor, 213, 217–218

K

Kadero cemetery, 35
Kalinga, 71–72
Kanishka I, 180–181
Kash kingdom, 69
Kaushambi, 68
Khadija, 232
khaghan, 177–178
khanates, 271–272
Khan, Genghis, 270–271
Khan, Kublai, 272–274
Khitan Liao Empire, 257–258
Khorezm, 179
Khosrow I, 183–184
Khufu, pharaoh, 48
Knossos, 85
kola nuts, 310
Kosala kingdom, 69
Koster settlement, 18
Kunlun Mountain range, 174
Kushan Empire, 179–181
Kushans, 186–188
Kushites, 304–306

L

landholders, 43
Land Survey and Equitable Tax System of 1072, 256
last glacial maximum, 9
Latin states, 120
Laurion mines, 98
learned behavior, xix

Lefkandi, 97
Levant, 86, 89
Levantine Mediterranean coast, 333
Libya, 116
loess soil, 28, 55
Lübeck, 296
Lu Buwei, 65
Luoyang, 167
luxury consumption, 185

M

Macedon, 116
Macedonians, 115–116
Madagascar, 303
madrassas, 331
Magadha, 69
magnetic compass, 333
Mahayana Buddhism, 180
maize cultivation, 347
Malia, 85
Mali kingdom, 313–314
Mamluks, 326–328, 331
    economy of, 334–337
mammoth hunters, 8–9
Mandate of Heaven, 62
Manichaeism, 178
manorial system, 216
Mapungubwe kingdom, 317–318
Marcellinus, Ammianus, 171
Martel, Charles, 278–279
Masada Fortress, 135
Maurya, Chandragupta, 69
Mauryan Empire, 69–72
    administration, 70
    capital, 70
    decline of, 72
    mixed economy, 70
    tax revenue, 70
Maya people, 351–352
meat consumption, 2
Mecca city, 233
Meccan tribes, 233
Mediterranean Sea, 101, 174
Mediterranean shipping, 229
Mehrgarh, 52
Mehrgarh settlement, 36
Memphis, 73–74
merchant oligarchy, 92
Meroë, 75–76
Meroitic kingdom, 75

Meroitic settlements, 76
Meroitic State, 75–76
Merovingian kings, 214
Mesoamerican cultures, 349–356
Mesoamerica, urbanization and state formation in, 77–82
Mesopotamia, 23, 40–45, 151
    agricultural settlements, 41
    gap between rich and poor, 43
    mixed economy, 41–42
    regional empires, 44–45
Mesopotamian kings, 42
Mesopotamian society, 41
Mezhirich, 16
Minoan states, 84–85
missi dominici, 280
Mississippian Culture, 345–347
Mitanni, 84, 87–88
mobile hunter-gatherers, 17
Moche culture, 357–359
Moche Warrior Tomb, 359
Mohenjo-daro, 52
Mongols, 328–330
    commerce under, 274–275
    conquests, 270–271
    khanates, 271–272
monotheistic concept, 91
monsoon, 67, 150
monsoons, 118
Monte Alban, 80–81
Morocco, 95
Moses, 91
Muhammad, Prophet, 231
    Constitution of Medina, 232
    mission of, 232–233
    revelations, 231–233
Musa, Mansa, 314
Muslim regimes
    commercial economy of, 332–341
    in North Africa, 324–328
    in Southwest Asia, 328–332
    luxury goods trade, 333
    major trading cities, 334
Muziris, 149
Mycenae, 85
Mycenaean citadels, 85–86
Mycenaean Greece, 85
Mycenaean kings, 86
Mycenaean pottery, 86
Mycenaean states, 85

N

Nabataeans, 152
Nanda dynasty, 69
Nanda, Mahapadma, 69
Napata, 73
Napatan Empire, 73–74
Napatan state, 74
Naqa, 76
Natufians, 16
Natufian villages, 16
Nazca culture, 357–359
Nazca Hummingbird Geoglyph, 358
Neanderthals, 4, 9
Nebuchadnezzar II, King, 96
Neoplatonism, 325
Nero, Emperor, 131
Niger River, 35, 311–312
Nile River valley, 34–35
Nisibis, 188
Northern Wei dynasty, 193
Nubia, 73, 308–309
Nubian farmers, 74
Nubian language, 75
Nubian society, 76

O

Octavian (Augustus), 128–129
Oldowan tools, 2
oligarchy, 122
Olmec societies, 78–80
Olympia, 102
Olympics, 102
Ordu Baliq, 178
Ostrogothic Italy, 212
Ostrogoths, 217
Ottomans, 330–332
    economy of, 337–339

P

pagan temples, 142
Palestine, 116, 132, 241
Palmyra, 153, 187
Palmyrene merchants, 152
Parthian Empire, 181–184
Parthians, 186–187
pastoralism, 35
Patagonia, 9
Pataliputra, 70
pax mongolica (Mongolian peace), 275

385

Peloponnese, 113
Peloponnesian War, 113, 115
pepper trade, 149–150
Periplus maris Erythraei, 150
Periplus of the Erythranean Sea, 315
Persepolis, 110
Persian Empire, 108–111, 115–116
Persian Gulf trade route, 335–336
Persian War, 112–113
Phaistos, 85
phalanxes, 98
Pheidon of Argos, 99
Philip II, 115
Phoenician artisans, 94
Phoenician city-states, 89–90
  decline of, 95–96
Phoenician Commercial Empire, 92–94
Phoenician kings, 91–92
Phoenician merchant ships, 93
Phoenician mortuary practices, 92
Phoenician oligarchs, 92
Phoenician war galleys, 93
Phoenician writing system, 90
Pilliya, 88
Piye, King, 73–74
Polo, Marco, 274–275
polytheistic, 141
polytheists, 91
Pompey, 127
Pope Leo III, 280
Portugal, 95
primate family, 1
primogeniture, 290
Ptolemy kingdom, 118
Punic Empire, 96
Punic Wars, 123–125
Pylos, 85
pyramids at Giza, 48
Pyrenees, 103

Q

qadis, 243
Qin empire, 64–65
  decline of, 66
Qin Empire, 61, 155–156
Qin Shi Huangdi, 65–66
Qin Xianyang, 160

Quanzhou, 207
Quran, 231–234, 238–239, 242, 250–251

R

Ra god, 48
Rameses II, 49
Records of the Grand Historian, 170
Red Sea trade, 151
Red Turban Rebellion, 274
republics, 297
Rhenish trade, 283
Rhodes island, 117
ritual specialists, 14
Roman Aqueduct, 140
Roman aristocracy, 210
Roman Cistern, 140
Roman city, 133
Roman countryside, 121
Roman Empire, 210
  aristocrats, 131–132
  barbarian invasions, 137
  census, 138
  ceramic production, 222
  characteristic of, 134
  city dwellers, 133
  civil administration, 138
  commercial agrarian economy, 132
  countryside and city, 131
  cultural traditions and religious practices, 141–142
  decline of, 210–212
  economy in western part of, 220–226
  effect of Bubonic plague, 221
  emperor and army, 134–138
  imperial tax system, 210–211
  infrastructures, 139–141
  networks of roads, 139
  peasants and slaves, 132–133
  persecution of Christians, 141–142
  ports and canals, 139–140
  Roman state, power of, 134
  tax collection and money, 138–139
  technological innovation, 222
  trade in West, 222–226
  vs Germanic tribes, 137

  waves of epidemic diseases, effect of, 137–138
Roman empire, 118–123
  civil and military power, 119
  civil wars, 126–128
  decline of, 128–129
  expansion, 120–122
  military campaigns, 122–123
  patricians, 120
  plebeian agitation, 121
  polarization of wealth and social unrest, 125–126
  population, 122
  republican constitution, 119–120
  Roman warfare and imperial expansion, 123–129
Roman Empire, economy of, 142–146
  agricultural production, 142, 144–145
  cash-based economy, 146
  coinage system, 143
  investment in grain production, 145
  markets, 146–148
  olive production, 145
  production and manufacturing, 145–146
  role of state in, 143
  state taxes and aristocratic rents, 144
  wine production, 145
  women, status, 146
Roman Empire, trade routes, 148–151
  Indian Ocean, 149–151
  Red Sea, 149–151
  to Arabia and Central Asia, 151–153
  to China, 148–149
  to India, 149–151
Roman freighters, 150
Roman imperial state, social hierarchy of, 215–216
  imperial bureaucracy, 215
  peasant society, 215
  social stratification, 219–220
Roman landowners, 212
Roman law, 141, 210, 217
Roman nobility, 119
Roman Republic, 122, 134
Roman Senate, 121–122, 131

Roman state, 120, 211
Roman wine, 149
Rome city, 211–212
royal tomb at Xin'gen, 59

S

Sahara, 34–35
Sahara Desert, 309
sahel, 300, 309
Salian Franks, 214
Salic Law, 214
salinization of soil, 43
Samarkand, 177
San Jose Mogote, 78, 80
San Lorenzo, 78–80
Sanxingdui, 58–59
Sappho, 101
Sardinia, 86
Sargon, 44
Sassanian dynasty, 181–184
Sassanians, 186–188
savannas, 300
Scandinavian cemeteries, 17
Scythian rulers, 105
sedentary foragers, 17
Seleucid kingdom, 117–118
self-interested households, 14–15
Seljuk Turks, 245
Senusret III, 49
Shabaqo, King, 74
shamans, 5, 14
Shanakdakhete, Queen, 76
Shang artisans, 57
Shangdi, 57
Shang kingdom, 56–58, 61
 military campaigns, 57
 power of Shang monarchs, 56–57
Shang society, 58
shanyu, 176
Shari'a, 239, 245
Shi'a, 239
Shi'a Buyids, 245
Shi Huangdi, 155–159
Sicily, 86, 102, 132
Sidon, 90
Silk Road, 148, 170–171, 176–178, 180, 184–187, 205–206, 248, 275
silt, 40
silver, 98

Sinai Peninsula, 3, 7, 91
slavery, 97–98, 220
 in Africa, 319–322
social inequality and warfare, 18
social relations, 14
social stratification, 17–18
socioeconomic inequality, 16
Sogdiana, 248
Sogdian merchants, 206
Sogdians, 195
Solon, 99–100
Song Dynasty, 254–256
 agriculture and urbanization, 261–263
 cities, 261
 civilian governance, 255–256
 commercial revolution, 265–267
 economic revolution, 260–269
 expansion, 256–260
 foreign trade, 268–269
 hemp cloth and silk fabric production, 264
 iron smelting, 263
 manufacturing, 263–265
 paper production, 264
 porcelain ceramic industry, 264
 state, role in trading and commercial activities, 262, 267–268
Soninke ethnic group, 311
Son of Heaven, 158
South Asia, empire building in, 66–72
 chiefdoms and kingdoms, 68–69
 chiefs and Brahmans, 67
 rise of Mauryan empire, 69–71
 untouchables, 67
South Asia, urban revolution in, 50–55
 agricultural intensification and craft production, 52–53
 political organization and urban decline, 54–55
 second urbanization, 67–68
 urban plans and public works, 53–54
Southwest Asia empires, 179–184

Southwest Gaul, 212
Spain, 95, 132, 215, 221, 235, 339–341
Sparta, 108
spice trade, 297
spiritual realm, 14
starvation, xx
stele, 45, 73
steppes, 30, 64, 173
 people of, 175–178
stone tools, 2–3
sub-Saharan Africa, 301
Sultanate, 325
Sumer, 40–41, 43
Sungir, 15
Sunnis, 239
supernatural entities, 14
surplus food, accumulation of, xix
synods, 280
Syria, 86–87, 132, 240–241, 295

T

Tabriz, 333
Taizong, Emperor, 273
Taizu, Emperor, 254–255
Takla Makan Desert, 169–170, 191
Talheim, 28
Tamerlane, 329–330
Tang dynasty, 177
 agriculture and manufacturing, 197
 armies and militia system, 194–195
 Buddhism in, 199
 cadre of career officials, 192
 civilian bureaucracy, 195
 coastal provinces, 207
 credit system and domestic trade, 205–206
 decline of, 253–254
 economic condition, 197–198
 emergence and consolidation of, 191
 equal-field system, 193–194
 governance, 191–193
 great estates, 198–199
 imperial weakness and collapse of, 195–197

long-distance trade, 206–207
manufacturing, 201
militarism and civilian governance, 194
porcelain ceramic industry, 201
rice and tea cultivation and consumption, 199–200
road network, 193
sea-based trade, 207
semi-independent kingdoms, 192
state regulation and commercial growth, 202–204
state salt monopoly, 201
Taizong era, 192
tax system, 193
technology, 200–201
woodblock printing, 200
Tanzania, 302
Tarim Basin, 174
Taurus Mountains, 40
taxation system, 70, 138–139, 144, 159–163, 193–194, 210–211, 220
Templars, 295–296
temples, 40–42
Teotihuacán, 349–350, 352
textiles, 45
Thebes, 85
Themes, 218
Third Dynasty of Ur, 44
Tian Shan range, 174
Tiberius, 152
Tiglath-pileser III, 95
Timur, 329
Tiwanaku Empire, 360–361
Toltecs, 352–353
Trajan, Emperor, 135
trans-Asian commerce, 181
trans-Saharan trade, 309–312
Trebizond, 295
tribute, 42, 80
Trinity doctrine of, 142
Tuareg nomads, 314
Tucson basin, 23
Türkic Empire, 177–178
Türks, 177–178, 186
Tutankhamun, 49
Tuxlas Mountains, 79
Tyre, 90–91, 93–96
Tyrrhenian Sea, 104

U

Ugarit, 86–88
Uighur tribes, 177–178, 186
Uluburun, 86
Umar, 238
Umayyad caliphate, 240–242
Umayyads, 243
umma, 232
untouchables, 67
Urban II, Pope, 292
Uruk, 41
'Uthmān, 238

V

Valley of Oaxaca, 77–78, 80–81
Vandal Africa, 212
Vandals, 211, 217
Veii, 120
Venetian gold ducat, 297
Venetians, 284, 296
Venus figurines, 13
Vespasian, emperor, 135
Vikings, 285–287
Visigothic Spain, 212
vizier, 47

W

Wang Mang, 157
Wari Empire, 360–362
warlordism, 157
Warring States period, 63, 65, 155, 165
wealth and power
  geographical center of, xxi
  in relative terms, xix
  relationship between political entities, xx
Wei Zhuang, 196
wergild, 214
West African sahel and savanna, 309
Western Han Chang'an, 160
Western Han dynasty, 156
Western Hemisphere colonization, 9–11
western Mediterranean, Phoenician colonization in, 94–95
William the Conqueror, 294

Wu di, emperor, 156, 161, 169–170
Wu Ding, Emperor, 58
Wu Zetian, Emperor, 193, 198

X

Xerxes I, 112
Xianbei tribes, 177
Xianyang, 160
Xianzong, 195
Xin dynasty, 157
Xiongnu, 163, 168–169, 174, 178, 186
Xiongnu Empire, 66, 176–177

Y

Yahweh, 91
Yangtze valley, 61
Yangzi valley, 31, 58–59
Yellow River valley, 31, 55, 57, 62
Yellow Turban Rebellion, 164, 165
Yuan Dynasty, 272–274
Yucatan Peninsula, 351
Yuezhi people, 176, 179, 186

Z

Zachariah of Mytilene, 221
Zagros Mountains, 44
Zakros, 85
Zhang Jue, 164
Zhang Qian, 169–170, 186
Zhao Kuangyin, 254
Zhao Zheng, 61
Zhao Zheng, king, 65
Zhejiang, 207
Zhengzhou, 56
Zhou dynasty, 254, 263
Zhou state, 61–62
Zhuangxiang, king, 65
Zhu Wen, 197
ziggurats, 41
Zongzhou, 62
Zoroastrian religion, 182

CPSIA information can be obtained
at www.ICGtesting.com
Printed in the USA
LVHW020914200722
723885LV00002B/4

9 781793 550866